PROFESSIONAL COUNSELING
An Overview

PROFESSIONAL COUNSELING

An Overview

Frank A. Nugent

Western Washington University

Brooks/Cole Publishing Company
Monterey, California 93940

Brooks/Cole Publishing Company
A Division of Wadsworth, Inc.

Printed in the United States of America

10 9 8 7 6 5 4 3 2 1

Library of Congress Cataloging in Publication Data

Nugent, Frank A   1921-
   Professional counseling, an overview.

   Bibliography: p.
   Includes index.
   1. Counseling. I. Title.
BF637.C6N84   158'.3   80-25726
ISBN 0-8185-0424-2

Acquisition Editor: *Claire Verduin*
Manuscript Editor: *Grace Holloway*
Production Editor: *Jennifer Young*
Interior and Cover Design: *Katherine Minerva*
Typesetting: *TriStar Graphics, Minneapolis, Minnesota*

To my wife, Ann,
and to our children,
Ellen, Laura, Mike, and David.

Preface

This book presents both a concise view of the counseling profession and a rationale for this view to students preparing to become professional counselors. My perspective arose out of my experiences in college, school, and community counseling and from my interpretation of the professional standards developed by national counseling professional associations.

After a long history of erratic growth, the counseling profession is developing the potential to offer a full-fledged, unique service to individuals in educational settings and in the community. No other group of people emphasizes working with persons who have conflicts and concerns about personal, social, or vocational/educational decisions arising out of everyday living. Few, if any, other professional workers have worked so diligently to develop professional and ethical standards that emphasize confidential, voluntary services focused on a person's right to privacy.

For the past few decades, counselor professional associations have defined counselor roles, outlined appropriate functions, and set standards for the training and ethical practice of counselors in schools and colleges. Recently these associations have emphasized the importance of upgrading professional training for community counselors and of establishing procedures for licensing them. This trend was highlighted by the recent inclusion of mental-health counselors as a division of the American Personnel and Guidance Association.

This book is based on my belief that counselor educators should not only make counseling students aware of these professional standards and trends but also help students understand the rationale behind the standards and actions of the professional associations. Understanding these professional standards and recognizing that mutual bonds exist among counselors in different work settings give graduate counseling students a number of advantages. First, this perspective enables prospective counselors to formulate meaningful personal counseling approaches, attitudes, and behaviors on which a sound, consistent, professional-counseling practice can be built. Second, prospective counselors become more capable of explaining and justifying their professional attitudes and behavior to counselees, to employers, to other professionals, and to the general public. Finally, counselors entering the field with an understanding of the mutual aims among counselors are more likely to recognize the need for working together to gain the professional strength necessary to implement effective professional counseling in schools and in the community.

In the first three chapters I have outlined and interpreted the philosophical and practical framework of an emerging counseling profession. The unique characteristics of the profession are identified and justified, and the communality of role definitions, training standards, and ethical practice of counselors in various settings is explained. In Chapter 2 the practical barriers that have hampered counselors from attaining professional status in the past are elaborated on from a historical perspective. The intent of this chapter is to give readers an understanding of the complex roots of contemporary problems in counseling and to demonstrate the need to strengthen the counseling profession if these problems are to be solved. Chapter 3 presents the standards developed by counselor professional associations to be used as guidelines for training and working and the problems or issues related to following these standards. I have included the reasoning behind the standards and used this reasoning to offer some resolutions to these contemporary problems and controversies interfering with the development of professional counseling.

Theories and techniques used in direct counseling and in the secondary functions of counselors, such as psychological education or consultations, are briefly summarized in Chapter 4. This chapter centers on the importance of developing a personal counseling approach based on one's view of human nature and environmental forces and on the relationship of this view to a counseling theory.

The remainder of the book describes ways of organizing and implementing voluntary, confidential, counseling programs in educational institutions and in the community consistent with the professional and theoretical ideas developed in the first four chapters. Examples of types of counseling interactions I have encountered in practice are discussed to give students some idea of the kind of problems and concerns that individuals bring to a counseling staff. Secondary functions or outreach activities of counselors are described with examples of how they apply in practice.

Although the book was designed primarily for students taking introductory courses that include school and community counseling, it can also serve as a supplementary text in courses about professional issues in counseling. In addition, it is my hope that practicing counselors struggling with professional identity or with environmental barriers to their development of professional programs can find some help in the suggestions in this book. The view of counseling presented here may also help teachers, administrators, or community-funding agencies better understand how counseling can contribute to educational and psychological programs in the community. Finally, my attempt to minimize jargon and to present a concise rationale may induce some nonprofessionals to try to gain an understanding of this complex service.

I would like to acknowledge the helpful suggestions from the reviewers of the manuscript: Jeannette A. Brown of the University of Virginia, Richard Dunlop of the University of Missouri, Thomas M. Elmore of Wake Forest University, Janet Craig Heddesheimer of George Washington University, Arthur M. Horne of Indiana State University, Lyle L. Miller of the University of Wyoming, C. H. Patterson of the University of Illinois, Richard J. Riordan of Georgia State University, Robert L. Smith of East Texas State University, Hershel Thornburg of the University of Arizona, Calvin Vraa of the Institute for Psychological Therapies, and C. Gilbert Wrenn.

My sincere gratitude is extended to my wife, Ann, who read the manuscript from its amorphous beginnings. Her constructive editing suggestions as well as her patience and encouragement were of inestimable value throughout the time it took to complete the book. I also want to express my appreciation to my children, Ellen, Laura, Mike, and David, who good-naturedly shared me with the book. Thanks are due my colleagues, Hayden Mees and Elvet Jones; Hayden carefully reviewed the chapter on counseling theories and techniques, and Elvet contributed a number of interesting activities related to ethical behavior and role-playing practice at the ends of Chapters 3 and 5.

A special word of thanks is extended to the Bureau of Faculty Research at West Washington University for their typing assistance. Finally, I wish to thank Jenifer Polak and Meredith Jacobson for their efficient typing of the many drafts and their cheerful and encouraging comments about the project.

Frank A. Nugent

Contents

Appendixes   *255*

PROFESSIONAL COUNSELING
An Overview

1

Counseling: An Emerging Profession

The Need for Counseling Services

Counseling services for people with normal conflicts and anxieties represent a rapidly emerging profession. Wrenn noted in 1970 (in Van Hoose & Pietrofesa, 1970) that counseling services not only continued to grow in schools and colleges but were also spreading to clients in employment services, hospitals, and rehabilitation centers. In 1975 Belkin wrote, "The profession of counseling is a relatively recent development still in its flowering stages" (p. 1). In 1978 Tolbert commented, "Counseling and guidance are well established in public educational institutions, community agencies, colleges and universities" (p. 8).

Most authors discussing the swift growth of counseling attribute it to increasing conflicts and anxieties in normal life that have resulted from rapid social, cultural, and economic change. Factors such as changing family patterns, the acceptance by society of various alternative lifestyles and sexual behaviors, the changing role of work, the new perceptions of women's roles, the increasing older population, the recognition of minority injustices, and increased drug and alcohol use are all believed to contribute to the possibility of increased moral and value conflicts in the general population (Belkin, 1975; Tolbert, 1978; Van Hoose & Pietrofesa, 1970).

These social changes during the past ten years have increased contemporary choices in sexual attitudes and activities, have broadened occupational choices for women and minorities, and have brought about a variety of possible lifestyles that are not dependent on an individual's age, sex, or ethnic background. The increase in options provides opportunities for a richer life for people at all life stages—preschoolers, students, workers in the labor market or at home, retired persons, and the aged. But as more choices in behavior become possible and as one leaves the security of a prevailing behavior pattern or custom, increased conflicts may occur. These conflicts are not neurotic or pathological. They are often legitimate, positive responses to feelings or situations that are potentially debilitating if they are not recognized, confronted, and resolved.

These sociocultural and economic conditions have undoubtedly contributed to a growing demand for counseling from the general public. However, it was not until professionals trained in psychology recognized the need for normally functioning persons to get help with problems that professional-counseling services began to expand in elementary and secondary schools, in colleges, and, more recently, in the community. This recognition became apparent in psychology circles when personality and counseling theorists developed theories and techniques for working with the prevailing concerns of normally developing individuals.

The Role of Professional Associations in Counseling

For the past two decades professional-counseling associations have attempted to set up guidelines for professional or psychological counseling. This task has not been easy. Wrenn noted in 1970 that the growth of counseling services was so rapid that smooth or systematic development was hardly possible (in Van Hoose & Pietrofesa, 1970).

Two major organizations have developed with the primary responsibility for establishing role definitions, training standards, and ethical procedures for professional counselors. These organizations are the American Personnel and Guidance Association (APGA) and its specific affiliates in counseling and Division 17 of the American Psychological Association (APA). The American Mental Health Counselors Association (AMHCA), composed of counselors in private practice and of marriage and family counselors, has played an important role in highlighting the need for upgrading community counseling. The AMHCA became an affiliate of the APGA, so its contributions will be discussed in that context. Another association not affiliated with either the APA or the APGA that has focused on family and marriage counseling is the American Association of Marriage and Family Therapy (AAMFT). In 1979 this association was chosen as the nationally recognized accrediting body for marriage and family counseling and therapy training programs by the U.S. Department of Health, Education, and Welfare, Department of Health and Human Services.

For a service to be accepted by society as a professional one, the group offering this service must demonstrate that its primary contribution is unique and that its members are specially trained to offer the service to the public. The APGA and its affiliates and Division 17 of the APA have published role definitions, training standards, accrediting and licensing procedures, and guidelines for ethical behavior for counselors based upon a unique function requiring specialized training.

APGA Professional Activities

The APGA and Division 17 have similar roots, as Chapter 2 will demonstrate. Their descriptions of counselor roles are thus similar. However, although the APGA originally was developed by members of the APA interested in counseling, these groups have not worked together on the professional development of counselors. The reasons for this lack of cooperative effort and the differences in emphasis will be elaborated upon in Chapter 2. A chief distinction to note now is that the APGA has considered persons with a master's degree as well as those with a doctorate as professional counselors, whereas Division 17 has come to reserve professional status for people with a doctorate in psychology.

The APGA focus on improving the professional status of counselors with a master's degree as well as those with a doctorate in counseling psychology and in counseling and guidance is evident in the APGA's overall descriptions of counselor role and function. Its major emphasis over almost three decades has been to outline roles, training standards, and ethical codes for counselors in elementary and secondary schools, in colleges, and in community agencies specializing in vocational counseling, such as rehabilitation and placement agencies. The APGA guidelines have been useful in the consideration of certification of counselors in these settings.

In the past few years the APGA has moved to the position that the profession of counseling encompasses working with normal concerns and anxieties of persons in the community. In 1977 the APGA developed a model licensing bill, which was updated in 1980, to be used in lobbying state legislators for the licensing of persons with a master's degree in counseling. The affiliation of the American Mental Health Counselors Association with the APGA in 1978 further involved the APGA in community mental health, for the AMHCA was founded for the specific purpose of professionalizing counselors with master's and doctoral degrees working in community clinics and in private practice. In July 1979 a national certification of counselors that had been fostered by the AMHCA went into effect under an independent board. This certification differs from the typical licensing of psychologists in that the professional group, rather than state legislatures, mandates and monitors standards (Messina, 1979). This certification, unlike licensing, does not have legal status.

APA Division 17 Professional Activities

Division 17 published a definition of the counseling psychologist in 1968. This document emphasizes the work of doctorate counselors in counseling, teaching, and doing research at colleges and universities and in handling psychological counseling at Veterans Administration hospitals. The duties of master's-degree counselors in schools, rehabilitation centers, and other community agencies are discussed, but until recently the main concern of Division 17 has in practice been college counseling (Pallone, 1977).

Division 17's most recent proposed *Standards for Providers of Counseling Psychological Services* (September 1979) emphasizes doctorate persons even more. These proposed guidelines follow the APA recommendation that only persons with a doctorate can use the term *psychologist*. The master's-degree person must use *psychological associate* or *psychological assistant*. These persons, it is contended, will require continuous supervision from doctorate counselors throughout their careers.

These standards indicate a growing interest on the part of doctorate counseling psychologists in entering private practice or working in community agencies as psychologists licensed under a state psychological examining board. The APGA and its affiliate the AMHCA are, of course, concerned with licensing for persons with a Ph.D or an Ed.D. in counseling psychology or counselor education, but they also support licensing for master's-degree persons, and they specifically want licensing as professional counselors.

The contributions of both the APGA and Division 17 to the definition of counselor roles and to counselor training standards and ethics will be considered in this book. However, I follow the philosophy of the APGA that professional-counseling services are needed in schools as well as in colleges and communities and that master's-degree persons in counseling are professional. Thus, I will emphasize the APGA standards in discussing school counseling and the standards of both associations when describing college and community counseling.

Definitions of Counseling

The numerous counseling definitions in the counseling and guidance literature have contributed to the definitions of counseling by the professional counselor. Pietrofesa, Hoffman, Splete, and Pinto (1978) and Shertzer and Stone (1980) discuss common elements in these definitions of professional counseling. These authors first note the loose usage of the term *counseling* in the occupational world—there are, for example, rug counselors, pest-control counselors, financial counselors, and camp counselors. They then analyze definitions of *counseling* used in a psychological sense.

Shertzer and Stone present a historical review of definitions that encompass similar characteristics. The review demonstrates that the counseling process has moved from an early stress on cognitive factors to an increasing inclusion of affective experiences as well. Professional counseling got its start in the highly cognitive areas of educational and vocational choice and changed its emphasis when personal counseling for mentally normal people became more acceptable and when vocational development began to be considered part of total personal development (Super, 1953). A standout in this review is Patterson's (1967) discussion of the unique, specific emphasis upon the voluntary nature of counseling, the importance of confidentiality, and the necessity of respecting the client's rights to privacy. These ethical issues were essential elements of successful counseling as defined by Rogers in his 1942 book on nondirective counseling.

After analyzing these various definitions, Shertzer and Stone arrive at a composite definition adapted from Blocher's (1974) developmental-counseling approach. According to Shertzer and Stone, "Counseling is an interaction process which facilitates meaningful understanding of self and environment and results in the establishment and/or clarification of goals and values for future behavior" (p. 20).

Pietrofesa and his colleagues (1978) point out a number of characteristics of professional counseling. These include: (1) counseling involves a professional relationship offered by a competent counselor; (2) in this relationship the client learns decision-making skills, problem resolution, and new behaviors or attitudes; and (3) the relationship is built upon a mutual enterprise. The authors conclude: "Counseling, then, . . . is a relationship between a professionally trained, competent counselor and an individual seeking help in gaining greater self-understanding and improved decision-making and behavior-change skills for problem resolution and/or developmental growth" (p. 6).

The APGA Definition of Counseling

Professional psychological counseling as defined by the APGA conforms to the definitions of counseling as a relationship between a professionally trained person and an individual needing help with normal anxieties or conflicts or with decision making. Loughary, Stripling, and Fitzgerald (1965) summarized the results of a nationwide study by counselors, administrators, and teachers under the auspices of the APGA and its affiliates the American School Counselor Association (ASCA) and the Association for Counselor Education and Supervision (ACES). In that report, ASCA presented a policy statement for secondary school counselors based on the survey in which counseling is defined as "a confidential, accepting, non-evaluative, permissive, face-to-face relationship, in which the counselor uses his knowledge and competencies to assist the pupil to resolve better those problems and issues which he would normally resolve less satisfactorily without counseling assistance" (p. 99).

In the rationale developed by the APGA and its affiliates since 1965 for counselor roles in schools and postsecondary institutions, the definitions become more specific about problem areas covered by counseling. These areas include helping individuals work through concerns in the personal, social, vocational, and educational domains (see Appendix A). The 1980 APGA Licensure Commission's model licensing bill developed to help convince state legislators to license counselors specified these areas directly when defining the proposed legal domain of professional-counseling practice as follows: "The practice of counseling within the meaning of this act is defined as . . . the application of counseling procedures and other related areas of the behavioral sciences to help in learning how to solve problems or make decisions related to careers, personal growth, marriage, family, or other interpersonal concerns" (p. 23a).

From my point of view, the APGA model licensing bill, which was designed primarily for counseling in private practice and in community agencies, exemplifies the similarities between counseling in educational settings and counseling for the general public. The normal concerns and conflicts of individuals in personal, social, and career domains are the focus of licensed professional counselors. Family, marriage, and couple counseling for normally functioning persons in conflict is emphasized rather than counseling for the dysfunctional individual, family, or couple with chronic long-term emotional disabilities. The emphasis is the same in counseling for schools and post-secondary educational institutions.

During the past few years, the American Mental Health Counselor's Association (AMHCA) has consolidated its aims with those of the APGA. Its areas of appropriate counseling concerns were similar to those of other APGA counselor roles. The AMHCA Certification Committee (1979) defined professional counseling as "the process of assisting individuals or groups, through a helping relationship, to achieve optimal mental health through personal and social development and adjustment to prevent the debilitating effects of certain somatic, emotional and intra- and/or interpersonal disorders" (p. 24). Career and educational counseling are not specifically mentioned, but the competencies of a certified professional counselor as defined by this group include vocational counseling.

The ethical code of the APGA (reproduced in Appendix C) further defines professional counseling by stating that it involves freedom of choice, rights to privacy, and confidentiality (Section B; Callis, 1976). The counseling relationship is also distinguished from an administrative relationship in the APGA code: "This section refers to practices involving individual and/or group counseling relationships, and it is not intended to be applicable to practices involving administrative relationships" (Section B). Thus, when a professional counselor is involved in an administrative, supervisory, and/or evaluative relationship with an individual seeking counseling, the counselor is expected to refer the person to another counselor.

The APA Division 17 Definition of Counseling

In the 1968 publication by the APA's Division of Counseling Psychology, *The Counseling Psychologist*, counseling is defined as work with individuals or groups with personal, social, educational, and vocational concerns. The final draft of proposed *Standards for Providers of Counseling Psychological Services* published in September 1979 by Division 17 states that counseling psychological services "are used by individuals, couples and families in populations of all age groups to cope with problems in connection with education, career choice, work, sex, marriage, family . . ." (Appendix A).

Division 17 members abide by the code of ethics of the American Psychological Association. This code, which appears in Appendix C, is geared to general psychologists, so that the process of counseling is not spelled out. Nevertheless, the code does include the APGA code's elements of free choice and confidentiality in discussing psychological services. The proposed 1979 standards say: "Counseling Psychologists are responsible for making their service readily accessible to users in a manner that facilitates the user's freedom of choice" (p. 16).

In summary, the definitions of counseling by the APGA and Division 17 are very similar. They specify a competent counselor working with conflicts, anxieties, or concerns related to personal, social, career, or educational decisions. Also, counselors are expected to have professional preparation and personal characteristics that will enable them to understand psychological processes and behavior dynamics in the client, in the counselor, and in the relationship between the two. Finally, counseling is based upon the free choice of the client and built upon confidentiality in the relationship.

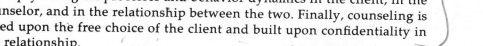

Definitions of the Counselor's Primary Role

The APGA Role Definition

A definition of the counselor's primary role in secondary schools was developed jointly by the APGA and its affiliates the American School Counselor Association (ASCA) and the Association for Counselor Education and Supervision (ACES) in a five-year national study reported by Loughary and associates (1965). This definition was first updated by the ASCA in 1974. In that year the ASCA also published separate role descriptions for elementary school counselors, middle school counselors, and postsecondary counselors (the only one not subsequently revised) that were very similar to the definition of the secondary school counselor's role. In 1977 the ASCA published a further revision of the secondary school counselor's role in the March issue of *The School Counselor* and a revision of the elementary and middle school counselor's roles in the February 1978 issue of *Elementary School Guidance and Counseling* (see Appendix A).

In all of these role definitions, direct counseling through development of a counseling relationship is the major function of the counselor. The counselor is described as uniquely prepared to work with individuals wrestling with developmental conflicts, concerns, or decisions in the personal, social, vocational, and educational areas appropriate to the age level and developmental needs of the individual.

The APGA proposal for licensing professional counselors is highly consistent with the ASCA role definitions. Similarly, the description of the major function of the mental-health counselor focuses on counselor competency to assist individuals and groups in gaining optimal mental health and personal and social adjustment.

The APA Division 17 Role Definition

The 1968 Division 17 publication about counseling psychologists states that they provide "individual and group guidance and counseling services in schools, colleges and universities, hospitals, clinics, rehabilitation centers, and industry, to assist individuals in achieving more effective personal, social, educational, and vocational development and achievement" (p. 1).

In the 1979 proposed standards for counseling psychologists mentioned earlier, the attempts of counseling psychologists to emphasize that they are psychologists become evident, and the role definition of the counseling psychologist appears less definite. The term *counseling* is used very sparingly. The word *intervention* becomes a key one. According to this document, the role includes evaluation, diagnosis, and assessment of the functioning of individuals and groups. These activities are those considered to be typical of the general applied psychologist. In addition, the counseling or therapeutic activities are perceived as interventions to facilitate overall personal development or to assist those individuals having problems with it.

Definitions of the Counselor's Secondary Roles

A counselor performs important functions other than direct counseling that contribute to the well-being of individuals in an educational institution or in the community. These functions indicate how counselors can use their special expertise to supplement or complement individual counseling.

The APGA and Division 17 role definitions include group counseling, family counseling, group interactions, consultation, psychological education, career education, and guidance activities as important secondary functions of counselors (see Appendix A). Also included is the responsibility of counselors to involve themselves in social-change activities designed to improve the environment and overall mental health of an educational institution or a community. Trained counselors or counseling psychologists supervise beginning counselors and counseling psychologists on jobs and are also responsible for supervising interns from college or university programs.

The emphasis upon specific types of secondary functions depends somewhat upon the setting in which the counselor works and the age range he or she is serving, the experience of the counselor, and whether the counselor has a master's degree or a doctorate. For example, family counseling might be expected in elementary and secondary schools and in community centers but be rare in a 4-year college. Marriage counseling would be considered essential in community agencies and colleges but would be less likely to occur in secondary schools. Appraisal activities, such as testing, would be more likely to be a function of a counselor in an educational setting than in a community agency. Involvement in graduate training and research would be expected more of doctorate persons.

Some counselors, after finishing preparation for professional counseling, decide to specialize in one of the secondary functions just described. A counselor may, for example, take intensive training in family or marriage counseling and concentrate on that. This action is not inconsistent with professional standards, since the person will have had the training to do overall counseling before specializing in one area.

Crisis Intervention

Although professionally trained counselors are geared to working with normal concerns of individuals, they must also be prepared to see persons who are experiencing emotional crises requiring immediate help. Persons experiencing emotional trauma or personal disorientation because of a life crisis will seek out or will be referred to a counseling staff with a good professional reputation. These counselors should know how to help people cope with immediate distress feelings that occur through the sudden death of a loved one, severe drug or alcohol reactions, a sudden break in intimate relationships, suicidal feelings, and incidences of anxiety reactions. After rendering immediate help, a counselor must determine whether to continue working with the client or to refer the individual to another professional person or to another appropriate community agency.

All role definitions do not include explicit recognition of this crisis service, but, in practice, counselors are expected to handle them. The

AMHCA has described the crisis function as a major one for community counselors.

The Professional Preparation of Counselors

Education and training standards for the preparation of counselors were recommended by the ACES in the 1960s and were updated and approved by ACES members in 1973. The 1973 document, *Standards for the Preparation of Counselors and Other Personnel Services Specialists*, outlines the standards leading to a master's degree. In 1977 the ACES approved the document *Guidelines for Doctoral Preparation in Counselor Education* (Stripling, 1978) (see Appendix B).

An understanding of sociocultural factors, behavior dynamics, and human development is at the core of these preparation standards. The standards also encompass perceptions about normal concerns and conflicts of individuals in their own development, in their interactions with others, and in their exploration and choice of careers. Professional, legal, and ethical issues related to counselor-client interactions are included as well. Thus, central to all recommended standards is knowledge of theories of personality; of theories of and techniques in individual, group, and family counseling; of systems of interpersonal skills; of legal and ethical codes; and of tests or inventories related to vocational, educational, personal, or interpersonal decision making. Finally, the keystone to comprehensive preparation programs is practicum at the college setting and internship experience in the selected work settings closely supervised by professionally trained counselors.

The ACES guidelines for a doctorate in counselor education expect graduates to have a strong background in the behavioral sciences and skill in individual and group counseling, consulting, and research. Knowledge of and skills in career guidance, learning theory, research, testing and evaluation, statistics, and research design are other expectations. The guidelines also suggest thorough preparation for supervision and administration of counseling programs or for clinical teaching. This program would require a minimum of 4 academic years of graduate work with at least 1 year of full-time internship (Stripling, 1978).

As a result of considerable work by the ACES Commission on Standards Implementation, an ACES Committee on Accreditation was formed in July 1978 to set up procedures for the evaluation and accreditation of both entry and doctorate programs in counseling. Five regional workshops were set up throughout the country to train evaluators of counselor education programs. In 1979 the APGA Executive Committee decided that the APGA would assume responsibility for accrediting counselor education programs.

The APGA licensing proposal (1980) sets a minimum of a master's degree in counseling. The board would also accept 3 years of supervised full-time experience in professional counseling. The 1973 *Standards for the Preparation of Counselors and Other Personnel Services Specialists* and the 1978 ACES Committee on Accreditation procedures are both used as guidelines. The national counselor certification standards launched through the AMHCA's efforts require a graduate degree from a college or university approved by a regional accrediting agency with 60 semester or 90 quarter hours of graduate study. Included on the evaluation examination for certification are counseling theories and techniques, rehabilitation, vocational and career counseling, abnormal behavior, theories of human behavior, learning and personality theories, group dynamics, appraisal procedures, professional identity and ethics, supervision skills, and supervised internships. Specialized experiences can be substituted for some academic work up to a point if acceptable to the board (Messina, 1979; Seiler & Messina, 1979).

The training recommendations of Division 17 in 1968 and in the proposed standards in 1978 do not differ significantly from those of the ACES in content to be covered and practicum and internships expected. Typical common areas of psychology—such as learning, perception, social psychology, personality theory, abnormal psychology, human development, and statistics—are included. Specialty areas in vocational development, assessment, individual and group theories, ethical considerations, consultation experience, and 1 year of full-time internship are also listed. However, in the 1979 standards, the training recommendations do not include specific curriculum expectations. Instead, the curriculum is left to the discretion of the university or professional school offering the doctorate degree in counseling psychology (see Appendix B).

Accreditation of programs through an APA Committee on Training Standards is reserved for doctoral programs only. When state licensing is granted to counseling psychologists, it most often comes through a board composed of psychological examiners. Some states, such as Washington and Oregon, offer limited licensing to master's-degree persons in counseling through the state psychological examining board. These persons are licensed as psychological associates or psychological assistants and are expected to do private practice only in consultation with or under the supervision of a doctoral psychologist.

Although counselors in private practice were not numerous, the APGA did establish the International Association of Counseling Services to evaluate standards and practices of agencies or of persons offering counseling services to the public. Generally, the standards developed by this association cover persons involved in vocational, educational, and personal counseling, including marriage and rehabilitation services. A certificate of approval is granted agencies meeting the standards.

Ethical Codes for the Counseling Profession

An ethical code for counselors was developed by the APGA in 1961 and updated in the 1970s. In 1973 the ASCA published a code of ethics similar to that of its parent organization to cover school counselors. (Both of these codes appear in Appendix C.) In addition to contributing to the definition of a counseling relationship as voluntary, nonevaluative, and confidential, the codes cover counselor professional and ethical behavior in other areas of functioning. These other areas are group counseling, measurement and evaluation, research and publication, consulting and private practice, personnel administration, and preparation standards.

Unless there is a clear-cut and imminent danger to the client or others, counseling must be kept confidential. Counselors must use valid and reliable tests, consider the client's cultural or ethnic background in interpreting test results, and keep the test results confidential. In research with human subjects, the research must not be harmful to the subjects, the purpose must be explained to the subjects at the beginning or end of the research, and participation must be voluntary. Consultation is described in the APGA code as "a voluntary relationship between a professional helper and help-needing social unit . . . in which the consultant is attempting to give help to the client in the solution of some current or potential problem" (Section E). These consultations must be within the expertise of the counselor, and decisions arrived at must be the client's free choice. The preparation standards for teachers of counseling outline their special ethical responsibilities. Among these is that varied theoretical counseling positions should be presented, so that trainees can arrive at their own position.

The APA's code of ethics (see Appendix C) emphasizes similar precautions and guidelines. The appropriate use of evaluative material, policies on testing, the importance of functioning only within one's area of expertise, and guidelines for carrying out consultation and research are covered. More emphasis is placed upon the assessment aspects of the profession than in the APGA's code.

The Association for Specialists in Group Work (ASGW), an affiliate of the APGA (1979d), has been working on formulating ethical conduct for group work. The APA in 1973 published guidelines on conducting growth groups.

Unique Aspects of Professional Counseling

The definitions of the counseling process are beginning to be more carefully spelled out in the standards of both the APGA and the APA. In particular, as the granting of credentials and licenses through state or national examining boards increases the need for specifying the unique contribution of counseling becomes more compelling.

Since the APGA definition focuses on counseling as a psychological process rather than on the psychologist practicing counseling, the unique professional contribution that counselors make to psychological and educational services stands out more vividly there than in the Division 17 definition. But in any case, no other professional workers in psychology, education, or social work are trained with a primary emphasis on helping persons of all ages resolve conflicts, problems, or anxieties related to everyday living. Nor does any other professional group specifically define the primary relationship as a voluntary, confidential, nonevaluative one.

A number of trained persons whose professional focus is not on normal anxieties and concerns do include counseling as a subsidiary function. Such people include some social workers trained primarily in casework and in working in community/home relationships, some clinical psychologists trained predominantly in behavior management and control of mentally aberrant or pathological behavior, some psychiatrists trained to treat mental illness, and some personnel trained to administer student services.

Whereas these professional workers have used counseling in a tangential or general way to supplement their major psychological or educational service, professional counselors have perceived their major function to be psychological or mental-health counseling and have attempted to define their specific activities and to describe the uniqueness of the profession. Their professional training and their internships have been immersed in working with normal developmental conflicts, concerns, and decision making and not with pathological processes or administrative personnel services.

Later chapters of this book will discuss counseling programs in schools, colleges, and community agencies based upon these standards. First, however, let us look at some of the reasons why counselors have had difficulties gaining sufficient professional strength to implement these standards and some possible ways to resolve the difficulties (Chapter 2), at some professional, ethical, and legal issues in counseling (Chapter 3), and at some counseling theories and techniques and their application to counseling practice in schools, colleges, and communities (Chapter 4).

Projects and Activities

1. *What behaviors or characteristics distinguish persons with normal conflicts and anxieties from those persons whose conflicts or anxieties are considered pathological, neurotic, or psychotic?*

2. *The position taken in this chapter is that counseling is an emerging and grow-*

ing profession. Some counselors argue that counseling is old fashioned and out of date and has proved to be ineffective. Explore and evaluate the arguments for both positions from the standpoint of professional definitions and standards.

3. *Consider the statement that an increase in options provides for a richer life. Consider also the comment that this increase may lead to more conflicts. Are these statements, in your opinion, contradictory? Why or why not?*

4. *What are the similarities and differences among a license, certification, and a credential? What are the relative advantages and disadvantages for members of a professional group considering each of these possibilities?*

5. *Compare the APGA/ASCA's definition of the counselor's primary role with that of the APA's Division 17. What are the similarities and differences for a nonlicensed person working in an educational institution or a community counseling center? What are the similarities and differences for a person in private practice?*

6. *Compare the APGA, ASCA, and APA codes of ethics as they apply to psychological counselors, on the issues of freedom of choice (voluntary counseling), the right to privacy, and confidentiality.*

2

Contemporary Problems: A Historical Perspective

Contemporary Confusion

The Inability to Implement Standards

In spite of the excellent work that counselor professional associations have done in developing standards, professional counseling is not available in schools and communities to the degree it is needed. Associations representing counselors have not, as yet, gained the power necessary to enforce their proposed standards or the influence to shape new programs.

Counselors who wish to adhere to professional standards have not been able to convince many school administrators of the value of supporting counseling programs based on these professional guidelines. Nor have they been able to convince enough practicing school counselors of the importance of joining counselor professional associations. Thus, many professionally trained secondary school counselors are assigned administrative or clerical duties that impede or even prevent the development of counseling relationships. Such counselors have little power to change the situation. Only recently have elementary school counselors begun to be hired in significant numbers. Even then, too many of them are assigned administrative, evaluative, and testing duties that take precedence over counseling.

School counselors' lack of professional strength has further deleterious effects. State departments of instruction in some states virtually disregard the professional standards of the APGA, the ASCA, and the ACES. In these states, counselor certification requirements may not include counseling functions. Rather, the requirements parallel teaching or administrative certification.

In the community, directors of mental-health clinics generally have preferred to hire professionally trained social workers rather than professionally trained counselors, partly because social-work training has been more consistent in quality. In some states clinical psychologists have controlled license boards for private practice and have excluded counseling psychologists.

College counseling centers, which originated as a response to needs described by counseling psychologists, have tended in the past decade to take one of two differing paths, both of which have decreased interest in professional individual and group counseling for normal conflicts and for vocational concerns. Some centers have hired increasing numbers of clinical psychologists and have emulated mental-health clinics. Other centers have begun to hire personnel specialists as counselors rather than professionally trained counselors and have become student-development centers emphasizing psychological education. The latter orientation has been particularly prevalent in 2-year community colleges.

Alternative Primary Counselor Roles

These huge gaps between professional standards and actual counseling practice have caused a number of counselor educators and practicing counselors to become very pessimistic about counseling as described by the professional associations. Some disillusioned counselors and counselor educators believe that counseling so described has been unsuccessful because it is old fashioned, inappropriate, and ineffective (Carroll, 1973; Cook, 1971; Warnath, 1973c). They recommend that counselors change their primary focus from direct counseling and work predominantly to improve the mental health of the system, institution, or society in which they are employed. The four primary counselor roles that appear most frequently in the literature as alternatives to direct counseling are counselor/consultant; psychological educator; trainer in communication, relationship, and human-development skills; and agent of social change (Carkhuff & Berenson, 1977; Ivey & Alschuler, 1973a; Lundquist & Chamley, 1971; Sprinthall, 1973).

These alternative ideas about the primary role of professional counselors have been suggested by counselor educators and practicing counselors in schools, colleges, and community agencies. The entire May 1973 issues of the *Personnel and Guidance Journal* and *The School Counselor* were devoted to describing psychological education as the prime function of counselors. In 1977 *The Counseling Psychologist* published an entire issue on the problems that counseling psychologists were having in arriving at a professional identity. In this issue, entitled *Professional Identity*, arguments for developing alternative roles for counseling psychologists as consultants or psychological educators or skill trainers were presented that are remarkably like those presented for school counselors.

Whereas all of these activities are accepted as appropriate counselor secondary functions by counselor professional associations, some professional counselors are recommending that one or more of these secondary functions take precedence over counselors' involvement in individual counseling. Other professionals go a step further and argue that one or more of these secondary functions should replace direct counseling by trained professionals. The first group believes that counselors can prevent the occurrence of many problems that require direct counseling if they educate the public about effective mental-health procedures through consultation and psychological education. These activities, they say, make more efficient and economical use of counselor time than does direct counseling. The other group of professionally trained counselors advocating new primary roles contends that counseling's lack of success stems from counselors' attempting to portray it as a highly skilled professional activity shrouded in unnecessary psychological mysticism (Ivey & Alschuler, 1973a). This group perceives counseling as a relatively simple helping process. Counseling skills are not differentiated from helping skills in the areas of communication, interpersonal relationships, and personal growth. These skills are considered universal, necessary, and sufficient conditions for successful counseling and are simple enough to be taught to almost anyone (Carkhuff, 1972b). According to this model, teachers, parents, community paraprofessionals, and peers do most of the direct counseling under the supervision of a trained counselor (Carroll, 1973).

Ivey has been a major spokesman for simplifying and deprofessionalizing the counseling process. Ivey and Alschuler (1973a) wrote, "We have too long kept our skills to ourselves through a mystifying process we term 'professionalism.' The true professional is committed not only to advancing knowledge but also to sharing it with the public" (p. 596). In the same paper, in discussing Ivey's work and that of Carkhuff, Kagan, and others, the authors comment that these persons have demonstrated "that the skills of counseling can be transmitted to such widely different audiences as medical students, teachers, junior high and elementary students and psychiatric patients" (p. 596).

Pine (1974) summed up the idea of relegating direct counseling to others in his article "Let's Give Away School Counseling." Hurst (1977) represents this view for college counseling. In a similar vein, Carkhuff (1972a) developed a human-technology delivery service called Systematic Human Relations Training for entire communities in which helpers at various skill levels do the majority of direct counseling.

Professional counselors who advocate simplifying counseling question whether the counseling process is a professional activity requiring a considerable amount of training in psychology and education. Their position is clearly one of questioning the professional standards of the APGA, the ASCA, and the APA's Division 17.

The Need to Strengthen the Counseling Profession

Other counselor educators do not believe that the implementation of counseling programs has been unsuccessful because the professional definition of and standards for counseling are out of date, inappropriate, or ineffective. Instead, they perceive the problem as a lack of power of counselor professional associations to insist that standards be enforced so that professional programs can be developed. Dunlop (1968a, 1969) and Patterson (1967) have argued for this view for years. More recently, APGA leaders have supported Dunlop's and Patterson's concerns. For example, Thomas J. Sweeney (APGA, 1979b) and Louise B. Forsyth (APGA, 1980), each of whom has served as president of the APGA, have urged the association to strengthen itself professionally. The APGA licensing guidelines and the establishment in 1978 of the Special APGA committee for Counselor Credentialing are indicative of this attitude.

This book is based upon the premise that failure to implement effective counseling programs results from lack of professional identity and unity, not because counseling is out of date. This chapter defends this belief from a historical perspective.

1900–1920: The Beginning of School Counseling

Vocational counseling and vocational-guidance activities early in the century greatly influenced the development of school counseling. In 1898 Jesse Davis was designated a high school counselor in Detroit. Davis helped students with vocational and educational problems in what was probably the first officially recognized school counseling program. In 1906 Eli Weaver published a pamphlet entitled *Choosing a Career* (Tolbert, 1978). Frank Parsons opened the Vocational Bureau in Boston in 1908 to assist young people in choosing, preparing for, and entering an occupation. He developed a process called vocational counseling to accomplish this task.

In these beginnings in counseling, Davis and Parsons laid the base for the contemporary view that vocational choice and development are related to total personal development. For example, Davis, in a group guidance approach, began to include moral guidance, interpersonal relations, and extracurricular activities in his vocational-guidance units (Mathewson, 1962). Similarly, Parsons (1909) dealt with the character and temperament of individuals in his book *Choosing a Vocation*. Parsons also emphasized self-determinism of the individual, who in turn worked to improve society (Cremin, 1961).

Parsons called himself a vocational counselor. He set up a training program for vocational counselors, and he spoke out about the need for vocational counseling in the public schools and colleges. Unfortunately, Parsons died in September 1908, before he could put his plans for schools into action. However, Stratton Brooks, Superintendent of Schools in Boston, was impressed with the Vocational Bureau and in 1909 designated 117 teachers in Boston elementary and secondary schools as vocational counselors.

School superintendents in other cities followed Boston's example—and with good reason. Society was becoming industrialized; school attendance became compulsory, and most students were no longer aiming at college, as they had in the 1800s. School staffs were thus interested in vocational planning and in job placement for students. By 1910, approximately 30 cities had either developed or were starting to develop programs in vocational planning and job placement. Training in vocational counseling began at Harvard University in 1911. In 1913 a professional association, the National Vocational Guidance Association (NVGA), was founded.

After Parsons's death the term *vocational guidance* began to replace *vocational counseling*. Parsons's stress on individual counseling, self-analysis, and counselee choice was replaced by an emphasis on distribution of occupational information. This distribution of information occurred through group guidance activities and inclusion of occupational courses in the curriculum. The emphasis on occupational guidance was strengthened when the federal government gave funds to public schools to support vocational education through the Smith-Hughes Act of 1917.

During World War I the development of group standardized tests led to a view of guidance and counseling that was somewhat different from the distribution of occupational information. The army asked psychologists to develop assessment devices to screen emotionally and intellectually handicapped draftees, to place draftees in appropriate jobs, and to select superior persons for officer training. Psychologists' efforts led to verbal and nonverbal group intelligence tests (the Army Alpha and Beta) and to Woodworth's Personal Data Sheet. Group testing and group assessment soon proliferated and became a significant force in the growth and direction of vocational guidance.

Counseling theories appropriate for work with people's normal rather than abnormal concerns had not yet been developed. Nor did most psychologists consider common human concerns or conflicts the province of psychology. Between 1900 and 1920, schools used clinical psychologists in college-based clinics for testing for mental retardation or for learning disabilities. Students with emotional problems were referred to community clinics usually staffed with a psychiatrist, a social worker, and a clinical psychologist using psychoanalytic methods and diagnostic testing and social-work case histories. Some schools hired social workers, called them visiting teachers, and used them for attendance problems and minor difficulties in home/school relationships.

1920–1940: The Influence of Progressive Education on Counseling

School Counseling

While vocational counseling was gaining a foothold in Boston, progressive education was being introduced into the public schools by its originator, John Dewey. School staffs, according to Dewey's progressivism, should foster the social, moral, and personal development of children rather than concentrate exclusively on intellectual growth. Dewey believed in a scientific approach to education that would have an impact on the child's total development in and out of school. School experiences were considered an integral part of the total life experience. Dewey recognized the importance of individual differences in children in the educational process. However, he believed that the major way to have positive educational experiences for children was to improve the social and environmental conditions influencing the children. Dewey was thus a forerunner of contemporary psychological educators who describe themselves as agents for social change, social engineers, or human technologists. Dewey (1929) said of education, "We may fairly enough call educational practice a kind of social engineering" (p. 39).

As progressive education flourished in the 1920s and 1930s, some educators continued Dewey's emphasis on social engineering. Others became interested in a highly permissive atmosphere in the classroom. More radical progressivists saw the schools' mission as reconstructing society (Woodring, 1953). Progressive educators differed somewhat upon a basic approach to social change, but all agreed that the school has a central responsibility for the personal, social, and moral education of children. Social and personal development were at the core of all curriculums. The teacher was the central person in helping social and personal development.

The present-day notion of psychological counseling for people's developmental concerns had not yet emerged. Consequently, counselor training continued to emphasize vocational counseling in the 1920s, with the first certification of trained school counselors occurring in Boston in the mid-1920s. In the 1930s faculty members at the University of Minnesota led the way in formulating the first theory of counseling to be used in counselor training. In 1939 E. G. Williamson's book *How to Counsel Students: A Manual of Techniques for Clinical Counselors* was published. In it he proposed a vocational-counseling theory based upon the assumption that personality consists of measurable traits that relate to occupational choice and success. The counseling process included a diagnosis of the individual's problem followed by an analysis of the problem and some alternatives for resolving the problem. The counselor depended upon the scientific measurement of personal traits through the use of vocational-interest and vocational-aptitude tests and upon any other objective data gained from interviews, tests, or other records.

The Progressivist Objection to the Vocational Emphasis in Counseling. Counselors trained in vocational counseling did not thrive in the schools in the 1920s and 1930s under the progressive-education system. Vocational counseling and vocational guidance were consistent with progressivists' ideas about broadening the scope of school beyond intellectual training for college and with their interest in individual differences. However, after some brief initial enthusiasm, progressivists, with some justification, rebelled against the narrow emphasis of vocational guidance. Their focus was on the total development of the child. Also, in spite of their interest in individual differences, their actual emphasis was upon changing the environment of schools through upgrading teachers' skills and through curriculum change rather than on individual counseling.

The Replacement of Vocational Guidance with Educational Guidance. Progressivists' ideas about including personal and social factors in education were crystallized by John Brewer in a book in 1932 entitled *Education as Guidance,* in which he proposed that the objective of education is to increase skill in living. In this text he argued that schools and colleges should guide young people in individual and cooperative activities in the areas of school and home life, citizenship, vocations, leisure and recreation, personal well-being, and religion (p. 17). He outlined special guidance classes, group guidance activities, homeroom discussions, and laboratory activity groups to handle these subjects. He recommended that teachers incorporate guidance into their subject matter by showing the relevance of the subject content to life.

For Brewer, as for most progressive educators, every teacher was a counselor. Teacher training institutions included heavy doses of life-adjustment techniques and life-skill units for both elementary and secondary teachers.

Some positive results arose from progressive ideas. Cumulative records were begun to keep track of the progress of individual students. Attempts to individualize teaching in the classroom according to the child's ability were initiated. It was recognized that emotional factors disturbing a child could inhibit learning. The importance of the relationship of the teacher to each class member was emphasized. And the curriculum offerings were broadened beyond preparation for college.

Attacks Upon Progressive Education. As progressive educational-guidance activities centering around life skills and the personal, social, and moral development of students mushroomed in public schools, these activities came under heavy attack from parents, teachers, educators, and the general public. Professional educators and the general public accused progressivists of being antiintellectual and overly permissive in teaching. They called for a return to fundamentals in education (Bestor, 1953). Other complaints were that schools, under the progressivists' influence, were taking over the development of morals, which rightfully belonged in the home or in churches. A small group accused progressivists of being pinkos or communists and set up witch hunting to find subversives in education (Woodring, 1953).

The Deterioration of Guidance Activities in Schools. These negative reactions were largely a result of some school personnel's preempting the personal, moral, and ethical development of children without sufficiently informing the public or parents of their intent. Rights of privacy and freedom of choice were not given due consideration by some progressivists who went beyond or misunderstood Dewey's proposals. Also, in their zeal for personal development, intellectual development was often neglected. This injudicious behavior on the part of some progressivists justified some of the public wrath. But the negative tide was so great that many of the benefits of the progressive movement in education were lost. Almost all guidance activities deteriorated. In teacher training institutions, courses in life adjustment, life skills, group interaction, and other progressive guidance courses, which had permeated the preparation of teachers, were severely curtailed by opponents of progressivism.

By the beginning of 1940, counseling and guidance services in schools had greatly decreased. Fewer than 10% of schools had one or more staff members assigned to one-half counseling. Two-thirds of the schools had no counselor at all. Brewer (1942, p. 86) estimated that there were probably more counselors in schools in 1915 than in 1942. Those few school counselors who were hired for helping students often functioned in secondary schools in paternalistic roles of schedulers, friendly but firm disciplinarians, or personnel clerks. Elementary counseling had not as yet been developed to any degree.

Students with learning or behavior problems were referred to school psychologists for testing and diagnosis during the 1920s and 1930s. School psychologists, modeled after clinical psychologists, developed as a professional group when clinical psychologists changed their emphasis from intelligence testing of children to diagnostic work with adults in mental-health clinics and mental hospitals after World War II. School social workers were trained as consultants and caseworkers on school/home problems but continued to be used for attendance problems. The numbers of school psychologists and social workers were small, and their work consisted mainly of trying to discover the reasons for student difficulties. School psychologists attempted to diagnose a student's problem through interviews with teachers and parents and through intelligence and personality testing of the child. Then recommendations were made on how to remedy the problem. Social workers used the case-study procedure to assess the home/school situation through home visits, home evaluations, and interviews and also made recommendations on how to improve the home/school interaction. School psychologists often ended up as psychometricians and school social workers as attendance clerks.

Counseling in Colleges and in the Community

Although student personnel work has a long history, going back to the late 1800s, college counseling as a profession did not get its start until the early 1930s at the University of Minnesota. In 1932 Williamson opened the University Testing Bureau, which had developed from research being done at the university on testing of the unemployed. Soon afterward the name was changed to the Student Counseling and Testing Bureau. The Minnesota point of view dominated the training of school and college counselors for the following two decades. Williamson put himself in the progressive camp because his theoretical framework rested on scientific measurement of individual differences and because, like other progressivists, he had a strong commitment to changing the environment of students. As such, he strongly identified counseling with student personnel administration.

Community counseling was still a rarity and remained aloof from progressive influence. Child-guidance clinics still emphasized clinical testing and psychoanalysis. Their staffs usually consisted of a psychiatrist, a clinical psychologist, and a social worker. The majority of private practitioners were psychiatrists, who held M.D.s and were trained in psychoanalysis. They were trained to work predominantly with neurotic complaints or psychotic reactions. Very few clinical psychologists were involved in private practice.

During the depression years the vocational counselors became an important commodity in the community. Since millions of people were unemployed, vocational counselors were needed by federal, state, and local agencies to help in job placement and to initiate retraining for persons out of work. Agencies interested in placement and job training hired school counselors who were trained in vocational guidance, which contributed to the disappearance of counselors from schools.

On a positive note for school guidance, the federal government began to give it support. An Occupational Information and Guidance Service was formed in the U.S. Office of Education. This service in turn established the first state guidance offices in state departments of education. Initial funding for these agencies came through the George-Deen Act of 1936.

1940–1960: The Origin and Development of Counseling Psychology

The Influence of Humanistic Psychology

In the 1940s a trend toward working with psychological concerns of the normal population began that contributed to the development of the profession of counseling psychology. Jewish humanistic psychologists and psychiatrists came to the United States to avoid extermination by the Nazis. Their emphasis on the human condition gradually made an impact upon the traditional scientific emphasis in U.S. psychology and gave impetus to the work of Rollo May, Abraham Maslow, and Carl Rogers. In addition, they began a trend toward a more accepting public attitude toward psychology.

Rogers became interested in humanistic self theory, and his epoch-making book on nondirective counseling, *Counseling and Psychotherapy*, was published in 1942. He defined counseling explicitly as a voluntary relationship with a predominantly normal population. Rogers, a clinical psychologist, attacked his own profession as being preoccupied with pathology and with diagnostic testing. He accused the majority of psychologists, psychiatrists, and vocational counselors of dehumanizing clients. He perceived counseling as a unique helping relationship. He carefully differentiated a counseling relationship from relationships with friends, parents, other psychologists, or social workers because of its nonevaluative, voluntary, and nonlegal nature. He denounced the use of diagnostic testing as being detrimental to developing a counseling relationship. As director of the counseling center at the University of Chicago, he developed a service exclusively based on client-centered, or nondirective, methods of counseling. Rogers challenged the strong position that Williamson's clinical counseling had held in counseling for almost 15 years. A series of debates were held starting in 1946 between Williamson and Rogers on the relative merits of directive counseling (Williamson) and nondirective counseling (Rogers). In 1951, while Rogers was at Ohio State University, his second book was published. In this book he used the term *client-centered counseling* and described what he considered the major components of a helping relationship as warmth, congruency, and empathy.

Rogers had little success in influencing most clinical psychologists. Many were not interested in working with clients with normal conflicts. One important reason was that a highly active group of clinical psychologists was much more concerned with challenging psychiatrists' claims that because they had had medical training they were the only professionals who should be licensed to do private practice with emotionally disturbed persons.

The Influence of Veterans Administration Training Programs

The Veterans Administration, near the end of World War II, provided the impetus that promoted the profession of counseling psychology. Many veterans expressed a need for vocational counseling and for help with personal concerns. Congress, under the GI Bill, provided college or vocational-training funds for any veteran desiring them. VA vocational guidance centers were set up in colleges and in the community to help veterans explore vocational aims. The VA funded doctoral training and gave paid internships and stipends for counselor training. In doing so, the VA rewrote specifications for vocational counselors and coined the term *counseling psychologist*.

Division 17: Counseling Psychology

In 1952 the Counseling and Guidance Division of the American Psychological Association responded to this VA action by dropping the term *guidance* and renaming itself the Division of Counseling Psychology. Super (1955), a member of Division 17, wrote that counseling psychology arose out of a merger of a broadening vocational counseling and the new humanistic therapeutic approach. He recommended that the term *vocational development* replace the idea of vocational choice and that vocational development be considered an integral part of total personality development. As such, counseling for vocational concerns was not perceived as separate from other developmental concerns. Super also distinguished clinical psychology from counseling psychology. Clinical psychology he described as being concerned with the diagnosis and treatment of psychopathology, whereas counseling psychology was concerned with the healthy, normal aspects of growth. Also, clinical psychologists were expected to intern in a mental hospital or mental-health clinic; counseling psychologists tended to intern and work in educational settings, such as college counseling centers, and in vocational-rehabilitation services in hospitals. Clinical and counseling psychologists, however, both followed a scientist/practitioner model in which the psychologist is trained for both services and research.

Professional Maneuvers and Their Influence on School Counseling

Until the 1950s the main professional group for school counselors and for other master's-degree counselors was the National Vocational Guidance Association (NVGA). With the expansion of counseling to include vocational development and other personal and social concerns of individuals, the NVGA was no longer broad enough to cover the interests of school counselors. However, APA and Division 17 membership requirements were stringent. At first a 2-year master's degree was expected and a Ph.D. preferred. Soon a doctorate was mandatory for full membership. Many school counselors were not eligible, nor was Division 17 particularly interested in incorporating school counseling into its organization. In fact, many counseling psychologists did not consider school counselors as psychological workers but perceived them as guidance or student personnel workers who might move into administrative jobs in the schools (Super, 1955). There was then no professional association with which school counselors could identify.

Some of the originators of counseling psychology sensed a need for and urged the development of a new association for counselors with training below the doctorate. In 1952 the National Vocational Guidance Association (NVGA), the American College Personnel Association (ACPA), and the National Association of Guidance Supervisors and Counselor Trainers (NAGS) merged to form the American Personnel and Guidance Association (APGA). Super (1955) pointed out that the APGA was an interest group, not a professional association like the American Psychological Association. The implication of that statement was that the association would not be expected to establish or monitor standards. This emphasis did prevail, so that membership requirements in qualifications or experience were lax. Members of Division 17 made strong statements that they were psychologists professionally prepared specifically for psychological counseling. Members of the APGA appeared content to see themselves as nonprofessionals in broad guidance activities that included counseling. The names of the merging associations indicate the strong identification of counseling with guidance to the practical exclusion of psychological understanding.

The American School Counselor Association (ASCA) was formed as a subdivision of the APGA, as was the American Rehabilitation Counseling Association (ARCA). The National Association of Guidance Supervisors and Counselor Trainers changed its name to the Association for Counselor Education and Supervision (ACES). Clearly, in the early 1950s counselors with a master's degree who were members of the APGA were not considered professionals by Division 17 although they grew from the same historical roots and although job descriptions of basic responsibilities were similar. For example, Super (1955), describing the reorganization in the early 1950s of counselor training programs at Teachers College, Columbia University, said that counseling psychology was allied with clinical programs in psychology and that "The Master's program for school counseling was merged with that in another, non-psychological, area called Student Personnel Administration" (p. 8). He added that many other universities followed suit. Most counseling and counseling-psychology training at master's and doctorate levels ended up in education departments or schools of education, with only a few programs housed in psychology departments, although the American Psychological Association presumably was the professional association "responsible" for counseling psychology.

Largely because of this professional maneuvering, counselor preparation and training became confusing and erratic. Persons with doctorates in counseling psychology, from either education or psychology, in counseling and guidance, and in student personnel administration all purported to be counselor educators. Graduates of counseling-psychology programs with a master's degree perceived themselves as psychological counselors, and graduates of guidance-oriented programs perceived themselves as guidance specialists doing primarily educational counseling. The latter were often called guidance counselors.

The Return of School Counseling to Vocational Guidance

In the 1950s, interest increased in counseling for people's normal concerns; Rogers's client-centered theory, geared to these concerns, continued to gain in popularity. Counselor training programs began to broaden the base of counseling from strictly vocational concerns to concerns and conflicts in personal and social areas. However, these new counseling approaches had little impact on school counseling practice. Secondary school counselors continued to be bogged down in administrative detail. Elementary school counselors were still practically nonexistent.

In 1957 an international event regenerated interest in secondary school counseling and refocused it on vocational guidance. The USSR launched Sputnik, the first space satellite. Concerned that the USSR was getting ahead of the United States in science, Congress pushed through the National Defense Education Act (NDEA) in 1958. The major purpose was to discover scientific and academic talent in schools and to encourage its development. Title V-A of this act provided funds to upgrade secondary school counseling programs. Title V-B provided funds and stipends to train counselors through counseling and guidance institutes.

As a result of these institutes, the number of secondary school counselors increased significantly. However, as might be expected in any crash program, neither the quality of counselor practice nor career guidance improved noticeably. Generally, counselor educators were hampered both by federal regulations that limited the scope of the programs and by the short-term training. On the positive side, elementary counseling received a boost when the NDEA was extended to include elementary counseling in 1964.

During these years state certification of secondary school counselors continued to increase. By 1960, 38 states had some form of certification (Wrenn, 1962). These certification standards were not consistent throughout the states. Some required only a few courses. Provisional certificates provided loopholes, so that administrators could hire untrained counselors without penalties or censure. Thus, counseling practice was not improved to any appreciable degree by this erratic certification.

1960–1970: Attempts at Professionalism

The Rapid Growth of Counseling Theories—Humanism versus Behaviorism

Humanistic psychology quickly gained favor in the 1960s. Humanists' focus on the feelings and emotions of normally developing persons and their emphasis upon relationships in individual and group counseling were consistent with counselors' emphasis upon normal counseling concerns and upon people's ability to resolve conflicts. Encounter and sensitivity-training groups began to mushroom. Personal-growth groups and workshops came into vogue. Gestalt techniques were added to the repertoire of counselors. The phrase *third force in psychology* was used to describe humanism as opposed to behaviorism and psychoanalysis.

At the same time, behaviorists became more interested in normal behaviors. Behavioristic techniques that had proven useful with schizophrenics, mentally retarded persons, delinquents, and hyperactive persons requiring social management began to be applied to normal behavior patterns. Smoking, overeating, nail biting, and fears of particular actions or objects (phobias) became suitable concerns for counseling. Krumboltz edited a book published in 1966 on behavioral counseling that he called *Revolution in Counseling*.

In the 1960s the major forces in counseling and guidance were agreed to be humanism and behaviorism. Rogers and B. F. Skinner engaged in debates on the merits of each position (Wann, 1964). Some counseling psychologists combined humanistic, behavioristic, and Williamson's earlier clinical counseling into developmental-counseling theories (Blocher, 1966; Tyler, 1969).

The Development of Role Definitions and Training and Ethical Standards

The leaders of the APGA, the ASCA, and the ACES responded to the new counseling trends in a highly professional manner. The APGA published a sound code of ethics for counselors in 1961. The ASCA and the ACES, under the aegis of the APGA, set up nationwide committees to define roles and establish training and ethical standards for counselors. Committees composed of counselors, teachers, administrators, and the general public contributed to these role definitions and training and ethical standards. After a 5-year study J. W. Loughary, Stripling, and Fitzgerald (1965) edited an APGA report summarizing the role definitions and training standards of school counselors based upon recommendations and training standards described in Chapter 1. All of these descriptions reflected the growing need to make counseling available to persons with normal concerns, the recognition that vocational concerns are part of total development, and the importance of honoring rights to privacy. These definitions were consistent with the Division 17 perception of counseling psychology rather than being statements aimed primarily at guidance or student personnel activities.

Division 17 also responded to the expanded view of counseling during these years. Various theories of vocational development were published by counseling psychologists in which personal and social conflicts were perceived as a part of some vocational conflicts. Counseling psychologists increased the range of normal concerns seen as appropriate for counselors. In 1968 the pamphlet *The Counseling Psychologist* was published by Division 17. Doctoral and subdoctoral job placements were discussed. It was mentioned that some subdoctoral counseling psychologists worked in public schools.

Journals about counseling issues and counseling research were published by the APGA and its affiliates and by Division 17. *The School Counselor*, the *Personnel and Guidance Journal*, *Counselor Education and Supervision*, and *The Vocational Guidance Quarterly* are examples of APGA publications. Meanwhile, the *Journal of Counseling Psychology*, a research-oriented journal, was developed by a group of counseling psychologists and later taken over by Division 17. In 1969 Division 17 started publishing *The Counseling Psychologist*, a journal dedicated to topical discussions of theory and practice.

Difficulties in Implementing Professional Roles and Standards

In spite of the prodigious, careful work done by the ACES and the ASCA in establishing professional standards, these associations were not able to implement or enforce them. The professional identity of counselors remained confused. Some members of the APGA were suggesting that the association increase counseling activities, while others recommended that the association increase its involvement in guidance activities. From a theoretical standpoint, the APGA had described itself in its standards as a professional home for counselors. From a practical standpoint, the APGA was not able to serve in that capacity.

Division 17, which was specifically set up as an association for professional counseling, was having its own difficulties in gaining professional recognition. Since large numbers of counseling-psychology preparation programs were in education rather than psychology departments, professional recognition was not strongly supported by the APA in general, by the APA's Division 12 (clinical psychology), or by some directors of college or community counseling agencies. In some states counseling psychologists with a doctorate from education departments were having trouble obtaining licensing as psychologists for private practice from state psychological examining boards dominated by clinical psychologists. Thus, many counseling psychologists with a doctorate trying to gain status from the APA and from other professionals did not find it expedient to support professional status for counselors with a master's degree. This attitude prevailed even though Division 17 had earlier included master's-degree persons in its official, published role description.

For these reasons, counseling psychologists with a doctorate who were interested in and involved in counselor preparation for a master's degree were placed in a dilemma when support for professional status of master's-degree persons became an issue. These professional struggles resulted in Division 17's having minimum impact on the growth and accreditation of counseling programs at the doctorate or master's level.

The Lack of Development of Professional Counseling

Although the APGA did have some impact on federal legislation, particularly in the vocational area, the development of the APGA as an interest group without monitoring ability left professionally trained counselors in schools and the community without strong professional backing. Not only was the APGA unable to monitor the training and practice of counselor members, but it could not influence nonmembers or apply sanctions to schools or agencies not following the standards. Also, since membership requirements were very broad, so as to include interests other than counseling, some APGA members themselves downplayed professional or psychological counseling.

School counselors tended to join education associations, which were more powerful politically than the counselor associations. Education associations had lobbyists to influence legislators, and they were strong bargaining agents for salary and tenure benefits. These groups also had some clout with state departments of education. Thus, many counselors opted to identify with teacher-dominated associations and did not join or identify with the ASCA. Also, unsuccessful attempts were made to move the ASCA from the APGA into the National Education Association. So school administrators continued to place teachers who were relatively untrained in counseling positions. These teachers often willingly accepted administrative and personnel tasks incongruous with counseling. Many counselors perceived themselves as teachers and resisted the ASCA's recommendation that a teaching certificate and/or teaching experience not be mandated.

Counseling in Colleges and in the Community

In the 1960s the number of college counseling centers continued to increase. The original strong emphasis on vocational counseling was broadened to include personal and social concerns not related to vocational choice or development. Group counseling became popular. Outreach programs increased. As humanistic existential theories became major forces in counseling practice, counselors in college centers gradually began to pay less attention to vocational conflicts and concerns.

Community mental health received a boost when Congress passed the Community Mental Health Act of 1963, which had been proposed by President John F. Kennedy. Federal funds became available to states for constructing community-based mental-health programs. The chief characteristic was the centralization in communities of all mental-health services, from hospitalization to counseling for typical conflicts in everyday living. A trend toward curtailing or closing mental hospitals began. Unfortunately, these comprehensive community mental-health programs were financed by gradually decreasing federal subsidies; the community was progressively to take over more of the cost. Most communities, even with state help, did not have the financial capability to maintain programs. Once more, clinic staffs emphasized or were totally involved with serious emotional problems.

Nevertheless, a need for professional counseling was becoming more evident. In the 1960s a cultural revolution occurred that brought about changing attitudes and behaviors related to sex, marriage, work ethics, education, and lifestyles in general. The popularity of drugs for increasing self-awareness led to a rise in the use and abuse of drugs. The gains in civil rights for ethnic minorities and women regarding career options and lifestyles created opportunities, conflicts, and the need to make decisions for these groups. Yet there was little professional counseling available. Some drop-in clinics and crisis centers started to develop in the late 1960s in metropolitan areas. However, because of lack of money and of trained personnel, these clinics were too often staffed by untrained individuals with interest in human concerns but with little consultation or supervision available. These clinics functioned on small salaries and meager operating funds.

The popularity of encounter, sensitivity, and personal-growth groups grew astronomically. A group craze hit colleges and the community. Most groups were led by untrained persons with missionary zeal who paid little attention to potential psychological harm. Some people believed that psychological health emerged by simply dropping all defenses through intimate self-disclosure.

States continued to approve licensing for doctorate psychologists to handle private practice, and increasing numbers of clinical psychologists

chose this route. During these years there seemed to be an increased willingness on the part of doctorate psychologists to discuss ways of professionally upgrading persons with a master's degree in psychological areas.

1970–1980: The Struggle over Counselor Professionalization

The Increase in Counseling Needs

Counseling needs in schools and in the community increased rapidly in
the 1970s. But the difficulty in getting quality counseling programs
launched in the schools continued. Drop-in clinics, self-help workshops,
personal-growth groups, and skills-training workshops of all sorts proliferated in the community. These clinics and workshops continued to be
run on small budgets and to be staffed by volunteers and paraprofessionals who lacked sufficient training. Many of these clinics and referral centers dealt with normal developmental conflicts of adolescents, postadoles-
cents, and senior citizens in the areas of careers, sex, social interactions,
and personal concerns. They could profitably have been staffed with
trained counselors, but even if a clinic wanted to hire some, they were not
usually available.

The Revival of Progressive-Guidance Activities

In the early 1970s, while professional counseling was having difficulties
gaining credibility in schools and in the community, a regeneration of interest in guidance activities in educational settings occurred. A surge of
interest in humanistic and developmental psychology gave rise again to
beliefs that developing students needed "humanized learning environments" and that teachers needed training in relationship skills. Progressive-education activities for the personal, moral, and social development
of students that had been extinguished in the 1940s and 1950s reappeared
in updated form. The term *humanistic education* was used in the literature
more frequently, and curriculums based upon affective components of
education were published (Patterson, 1973a; Stanford & Roark, 1974).

Counselors as Psychological Educators: A Misperception of Counseling

This renewed interest in humanistic education and progressive-guidance
activities was bolstered by the development of systems of communication
skills. Truax and Carkhuff (1967), former students of Rogers, and Ivey

(1971) had developed theories concentrating upon relationship and communication skills, which they called helping skills. Some of these systems will be discussed more fully in Chapter 4. At this point a brief description should suffice. Based upon various human-development models, these theories were actually sets of skills systematically organized to be used by counselors in training and in the training of paraprofessionals. Most of these systems of skills included relationship factors, such as warmth, congruency, and empathy, or communication skills, such as listening, which were based on Rogers's early definition of a helping relationship. In the 1970s relationship-skills and communication-skills systems like those originated by Carkhuff and his colleagues and Ivey began to multiply. It was at this time that the misperception of the counselor's primary role described earlier in this chapter began to surface. Counselors were defined by some counselors as primarily psychological educators or consultants with the primary function of training teachers, peers, and parents in relationship and counseling skills and/or developing psychological curriculums relating to the personal, social, and moral growth of students and the general public.

These ideas about school counseling were considered revolutionary by some counselor educators (Carroll, 1973; Cook, 1971; Ivey & Alschuler, 1973b). In reality, like the humanistic-education curriculum, these ideas were an updated revival of progressive activities in the schools in the 1940s and 1950s (Arbuckle, 1976). Then every teacher was a counselor, curriculums included life skills, and social change was crucial. A chief difference was that then teachers got training for these activities in their college preparation, while now counselors presumably were to train teachers on the job.

Moves to Deprofessionalize Counseling

To justify claims that counseling is composed of simple, teachable, measurable skills, vigorous attacks upon professional counseling were launched by persons who perceived counselors as psychological educators. Ignoring the history of counseling, they described counseling as being preoccupied with pathology. They claimed that paraprofessionals frequently were more effective counselors than were trained counselors. A general impression was conveyed that the more training one had, the less effective one became. The blame was placed in part upon the stifling effects of professionalism. Some counselor educators set up businesses to sell training kits to teachers and the general public on how to train oneself and others in various helping skills. Human-service programs were developed to prepare undergraduates to become helpers in the community. Ivey (1970) recommended changing the APGA's name to the Association for Human Development. Egan (1975), and J. W. Loughary and Ripley (1979) published books on skills for helpers. In almost all of these activities, the distinction between professional counseling and helping relationships of paraprofessionals or volunteers was not clear.

Moves to Strengthen Professionalism

Professional-counseling associations made some moves in the 1970s to counter these attempts to deprofessionalize counseling. The APGA, the ASCA, and the ACES updated counselor role definitions, developed training standards for master's-degree and doctorate counselors, and established accrediting procedures for counselor training programs (discussed in Chapter 1). Also, movements of the APGA and the AMHCA to improve the status of community counseling led to their merger in 1979.

Meanwhile, Division 17 was working on its proposals for providers of psychological-counseling services in an effort to upgrade the status of doctorate counseling psychologists. Another move toward improvement of the status of counseling psychologists occurred when the Executive Committees of the APGA, the APA, and Division 17 met to work cooperatively on correcting a long history of inequitable treatment of counseling psychologists by state licensing boards dominated by clinical psychologists.

Professional Licensing

In the early 1970s the demand for counseling in the community increased rapidly. Counselors and counseling psychologists took action to try to provide quality services to the public. The nonprofessional use of the title of counselor and the lack of protection for the public led to some attempts to license counseling in various states (Cottingham & Swanson, 1976). Virginia passed the first licensing law that specifically related to counselors. In some states, such as Washington, counselors with a master's degree, including school counselors, were given the opportunity for limited licensing for counseling through the state psychological examining board.

Concerned about unqualified persons handling counseling and about the possibility of a nonproductive proliferation of counseling licenses, the APGA in 1976 proposed its guidelines for the licensing of counselors mentioned in Chapter 1. The *Licensure Commission action packet* was published in 1977 for distribution to regional personnel guidance associations to use as guidelines in the various states. This packet was expanded and updated in 1979 and again in 1980.

A strength of the document is that professional counseling is defined, so that it can be distinguished from guidance activities. The importance of vocational concerns is reemphasized. Master's-degree persons are included as eligible for licensing, and special certification for trained paraprofessionals in specialty areas is suggested. The state legislature of Arkansas approved licensing for counselors in July 1979, thus becoming the second state—after Virginia—specifically to license counselors. The Arkansas Personnel and Guidance Association used the APGA model licensing document to help gain this recognition (APGA, 1979c). In August 1979 Alabama became the third state to legislate licensing for counselors. At about the same time Florida, South Dakota, and Alaska repealed licensing for psychologists through sunset legislation. Under this legislation, laws that the legislature considers unnecessary or unimportant are allowed to lapse.

The Influence of Mental-Health Insurance

The rapidly growing interest in providing mental-health services to the general public has contributed in part to health-insurance carriers' giving their subscribers more coverage for emotional problems. This move is considered necessary by most persons working with emotional concerns in the community. However, it has become a divisive factor in the development of professional psychological and/or mental-health counseling.

Historically, health-insurance benefits have fallen under medical benefits. Thus, health-insurance carriers granting benefits for emotional problems have tended to give first priority to psychiatrists, who are also physicians. Doctorate clinical psychologists in private practice who have been trained in pathology have emulated psychiatrists and after some bitter struggles with psychiatrists have been accepted as professionals qualified to treat emotionally disturbed persons. Counseling psychologists who have strengthened their position by obtaining licensing for private practice believe that they should qualify as providers of psychological services for health-insurance plans that include mental-health benefits.

As this concern about licensing for private practice and insurance benefits has increased, counseling psychologists are taking the position that master's-degree persons in psychology should not be considered as qualified professional providers of mental-health services and are making strong efforts to dissociate themselves from other persons or groups doing counseling. In January 1977 a Division 17 Ad Hoc Committee on Licensure met with the Educational Standards and Accreditation Committee of the American Association of State Psychology Boards (AASPB). In that meeting Division 17 affirmed that counseling psychology was a discipline of psychology as a whole, that the training should be a coherent doctoral program, and that counseling psychology should "be distinguished from other related disciplines, such as counseling and guidance, counselor education, and counseling, both in regard to professional preparation and practice" (APA, Division of Counseling Psychology, 1977, p. 3). This attitude reflects the view of the Executive Committee of the APA.

Asher (1979) interprets this view as follows: "master's and doctoral level counselors face exclusion from the mental health care system because of the trend toward funding by health insurance. Organized psychology is moving to bar doctoral level counselors and counseling education graduates from participation in licensure" (p. 53). In the same article she asks, "Why should counselors, and for that matter, master's level psychologists, be accorded lower status than clinical social workers and nurses" (p. 59)?

These attitudes about licensing led the AMHCA to initiate procedures for national certification of counselors. The result was the establishment of the National Board of Certified Clinical Mental Health Counselors in July 1979. This certification does not have the statutory status of state licensing for psychologists in that the applicant must meet standards set by the professional association rather than standards set by the legislature in each state. The certification board is a corporate group independent of the AMHCA or the APGA. This independence meets the requirements of the National Commission for Health Certifying Agencies (APGA, 1979a). This independent board for examining and monitoring professional counseling may help counselors in their attempts to qualify as providers of mental-health services with health-insurance carriers.

One further move by the APGA to upgrade professional standards was a decision by the APGA Registry Committee in February 1979 to develop standards for a national registry of counselors in the following 2 years (APGA, 1979a).

The 1980s: The Need for Professional Unity and Flexibility

To accomplish professional growth and to keep it creative, counselors must avoid falling into a narrow, sterile professionalism designed more to protect elite professional membership than to protect the public from charlatans. On the other hand, counselors must avoid remaining so professionally weak that protection of the public from unprofessional behavior cannot be maintained. Until recently, the APGA had little success in implementing its standards. Narrow, limiting professionalism can be decreased if professional standards are not solely based on licensing doctorate persons in private practice. This view has been traditional in the APA for psychological work. Instead, the training and behavior standards for psychological workers in schools, colleges, and community agencies and clinics should be at least equal to those for private practice. Children who are minors and must by law attend school probably need more protection from unprofessional behavior of psychological workers than do adults seeking private help. Similarly, the effective professional strength that has eluded the APGA would have a much better chance of materializing if doctorate and master's-degree counselors working in community agencies, in schools, and in private practice combined efforts to insist upon the professional standards that the association has developed.

The APGA and Division 17 descriptions of the counseling process, counseling standards, and counselor training are very similar. The process can best be described as psychological counseling. This designation best differentiates professional counseling from clinical psychology and from student personnel work. In most states that license psychologists for private practice, the term *psychologist* applies only to persons with a doctorate. This idea has been expanded to include the adjective *psychological*. The APGA may well need to test the legality of state licensing laws that only persons with a doctorate can use the term *psychological counseling*. The term *psychological education* does not have this limitation.

Because of professional similarities, it makes sense that these associations should collaborate on licensing and certification of counselors. Such joint efforts could help a great deal in gaining professional recognition for school, college, and community counseling. This collaboration, however, would require some significant changes in attitudes on the part of Division 17 and the APGA. Division 17 would have to agree to work toward professional recognition of persons with a master's degree in counseling in addition to working for licensing parallel to that of clinical psychologists. Also, Division 17 would need to increase its responsibility for the quality of school counseling. The APGA, for its part, would have to resolve whether the primary group it represents is professional psychological counselors or whether it more truly represents advocates of human development and guidance and personal activities, as some APGA members claim. The APGA would also need to spell out specific differences in level of expertise between professional counselors with a master's degree and those with a doctorate.

The APGA and its affiliates have tried to professionalize counseling in a number of ways. The APGA is continuing its efforts toward licensing of counselors and strengthening counselor certification nationally. The American Rehabilitation Counseling Association has set national standards for training. The ACES in 1978 published guidelines for evaluating counselor training programs at the doctorate level. The decision by mental-health counselors in 1978 to affiliate with the APGA shows the APGA's interest in expanding its involvement in professional counseling to community mental-health work.

For members of the APGA, the ACES, and Division 17, perhaps some coordinated efforts could prevent counselors from organizing another counselor professional association. Pine, who earlier called for giving school counseling away, recently advocated that counselors return to their primary commitment of direct counseling (Boy & Pine, 1979). Ivey, who had urged counselors to demystify and deprofessionalize counseling in the early 1970s, more recently called for increased professionalization of counseling psychologists (Ivey, 1979). Also, in their latest book, Ivey and Simek-Downing (1980) made distinctions between counseling and interviewing that were not clear in earlier writings. Division 17 and the APGA have made joint efforts to increase licensing for doctorate counselors. Perhaps the APGA could become the main affiliation for those interested in counseling practice and Division 17 the association for scientific study of the field. In any event, the decrease through sunset laws in the number of states providing licensure for psychologists should motivate the APGA and APA to work together toward new licensing procedures. These procedures should be perceived by the legislature as beneficial primarily to the public rather than to the professional groups.

Division 17 grew out of a resistance to psychologists' preoccupation with mental illness and medical approaches. Thus, it would be consistent for professional counselors in private practice to look for funding for clients from sources in the Department of Education, and the Department of Health and Human Services that are not medically based. An alternative would be for professional counselors to try to convince Congress and health-insurance companies that counseling for normal concerns helps prevent mental illness. Perhaps then counselors would be eligible providers of mental-health services in present health-insurance programs and could be included in any future national health-insurance program.

The importance of counseling, career choice, and career education for schools, colleges, and communities has recently been receiving attention from the federal government. This interest may lead to funding of some counseling activities. A Career Education Incentive Act (PL 95-207) was passed in 1977. This act provides funds to set up model career-education programs in public schools, higher education, and adult education. If these programs are adequately funded, more professionally trained counselors will be essential in both schools and communities.

It is obvious that counselors with a doctorate cannot possibly handle the increased demand for professional psychological counseling in schools, colleges, and communities, nor can persons with a doctorate in other specialized areas of psychology meet this demand appropriately. The logical steps for professional-counseling associations to take are to continue to upgrade the training and practice of doctorate counselors while strengthening the training and status of master's-degree counselors. In this way counseling programs will be enhanced, and clients will have some protection from unsound psychological practice regardless of where the counseling takes place.

Projects and Activities

1. *Trace the influence of federal funding upon the development of counseling from its origins to the present. Explore federal programs currently pending in Congress that relate to counseling. How might these programs affect the profession of counseling if they are passed?*

2. Describe the differences and similarities in vocational counseling as defined by Parsons (1909) and by Super (1955). How did the notion of vocational development influence the direction of counseling?

3. Explore the roots of behavioristic and humanistic psychology. What has each contributed to the development of the counseling profession?

4. Super (1955) made a distinction between clinical and counseling psychologists. Look up preparation programs for each profession at well-known universities. Are the distinctions Super made consistent with contemporary Ph.D. and master's-degree training programs at these universities?

5. Evaluate the positive and negative influences of progressivism in education upon the development of counseling as a profession. Discuss how those contemporary psychological-education activities that are based upon progressivism can avoid the pitfalls of the earlier progressivist activities.

6. A back-to-basics-in-education movement has surfaced in various parts of the United States. Compare these complaints with the complaints about progressive education in the 1930s. What were the effects on guidance activities then? How should counselors respond constructively to contemporary complaints?

7. Interview some senior citizens about their perceptions of psychologists, psychiatrists, and counselors. Compare their reactions with those of a group of college students and a group of young adults not in school.

8. Community mental-health clinics originated in the early 1900s. At that time a psychiatrist, a clinical psychologist, and a social worker constituted the staff in most cases. Major concerns were working with delinquents and disturbed children and their families. Look up your central regional community clinic and trace its history in terms of staffing and types of problems handled.

9. Some people consider vocational counseling as a function of specialized counselors who cannot handle personal counseling. Others perceive counseling for vocational concerns as a form of personal counseling that all counselors should be able to handle. Discuss how these positions relate to professional standards.

10. School counseling and counseling psychology stem from similar historical roots and from similar social needs. Recently, Division 17 has moved to dissociate itself from responsibility for professional counseling in the public schools. Does this position make sense professionally and ethically? Present arguments for overall monitoring of a profession and arguments for monitoring only those professionals in private practice.

3

Professional, Ethical, and Legal Issues

The essential criteria for determining whether an occupational group constitutes a profession are generally agreed upon (Dunlop, 1968b; McCully, 1963). These characteristics are that the professional group and its members (1) can clearly define their role, (2) offer a unique service, (3) possess special knowledge and skills, (4) have an explicit code of ethics (5) have the right to offer the service as the profession describes it, and (6) have the ability to monitor the practice of the profession.

As the first two chapters showed, the APGA and its affiliates and Division 17 of the APA have met the first four specifications: the counselor's role and the service have been described, training has been specified, and ethical behavior for members has been carefully spelled out. But counselors have not yet attained the right to be primarily responsible for defining their role and monitoring their practice, so they have not been able to insist upon standards in agencies in which counselors work. Physicians and lawyers, for example, have been granted licenses by state legislatures to describe their expertise and to spell out a code of ethics that members must follow. Whether in private practice or in community agencies, doctors and lawyers are expected to conform to these standards. In contrast, counselors in schools are often assigned duties by administrators that are contrary to their training and ethical standards. And some administrators look for loopholes in certification standards in order to avoid hiring fully trained counselors. Moreover, counselors attempting to engage in private practice often find licensing impossible to attain.

I suggested in Chapter 2 that strengthening certification laws and licensing trained counselors would give added leverage for counselors to monitor the profession. But it is equally important that counselors develop a clear rationale for their standards in order to educate administrators, teachers, clients, parents, and the general public about why certain roles, training requirements, and ethical behaviors are being insisted upon. If explanations of standards make logical and practical sense, then it is highly likely that employers and the general public will support the professional growth of counselors and grant the group the autonomy to carry out its work with minimal interference from employers.

A rationale for role definitions and standards that includes distinctions from other professionals in psychological work, in guidance, or in psychological education might also help reduce friction and increase cooperation among these various psychological specialists. In addition, differences between the counselor professional associations and among their members might be more easily reconciled. For example, the differences in opinion between Division 17 and the APGA over the professional status of master's-degree counselors might be settled. Finally, sharp differences exist among groups of counselors and between professional counselors and other professional workers over what the unique, primary, or most important function of professional counselors should be. A well-thought-out rationale might contribute to more productive discussions about these differences.

This chapter offers one interpretation of the reasoning underlying professional standards. I hope that other professional counselors will present their viewpoints on the logic of the standards.

The Counselor's Role

In the first chapter the counselor's role was interpreted as follows. Professional counselors should be primarily engaged in direct counseling with individuals or small groups having normal developmental conflicts. Consulting and other outreach activities should supplement counseling. Counselors serve a unique function and are specialists distinct from other personnel and psychological specialists.

As Chapter 2 indicated, objections to these standards have led to continued role confusion. Some counselors and counselor educators believe that counselors should function primarily as consultants and agents of social change. Other critics have suggested that counselors dissociate themselves from working with conflicts or problems of students because counselors are not concerned with pathology. Instead, these critics recommend that counselors emphasize working with personal growth by teaching communication and relationship skills. Still other individuals perceive counseling not as a unique, specialized function but as a function generic to all human services. These people thus ignore or minimize differences between counselors and other personnel and psychological workers, such as student personnel administrators, vocational counselors, school psychologists, and psychotherapeutic interventionists. Finally, similarities and differences in the functions of master's-degree and doctorate counselors remain confusing both to professional counselors and to agencies hiring them.

Another issue related to the counselor's role is the appropriate use of paraprofessionals by counseling staffs. Many counselors are questioning how best to use paraprofessionals and to determine their effectiveness. Other professional counselors, particularly those who are advocating the psychological-educator role for counselors and who use the term *helping skills* to describe all psychological interactions, raise more controversial issues. One is the claim that paraprofessionals with as few as 20 hours of training in communication skills can be as effective or more effective than trained professionals in counseling. Another is the recommendation that paraprofessionals do the major share of direct counseling, so that trained counselors can spend most of their time training and supervising paraprofessionals and volunteers.

Some persons believe that counseling defined as a voluntary, confidential relationship is a White, middle-class idea that will not work for minorities or for persons from lower socioeconomic groups. The recommendation is that intervention strategies will be more effective. A corollary is whether a White, middle-class counselor can work effectively with a member of a minority group or a person from a lower socioeconomic background. A similar issue has been raised about the ability of male counselors to work with female clients.

Direct Counseling versus Consultation as Primary Role

Clients require direct counseling interaction with professionally trained counselors to develop resolutions to their conflicts or concerns. Consultations with others involved in a conflict may be useful when the client agrees, but they are not always a necessary ingredient of a counseling interaction. In fact, overemphasis on consultation may retard the client's progress. One reason is that consultation may prevent clients from developing an understanding of the attitudes and behaviors necessary to work through their present conflict or to generalize to similar conflicts in the future. Overuse of consultation may also diminish the opportunity for clients, even at a young age, to comprehend and label emotions they are experiencing. Further, consultation may prevent clients from gaining the skills to change their environment and instead make them depend upon the counselor to improve it.

The experience of trying to be an agent of change in one's own life is an essential component of effective counseling. Sometimes, however, clients find it difficult to change environments on their own. In these cases, counselors can work jointly with the client and, for example, the teacher, parent, or employer, if both parties are willing, to change environmental circumstances.

Counselors performing secondary roles involving outreach can also work on educative programs designed for social change. Improvements in policies about student rights and responsibilities, curriculum suggestions, and workshops on drugs or on career awareness are examples of change programs. Similar programs can be handled in the community.

Counselor Responsibilities in Normal Developmental Conflicts

Normal conflicts arise when an individual has difficulty fulfilling his or her needs and society's expectations to the satisfaction of both. These conflicts arise from different sets of circumstances. Sometimes they emerge because of contradictions between or uncertainty about motivations, impulses, attitudes, or feelings. For example, individuals might have mixed feelings about premarital sex, about attending college, or about appropriate care of their aging parents. Sometimes conflicts may result from discord between an individual and important persons in the individual's life. Parents and children or husband and wife may have contradictory values or different role expectations. Sometimes the conflicts are related to environmental barriers that are frustrating the individual in potential growth. For example, financial problems or the physical illness of a loved one may inhibit the pursuit of certain life goals. Also, feelings of loneliness or of indifference may cause difficulty in coping effectively with one's needs or with society's demands. Individuals may feel as though they are drifting through life. Such conflicts may cause sufficient tension or anxiety to interfere with the ability to make decisions or to take action appropriate for the productive growth of oneself and of society.

Developmental conflicts, as I prefer to call them, are often realistic reactions to environmental pressures or to ambivalences in an individual's drives. They often represent a healthy recognition that all is not well in one's interactions with others or in one's feelings about oneself. Recognition of the conflict is potentially constructive because it often motivates attempts to change patterns of behavior that are stifling occupational, personal, or social growth.

Professional counselors who object to using the term *conflict* have failed to distinguish the potentially constructive nature of the normal conflicts with which psychological counselors work from pathological conflicts anticipated in psychotic, neurotic, or delinquent behavior. Pathological conflicts tend to be chronic and to inhibit or immobilize the individual, so that motivation to change is limited and growth is stifled or maladaptive. When this behavior becomes overly disruptive to others or severely debilitating to the individual, psychological intervention, behavior management, or institutionalization may become necessary.

Unfortunately, avoiding the word *conflict* has contributed to the confusion of professional counseling with personal-growth and social-engineering activities in guidance and student personnel work. Counseling goes beyond social interactional exercises. Counseling includes working with the dynamics of individual and interpersonal behavior that cause conflicts and ambivalence.

A Comparison of Counselors with Other Specialists

Psychological Counseling and Personnel Work.   Student personnel workers are hired by colleges to administer student services that contribute to an integration of academic work and personal progress. Vice-presidents of student affairs, deans of students, financial-aid officers, placement officers, residence coordinators, admissions officers, registrars, and coordinators of special programs for minorities and the handicapped are responsible for coordinating and administering policies and regulations in their special areas of expertise that lead to students' smooth progression through their academic life.

Although all of these workers are interested in and initiate activities related to students' personal growth, their primary function is to handle their specific administration services. Thus, for example, the primary duty of a financial-aid officer is to advise students about financial aids and scholarships and to decide upon students' qualifications for aid. The placement officer's main reason for existence is to help in job hunting; a residence coordinator is responsible for the management of a residence complex. Deans of students and their assistants are interested in helping enrich student life through psychological-education activities, but they are ultimately responsible for disciplinary policies, procedures, and adjudication and for procedures and decisions involving scholastic probation or dismissal.

In contrast, counseling-center staffs are trained primarily for professional counseling. Their unique function is professional psychological counseling. They are not involved in administrative decisions, nor do they establish policies or procedures about student behavior. It should be clear from the professional descriptions of counselor duties that personnel workers are not trained as counselors to handle vocational/educational, personal, and social conflicts, nor are counselors prepared to handle personnel administration. The attempt to make the two activities synonymous does not do justice to either group of professionals.

Student personnel workers offer important services in an educational setting. Unfortunately, these services have been neglected in public schools. During the 1950s, deans of men and women were hired in some larger high schools to handle some of these personnel activities. In the 1960s, these staff positions gradually disappeared or were converted into vice-principalships. The general practice was, and has been, to assign counselors to guidance and personnel activities rather than hiring trained personnel administrators. For this reason, counselors have been held responsible for all of those activities that can be classified as personnel and guidance ones. They have become the schedule makers, the keepers of records, the attendance monitors, the directors of student affairs, and the like at the expense of handling necessary counseling duties.

Counselors can handle some guidance activities that are appropriate to their training as secondary functions to improve the social climate of the school. I certainly do not object to consultation activities, such as involvement in curriculum planning, but these activities should supplement, not replace, counseling. Other guidance and personnel activities that are not within the expertise of the counselor or that interfere with the development of counseling relationships should be handled by other specialists or administrators who are trained in personnel work.

Some school districts across the country have recently hired deans of students to coordinate some of the personnel activities. This trend should be encouraged, so that public school students can receive the full range of professional services.

Psychological Counseling and Vocational Counseling. A recent trend toward certifying individuals as vocational counselors has contributed further to the confusion in counseling. Most training for vocational counseling is geared specifically to the important considerations of vocational-placement opportunities and the distribution of occupational information, in the tradition of earlier vocational counseling. People with this sort of training can be very useful additions to a school staff in helping develop work/study programs, in analyzing the local job markets, in managing occupational files, and in keeping abreast of scholarship and apprenticeship opportunities. They are not usually prepared to work with conflicts over career choice or to work with other personal or social concerns and conflicts of students, as professional psychological counselors are. My preference is to call this group career guidance specialists, since this name more clearly spells out their unique area of expertise.

Psychological Counseling, Psychotherapy, and Psychotherapeutic Intervention. Although Brammer and Shostrom (1977) see an overlap between counseling and psychotherapy, they agree that there are theoretical and practical differences in the two processes. Counseling emphasizes rationale planning, decision making, and situational pressures in everyday living and is shorter in duration than psychotherapy. Psychotherapy stresses alleviating pathological problems, which are more intense and which usually require more time to work through. Tyler (1969) has consistently taken a similar point of view. Patterson (1973b) perceives no essential differences between counseling and psychotherapy in the relationship, goals, methods, or types of clients. He suggests that the distinction that counselors work with less disturbed clients in a nonmedical setting while psychotherapists work with more disturbed persons in a medical setting arises out of convenience or practical or political factors. Overlap does exist in the work of persons calling themselves counselors and of those termed psychotherapists. However, there are differences in the training and supervised experiences of the two groups because they serve persons with problems of differing severity that require different approaches and involve different ethical considerations.

Traditionally, clinical psychologists and psychiatrists have used the term *psychotherapy* to describe their work of diagnosis and treatment of persons with severe, chronic emotional distress or persons whose behavior is severely disruptive to themselves or others. They are trained to recognize and handle pathological, deviant, or incapacitating emotional problems or behavior. Internships emphasize diagnosis and treatment of psychotic patients, severely neurotic persons, and persons who require behavior management, such as juvenile delinquents, autistic children, or children who are mentally retarded. Often such persons' behavior becomes so disruptive or debilitating that they may require psychological intervention against their will for their own protection or for the protection of society. This forced intervention may require assessment of the behavior to help determine what treatment is necessary. The intervention may lead to enforced, prolonged institutionalization, social controls, or drug therapy.

The skills necessary for making judgments about the need for enforced therapy mean that clinical psychologists receive training to become psychological consultants for social agencies in the community. Similarly, social workers are prepared for social intervention when home and community relationships become disruptive or incapacitating. The primary client of both of these workers often is the institution or social agency for which they consult rather than the person needing treatment. Assessment or treatment is often not at the individual's option. Because of these emphases, clinical psychologists and psychiatrists receive little preparation for working with people's normal concerns.

In contrast, counseling has been defined as the process used to work with individuals who are struggling with normal anxieties and concerns or situational crises occurring in everyday living. Diagnosis is done with the client for the purpose of helping both client and counselor understand the problem. Whether to receive counseling is up to the individual. Clients are usually normally functioning persons; if counselors work with persons who have had a serious emotional trauma, the purpose is to help them make the transition back to everyday living.

Similar differences exist in the public schools. The training of school psychologists is patterned after that of clinical psychologists. As administrative psychological consultants, they are trained primarily to handle the assessment and treatment of learning or behavioral difficulties occurring in the classroom that require administrative intervention. Similarly, school social workers are prepared to intervene when home/school conditions become disruptive to the school or the home or incapacitating to the student. Their primary responsibility is often to the administrator of the school (Nugent, 1973).

Counseling psychologists and school counselors should not work as psychological consultants to administrators for purposes of screening or evaluating people. Their unique function lies in working with problems of persons not requiring forced psychological intervention. Their primary responsibility is to their clients, whether they be public school students, college students, or the general public. Their consultation work with agencies is done in the area of normal concerns and with the knowledge and consent of the individual being evaluated.

Psychological Counseling and Psychological Education.   Psychological counseling is definitely distinct from psychological education in spite of the recent attempt to equate the two. Counseling involves working with the dynamics of individual and interpersonal behavior that contribute to the conflicts, ambivalences, and anxieties in everyday living. It focuses on concerns that persons present to counselors. The individuals hope that they can get some help in resolving the dilemma confronting them. Psychological education involves teaching communication, social-growth, and personal-growth skills in schools through in-service workshops or through curriculum involvement. These counselor activities are directed toward training teachers to become more effective in their relationships with students, increasing teachers' abilities to expand subject matter beyond intellectual factors, and teaching psychological-education courses, such as self-awareness, assertiveness training, and career education.

Today there are justified concerns that teachers and administrators are not given sufficient college training in human relationships, communication, use of tests and records, and group interaction. This gap in training resulted largely from the sharp criticism of progressive education in the 1940s, which led to large cutbacks in affective education. The answer does not lie in training counselors primarily to handle the training of teachers in human-relationship skills. Rather, teacher training in colleges needs to be expanded to include these skills. People like Carkhuff (1972a, b), Carroll (1973), and Ivey and Alschuler (1973a) could devote their efforts to humanizing teacher education programs in colleges. A curriculum coordinator professionally prepared as an affective educator or psychological educator could be developed. This new specialist could work on expanding curriculums to include personal and social areas. But these educational experiences should not be confused with counseling or be designed to replace it. Also, communication and relationships skills taught to prospective teachers should focus on improving interaction in class and not be considered sufficient for teachers to engage in counseling.

Psychological Counseling and Helping-Skills Systems.   The major systems of helping skills will be discussed in Chapter 4. At this point the problem of confusing technical interviewing and communication skills with professional-counseling knowledge, skills, and procedures is at issue. Systematic skills training is presented as a training package in helping skills. The degree of professional competence in these systems is determined by how high the helper is rated by expert raters in these skills.

In the June 1977 issue of the *Personnel and Guidance Journal*, packages of skills by Carkhuff, Ivey and Gluckstern, and Hosford and Kagan are reviewed and evaluated by Brammer and Allmon. They indicate that these training packages can be useful in improving interviewing and communication skills for paraprofessionals working as counselor aides or for persons in programs such as nursing, medicine, social work, and teaching. Brammer and Allmon conclude that there are advantages in specifying skills and processes in such a way that novices can use them. But they say, "One price for this game, however, is the risk that learning to counsel will be viewed as the application of simple relating skills. Counseling is a complex act of which helping skills and attitudes are only a part" (p. 616).

Mahon and Altmann in 1977 gave an overview of research on helping skills. They expressed serious concern about overestimating the value of helping-skills training and cautioned that they not be taken as ends in themselves in preparing persons for the helping professions. The skills, they assert, are insufficient for understanding behavior, which is essential for behavior change. They recommend that the skills be integrated with a theory such as perceptual psychology.

The Appropriate Use of Paraprofessionals in Counseling

Few professionally trained counselors question the need for paraprofessional help. However, serious questions can be raised about the quality of research that has been used to demonstrate paraprofessional effectiveness in counseling. Also, the evidence that paraprofessionals have been shown to be as effective, if not more effective, than professional counselors is highly questionable on a number of statistical grounds.

A considerable body of literature exists on the effectiveness of paraprofessionals (Brown, 1974; Hoffman, 1976; Peth, 1971). The reviews just cited include numerous examples of studies concluding that paraprofessionals are highly effective in various activities. However, some of the most supportive persons reviewing the literature agree that the research designs raise questions about the statistical validity of the studies. Peth notes:

In even the most objective studies cited, there exist numerous uncontrolled variables and questionable assumptions and conclusions. Counselor "effectiveness," for example, a thorny problem of long standing, at best remains at the mercy of subjective evaluation and so-called expert ratings. In addition, most studies reveal a noticeable lack of objec-

tive, quantifiable data, thereby remaining in the more descriptive, subjective realm and offering little possibility for replication or validation
[p. 229].

Brown, a strong advocate of the value of paraprofessionals, admits, "Most
of these studies, however, are plagued with the design inadequacies that
characterize much of the research published in educational and psychological journals" (p. 258). McArthur (1970) and Gruver (1971) point out
similar flaws in the research designs they have reviewed and include, in
addition, that the Hawthorne effect has not been controlled (attention
alone may cause improvement in behavior or attitude). Gruver found that
fewer than 25% of the studies on the use of college students as therapeutic
agents were designed appropriately. He concludes that "most of those investigations that have been conducted are so methodologically inadequate that it is impossible to draw firm conclusions about the relative effectiveness of college students as therapeutic agents" (p. 123).

These poor research designs make it virtually impossible to conclude
from a statistical standpoint that paraprofessionals are effective workers.
This does not mean that the use of paraprofessionals should not be encouraged or that appropriate use should not be thoroughly explored. The
positive response by agencies using paraprofessionals in itself warrants
further serious consideration of their use. However, it is reasonable to
suggest that studies of paraprofessional effectiveness should be held to
the same rigorous design standards as studies about professional counseling.

As professional counselors explore reviews of paraprofessional effectiveness, another important consideration emerges. Only a very small
portion of the paraprofessional activities reported are counseling-related
activities as defined by the counselor professional associations. In the
1976 review by Hoffman are examples of paraprofessionals used as psychotherapeutic agents for moderately disturbed children, as workers with
chronic schizophrenics, as community behavior-modification consultants,
as technicians treating reading defects, and as academic advisors as well
as crisis workers on hot-line telephones and in community clinics. Peth's
(1971) review includes convicted felons functioning as therapists and re-
formed alcoholics and drug addicts working with problems of addiction
as well as other paraprofessionals working as instructional aides for minority groups. Brown (1974) reviewed paraprofessional use more specifically in college settings. Most of the work evaluated, including his
own studies, was academic advisement, tutoring, and informational interaction. His review and those by Peth and by Gruver (1971) indicate the
difficulty in generalizing from these studies to counseling-related activities because of the diversity in training, in work settings, in tasks, and in
client populations.

The contention that paraprofessionals are as effective, if not more so, than trained counselors is particularly provocative. Surprisingly, very few studies have compared paraprofessionals with professionals (Lamb & Clack, 1974; Shelton & Madrazo-Peterson, 1978; Truax & Lister, 1970; Zunker & Brown, 1966). All but the Truax and Lister study had a methodologically sound research design. In three of the studies, paraprofessionals were compared to counselors on activities that cannot truly be called professional-counseling activities. Zunker and Brown used comparisons on academic advisement, scholarship data, and study skills. Lamb and Clack compared paraprofessionals and professionals on freshman orientation, Truax and Lister on giving rehabilitative information to clients. Shelton and Madrazo-Peterson compared professionals and paraprofessionals on a specific, trainable technique, systematic desensitization. In all of the studies, paraprofessionals performed as well as professionally trained counselors. However, one cannot conclude from these studies that paraprofessionals are more effective than professionals in counseling. Rather, Brown believes that paraprofessionals can be trained to do specific tasks that counselors prefer not to do because they interfere with their major professional functions. Shelton and Madrazo-Peterson assert that paraprofessionals can be trained to handle highly structured behavior-therapy techniques as well as professionals, thus freeing the professional to handle more complex professional-counseling interactions.

The systematic human-relations training for a given group of helpers described earlier, based upon Truax and Carkhuff's (1967) mechanizing of Rogers's relationship skills, contributes to confusion about paraprofessional effectiveness. Carkhuff is cited by most writers about paraprofessionals as having proved through research that paraprofessionals are as effective, if not more so, than professionals in counseling. Actually, the majority of citations refer to Carkhuff's theoretical expositions about the reliability and validity of the scales he devised rather than to an experimental verification of his system. He based his verification on the type of studies just mentioned, which have methodological problems and draw unwarranted conclusions. All the studies he pointed to include subjective scales used by raters assumed to be experts. These scales are those he devised, based upon concepts he described as proven to be universal, systematic, helping skills. Calia (1974) agrees that this system has influenced the practice of a considerable number of counselors. Nevertheless, he presents serious reservations about the theoretical underpinnings of the concept of training used by Truax and Carkhuff and about their assumption of definitive, universal, helping attributes. Calia says, "Carkhuff presents his conceptions of counseling as dogma. . . . Such a presentation discounts the possibilities of alternative approaches. . . . Carkhuff's concept of the 'effective' person as a helper-warrior goes beyond counseling and has perturbing overtones" (p. 92). He asserts also that Carkhuff's system may end up training therapeutic technicians and program one to look like Rogers, Truax, or Carkhuff.

The question of the need for improving studies of paraprofessional effectiveness aside, some writers have discussed ways of using paraprofessionals consistent with the counselor's role. Hoffman (1976) suggests that
paraprofessionals in counseling and guidance should be used in the areas
of reading and study skills, academic advisement, and the exploration of
careers. Brown, Wehe, and Zunker (1971) have used paraprofessionals in
college settings to help with academic adjustment. For example, they have
developed a guidance sequence consisting of freshman orientation, test
interpretation, study-skills instruction, and study-habits evaluation.

D. J. Miller (1979) discusses the general-guidance associate recently developed in Texas who functions as a form of counselor aide. This person
must have a B.A. degree, a teaching certificate, and 24 hours of guidance
courses. Required skills include gathering and distributing educational
and vocational material, working in a testing program, conducting group
guidance activities, consulting with students and parents about educational programs, doing follow-up studies, and identifying children with
special needs or concerns.

Colleges have also used student residential aides for paraprofessional
help and have initiated drug, sex, and birth-control referral and information services staffed by paraprofessionals supervised by counselors (Warnath, 1971). All of these activities seem appropriate adjuncts of counselor
functions.

In the community, paraprofessional tasks that relate to professional-
counselor roles have not been clarified, despite the variety of services
available. Crisis clinics, telephone hot lines, birth-control, drug, and alcohol services, and centers for women's concerns, teenage problems, and
runaways have all been developed.

An important criterion for appropriateness of paraprofessional activities in schools, colleges, and the community is that they relate to the professional counselor's role sufficiently that counselors have the expertise to
train and supervise the paraprofessional. Also, assuming that paraprofessionals will reduce the counselor's work load is unrealistic if the professional truly holds to the close, quality supervision required. Supervision
is time consuming.

Master's-Degree and Doctorate Counselors

Any person working toward a master's degree or a doctorate in counseling requires certain basic knowledge and skills. These include understanding the dynamics of individual and interpersonal behavior that
cause conflicts and ambivalences. This understanding comes from exposure to behavior dynamics, learning theory, personality theory, and counseling theory and techniques as well as theories of human development.
In addition, the student must have the opportunity to develop the personal philosophy about behavior and about counseling techniques that un-

derlies the choice of techniques used. A theoretical orientation also helps counselors develop a systematic rationale about why they do or do not function in certain ways in counseling. Internships and closely supervised practicums are essential to provide opportunities for prospective counselors to work with a variety of clients with a variety of problems.

Sufficient understanding and skills can be gained in a master's-degree program directed by counselors with a doctorate for professional counseling. Persons with a doctorate in counseling have had more study of theory and longer internships. Therefore, they should be able to handle a broader and more difficult range of problems and to develop original research on the counseling process and its outcomes. Because of the increased training, consultation with schools and community agencies would be anticipated, as would be the ability to supervise, coordinate, and teach in counselor training programs. Obviously, any comparison of the training standards for master's-degree and doctorate counselor education programs would highlight the increased amount of research skills and experience, consultation skills, and supervised practical experience expected of doctoral candidates. See Appendix B for a more complete comparison of the training standards for professional counselors and for counseling psychologists.

Counseling with Lower Socioeconomic Groups

Counselors who believe that all or most persons from lower socioeconomic groups require direct intervention by counselors rather than having voluntary counseling available contend that these persons will not voluntarily seek counseling and that they cannot express themselves sufficiently to profit from counseling relationships. My experience with these groups has been that they are weary of being directed and manipulated by psychological specialists. They become suspicious of the motives of psychological workers. If they trust counselors, they will use counseling services and express their emotions as directly and genuinely as do members of the middle and upper socioeconomic groups.

It is true that significant changes in the school system and in society are essential for ultimately helping students in the lower socioeconomic groups to develop their potential more fully. Outreach programs are essential to help make these changes. However, these activities should supplement rather than supplant voluntary counseling.

Counseling with Minority Groups

I would want representatives of different ethnic groups on any counseling staff with which I worked, but would not favor these counselors' working only with members of minority groups. They should be available to all clients. Counselors from minority groups can organize and coordinate in-service training of the counseling staff in the values, traditions, and attitudes of various minority groups. Also, they can offer psychological-education workshops and seminars for students and the general public about the effects of prejudice and of stereotyping.

In many instances it may be wise to arrange for a minority client to work with a minority counselor. For example, the prospective client may specifically request a minority counselor. A counselor of the same ethnic group as the client may be advantageous when a client's family interactions are important and the family is resistant to working with, say, a White counselor. If a member of a minority group is having serious difficulties with other members of his or her minority group, selection of a minority counselor may be sensible. However, the assumption that a counselor and a client of the same ethnic group will automatically develop an effective counseling relationship does not hold. Clients may believe that a member of their own ethnic group has joined the Establishment and has lost contact with their culture. Such beliefs could lead to client resentment.

Effective school counseling is particularly important for minority students. The literature shows that these students have the same normal developmental concerns that Whites do but that these problems are compounded by factors related to being a member of a minority group. A number of authors have also pointed out that minority students experience severe conflicts during adolescence (Kincaid, 1969; Martin, 1978). Henderson (1979), Marsella and Pedersen (1980) and Pedersen, Draguns, Lonner, and Trimble (1980) have recently written texts devoted to counseling with various ethnic groups.

Counseling with Women

The literature shows that much sex bias and sex stereotyping have occurred in counselor interactions with women. Considerable improvement has been noted in the past few years as studies on the effects of bias and stereotyping upon women clients have appeared in the literature, but there is still a need to work vigorously for continued improvement (Blimline & Birk, 1979). At this time there appears to be general agreement among professional women counselors that having female clients see only female counselors will not resolve these problems. Tanney and Birk (1976) indicated that empirical evidence did not support the idea that female counselors are better for women than male counselors.

In a similar view, there is no evidence that male counselors are more effective with males than are female counselors. However, at times a male client may have trouble relating to a female counselor if he has just experienced a traumatic divorce or has had a series of difficulties with various important women in his life.

Counselor education programs should include course work and practical experiences designed to eliminate sexual biases for all counselors.

As with minorities, there are times when it may be wise for a female client to see a female counselor. Obviously, a request by the client should be honored. In addition, a woman who has just experienced assault, battering, incest, or rape by a male will most likely find it more difficult to relate to a male counselor than to a female counselor.

Ethical and Legal Considerations

An ethical code is developed by a professional association to help clarify a professional's responsibility to clients, to the employing institution, and to society in general. An important purpose of the code is to protect the client when conflicts arise between the counselor's primary responsibility to the client and his or her responsibility to society. The APGA has assumed the responsibility of developing an ethical code for counselors. The ASCA has dealt specifically with school counselors. Counseling psychologists of Division 17 follow the APA code, which is similar to the APGA code.

Although all of the codes are similar, the APGA and ASCA codes, in my opinion, are more tailored to the ethical concerns of all psychological counselors than is the APA code. The counseling relationship is defined. The emphasis upon free choice of the client and upon confidentiality of the counseling sessions is clear-cut. The obligation of counselors not to impose their own values on clients is unequivocal. The ASCA code says that the counselor "must not impose consciously his attitudes and values on the counselee though he is not obligated to keep his attitudes and values from being known" (Section IA.2).

The APGA ethical code specifies that the members' primary obligation is to respect the integrity and promote the welfare of the client (Section B1). Responsibility to the employing agency is not ignored, but this responsibility must not interfere with the counselor's ethical and professional responsibility to the client.

Ethics in group work as well as with individuals has received attention from professional associations. The APGA code was revised in 1974 to include group guidelines. The Association for Specialists in Group Work (ASGW), a branch of the APGA, has been developing ethical guidelines for group work, and in 1973 the APA published its ethical recommendations for growth-group leaders.

In the APGA code of ethics, as I noted in Chapter 1, a professional-counseling relationship is differentiated from an administrative relationship. An administrator has important and necessary legal and authoritative responsibilities that often preclude voluntary interaction and confidentiality in the administrative relationship. In contrast, counseling relationships are singled out as involving free choice and guaranteeing confidentiality. The code says, "To the extent that the counselee's choice of action is not imminently self- or other-destructive, the counselee must retain freedom of choice" (Section B). Confidentiality is expressed in the following way: "The counseling relationship and information resulting therefrom must be kept confidential . . ." (Section B2).

According to Shah (1969), confidentiality relates to matters of professional ethics whereby the client is protected from unauthorized disclosures by a professional without the consent of the individual. This protection is guaranteed by the profession rather than by law. Sanctions for violations are supposed to be imposed by the professional associations in the form of fines or revocation of certification or licensing.

Although the voluntary nature of counseling is guaranteed by the professional codes of ethics, the constitutional right to privacy has only recently become increasingly important in our society. The right to privacy is an evolving legal concept that "recognizes the freedom of the individual to pick and choose for himself the time, circumstances and particularly the extent to which he wishes to share with or withhold from others his attitudes, beliefs, behavior and opinions" (Shah, 1969, p. 57).

Privileged communication is defined as "the legal right which exists by statute and which protects the client from having his confidences revealed publicly from the witness stand during legal proceedings without his permission" (Shah, 1969, p. 57). In essence, privileged communication is meant to preserve a relationship, such as that between attorney and client, physician and patient, or psychologist and client, in which it is important that the client talk freely without fear of disclosure in court. Shah points out that the crucial factor is whether the injury to the relationship from disclosure would be greater than the loss of justice if the information were presented in court.

The APGA and ASCA codes are predicated upon the idea that confidentiality is essential to successful counseling. Thus, privileged communication seems a natural follow-up, as legislative action in the past ten years demonstrates. In 1968 only two states, Michigan and Indiana, had legislated privileged-communication rights for clients. In 1974 the Privileged Communication Committee of the ASCA published the results of a national survey, to which 47 states responded, on the status of school counseling and privileged communication. Litwack summarized this report in admirable fashion in *The School Counselor* in 1975. He reported that 18 states provided full or partial coverage of testimonial privileged communication, with an additional 14 states having made attempts to pass legislation. Five states—Idaho (1971), Nevada (1973), North Carolina (1971), North Dakota (1969), and South Dakota (1972)—legislated full privileged communication for clients in that counselors cannot testify without the student's consent. Montana (1971) requires the consent of both student and parents. In Michigan (1963), Oklahoma (no date given), and Pennsylvania (1972), the parents must give their consent. In the remaining nine states that passed legislation, varying degrees of limited privilege were granted—for example, specifically for records or for counseling on drug usage. By 1979, it was estimated that 21 states had passed privileged communication laws protecting clients of school counselors (Shertzer & Stone, 1980).

Not all counselors, counselor educators, or persons hiring counselors agree with these standards. Some argue that persons who need counseling may not ask for it, so that intervention is necessary. Confidentiality is viewed by some individuals as nonproductive secrecy that handcuffs counselors when they want to share helpful information about a client with others in the client's life. Some counselors object to legal confidentiality or privileged communication for minors. They argue that young people do not have the experience or the judgment to permit counselors to give up their control over counseling information. Also, in direct contrast to the standards I have discussed, some people have proposed that it may be advantageous to influence the values or behavior of clients in the direction preferred by the counselor (Mosher & Sprinthall, 1970). The notion that counselors should be responsible primarily to their clients makes some counselors, particularly those in schools, very uncomfortable. Some counselors who agree to all of these ethical considerations with adults are uncertain whether they should apply to minors.

Free Choice, Confidentiality, and Privileged Communication

Free Choice. Counselors are primarily concerned with persons who are not disruptive enough to endanger or disturb others, not with individuals who are so severely handicapped emotionally or mentally that the state or a community agency must move in to protect them or society. Thus, counselors give increased attention to the right of people to choose whether they need psychological help or not. On this basis, imposing counseling on individuals who are not disruptive or severely disturbed has been considered a breach of professional ethics. More recently, the constitutional right to privacy has become an important consideration in our society. In this sense, imposition of counseling goes beyond professional ethical courtesy; it could constitute a violation of the person's civil rights. Therefore, counselors must begin to consider the legal implications of involuntary counseling in addition to the professional ethical ones, for they might be subject to civil suits for invasion of privacy.

Aside from the legal and ethical considerations regarding voluntary counseling, experience has shown that most persons profit more from counseling when they agree to or seek out counseling. Motivation to change behavior is considered in almost all counseling theories as a first essential step toward a successful counseling outcome. For those who are concerned about individuals who need counseling but will not seek it, I recommend making counseling easily available and highly attractive to potential clients rather than prescribing mandatory contacts with counselors.

When students or members of the community require forced psychological intervention because of behavior dangerous to themselves or others or because of conditions severely detrimental to their well-being or education, then school psychologists, clinical psychologists, psychiatrists, or social workers should be available in schools or communities. These specialists have learned strategies and have received supervised experience in evaluating, managing, and treating persons who require forced psychological intervention or who have severe learning or behavioral problems.

Confidentiality.   Violations of confidentiality in schools, colleges, and community agencies occur too frequently. Some breakdowns happen because people give in to the temptation to share some juicy bit of information. More often, broken confidences result from ignorance of the reasons for confidentiality and of the potential consequences of breaking it for counseling relationships and the image of the counseling staff. Insufficient exposure in counselor training to ethical considerations thus contributes to confidentiality breakdowns.

Confidentiality is based upon the idea that individuals are freer to explore conflicts if protection from disclosure without consent is available. Attitudes, feelings, and thoughts about oneself or about others that are painful, guilt-ridden, or otherwise emotionally charged are more apt to be expressed. Clients often need to express resentment, anger, hostility, or ambivalence toward authority figures, loved ones, and peers without fear of reprisal in order to work toward good feelings about themselves and productive relationships with the significant people in their lives. If confidentiality is not guaranteed, these intimate emotional concerns might not be brought out.

Some counselors believe that confidentiality inhibits the amount of help a counseling staff can give. They actually believe that the professional can help a client more by communicating information to teachers and parents or to staff members of other community agencies. In an interesting twist the confidential relationship is often formed between the persons sharing information about the client. There is no question that this behavior is not only unethical but also unsound professional practice. Too often counselors who took teachers or parents into their confidence are shocked to find that the client in question was later informed of the interaction by the teacher or parent involved. Appropriate exposure to potential incidents of this type in counselor training would reduce such unproductive counselor behavior.

Counselor behavior of this sort often stems from a false assumption that confidentiality involves secrecy that impedes the flow of information that can ultimately help a client. To me, confidentiality is not synonymous with secrecy in definition or intent. Confidentiality emphasizes trusting that another person will not share information without the person's knowledge and consent. It does not include the elements of furtiveness and covertness also associated with secrecy. If handled correctly, confidentiality can increase rather than decrease communication.

Some school counselors feel in an ethical bind when the principal asks them to share information gained in counseling because they are uncertain whether their first responsibility is to the client or to the chief administrator. The ethical bind increases when students reveal involvement in such acts as shoplifting, taking drugs, drinking, or cheating on exams. Counselors need to reaffirm the importance of keeping confidences in order to maintain the trust of the student or of the total student body. Then students with similar problems will feel free to get counselor help. Counselors should clarify with students that they will not intervene to reduce penalties that result from illegal or asocial behavior. Rather, they will continue to assist them in changing behavior. This attitude cuts down on attempts by some students to manipulate counselors in order to beat the system.

In addition, counselors can reassure the principal that they have an ethical obligation to report a student's behavior when it indicates an imminent danger to the student or to society. Counselor judgment is involved, and both administrators and counselors must learn to trust it. Distinctions regarding danger to self or others based upon counselor judgment can be discussed with the principal. For example, a student who reveals that he or she set a fire in a wastebasket in school might be handled differently than a student who reveals a compulsive drive to set fires and who admits to setting numerous ones. Counseling with no report may suffice for the first student. In the second situation the counselor and the student need to discuss the necessity for involvement of other persons because more intensive treatment is needed and because of the danger to others.

If counselors break confidence with clients in spite of warnings, they are supposed to be subject to disciplinary action by a professional association. However, because of lack of professional controls, professional counselors have little recourse if they see another professional violating confidentiality. The proposed APGA licensing law recommends suspension or revocation of a license for licensees found guilty of violating ethical standards. I support this move. Also, counselors should be aware that they can be sued for slander or libel.

Privileged Communication.   Counselors should have a clear understanding of the differences between ethical confidentiality and the confidentiality involved in privileged communication. Privileged communication is specific to counselors testifying in a court of law. It is a legal right granted to clients by a specific state law rather than a professional behavior guaranteed by a professional association's ethical code. It is important to remember that privileged communication is the client's right, not the counselor's.

Some counselor authorities (Bangs, 1971; Goldman, 1969) resist the idea of privileged communication for students in counseling with school counselors because they believe that students are too young or unsophisticated to comprehend fully their legal rights. Goldman suggests that the young would be better served by strengthening the ethical code. Some critics of privileged communication believe that it puts too much power in the hands of students to control the flow of information from counselors to authorities. Counselors would then be reluctant to share necessary information with authorities when illegal acts are involved. The use of drugs by high school students has made this issue an especially provocative one. Nelson Rockefeller, when governor of New York, in 1973 vetoed a privileged-communication bill for students on the grounds that it would inhibit counselors from reporting drug usage.

Opponents of privileged communication who present these arguments either disregard or misperceive the nature of a counseling relationship. Since counseling is geared to voluntary involvement and to ethical and legal confidentiality, students who admit difficulties with drugs, alcohol, or other asocial or illegal impulses or behaviors obviously see counselors out of a need to get help to control or to change these behaviors. If, in addition to guaranteeing confidentiality, counselors can guarantee that they can refuse to testify in court about information gained in counseling unless the client agrees, students will be even more likely to share concerns about illegal or asocial acts or impulses. Similarly, if child custody is involved in a divorce suit and a counselor is not forced to testify in court about counseling sessions with the child, students with this type of problem will be more likely to seek counseling help.

For some reasons, reluctance about privileged communication relates to fears that a rash of malpractice suits may be launched by clients. Counselors must be willing to assume the risk if they are to gain the autonomy to function professionally.

The Nonimposition of Counselor Values

Values are standards or ethical guidelines that influence an individual's or a group's behavior, attitudes, and decisions. Lifestyles are based upon a value system. Various lifestyles based upon different religious, philosophical, social, economic, and personal values are accepted or tolerated in the United States. These lifestyles may be fostered by families, ethnic groups, churches, or schools, or they may be arrived at through an individual's personal searching. Most counseling related to values occurs when individuals have mixed motivations about choices they must make or when their choices conflict with the values of family members, peers, or society.

A counselor's job is to help clients arrive at a resolution of these value conflicts by searching out various alternative behaviors or attitudes and deciding which best contributes to their personal satisfaction and development and still permits effective social interaction. The counselor's task is complex because this search may involve a number of value systems: the client's, the counselor's, the school's, society's, the client's peer group, and the client's family. These value systems may all be different, including the values of each parent. Counseling is further complicated by the recognition that counselors cannot keep their values entirely out of the counseling sessions. Their lifestyle and general behavior give some explicit clues to their beliefs about values in general and about controversial behavior.

Counselors follow the ethical codes when they help clients search out alternative value systems and openly indicate when their own biases may unduly influence a client. In these situations the counselor should decide whether to continue working with the client or to refer the client to another counselor. Counselors, I believe, should also indicate to clients when client goals run contrary to their own ethical beliefs, so that counseling might be impeded. These differences are quite likely to occur when either the counselor or the client has strong religious beliefs. A very strict Catholic counselor, for example, might find herself or himself in an ethical bind when a pregnant client contemplates abortion. The counselor must determine whether his or her religious convictions permit an objective discussion of the option of abortion. If not, the counselor should refer the client to another counselor. On the other hand, a counselor should not try to convince a client with strong religious objections to abortion that it is a wise alternative to consider in spite of the client's moral convictions. Such persuasion constitutes unethical behavior.

Counselors who urge the teaching of productive values or who support directly influencing clients with such values are saying that they have discovered a set of values that is right for everyone. These values may be their own and/or the values of contemporary society. In either case the assumption is highly questionable morally, ethically, and theoretically. Counselors who believe that they are experts in behavior who should teach or model appropriate values and counselors who support the idea that they should transmit established values of the school or society usually experience few ethical dilemmas. One can question whether their interactions are truly counseling.

Counselors who follow the guidelines on nonindoctrination of some preconceived set of values will continue to find that one question of values becomes so intertwined with one's lifestyle and general behavior that it becomes practically impossible to divorce their values completely from the counseling process. As Patterson (1958) has suggested, counselors should be open about their values but insist that clients make their own decisions about alternative values if they are to become genuinely productive persons.

As with values, counselors must recognize the potential influence of their personal needs upon clients. Corey (1977) points out, "Therapists must develop a sensitivity to their own unmet needs so that they don't use the therapeutic relationship as a main avenue of satisfying those needs. By recognizing and working through their own personality problems, there is less chance that they will project them onto the client" (pp. 225–226). Counselors must also be aware of any of their needs for power, needs to nurture others, or impulses to manipulate or control others that might influence counseling.

The Rights of Minors

Neither the APGA nor the ASCA standards deal with students' rights versus parents' rights. The APGA code does include a statement that is ambiguous: "When the counselee does not have full autonomy for reasons of age, mental incompetency, criminal incarceration, or similar legal restrictions, the member may have to work with others who exercise significant control and direction over the counselee" (Section B). The ASCA code does indicate that parent/counselor contacts are to be held in confidence, just as student/counselor interviews are. This stipulation allows counselors to have joint sessions with students and parents without feedback to administrators or teachers unless students and parents give their consent. However, it leaves open the possibility that counselors will hold interviews or consultations with parents without the students' knowledge or consent, which would be inconsistent with the code of ethics.

There has been a steady trend toward rights for minors in schools and in community agencies. The increase in privileged communication for minors in counseling provides one example. Students' rights, including freedom of speech, due process regarding disciplinary actions, and the right to legal counsel regarding accusations about illegal behavior, have been mandated by the courts. Minors in some states have the legal right to see physicians or other professionals about contraceptives, abortion, use of drugs, or venereal disease without the requirement that parents be informed. The question of young people's seeking counseling without parental knowledge or consent involves more education of parents and better trained counselors, so that parents will be willing to trust the professional groups.

There have not been many parental objections to confidential counseling in high schools when counselors have insisted upon it. Since high school students are either of legal age or close to it, parents can more easily see value in confidential counseling. In elementary school, when parents have more legal responsibility for children, parents are more likely to question counseling without their consent. Some schools send out letters at the beginning of the year informing parents that children are encouraged to talk with counselors in confidence. If parents object to this procedure, they are invited to the school to discuss their objections more fully. If a child requests counseling and the parents refuse to allow it, I recommend a three-way conference with parents, student, and counselor to determine whether the parents will change their minds.

Further legal precedence has been set for minors' rights to confidentiality by the Family Educational Rights and Privacy Act (the Buckley amendment), passed by Congress in 1974. All school records are open to parents. However, counselors' private notes on counseling sessions are exempt as long as they are not considered official school records or shared with anyone. Protection of information gained in counseling has been given this legal sanction so that students will feel free to share intimate or disturbing emotions about themselves or others without fear of reprisal. The Buckley amendment substantiates the contention that confidentiality, privileged communication, and the right to privacy are important conditions for effective counseling.

Education and Training Standards

Education and training standards for counselors were discussed in Chapter 1. A brief overview should suffice to help focus on some prevailing issues.

Standards for the preparation of school counselors were issued in 1964 by the Association for Counselor Education and Supervision (ACES) as a result of a 5-year study conducted jointly by the APGA, the ASCA, and the ACES. The training standards were revised in 1967. In Division 17's 1968 description of counseling psychologists, the preparation standards are similar to those for school counselors. In 1979 Division 17 published proposed *Standards for Providers of Counseling Psychological Services*, and the ACES developed training standards for doctoral programs in counseling.

Objectives in these documents are consistent with the idea of counseling as the professional's primary role. Graduate-degree programs are recommended. Qualifications for entrance into a training program and for certification are spelled out. The importance of quality supervised experiences is stressed. Supervised practical work at the college counseling clinic or laboratory under close supervision of faculty followed by an internship in an institutional setting supervised by a qualified practitioner in the field is expected.

In 1973 the 1967 standards for the preparation of school counselors, the 1968 standards for elementary school counselors, and the 1969 guidelines for graduate programs for student personnel workers were combined. The guidelines now are entitled *Standards for the Preparation of Counselors and Other Personnel Services Specialists.* I agree with the idea of a core program for counselors in various settings. Also, this core program is highly consistent with school counselor and counseling-psychology roles and with earlier training standards. However, as a member of the ACES, I voted against the adoption of the 1973 standards because I believe that special training in skills to fulfill the unique role of counselors is not sufficiently distinguished from special training in skills to fulfill the roles of other unique personnel specialists. Moreover, the special training differences for these other specialists are not specified at all. Finally, there is a serious contradiction between the idea expressed in the 1973 training standards that counseling is generic to all the duties of personnel administrative specialists and the specification in the 1976 APGA ethical code that counselors should not become involved in administrative functions with clients (Section B12).

In a section on environmental and specialized studies in the 1973 standards, it is recommended that a personnel-service educator might need additional course work in specialized areas, such as financial aid. I contend instead that the ACES should once again separate counselor core preparation from that of personnel-service administrators. The APGA model licensing proposal specifies professional-counseling training consistent with the counselor's role. The ACES, in my opinion, should follow this model in revising preparation standards.

There are some guidelines that I believe strengthen training standards. According to the APGA ethical code's section on the preparation of counselors, counselor educators "are expected to present thoroughly varied theoretical positions so that trainees may make comparisons and have the opportunity to select a position" (Section G10). This guideline is to prevent indoctrination of students. The training guidelines emphasize that supervised practicum and internship experiences are needed in a college laboratory, a clinic, and a setting in which the prospective counselor is contemplating working. The need for continuing training and upgrading of knowledge and skills after one graduates and begins working in the field is stressed. Teacher training or teaching experience is not considered essential for counselors.

As in the other areas I have discussed, not all professionals or employers agree with these ideas, nor have all these standards been implemented. Some persons are looking for a counseling theory or system for all counselors, some counselor educators do not provide sufficient supervision in schools or in work settings, some counselors and counselor educators still insist that teaching experience is necessary to be a successful counselor, and most counselor preparation programs do not include or are weak in experience with minority and opposite-sex clients.

As discussed in Chapter 2, an emerging, very provocative issue is the amount and type of training needed to qualify for licensing by state legislatures to engage in private practice, particularly as it relates to eligibility for health-insurance payments for counseling and therapy. Arguments have been presented that licensing will hurt rather than help the counseling profession. Tiedeman (1979), in an ACES newsletter, vehemently rejected the idea of licensing, believing it contrary to counselors' ideas of self-growth.

I have already dealt with this issue and with the rationale for the difference between personnel workers and counselors. Thus, the rest of this section concentrates on questions related to the other professional guidelines: the need to expose trainees to a variety of theories, the importance of quality supervision, the reasons that teaching experience should not be required for school counselors, and the importance of including work with minority and opposite-sex clients in counselor training programs.

Developing a Personal Philosophy of Counseling

Professional guidelines indicate that it is unethical for counselor educators to expose trainee counselors to only one counseling theory. Instead, a variety of counseling approaches, based upon varying perceptions of human nature, human behavior, and human experience, should be part of the curriculum. This type of educational experience gives counseling students the philosophical and psychological background to help them independently assess the value of contemporary counseling positions. From these personal evaluations, counselor trainees can select a theory similar to that of their instructor, select a different theory, or develop a systematic eclecticism rather than accepting the instructor's theory on faith. In addition, this type of orientation gives practicing counselors the background to evaluate new counseling theories and techniques. The rationale for this type of preparation is that no one counseling theory has proved to be satisfactory for all clients. It is also based upon the idea that people who learn only one set of skills are technicians rather than professionals. As technicians, their backgrounds limit their ability to expand their knowledge and skills as new discoveries are made in counseling theory and practice.

Supervised Experience

For school counselors the amount and quality of supervised internship has undoubtedly been the weakest part of training. Many schools do not have counselors trained to supervise interns. Some interns get bogged down in emulating ineffective counselor roles carried out by poorly trained counselors or by counselors trapped in inappropriate functions. Counseling offices for interns are often not available. Audio or videotaping equipment also is not on hand to help in supervision. But the resolution of these problems does not lie in refusing to put student counselors in school internships. If trainees receive supervision only at the college or university, they are not sufficiently acquainted with schools to handle themselves effectively in interactions with teachers, parents, and administrators. Also, experience in important outreach activities is not possible. A better approach appears to lie in a joint effort by professional associations and preparation institutions to upgrade the supervisory skills of practicing school counselors through workshops or postgraduate training.

On the other hand, counselors who intern in community clinics are sometimes given heavy caseloads with minimum supervision from either the college or the clinic staff. Effective supervised experiences seem to work best if all counselor trainees first engage in practical work at a college training clinic with close supervision by the college faculty. Then, supervised internships at the selected work setting with gradually increasing caseloads should follow. Supervision then can be handled by the agency in which the student is interning.

Internships for both master's-degree and doctoral counselors need to be intensive and of sufficient duration for the prospective counselors to be exposed to a variety of potential clients and activities. Doctoral candidates in counseling should be expected to have more advanced and prolonged internships than master's-degree candidates. The roles of doctorate counselors include training of and consultation with master's-degree counselors, consultation with community agencies, and overall responsibility for the development and implementation of counseling programs.

Practicing counselors need continuing opportunities for consultation and supervision. I strongly recommend that counseling staffs have psychological consultation available on a regular basis. Different cases can be discussed, and counselors can share new and different approaches to handling clients' concerns. This consultation is more likely to occur if there is joint responsibility for continued training through professional associations, school districts, and training institutions. Psychiatric consultation should be available about clients who have had severe emotional crises or who may require psychotropic drugs (tranquilizers).

Teaching Experience

There has been a decrease in requiring teaching experience for school counselor certification. In 1979, 14 states required teaching experience and 8 other states expected the prospective counselor to qualify for a teaching credential but did not require teaching experience (Woellner, 1979). I do not believe that teaching experience should be a necessary component of counselor preparation. A number of years ago, I expressed the view that counseling and teaching are different relationships (Nugent, 1966). Good teachers must be effective evaluators, and have a thorough command of group discipline and instructional techniques to get their subject matter across. Counseling involves a nonauthoritarian relationship in which grading, discipline, and teaching skills are not important. In fact, it has been my experience, backed by some evidence (Campbell, 1962), that the longer teachers are in the classroom the more difficult it becomes to establish a counseling relationship. The most important components for counselor selection are an interest in children and the ability to establish effective counseling relationships. I do believe that experiences in a school are important but prefer to put counselors into a year-long practicum in the school.

The continued administrative demand for prior teaching experience for counselors seems to relate to administrator and teacher persistence in perceiving counselors as upgraded teachers who are friends of the students rather than as counseling specialists. If the counselor's role is clarified, appropriate training is insisted upon, and the counseling relationship is differentiated from the teaching relationship, the demand for teaching experience will probably drop. Most counselors will still come from the teaching ranks, but opportunities for individuals who have the potential for counseling students will be open without the necessity for teaching experiences.

It has been argued that teachers will be more responsive to counselors who have had teaching experience because they will understand teachers' problems in the classroom. History does not support this contention. Almost all school counselors have been teachers, and the relationship between counselors and teachers over the years has generally been poor. Good teachers will respect persons who are knowledgeable in counseling whether they have taught or not. School nurses and school physicians function in schools without having had to teach.

Counselors have been reluctant to disengage themselves from teaching certification, since job tenure has been dependent upon teaching rather than counseling certification. Recently, in Washington, counselors and other specialized personnel were given tenure rights similar to those of teachers. Also, counselors must now have certification for counseling positions; teaching certificates are not appropriate. If counselors continue to gain benefits as members of the counseling staff rather than the teaching staff, the identification of counselors with teachers will decrease.

Counselor Training and the Needs of Minorities

In 1977 a special issue of *Personnel and Guidance Journal* was published under the editorship of Darrell Sue, an Asian-American counseling psychologist. This publication contains articles written by professionally trained counselors about the particular concerns of Asian-Americans, Blacks, Latinos, Haitians, and Puerto Ricans. In most cases the counselors are from the ethnic group about which they were writing. The articles point out a basic feature of all minority groups, that of oppression. However, the articles also focus on the importance of recognizing that each group has a history, a cultural background, and values that make each unique. Therefore, no one counseling approach applies to all.

There are suggestions in these articles and in earlier papers that different ethnic groups need different types of intervention. Smith (1977), in writing about Black clients, objects to this prevailing idea. She first points out the frequency with which intervention techniques of various sorts are recommended specifically for Blacks. These strategies include task-oriented counseling, reality-oriented techniques, and a direct and confrontative manner on the part of the counselor. Her view is that "once the members of the counseling profession start proposing techniques on the basis of race and socioeconomic class alone, they are surely treading in dangerous waters" (p. 393). She continues, "Black clients should be treated as individuals first and secondly as members of a particular racial group" (p. 394). She suggests finding a common core of effective counseling rather than concentrating on differences in race. This idea, it seems to me, should apply to all clients.

Nevertheless, many counselor education programs do not adequately prepare counselors for working with minorities. Master's-degree and doctorate programs should have faculty members from various ethnic backgrounds. Courses and seminars dealing with different customs and values of minorities and with specific problems related to minority groups need to be included in the curriculum. Field work and supervised experience with minorities are essential.

When preparing minority persons to become counselors, it is imperative that program directors do not inadvertently short-cut their training and prepare them at a paraprofessional level.

McDavis and Parker (1977) have developed a model course on counseling minorities. First they collected syllabuses from various universities offering courses in minority counseling. Then a bibliography was drawn up. From these data and from discussions with students, they outlined a course consisting of 22 hours of class. Included are an awareness-group experience, the facilitation of interracial groups, discussion panels with minority students, and techniques for counseling with minority groups.

Counselor Training and Counseling with Women

The knowledge, skills, and attitudes needed to remedy deficiencies in the training of counselors for working with women are discussed in a 1979 issue of *The Counseling Psychologist*, "Counseling Women III." A set of 13 principles about counseling women that was developed by the Ad Hoc Committee on Women in Counseling Psychology (Division 17) is included. In addition, principles for working with various kinds of women's problems are outlined (examples are aging, divorce, and rape).

In the same issue Haraway summarizes her views on the training changes needed to improve the ability of male counselors to work with women. She concludes that roughly half of the faculty should be women, that an equal number of men and women graduate students should be accepted, and that a course on the psychology of women and supervised experiences with women clients should be required. Other curriculum suggestions are that personality theories and materials on careers should be presented and that trainees should be given the opportunity to explore their own biases and the biases present in contemporary counseling. Essential, too, are continuing education about women's issues and continued research on factors related to women and to the counseling of women. Similary, training institutions should include courses, experiences, and practicums that will help female counselors understand problems, concerns, and ambivalences of males of all ages. Male concerns about personal adequacy, relationships, career choice, aging, retirement, and sexual adequacy should be understood by female as well as by male counselors. These and other similar concerns are discussed in a 1978 special edition of *The Counseling Psychologist,* entitled "Counseling Men" (Skovholt, Schauble, Gormally, & Davis, 1978).

Professional Autonomy

For years Dunlop (1968b, 1969, 1971) has been one of the few persons who has objected to the weak professional status of counselors and their inaction on strengthening it. Dunlop (1968b) objected to the failure of school counselors to insist upon performing counseling in the schools. He asked, ". . . how many [counselors] are willing to insist upon autonomy to function within their area of expertise, on their own responsibility, without interference from unqualified persons" (p. 178)? Dunlop's concerns are still valid.

During these years Dunlop has presented well-thought-out recommendations for improving the professional status of counselors. These include developing a rationale for counseling, issuing licenses through examinations, and instituting penalties for unprofessional and unethical behavior. Then, he believes, counselors could gain professional recognition. Professionally prepared counselors who are able to present a rationale to administrators, teachers, parents, and students for their counseling roles will be much more likely to be granted the autonomy to carry out their duties professionally. Counselors should be prepared by training institutions to present a clear, thorough explanation of what they should do and why. They should also be prepared to anticipate unrealistic expectancies of administrators and others and convince these persons to change them.

In addition, strong professional affiliation is needed. Through it, counselors can insist that schools hire professionally trained counselors. Counselors in schools, I believe, should be legally held to the same professional preparation and ethical behavior as counselors in private practice. Thus, I favor either licensing of school counselors or certification paralleling the licensing requirements for private practice. These requirements should include similar penalties for violation of ethical or professional standards whether one is a school counselor or a counselor in private practice. Then school counselors will be strengthened as a professional group, and protection will be available to schoolchildren from unprofessional, unethical, and incompetent counselor behavior.

Effects of Professional Trends on Evaluation and Research

A professional group offering a public service has a responsibility to assess continually the quality of the service, the degree to which it is helping the public, and its overall effectiveness. In counseling these assessments frequently take the form of program evaluations, accountability, and research.

Program evaluations are aimed at determining how effectively counseling staffs carry out their objectives. Program evaluations also can be applied to counselor education programs. Accountability requires a justification, most often financial, to a state or local budgetary agency or to the public, which is footing the bill for services through taxation. Research efforts are usually scientific, objective studies of the effectiveness of counseling methods.

The counseling profession has had difficulties in all of these types of assessments. Program evaluations in schools have not been conducted in any consistent manner with some uniform guidelines. Neither have most counselor education programs been evaluated on the basis of professional-association expectations.

The need in accountability studies to justify money and time spent in counseling has tended to make some counseling staffs emphasize numbers of students seen regardless of the reasons. Also, some counseling staffs have taken on highly visible, concrete activities as a demonstration of their usefulness. These actions reinforce counselor involvement in administrative and clerical tasks at the expense of counseling contacts.

Researchers attempting to determine the effectiveness of counseling have had difficulties developing appropriate experimental designs. Essentially, the major question is what criteria to use to demonstrate counseling effectiveness. Shertzer and Stone (1980) point out the need to find definable, stable, and relevant measures to demonstrate counselor effectiveness. Most criteria used in counseling have weaknesses. Ratings of counseling success by counselors and clients are subject to the halo effect, the tendency of a favorable or an unfavorable general impression to spread to specifics. The rater may also be biased by feelings about the other person that develop in counseling. With students, improved grades, improvement between precounseling, and postcounseling tests, and behavioral improvement in the classroom are not always appropriate measures of counseling success. Finally, the results of follow-up studies are criticized as being contaminated by influences unrelated to counseling sessions.

These problems result in part from the difficulties inherent in any evaluation of or research on human behavior. But in counseling these problems have become even more complicated because some counselors have had insufficient training in research or evaluation, counselor selection and training have been spotty and erratic, and counseling programs in schools and communities often do not include sufficient professional counseling as described here.

A strengthened, unified, professional group agreeing upon primary counselor functions and upon counselor training and insisting upon maintaining professional standards could have a refreshing, salutary effect on counseling evaluation. Such a group would provide the necessary control over the quality of counseling and the definition of counseling and thus make the counseling researcher's task easier. If these factors were controlled, the profession could turn to tackling problems that are inherent in evaluating the effectiveness of human interactions.

Program evaluations that are used to determine how effectively a staff is carrying out objectives could become more meaningful. Counseling experts could conduct evaluations using guidelines developed by national, regional, or local counseling associations rather than depending upon state agencies to develop guidelines.

A well-trained staff could insist that accountability be based on the quality of counseling services rather than on a computer cost analysis of the number of counselor contacts with people.

Research on the effectiveness of counseling methods could be carried out with considerably less contamination of the results because of disparities in the training of counselors. Counselors in practice could collaborate with counselor educators in colleges and universities to improve research designs, to develop criteria to measure counselor effectiveness, and to set up controlled experiments comparing counseled and noncounseled subjects.

If trends such as these began to flourish, conclusions about the ineffectiveness of professional counseling resulting from an inappropriate definition of counseling would change. Eysenck (1952), for example, conducted a survey of therapeutic outcomes as judged by psychiatrists working with psychotic and neurotic patients in hospitals and mental-health clinics. He concluded that no therapy was just as effective as therapy. Some counselor educators (Berenson & Carkhuff, 1967; Carkhuff, 1972a, b) have generalized these results to include counseling. Even if we disregard the heavy criticism of the experimental design used by Eysenck, the population and type of treatment he studied were in no way similar to those in psychological counseling. Professional strength leading to improvements in assessment and research would give much more substantial evidence

on the effectiveness of counseling and should lead to continual improvements in the counseling field (Peters & Shertzer).

Projects and Activities

1. Write or phone your state attorney general's office and ask about the legal status of college, school, and community counselors regarding privileged communication. Are minors covered? Are there special regulations for drug treatment and pregnancy with minors? Ask for copies of any existing statutes. Start a looseleaf notebook on legal concerns.
2. Compare the ethical codes of the APGA, the ASCA, and the APA as they pertain to professional counseling. Which code, in your opinion, best fits the practice of counseling in the setting in which you want to work or are working?
3. Write or phone the president or executive secretary of your regional or state professional associations about procedures for reporting unethical behavior of members of the associations. Find out what sanctions, if any, can be applied. Also explore whether the counseling department of your state department of public instruction has policies on unethical behavior of school counselors.
4. Organize a panel of counselors with master's and doctoral degrees in counseling who are working in private practice, schools, colleges, and community agencies to discuss licensing of counselors with a master's degree.
5. Check with your state affiliates of the APGA and the APA about the licensing of counselors in your state. If licensing exists, what are the stipulations for doctorate and master's-degree counselors? If not, are plans to license counselors being considered?
6. Interview some professionally trained counselors in the community, at a college, or in a public school. Ask them to read the definition of the counselor's role as developed by the APGA, the ASCA, or the AMHCA and the APGA or APA code of ethics. Do they agree with the standards? What problems do they see in trying to function in the manner described by the professional associations?
7. Compare the standards of associations representing professional counselors (the APGA or Division 17) with those for other recognized professional workers such as social workers or clinical psychologists in terms of role, training standards, and ethical codes. Which are most clearly delineated?
8. Division 17 has recommended that counseling psychologists distinguish themselves from other professional counselors as described by the APGA. Look over the standards and role definitions. In your opinion, do significant differences emerge? If so, what are these differences? Do they outweigh similarities?
9. Select several agencies with different emphases, such as a child-guidance clinic, a halfway house, a crisis clinic, and a public school. Find out whether they employ any paraprofessionals. If so, compare their training programs and duties. How do these duties relate to the duties of professional persons?

10. *Invite professionally trained counselors from various minority groups to discuss with your class or group issues related to the counseling of minorities— for example, counseling by Whites, differences and similarities in minority-group values and their influence on counseling, and the problem of culturally biased tests.*

In the following three incidents, assume that you are a certified counselor. In each case write a response indicating what you would say or do.[1]

11. *A principal (or agency head) who was once a professional counselor confers with you and tells you that because drug problems in your area have now reached "epidemic proportions" it would be wise for you to let him know about any client who comes to you with such a problem. What do you say to your principal or agency head? (Compare your answer with the author's comments below.)*

12. *A 17-year-old comes to see you for the first time. He appears very depressed. He tells you that on May 16, his 18th birthday, he plans to commit suicide and tells you in great detail why and how he intends to do so. He further says that he is telling you this because he wants to be sure no one is accused of doing him in and that since he does not belong to any church and has no priest or minister you are the only person who will not tell anyone. In light of your role as a counselor and considering the code of ethics, do you tell anyone? (Compare your answer with the author's comments below.)*

13. *A large, local business firm calls you about a former client, now 19 years of age. He apparently is on a trip out of the country with his entire family for at least a month and cannot be reached. He is being seriously considered for a good job, but the company wants to make a decision within 30 days. What they wish to get from you are his school records and an evaluation of his personal and emotional adjustment. How do you respond to the company's request for information that could lead to this young man's getting a good job? (Compare your answer with the author's comments below.)*

Author's Comments

Activity 11.   *The code of ethics is very clear in regard to this activity question. For the counselor to give the agency head or principal the names of clients with a description of the areas of the clients' concern would be a clear violation of the counselor's professional responsibility. In some states, such as Washington, revealing the name of a client to the agency head or anyone else would also be a violation of the civil rights of the client because state law grants privileged communication to clients who voluntarily go to professional counselors to discuss drug problems. In this illustration it might well be that the administrator, after being*

[1]These activities and comments were written by Dr. Elvet G. Jones, professor of Psychology at Western Washington University.

told of the ethical and legal restrictions, would be happy to follow a suggestion that keeping a record of the number of certain types of problems, as long as the clients remain anonymous, might be all that the administrator really needs to know. It is important, however, that counselors hold fast to ethical and legal responsibilities and not justify their violation on the basis of "the administration asked me to do it."

Activity 12. *In this case the client presented a problem in such a manner as to indicate clearly that his behavior falls well out of the range of the normal. In fact, the case would lead one to suspect a possible psychotic condition as well as the high suicide risk. Under these conditions the code of ethics permits (and experience would strongly recommend) that the counselor take action for the welfare of the client, which becomes the overriding principle in this case. Even though one might hold the personal view that individuals have a right to take their own lives, we live in a society in which this view is clearly rejected even legally. In addition, research shows that the majority of people comtemplating suicide who go to someone to discuss the possibility are not beyond wanting help. Most well-organized counseling agencies have policy statements and guidelines on how to handle this type of extreme situation. The beginning counselor might feel that he or she would indicate that it is not a breach of professional ethics. However, to leave the individual with the impression that you are not going to involve others when you are would be considered poor professional practice, with the exception of those cases in which individuals are so disturbed that telling them might precipitate immediate violence against themselves or others.*

Activity 13. *In responding to this activity question, it certainly would be easy to think that since it would appear to be in the client's interest to send the information requested, it would be a simple act of human concern to do so. However, it would be a serious technical error and not consistent with ethical or legal standards to send any of the requested information. By way of explanation, ever since the passage in 1974 of a federal law known as the Family Educational Rights and Privacy Act, it has been illegal to send school-file information to another agency or person without the* written *permission of the parents or the student if he or she is of age. Sending an evaluation of the student's personal adjustment would also be covered by this law and would raise serious questions about the violation of professional confidence, no matter how good one's intentions. Even though you might be convinced that the student will not get the job because of the lack of information, you and the school would be forced simply to inform the company of the dilemma. Written permission from the client for the release of information would be required.*

4

Theories and Techniques
Used in Counseling

A Definition of Counseling Theory

Brammer (1971) describes a theory as an orderly set of assumptions, concepts, and models to help describe and explain phenomena. For psychological counselors, the phenomena to be described are the elements that make up the counseling process. Foremost among these elements are views about human nature and the environment and the influence of each upon human behavior. Thus, assumptions about growth, development, and learning, accounting for problems in decision making, and descriptions of socialization processes are essential components of counseling theories. In this sense, counseling theories are like personality theories. But counseling theories go beyond personality theories by emphasizing a systematic description of difficulties that may arise in the individual's interaction with the environment and require professional assistance. Further, counseling theories include techniques for helping individuals resolve these difficulties.

The Purpose of Counseling Theory

An integrated system of beliefs about the counseling process can help counselors improve their professional practice, increase their professional knowledge, and enhance their personal development. In counseling practice, an integrated theory provides a more coherent definition of the counseling process, more clear-cut statements of counseling goals, a rationale for selection or rejection of particular counseling techniques, a basis for determining ethical counseling procedures, and a framework for evaluating and conducting research on counseling processes and outcomes. Counselors' professional growth can be enhanced because they can evaluate whether new theoretical models or new techniques are sufficiently worthwhile to be incorporated into their own theory or into their practice. Practicing counselors become true professionals who can make some studied judgments about new ideas and new techniques. A personal theory of counseling relates to one's philosophy about life and about human nature. Thus, both counselors in training and practicing counselors experience personal growth when they are literally forced to search out their own beliefs and values as they relate to various counseling theories.

Developing a Personal Counseling Theory

The Search for One Comprehensive Counseling Theory

When counseling psychology began in the late 1940s and early 1950s, two major theories dominated counseling training: Williamson's clinical-counseling approach (directive) and Rogers's client-centered counseling approach (nondirective). Psychoanalysis, which was offered as a general background for counselors, was the major theoretical approach taught to psychiatrists, clinical psychologists, and social workers.

This limited choice made professional life easier for counselor educators, counselors in training, and practicing counselors. Counselor educators could present fairly clear-cut comparisons of theories. Student counselors could make simpler and more definite discriminations about what theoretical leanings they preferred. Practicing counselors could keep up with trends by continued reading and by attending workshops at regular intervals in familiar areas of counseling theories and techniques.

As information about development and behavior increased and as the need for help with normal developmental conflicts became more acceptable, different approaches to human problems began to influence counseling practice. In particular, humanistic psychological theories, new approaches in behaviorism, and the advent of developmental approaches in counseling added many new and challenging possibilities for counselors in training or in practice.

As theoretical possibilities grew at a bewildering pace, some counseling theorists began to present approaches that they believed would be appropriate for anyone in the counseling profession. In the 1950s Dollard and Miller reconceptualized psychoanalysis into behavioral concepts and Pepinsky and Pepinsky developed a counseling theory based on learning principles. Krumboltz edited a 1966 book called *Revolution in Counseling*, which was a major attempt to apply behaviorism, particularly operant conditioning, specifically to counseling.[1] His hope was to convince most counselors of the value of this approach. But in the same year Blocher pulled together an emerging interest in development processes in a book called *Developmental Counseling*. Again the hope was to develop a theoretical system particular to counseling that could provide professional theoretical unity. Neither the behavioral nor the developmental theory has proved sufficiently comprehensive for all counseling practitioners. Neither covers the range of client problems, and neither is compatible with the total range of personal characteristics that counselors and clients bring to the counseling relationship and that influence their interactions. Also, some theories originally developed for psychotherapy with persons with neurotic or severe problems of adjustment have been expanded to include work with normal developmental conflicts. The neopsychoanalytic, Gestalt, rational/emotive, and existential theories are examples. To compound the complexity of the theoretical picture, derivatives of behaviorism, such as social-learning theory, have become popular.

Thus, even though some professional counselors are still hoping for one comprehensive theory, it is not likely to appear for quite some time, if at all. History has shown that other professional groups that latched onto a specific approach to therapy have had to abandon total dependence on the approach. For example, psychiatrists were almost all trained in psychoanalytic theory or its derivatives until recently. Also, clinical psychologists were at first trained almost exclusively in psychoanalytic theory and, more recently, in behavior modification.

Reasons for Developing a Personal Counseling Theory

Considering the number of counseling theorists existing today, the most reasonable professional procedure for counselor educators is to expose students to various approaches and to give them guidelines on how to develop their own personal theory. Not only is this good professional practice, but it is also consistent with good ethical practice. The ethical responsibility not to indoctrinate students is stated clearly in the APGA code of ethics: "Members are expected to present thoroughly varied theoretical positions so that trainees may make comparisons and have the opportunity to select a position" (Section G10). Under this guideline, students could follow a particular theorist after comparing theorists, or they could select ideas from various approaches and integrate them into their own personal, eclectic theory.

In spite of these professional and ethical considerations, it is tempting for counselor educators to teach only their particular theory to students. They believe in it, and using it makes for simpler, more efficient teaching

---

[1] Guthrie wrote about the application of operant-conditioning techniques to applied problems in psychology in the 1930s. Krumboltz wrote specifically about behaviorism and counseling.

and causes less initial confusion for students. But counselor educators who unilaterally push their own theory in counselor graduate programs are essentially being unfair to the students. Most well-prepared counselor educators have been exposed to numerous views about personality, development, and the dynamics of human interaction. They have learned various ways of incorporating these concepts into a personal theory of counseling. It might be a literal compliance with a contemporary theorist like Ellis or Perls. It might be an eclectic position based upon some studied decisions of various theorists' ideas. In either case, because consideration has been given to various views, the theory is open to revision as the professional gains new concepts, learning, or insights.

If counselor educators do not provide students with similar opportunities for theoretical searching, they end up preparing technicians capable only of carrying out a particular set of communication, relationship, or behavioral skills deemed appropriate by their professors. Some of these technically trained persons become bewildered by the many theories. Others become victims of passing popular fads in counseling and move indiscriminately from one to another. Still others hold rigidly to the learned techniques and fail to profit from new ideas. These people lack the professional capacity to make independent judgments on what they wish to accept or reject in their practice. Further, confusion occurs in the counseling profession over the difference between paraprofessionals, who should be prepared in specific, circumscribed skills, and the professional psychological counselors, who have a broad theoretical base.

A Method for Developing a Personal Counseling Theory

To help counseling students develop their own counseling theory counselor educators must provide them with some method of analyzing the many existing theories. This analysis enables students to make more sophisticated judgments about what they want to include in their own theory. The analysis becomes easier if the theories are divided into categories based upon some common characteristic rather than considering each theory as completely distinct from one another.

A classification system that has proved useful to me focuses on the theorist's philosophical views about human nature and human interaction. This type of classification has the advantage of being consistent with the major contemporary influences in psychology, which have usually been described as behaviorism versus phenomenology or behaviorism versus humanism. Behaviorists usually believe that human behavior results predominantly from the individual's responses to external stimuli. Human behavior can be manipulated through appropriate control of these stimuli. Behavior as a result of mental processes is given little, if any, attention. Humanists usually perceive potentialities in humans as the primary sources of behavior. Humans can make choices on how to act in different situations. Mental, perceptual, and other inner processes are considered influential in behavior development (Hitt, 1972). As you will recall, Rogers and Skinner held debates on the relative value of behaviorism and phenomenology (Wann, 1964).

Allport (1962) and Barclay (1968) offer philosophical frameworks in which counseling theorists can be placed upon a continuum from those who strongly hypothesize environmental forces as determinants of behavior to those who strongly perceive humans as active beings with potentialities for influencing their own behavior. By exploring such a continuum, students can attain a more comprehensive and explicit analysis of the relationship of their beliefs to the beliefs of various theorists. A personal counseling theory built from this analysis will more likely show a consistency between the goals and methods used in counseling and the theoretical base for these goals and techniques. Also, this approach prepares students to make professional judgments about new theories and techniques as they arise in the field of counseling.

At this point I will review the major theorists influencing counseling. Barclay (1971) has recommended using the terms *environmentalists* and *humanists* because he believes that they more accurately describe the underlying distinction in theories than do either *behaviorists* and *humanists* or *behaviorists* and *phenomenologists*. I agree with this suggestion, so I will distinguish theorists first on the basis of whether they assume that environmental influences or human potentialities are more important determinants of behavior. Then I will consider a more specific breakdown of theories based upon the degree to which counselors are committed to either view or to an eclectic combination of some elements of each view.

In this overview only a relatively simple discussion of a complex issue can be presented to give beginners in counseling a start toward analyzing their own views. For readers with a more advanced theoretical background, I recommend reading Allport (1962), Barclay (1968, 1971), and Hitt (1972). In particular, Barclay has outlined a bipolar model to analyze more complex considerations of philosophical views than can be presented here.

A Comparison of Environmental and Humanistic Influences on Counseling

Theorists with an Environmental Orientation

General Orientation.   Environmentalists define humans as being predominantly reacting organisms having little or relatively limited control over their lives. External reality in the form of events, circumstances, and social influences are the significant factors contributing to the individual's behavior and development. Cognitive processes, if accepted, are described as intellectual or reasoning abilities that help people cope with the environment or make more effective responses to the environment through improved problem-solving skills. If inner characteristics such as traits are hypothesized, only those that can be measured scientifically by valid and reliable tests or inventories are acceptable. Basically, human nature is described as neutral. Adaptive or unadaptive behaviors result from responses shaped by, or learned from, other significant persons in one's life or through significant social influences. Values are based upon cultural norms or natural laws that have been conceived primarily to help society survive.

From the above summary, it becomes clear that counselors with environmental leanings emphasize traditional empirically-based scientific methods in counseling practice. Humans are alike and predictable in behavior. Overt, observable, or measurable behaviors are the prime consideration. Emotions are inner phenomena that are difficult to observe or measure scientifically. Therefore, they are ignored or given secondary status, or attempts are made to measure them before using them in practice. Environmentalists interested in research on social management are often called social engineers.

Counseling Goals, Methods, and Evaluation. Counselors who emphasize environmental and/or social influences are called behavioral counselors, rational counselors, or developmental counselors. They define counseling as a learning process in which the counselor functions as a teacher. The most significant behavior in a person's repertoire is learned. Unadaptive or ineffective behavior is a result of insufficient, inappropriate, or distorted learning experiences.

The goals of counseling are to improve clients' adaptation to their environment and to help them work toward socially desirable behaviors. These more appropriate and adaptive behaviors can be learned by changing clients' reactions to environmental influences, by changing their environment, or by teaching them more logical ways of behaving.

The counseling process becomes essentially a learning environment. Establishing a good relationship is important but is insufficient to carry out effective counseling. Counselors believe they have special expertise about human behavior based upon sound scientific principles that can be used to help clients learn new ways of behaving. Counselors prefer to work with specific problems, symptoms, and complaints. If the presentation of the problem is not specific enough, counselors tend to begin the counseling process by helping clients pinpoint their concerns.

The emphasis on external factors makes possible a wide range of techniques. Counselors may demonstrate culturally appropriate behavior by serving as models or by using other persons to model behavior. Problem-solving or logical-reasoning skills may be taught. Role playing, in which the counselor and client assume the roles of other persons in the client's life and practice appropriate responses, is another popular approach. In addition, clients are given reinforcement for or are taught to reinforce themselves for desired behavior. Clients may also be trained in specific social skills, such as assertiveness. Homework assignments are considered useful. Finally, counselors may try to influence clients toward socially desirable behavior when they consider it necessary.

The criteria for evaluating the success of counseling are often based upon whether a specified behavior or attitude outlined as a goal of counseling has been achieved. Also, counselors are interested in whether the client is functioning more efficiently or effectively in society.

Theorists with a Humanistic Orientation

General Orientation. Humanists perceive people as active beings with inner capacities to make a significant impact on the environment. Conscious behavior is important. Purpose, the ability to organize experiences into meaningful patterns, motivations, and the freedom to choose are the major influences in human behavior. Events, circumstances, and social influences are realities in the material world, but the perception and interpretation of these realities give meaning to the environment. Thus, the subjective reality of the individual's inner world (intuitions, feelings, emotions, and thoughts) is not only a respectable source for understanding persons in their world but the only one. Cognitive processes, when accepted, are perceived as perceptual processes that contribute to people's insight into their feelings, attitudes, and behavior. The tendency is to perceive human nature as positive. Positive or negative behavior results from the degree to which people accept and understand the legitimacy of their needs, drives, or attitudes in light of environmental demands or social pressures. Values arise from searching the inner self or are created through the human existence in the environment and are conceived primarily to help individuals survive with integrity in society.

The humanists' beliefs that human behavior is purposeful and that the subjective reality of inner processes is important tend to make them reject traditional scientific methods. People are capable of developing unique lifestyles, so that behavior becomes difficult to predict and can be studied only in terms of the total human being. Human behavior is too complex to be fully understood, and attempts to do so might dehumanize the individual. Rogers has argued for years that humanists should develop scientific, but not dehumanizing, approaches to the study of human processes and human relationships. Historically, phenomenological and Gestalt psychologists have carried out laboratory research on introspection, on insight in animals, and on perceptual processes in humans. Some of these procedures might be explored to determine whether they can be applied to the study of an ongoing counseling process.

Counseling Goals, Methods, and Evaluation. Counselors emphasizing the importance of human characteristics are called phenomenological, Gestalt, self, existential, or relationship counselors. They believe that human potential and predispositions are the major forces developing behavior. Problems arise when people do not fully use their potentialities to resolve inner conflicts or anxieties or conflicts with others. Increased perception about oneself or about reactions to others involves exploring feelings, attitudes, and emotions in general. Counselors believe that the degree of awareness relates to the type of conditions developed in counseling interactions. Therefore, they define counseling as a relationship in which clients are helped to capitalize on their own capabilities for resolving conflicts and assuming responsibility for changing their own attitudes or social circumstances.

The goals of counseling are perceived as improved self-direction, self-understanding, or self-reorganization or as improved insight into one's own motivations or into the dynamics of conflict with others. Improved decision making and willingness to assume responsibility for one's own behavior are anticipated.

Humanists who believe firmly in an innate, healthy, potential-growth force rely on few techniques. They stress such counselor characteristics as warmth, empathy, and genuineness as necessary and sufficient conditions for counseling. Other humanists, such as Gestaltists, use immediate, ongoing interaction in the counseling relationship to help clients understand their own behavior. They use a variety of techniques to activate clients, such as confronting them with their contradictory behavior or asking them to act out various social roles. These techniques are assumed to help develop the self-understanding necessary to resolve conflicts. Because of this orientation, feelings, attitudes, beliefs, and perceptions are major considerations in counseling interactions.

The criteria for determining the success of counseling are various measures related to self-understanding. Measures of congruency between one's aspirations and reality or between perceptions of oneself and how one would really like to be are other criteria.

It should be noted that other classifications of theories used in counseling have been recommended in the literature. For example, London (1964) divides theorists on the basis of whether their goal in counseling is primarily client insight, or client action. Patterson (1980) prefers to distinguish theorists by whether they emphasize rational problem-solving procedures or affective processes in the counseling relationship. I have found the environmental/humanistic comparison to be the most useful and flexible approach both in teaching theories and in continuing to modify my own personal theory.

Counseling Theories

Counseling theories will be discussed on a continuum from those that are most environmentally oriented to those that are most humanistic. This continuum is an arbitrary one. Readers might make different decisions on where they would place theorists. Theoretical approaches that have had an impact on counseling practice will be included. These are behavioral, rational, developmental, phenomenological, and existential theories. Specific theorists who have made important contributions to counseling will be handled individually. In other categories a broader description of a theoretical group will be more useful.

In an overview, as this book is, only short descriptions are possible. For more comprehensive treatments, readers should consult the references cited in this chapter. I also recommend reading the original writings of the theorists in order to make one's own judgments.

⮑ Behavioral Counseling

Behaviorists most closely follow the extreme environmental position presented earlier. Actually, behavioral theories are a cluster of theories, all of which use some form of learning theory as a basis for the counseling theory.

Behavioral counselors believe that counseling goals must be those desired by the client that are not contrary to the values of the counselor and that are possible to achieve. Once these goals are agreed upon, the goals are specified in such a way that appropriate methods for working toward these goals can be determined and the degree of attainment of these goals can be measured at the completion of counseling.

Krumboltz (1966) has described four approaches in counseling based on learning theory: operant conditioning, imitative, or social, learning, cognitive learning, and emotional learning. For those behavioral counselors to whom behavior is primarily the product of operant conditioning, symptoms in terms of observable behavior are the main concerns in the counseling process. People respond to events in the environment. If a behavior is reinforced by some reward, the behavior will tend to continue. If the behavior is not reinforced, it will tend not to be repeated. Thus, behavior is conditioned by its consequences. Ineffective behavior is extinguished by eliminating the conditions that reinforce it. New behavior is

then introduced and appropriately reinforced. The counselor is essentially a teacher who helps clients learn new and more adaptive responses to
old situations.

More recently, other behaviorists have considered the conditioning
procedures just described as too limited to explain all behavior. These
theorists suggest that some learning can occur when individuals imitate
the behavior of others even though the imitation is not directly reinforced. Bandura and Walters (1963) have been major spokesmen for this
form of social learning. Counselors expose clients to live or filmed actors
who model socially desirable or socially effective behavior. The clients
observe and imitate the models' behavior. This approach has been used to
treat phobias. For example, a client who fears snakes observes a model
petting a snake. Tape recordings, autobiographies, and typescripts can be
used to demonstrate problem solving.

In cognitive learning the emphasis is upon telling a person what to do.
Counselors may give direct verbal instructions for clients to follow. They
may develop a behavioral contract with clients in which it is agreed that
certain behaviors will be rewarded. Or they may help clients learn more
effective ways of interacting socially by teaching them to role-play new
behaviors. The term *cognitive restructuring* is sometimes used to describe
these processes.

Wolpe (1973) has been interested in emotional learning. He developed
the technique called systematic desensitization. The term *desensitize* refers
to gradually decreasing sensitivity to an anxiety-provoking emotion by
pairing the emotion with relaxation responses. Wolpe assumes that a person cannot physiologically be anxious and relaxed at the same time. Let us
take a common example, the fear of dentists. A client tells a counselor
about an unreasonable fear of dentists. The fear is preventing the client
from keeping necessary appointments with the dentist. The counselor
first helps the client develop a hierarchy of gradually increasing anxiety
situations related to visiting a dentist. The client is taught how to relax
through a series of relaxation exercises and is told to imagine gradually
increasing anxiety-provoking images about dentists. In this way the client
learns to visualize being worked on in a dentist's chair without anxiety.
Ultimately it is assumed the person will be able to see a dentist without
fear.

Some behaviorists are attempting to broaden the base of their work by
including a quantification of some of the inner processes that humanists
have specified. Training clients in self-control and self-determination and
changing self-concepts through reinforcement, modeling, and other behavioral techniques, then, are considered legitimate behavioral activities
(Thoresen & Mahoney, 1974).

The most common criticism of behaviorists is that they work with a
fairly narrow range of problems because they insist on specifying the

problem. This specificity, however, increases the opportunity for them to become active in research on counseling outcomes.

Rational Approaches to Counseling

Rational-counseling theories are popular with counselors who prefer logical, intellectual approaches. For these counselors, people have potentialities for effective or ineffective behavior. However, these potentialities are influenced by social and environmental forces to the extent that individuals have only limited choice in and control over their lives. Most client problems, including emotional ones, result from inefficient learning modeled after or shaped by inappropriate behaviors of significant persons in their lives. Social learning, then, is an important component of these theories.

Counselors perceive themselves as very active teachers who apply scientifically based techniques to help clients learn problem-solving skills. Since social influences are a strong determinant of behavior, rationalist counselors are not reluctant to persuade or socially influence a client toward some behavior that they deem to be psychologically or socially desirable. Ellis and Williamson are representative of this group.

Ellis's Rational/Emotive Theory.   Ellis (1973) is very straightforward in his description of why people have problems and how counselors go about helping them. He hypothesizes that most problems relate to irrational beliefs that arise because of illogical reasoning and insists that thinking and emotion are not separate processes. Emotional problems result from illogical thought processes. Ellis lists about a dozen irrational beliefs that he believes plague most people in our culture. These beliefs relate to unrealistic ideas or expectations about oneself, about others, and about the world in general. For example, it is irrational to become very upset over other people's problems or to believe that the world is a catastrophic place when things are not how one would like them to be. These ideas form and are reinforced when a child is exposed to parents and others who model irrational thinking. The goal of counseling is to help clients attain logical approaches to solving problems.

Ellis takes a phenomenological position in explaining the roots of problems and uses highly behavioristic techniques to treat the problems. His famous *ABC* principle emphasizes the importance of the perception of a stimulus. *A* represents the stimulus, *B* is the belief related to *A* (perception of the stimulus), and *C* is the consequence. For example, a male student comes to counseling complaining he feels worthless (*C*) because he did poorly on a math test (*A*). The counselor will try to show that the failure is not what is really giving him these feelings but rather his perception of the failure (*B*). Ellis believes that people use illogical internalized sentences. In this case the student thinks, (*A*) I failed my math test; (*B*) I should not have failed, for only worthless people fail; (*C*) how worthless I am for failing. The counselor helps the student see that Belief *B* is irrational.

Counselors using Ellis's approach confront clients with their irrational beliefs and proceed to teach more rational belief systems. Persuasion, cajolery, provocation, and subtle coercion are used where necessary. Homework assignments may be given to help clients practice thinking rationally.

Williamson's Trait-Factor Theory.   Williamson (1939) developed the original theory labeled counseling theory. Elaborating on Parsons's (1909) vocational-counseling ideas, he geared his approach to colleges and high schools. The original focus was predominantly on vocational and educational problems related to schoolwork. The theory was first called vocational guidance, then vocational counseling. More recently, Williamson used the term *clinical counseling* and presently prefers *trait-factor counseling* (Williamson, 1965).

Personality is conceived of as an organized constellation of trait factors and potentialities that can be measured through standardized measures of interests, achievements, aptitudes, and other personality attributes. People seeking counseling have not used their potentials effectively. The counselor functions like a physician; the client presents problems, and the counselor gathers data through a history-taking interview, arranges for appropriate tests, and makes a diagnosis.

After the diagnosis the actual counseling begins. In this process the counselor carefully explains the diagnostic data accumulated and presents alternative solutions. The selection of an alternative is ultimately the responsibility of the client. However, the counselor does not hesitate to offer advice or to influence the decisions or values of the client if the counselor believes it necessary. Once a plan is decided upon, the counselor is willing to provide direct assistance in carrying out the plan. The counseling outcome is judged predominantly by follow-up studies.

Developmental-Counseling Theories

Developmental theories, like behavioral theories, are a cluster of theories. The concept that ties them together and differentiates them from other groups of theories is the importance placed upon normal developmental stages in the human life span. These theories are all based upon the idea that every human goes through ordered and sequential developmental stages. Society demands that individuals perform particular tasks appropriate to their stage of development. For example, when people reach late adolescence, they are expected to break away from dependence on the family and be able to function independently in society. People run into difficulties when they do not pass smoothly through a stage of development or remain fixed at a particular stage.

Though all developmental theorists agree on the idea of universal stages of normal development, they are not agreed on what these universal stages are. Some developmental counselors (for example, Tyler, 1969) base their theory on a pattern consistent with types of problems handled. Most developmental counselors combine a number of systems into an eclectic model. Some of the more popular systems covering systems of general development are Havighurst's (1953) developmental tasks and Erikson's (1968) stages of identity crises. Some commonly used developmental models based on the development of specific attitudes or skills are Kohlberg's moral-reasoning stages and Piaget's cognitive stages (Shaver & Strong, 1976).

The idea of developmental stages is not new to psychology. Freud's theory was based upon oral, anal, and genital stages (Hall, 1954). But the specific application of developmental theory to counseling on normal problems is relatively recent. The roots of developmental counseling are similar to those of rationalist counseling and are in part the result of attempts to combine social-influence forces and individual potentialities into a workable theory. Like rationalist counselors, developmental counselors believe that humans have potentialities to be active in their environment but that social or environmental influences severely restrict individual choice and development. Also, most developmental counselors describe themselves as teachers, with counseling an educative process. Their goals are similar to those of rationalist counselors in that clients are to be helped to attain effectiveness in society as defined by standards decided upon by the counselor.

Developmental counseling followed Williamson's lead in that the theories were designed primarily for work in educational settings. As with Williamson, educational and vocational choices and problems are major considerations of most developmental counselors. But vocational development has been broadened and defined as an ongoing life process that is part of total personality development (see, for example, Super, 1953).

Blocher and Tyler will be presented as somewhat contrasting developmental counselors. These counseling theories should be differentiated from developmental-guidance approaches, which are permeating psychological-education activities. These approaches will be discussed later in the chapter.

Blocher's Developmental Counseling.   Blocher (1974) assumes that personality develops in a largely healthy interaction between the growing organism and the culture or environment. His theory is an eclectic one that includes developmental, relationship, cognitive, and behavioral models.

The goal of counseling is to help individuals maximize their freedom within the limitations of their capacities and their environment. This freedom is attained by maximizing their effectiveness so that they can gain the greatest possible control over their environment and over their own emotional responses to the environment.

Blocher's counseling theory is based upon a human-effectiveness model that includes three concepts: effective social roles and relationships, coping behaviors, and developmental tasks. He divides development into five stages. These stages are organization (infancy to adolescence); exploration (adolescence to young adult); realization (30 to 50); stabilization (50 to 65); and examination (65 and over). Blocher lists principal roles, developmental tasks, and coping behaviors for each stage. For example, in the realization stage one has leadership, helping, creative, and accomplishment roles. Developmental tasks include learning to be inner directed, interdependent, and emotionally flexible and to develop creative thought processes and effective problem-solving techniques. Some coping behaviors for this age are objectivity, logical analysis, tolerance of ambiguity, concentration, and suppression.

Blocher assumes that developmental tasks must be handled effectively at each life stage before the individual can move smoothly into the next stage. He believes that the central developmental task is identity formation, by which he means an organization of personality that gives meaning and consistency in life. People run into problems when discontinuities occur in their move from one developmental stage to another because of environmental barriers. Counseling can then help the individual attain the necessary effectiveness through a counseling relationship that includes diagnosis, interest and aptitude testing, or problem solving when necessary. Vocational concerns are important, since work constitutes a developmental task.

In his later writing Blocher (1974, p. 7) said more definitely that social influences severely limit freedom. This belief has led him to focus on social systems and learning environments in counseling. He sees counselors as social engineers who intervene to improve the environment for an individual. In these ideas Blocher represents a growing trend of developmental theorists to move toward a human technology in which social management takes precedence over professional individual and group counseling.

Tyler's Psychology of Possibilities.   Tyler has devoted much of her time to counseling theory and practice. She has not written a book exclusively outlining a theory of counseling but has developed a "blueprint for a counseling theory" in her *The Work of the Counselor* (third edition, 1969). In this blueprint she outlines a developmental approach that includes trait-factor, client-centered, and learning-theory concepts and techniques as well as developmental concepts. In a sense her theory is an updating and expansion of Williamson's trait-factor theory, discussed earlier. Like

Williamson, she believes that people have some capacity to control their lives but that internal and external structures set limits on possibilities of choice.

Counseling is a decision-making process. People come to counselors when confronted with the need to make a decision. The goal of counseling is to help clients accurately assess the possible alternatives open to them and to choose the alternative that holds the best promise for future development.

Tyler uses a two-dimensional system for categorizing developmental life stages proposed by Gilmore (1973). Five orderly, sequential stages are hypothesized from infancy through old age. In each life stage three central developmental tasks must be mastered: work, interpersonal relations, and aloneness. For example, in old age, retirement, coping with loneliness, and facing one's own death are life tasks. Tyler makes a further distinction in her theory by dividing problems into three categories: choice cases, doubtful cases, and change cases. The distinction is based on the degree to which possibilities are open to individuals.

Tyler recommends using different approaches for each category of problems. When a client has a simple choice decision and when present possibilities appear adequate, Tyler gathers information through interviews and tests to help the person make a decision. When a client is confused or doubtful about choices and when possibilities cannot be evaluated without a better understanding of the individual, Tyler starts with client-centered interviews before moving to diagnosis, testing, and information gathering. When significant change is required in behavior or environment and the client's present possibilities appear inadequate and unpromising for future development, Tyler uses deeper-level counseling or therapy or some behavioral technique to change the person's environment or responses to the environment.

In contrast to many other developmental theorists, Tyler does not favor the notion of maximizing human effectiveness to achieve full potential. She believes that many potentialities are not used in order to actualize a few significant ones.

Phenomenological Theories

Phenomenological theorists have a common belief about the importance of the perceptions or the perceptual field of the individual. People are active in their interactions with the environment. They have potentialities, such as actualizing tendencies or perceptual tendencies, that help make experiences meaningful and that enable them to develop purpose and to make choices in life. The importance of environmental and social forces for human behavior is not denied. In fact, these theorists tend to look at human behavior in one total interactional field. However, people's inner forces are the major determinant of behavior. Rogers's client-centered theory and Gestalt theories have had a considerable impact on counseling.

Rogers's Client-Centered Theory.   Rogers (1951) perceives humans as possessing an innate growth force that is basically positive, forward moving, constructive, and trustworthy. This force is called the self. People have a basic need for high self-regard. If unhampered, the individual will organize all of his or her inner and outer experiences into an integrated person through a process called self-actualization. Inner characteristics do not block a person from a productive, happy, or creative life. Rather, unhealthy social or psychological influences prevent individuals from realizing their potentials.

Humans have the ability to resolve conflicts but are limited predominantly by lack of knowledge about themselves. Conflicts arise when there is a disparity between an individual's organismic or basic growth needs and the needs of the self to gain approval or positive regard from significant others in the environment, such as parents, other authority figures, and peers. The self may then grow, or actualize itself, to satisfy others' demands rather than satisfying its own true organismic needs. For example, a child experiences natural, pleasant, sexual feelings (organismic need) but denies them integration into the self because of apparent or real disapproval of his or her parents or of other significant persons. Incongruency then occurs between authentic self-actualizing and experiencing. Note that the disapproval may not actually occur but may be perceived. The perception of others' reactions, Rogers believes, is the most important reality for the individual.

Clients are capable of correcting misperceptions or incongruencies between self and experience in the accepting environment of a counseling relationship if the counselor possesses certain personal qualities. In Rogers's client-centered counseling these characteristics are described as congruency or genuineness, unconditional positive regard, and empathy. Rogers considers them necessary and sufficient conditions for counseling or therapy. Congruency relates to the counselor's being an authentic, integrated person. Unconditional positive regard, sometimes called warmth, is the nonevaluative counselor attitude whereby any client thoughts, feelings, or behavior are accepted without judging them as good or bad. Empathy is the counselor's ability to know the client's world as the client does and to convey that understanding.

When these conditions are present, clients can arrive at self-understanding, resolutions to conflicts, and positive values because their natural tendency to grow positively is enhanced. The implication is that the counselor does not need to be familiar with behavior dynamics, problem-solving techniques, or developmental processes.

Rogers rejects the use of diagnosis, testing, and most other techniques, believing that these act as a hindrance to the client's natural growth. His interview methods are indirect ones that include listening, paraphrasing, and reflecting client comments rather than interpreting, direct questioning, or probing.

Research on counseling processes and outcomes has been of great interest to Rogers. He and his students have pioneered evaluation of counseling processes through use of recorded counseling interviews. He has also compared degrees of congruency between the counselee's self-perception before and after counseling.

In recent years Rogers has moved to a more existential view, with considerable interest in encounter. However, his earlier client-centered methods are still used a great deal. They are popular in schools and in community agencies.

Rogers's client-centered theory has been criticized as portraying humans as having little self-determination in spite of the humanistic label. The innate, positive, unfolding, growth capability he hypothesizes can be interpreted as an inner, robot-like force that automatically propels people to positive values if the environment is sound.

Gestalt Theories.   Perls was the major spokesman for Gestalt theories. After his death Kempler became the major spokesman. The emphasis in the Gestalt approach is on the oneness of people's inner reality (thought, perception, emotions) and outer reality (environment). People's experiences are always in a phenomenal field in which the inner and outer forces are integrated into a whole (Gestalt). Humans have potential for functioning in a responsible, genuine way. Conflict, indecision, or anxiety arises when there is an inconsistency between inner perception and outer reality, or between the organismic and environmental fields. The term *contradiction* is used to describe inconsistency between inner and outer reality. Potentially, these contradictions can lead to a continual battle between individuals' drives to function authentically consistent with their experiencing (self-actualizing), or to function as they believe they should or must according to expectations of others (idealized self-actualization).

The goals of counseling are to teach people to use their ability to be fully aware of themselves and the world and to be more mature and responsible for their own lives. The Gestalt counselor is a teacher who helps clients learn to understand themselves, correct misperceptions, and take responsibility. The major emphasis is upon responding to immediate experiences in life and in counseling. To make clients do so, the counselor confronts them with inconsistencies and with the need to take constructive action regarding unresolved problems related to past experiences (unfinished business). This action permits the individual to devote more energy and more awareness to resolving current problems. Manipulation, persuasion, or some form of coercion may also be used to provoke clients into facing themselves. Games, gimmicks, and body massage are other means to get people to become more aware of their emotional and physical feelings. Role playing, role reversal, and role rehearsal may be used. However, in contrast to behaviorists' use of role playing, the emphasis is upon understanding one's feelings and the feelings of others rather than practicing behavior.

Belkin (1975) believes that the wide repertoire of techniques available makes this a potentially useful approach for school counselors. This approach usually appeals to counselors who are naturally outgoing, who enjoy using instructional techniques, and who are comfortable with encouraging clients to sound off. Also, the Gestalt approach appears to work better with clients who have fairly strong egos or ego defenses.

Existential Counseling

Existentialists stress experiencing and experiences in inner, subjective reality and the highly active, purposeful nature of humans. Individuals are unique and have not only the capacity but also the responsibility to make choices. The well-functioning person is authentically experiencing and expressing needs in a manner not determined by others. People have conflicts or anxieties when they do not take actions they should take or when they do not act responsibly and authentically. Problems also arise from an inability to perceive purpose or meaning in life. However, anxiety is not necessarily neurotic; some anxiety is an essential part of life.

The goal of existential counseling is to help clients explore and develop meaning in life. The counselor can help clients to recognize their choice-making potential and to understand and accept the consequences of choice for their lives and for the lives of others. Counseling is essentially an encounter for therapist and client. The emphasis in the relationship is upon understanding and experiencing each other's being in an existential partnership.

The techniques used, as you might expect, are varied because of the insistence upon individuation in existentialism. Like Sartre and May, some theorists have a psychoanalytic orientation and use free association and interpretation. Others see attitudes as more important than techniques. Introspection and expression of inner feelings to get to the raw data of a person's consciousness are hallmarks of these theories. Group experiences are encouraged that enable clients to feel emotionally safe enough to expose their feelings to others. The purpose of these experiences, often called encounters, is to increase self-awareness.

Counselors who can function with little structure and who themselves approach life philosophically and with broad, sweeping concern find this approach compatible. Similarly, clients who are verbal and expressive or who are looking for close relationships may prefer this approach.

One might anticipate considerable client response to an existential approach in public schools. The question of the meaning of life, of the purpose of it all, of who I am, is generic to adolescents' concerns. Van Kaam (1962) and Arbuckle (1975) have been interested in applying existential approaches in the schools.

Attempts at Reconciling Environmentalism and Humanism

Some behaviorists are attempting to broaden the base of their work by including a quantification of some of the inner processes that humanists have specified. Training people in self-control and self-determination and changing self-concepts through reinforcement, modeling, and other behavioral techniques are considered legitimate behavioral activities.

These behaviorists tend to incorporate new techniques gained by the merger of environmentalism and humanism into their counseling and therapy interactions. Thoresen and Mahoney (1974), in their book *Behavioral Self-Control,* and Lazarus (1971), in his text *Behavior Therapy and Beyond,* are examples of this trend.

Some humanists have also tried to reconcile the humanistic and behavioristic approaches by combining what they consider the best features of both. Their attempts center around quantification of inner processes, but rather than increasing or improving counseling or therapy skills, they want to arrive at measurable interpersonal skills that can be taught to anyone, largely through group interaction or instruction. Human-development specialists have moved in this direction, particularly in the public schools, as have advocates of psychological education. Carkhuff (1972a, b), in his human technology, and Ivey and Authier (1978), in their microcounseling-skills approach, represent humanists attempting to incorporate behavioral methods into the guidance and counseling field.

The Influence of Psychoanalysis and Neopsychoanalysis

Although Freud's theory has had little direct effect on counseling, some of his ideas still influence psychological thought and practice. Berne's transactional analysis is directly related to this theory. Erikson's (1968) theory of developmental stages, which has been accepted by many developmental counselors, derived from Freud. In addition, different forms of psychoanalysis developed by some of Freud's colleagues, such as Adler and Rank, have had a direct bearing on counseling practice.

Freud hypothesized that unconscious instincts over which individuals have little control motivate human behavior. Humans are assumed to be potentially destructive by nature. Environmental control through the ego (reason) and the superego (conscience) exerts a socializing influence on the primitive id that prevents humans from destroying themselves and society (Hall, 1954). Some of Freud's colleagues and most neopsychoanalysts rejected destructiveness in people and incorporated humanistic concepts into their psychoanalytic theory, such as self, purpose, and self-actualization. Rogers used some of Rank's beliefs about the nature of humans and about free will in his development of client-centered counseling. Adler's combination of psychoanalysis with humanistic, phenomenological concepts has had a strong impact on family counseling.

I will briefly discuss Adler's theory and transactional analysis, since they are the psychoanalytic theories that most counselors hear about. Both can be used in individual counseling, but they have received most attention in schools and in communities in their application to family and group interactions.

Adler's Individual Psychology

According to Adler (1959), humans are social beings with a basic motivation to belong to a group in which they can function and participate. People obtain meaning from how they perceive their environment. Their degree of normality can be determined by the degree of their social interest. A well-functioning individual would have sufficient social interest to develop abilities to function in society. Lack of social interest causes people to fail, to feel deficient, and to develop problems.

Humans are perceived as responsible, goal-directed beings with some limited choice in life. They set up goals and a lifestyle to attain them. Children have an inferiority complex because they are dependent upon adults for the satisfaction of most of their needs. To compensate for this inferiority, people strive for superiority. Problems occur when people become discouraged and cannot compete in a socially unified way. This discouragement is learned or is based in misperception of social interactions. People then strive for inappropriate goals such as gaining attention or power, getting revenge, or acting inadequate or inept. The counselor functions as a teacher, so the counseling process is an educative one. Counselors diagnose goals of behavior, help clients develop insight, and then provide plans of action. Methods include letting children experience natural and logical consequences of their behavior and providing encouragement.

Transactional Analysis

Transactional analysis, a theory developed by Berne, has its roots in psychoanalysis. Berne (1961) believes that interpersonal behavior consists of social transactions between people. He assumes three ego-type states: the parent, the adult, and the child. These constitute a person's makeup. The parent is the conscience, or a group of do's and don'ts learned as a child; the adult is the commonsense, reality-oriented portion of the personality;

and the child is composed of spontaneous, impulsive feelings and emotions. The goal of counseling is to disengage the adult from an overly inhibiting parent and from an overly troublesome child.

Clients are taught first to analyze the structure of ego states. Then they learn to analyze social transactions, starting with simple ones and moving to more complex ones. The aim is to get an effective balance among the three components of the personality, so that one does not interact consistently as a boss and parent, an immature child, or a stuffy adult. Repetitive or stereotyped interactions are examined. Repetitive sets of social manipulations are called games and pastimes. More complex repetitive lifestyles are called scripts. In counseling, clients learn more about how they are reacting to other people and learn practical suggestions for changing lifestyles.

Characteristics of the Counseling Process

In addition to studying counseling theories, counselors in training need to study how counselor characteristics, counselor techniques, and the nature of the counselor/client interaction relate to the quality and the effectiveness of the counseling relationship. As new counselors examine the attempts of professional counselors to discover and describe characteristics of the counseling process, they can learn better to select counseling techniques consistent with their own counseling orientation.

Robinson (1950) and Rogers (1951) were pioneers in efforts to isolate and understand various components of the counseling relationship that go beyond the expected conditions of confidentiality, privacy, and free choice. Their efforts stemmed from almost opposite views about counseling theory.

Robinson, who followed the thinking of the Minnesota school of counseling, worked largely with factors related to vocational and educational counseling. He examined behaviors of both counselor and client and explored the interactions of the two in the counseling relationship. For example, he investigated the relationship of client behavior and attitudes to counselor leads and to divisions of responsibility that counselor and client arrive at in the counseling sessions. Effective leads are defined as counselor comments that are geared to what the client is ready to accept rather than being behind or ahead of the client's thinking or emotional maturity. Robinson categorized counselor leads on a continuum from low leads (nondirective) to high leads (directive). Examples of low leads are silence, acceptance, and restatement or clarification of the client's remarks. High leads include tentative analysis, interpretation, urging, and introduction of new aspects of a problem. Division of responsibility is defined as the amount of responsibility the counselor and the client accept for decision making in counseling. Robinson believed that the degree of the client's motivation and insight and the nature of the client's behavior dynamics may call for different leads and different divisions of responsibility in counseling sessions.

One further contribution of Robinson was his classification of client problems into the diagnostic categories of adjustment, skill, and maturity problems. Following up on Bordin's (1946) and Pepinsky's (1948) earlier work on diagnostic categories, he hypothesized that differing counseling techniques may be necessary depending on the client's problem as well as the client's motivation or insight. Callis (1965) and Tyler (1969) did later work on refining diagnostic categories.

Rogers (1942, 1951) also explored the counseling relationship, but he and his followers concentrated on counselor characteristics. Very little, if any, attention was given to client motivation, or behavior dynamics. Nor were types of client problems considered an important factor in the counselor's use of techniques. This emphasis developed because Rogers believed that the innate, unfolding, positive, growth force of clients requires only certain appropriate attitudes from the counselor to assure a climate for counseling success. Therefore, counselor characteristics such as warmth, empathy, and genuineness are considered necessary and sufficient conditions for effective counseling. Low leads are considered most effective for counselors to use. Thus, Rogers's techniques emphasize silence, reflection, or restatement or clarification of the client's remarks. Response to feeling has higher priority than response to the content of the client's remarks. Listening attentively is also a paramount technique.

Rogers's students followed up his work with studies trying to quantify and rate counselor characteristics of warmth, empathy, and genuineness (Truax & Carkhuff, 1967). Ivey (1971) quantified some of Rogers's early counseling leads, such as listening, attending, paraphrasing, and reflecting. Carkhuff and Ivey recently developed systems of skills based upon these techniques into human technologies. I will discuss these systems later in the chapter.

Obviously, theorists with orientations different from those discussed in this chapter have developed techniques specific to their counseling theory. Counselors should examine these techniques to determine whether they are consistent with their own views and to explore whether the techniques would need modification before they could become part of their counseling repertoire. L. L. Miller (1970) has compiled a glossary called *Counseling Leads and Related Concepts* that may prove useful in distinguishing various counseling leads and techniques.

Theories and Techniques Used in Counselor Secondary Functions

In Chapter 1 I described counselor functions that I consider secondary to the primary function of individual counseling. These activities include group counseling, family counseling, psychological-education training, and consultation. In this section I will briefly discuss some of the latest trends in theory and techniques related to counselor secondary functions.

The Classification of Group-Counseling Theories

Almost all counselors offer group counseling for clients. As one might surmise, the rationales for group interactions are similar to those for individual counseling.

Gazda, more than anyone else, has tried to pull together the group-counseling and group-psychotherapy theories based upon individual theories. In *Basic Approaches to Group Psychotherapy and Group Counseling* (1975), he presents examples of group counseling based upon rational/ emotive, reality, client-centered, Gestalt, behaviorist, developmental, existential, and psychoanalytic ideas. For people who are trying to sort through a myriad of group-counseling theories, the knowledge that many theories for individuals have been expanded to fit groups can cut through some of the confusion. In *Theories and Methods of Group Counseling in the Schools* (1976), Gazda discusses varied approaches appropriate for school counselors.

Some theories that started with a focus on individual counseling have become more popular for groups. As mentioned earlier, transactional analysis and Adler's theory are used much more for groups than for individuals. Some Gestalt and existential theorists also have been encouraging group sessions as a means of providing a safe environment for clients to explore their feelings and attitudes in order to arrive at enhanced self-awareness.

Family Counseling

Family counseling has become an important area of concern in elementary school counseling. Since their inception in the early 1900s, community clinics have been working with child and family. As counselors in schools become more professionally trained, the possibility of some family counseling will increase, particularly for elementary school counselors. Even if secondary school counselors do not have opportunities for carrying out full-blown family counseling, awareness of some of the ideas about this area can be helpful, for the effective counselor can expect some interactions with parents of teenagers. In addition, if school counselors become licensed as professional counselors, they may be able to handle family counseling in the community.

Many practitioners who have clients for individual counseling will also work with families when they feel it necessary. As with groups, they tend to use or modify the same basic theoretical orientation they use in individual and group counseling for working with families. Environmentalists, because of their strong feeling that social influences affect individual behavior, tend to move quickly into family counseling. They perceive intervention as natural. For example, some social-learning theorists have engaged in family-counseling work in which social reinforcement is given to the client (the child or adolescent) for desired behavior rather than focusing attention on negative behavior.

Developmental counselors such as Dinkmeyer (1966) have emphasized the importance of involving families in elementary school counseling using an Adlerian approach. Adlerian groups who emphasize working with families and parent groups have begun to flourish. Also, Dreikurs (1971) has modified and updated Adlerian theory and applied it to families, particularly in school situations. Humanists generally have not been as prone to intervene in family relationships because of their emphasis upon individual responsibility and choice. Some humanistically oriented counselors prefer to have another counselor work with the family while they work with the individual's development as well as family interaction.

Three forms of family counseling can be used: concurrent, collaborative, and conjoint (Goldenberg, 1973). In concurrent family counseling the counselor works with different family members in separate sessions. In collaborative family counseling one counselor works with the entire nuclear family in an effort to increase communication. Satir is the best-known conjoint family counselor. She is an active interventionist who diagnoses the family situation, sets up purposes based upon input from the family, and then in a direct manner teaches open communication to the family.

Theories and Techniques in Psychological Education

Some theorists with an interest in human development have tried to combine features of environmentalism, humanism, and development theories into systems of relationship and communication skills that can be quantified, measured, and taught to anyone. Using the term *human technology,* some theorists have proposed that entire communities or school populations can profit from training in these skills. In addition, skills-training workshops and affective curriculums have been developed. Human-development specialists have moved in this direction in schools and colleges and, more recently, in communities. These informal and formal training experiences have been called psychological education. Used wisely, these skills can broaden the counselor's repertoire of skills. They can also be used in counselor secondary functions to help improve an environment. In addition, they can contribute to increased proficiency of counselor aides. Used unwisely, these skills can contribute to wariness on the part of the public toward counselors and to some emotional harm to the public. I will discuss appropriate use of these skills in Chapter 9. In this chapter brief discussions of the better-known systems will be presented. We will start with examples of systematic skills and then look at a sample of psychological-education activities that have been recommended as curriculum experiences.

Human Technologies.   As described previously, Truax and Carkhuff (1967) made an early effort to quantify and measure components of the counseling relationship with the primary intention of improving counseling and therapy skills. They started with the assumption that counselor characteristics almost solely determine the effectiveness of counseling. Both followers of Rogers's client-centered approach, they developed standardized rating scales to measure his necessary and sufficient conditions for counseling (warmth, genuineness, and empathy) in which counselor educators and counselors rated videotapes of counselor interviews. During 1969–1972 Carkhuff outlined a model for helping services in which he expanded on Rogers's thinking. Carkhuff added new scales to the three original ones: respect, self-disclosure, concreteness, confrontation, and immediacy of a relationship. He called these universal helping-relationship skills that could be taught to almost anyone. In this period he changed his emphasis from training counselors to training paraprofessionals.

Carkhuff (1972a, b) published his system of human-resource development (HRD) in *The Counseling Psychologist* and labeled it human technology. Two major steps were outlined in his proposal: facilitating individuals' understanding through self-exploration and then facilitating action by the individuals through confronting them with reality and the necessity for action.

Ivey (1971), using a similar theoretical framework and rationale, took a somewhat different tack. He isolated some of Rogers's interviewing skills, such as listening, attending, paraphrasing, and clarifying, and proceeded to teach them to counselors in training and to paraprofessionals. More recently, Ivey has added skills in social influencing, which are used once clients attain awareness of themselves. The purpose of social influencing is to assure that clients will take action after gaining awareness. These skills include self-expression, directionality, self-exposure, and interpretation. Egan (1975) used a combination of Carkhuff's and Ivey's skills to develop his system of helping skills.

In all of these systems, the helping relationship is seen as a dual process. Simultaneously, while getting help, the client also is receiving training as a helper in these universal relationship and communication skills.

Systematic skills training presents some potentially useful tools for the initial training of psychological counselors in interviewing. Also, if professional and ethical considerations are met, they can be useful for training paraprofessionals in some circumscribed interviewing skills consistent with their psychological background. Finally, they can help improve the communication and relationship skills of professional people who are not professionally trained as psychological counselors, such as teachers, administrators, and student personnel administrators.

Paraprofessional aides can be taught such initial interviewing skills as listening and looking directly at the clients. They can also be trained to phrase questions so as to elicit responses from the client that will help them determine whether information is needed or whether a referral to a professional counselor is required. Teachers and administrators can gain skills to improve communication and relationships and to determine when they can handle people's requests for help and when they should refer them for counseling. None of these groups should be trained in eliciting high degrees of self-disclosure, in setting up confrontations, or in interpreting behaviors. These activities require a theoretical knowledge of behavior dynamics and of conflict and long-term internships that these persons do not have. Moreover, the idea that the person being helped is at the same time becoming a helper encourages many untrained persons to offer counseling services to others on the basis that counseling is a very simple process requiring little training.

Training in Specific Human-Relationship Skills.   Some sets of training skills arise from a specific technique that is part of a larger counseling orientation. For example, the assertiveness training used by Wolpe is quite commonly offered in workshop form in schools and in communities. Confrontation, body awareness, and consciousness raising, which are basically Gestalt and existential techniques, are other examples of specific techniques offered in workshops.

As with other skills, persons with professional training in counseling or therapy should be responsible for these workshops. The use of these techniques still needs to be considered in the broader concept of the total theory if psychological protection of individuals is to be maintained. Persons with training can also screen workshop members and offer counseling to those who need it. The best use of these workshops is to upgrade professionals in practice.

Specific Skills for Parents, Families, and Teachers.   Some training skills have been designed specifically to help parents, families, and teachers learn how to manage children. These skills are used in school counseling and by community agencies but infrequently in colleges.

The best known is Gordon's (1970) Parent Effectiveness Training (PET). Dinkmeyer and Dreikurs also have developed parental-skills programs based on Adlerian theory. In addition, various Adlerian groups offer courses in parental skills in communities. Gordon's PET will be discussed as an example.

Gordon calls his system the no-lose method of resolving conflicts. Parents learn effective management of conflicts by learning how to listen in a nonevaluative way and how to communicate feelings honestly. Techniques on how to change unacceptable behavior by changing the environment are also spelled out. Parents are taught in steps to identify the conflict, generate and evaluate alternative solutions, and decide on the best solution. Then ways are worked out to implement the solution and follow-up is arranged.

Encounter, Sensitivity, and Personal-Growth Groups.   Some groups developed in the 1960s were not designed for counseling or for therapy. Instead, the emphasis is upon offering essentially psychological-training or educational-training groups designed to develop either self-awareness or improved social systems. The first type are called encounter or personal-growth groups. The second are called sensitivity-training (T-groups) or organizational-development groups.

Lakin (1972) has compared these two types of groups. The first he calls training for expanded experiencing. The second he terms training for interactional awareness. The goal of expanded-experiencing training is to increase authenticity, openness, or flexibility in individuals. The group helps the individual attain self-awareness in a safe, nonjudgmental atmosphere. The goal of interactional-awareness training is the development of an efficient social system by using a democratic process to increase communication, to cultivate leadership qualities, and to improve decision making. These groups require professional leadership, in my opinion, because the training experience may trigger a need for professional counseling.

Personal-growth groups have been popular in colleges and in communities but have not been used to any degree in public schools. Organizational-development or sensitivity-training groups have become acceptable in the schools because the experiences are designed for social systems such as educational institutions. They also have been used by businesses, churches, and other organizations in the community.

If personal-growth groups are offered, a professionally trained counselor should be involved for the reason just given. If an organization in which the counselor is a staff member desires sensitivity training, an outside leader should be used. Since the counselor is professionally involved in the system, he or she would not have the objectivity necessary to conduct the social interactions in the group successfully.

Psychological-Education Curriculums.   Instructional materials for increasing the affective content of school and college curriculums have recently flourished in the counseling and guidance literature. Commercial kits, canned teaching units, recordings, and videotapes are available to counselors and teachers. The activities for which these materials are designed are usually called humanistic education to differentiate them from intellectual, or traditional, subject matter. Actually, most of these activities are based on one developmental model or another and make use of humanistic and/or behavioristic techniques. The common term in the current counseling and guidance literature is *psychological education.*

Simpson and Gray (1976) have done a notable job of pulling together a 200-page annotated bibliography of these materials. Stanford and Roark (1974) have described classroom activities, games, commercial kits, and instructional techniques that they believe will increase meaningful interaction in the classroom. Shaver and Strong (1976) have done an effective job in evaluating educational programs related to value decisions.

Professional counselors need to be aware of these curriculums because they are presently being added to teacher training throughout North America. Counselors may be asked by teachers to visit classes and initiate some of these programs; they may serve as consultants for teachers who want to broaden their curriculum; or they may work with teachers as co-leaders. Concurrent with these functions, counselors can also serve as a backup referral source in case any of these activities indicates that a student may need or want counseling.

Alschuler (1973) divided these activities into congruent, confluent, and contextual curriculums. Congruent curriculums focus on a well-defined, specific aspect of psychological growth (self-esteem or achievement motivation, for example). Confluence courses are those in which traditional subject matter is made more relevant by introducing personal factors. Contextual curriculums are intended to improve personal growth by changing the environment of the class.

Some of the more popular programs include valuing processes (values clarification); processes in moral development (Kohlberg's moral development); activities to improve personal growth and social interactions (Bessell and Palmores's structured Human Development Program for elementary grades, and Dinkmeyer's kits, called Duso kits, of puppets and games to develop understanding of self and others for grades 4-6); games to change a behavior (achievement motivation); and various strategies to change the classroom environment (sensitivity modules) (Simpson & Gray, 1976).

Much enthusiasm has been generated about these programs in educational and guidance circles. They are perceived as satisfying a need to make education more meaningful and more relevant. Unfortunately, insufficient attention has been given by many of the designers of these programs to the ethical and professional issues that always accompany psychological work with individuals or groups. Guidelines on privacy of students, protection from psychological harm, and backup professional-counseling service are not usually given to teachers. Shaver and Strong (1976), for example, are concerned that the designers of values clarification did not pay sufficient attention to the type of values that teachers should feel free to probe, for they may unwittingly invade the personal

privacy of students. It is important to remember that similar guidance activities came under severe attack in the 1930s and 1940s because not
enough attention was paid to guidelines on appropriate use.

Counselors need to become familiar with these curriculum activities to
help teachers determine appropriateness for use in the classroom. Counselors must also develop their own guidelines on how they can become
professionally involved in an ethical manner. In Chapter 9 some guidelines on evaluating these activities will be presented.

Implementing a Personal Theory of Counseling

It is crucial for counselors to remember that counseling involves voluntary, confidential interactions in which the right to privacy is assured.
These conditions apply to both the primary and the secondary functions
of counselors. Thus, techniques involving control of behavior, management of the environment, and teaching of specific skills or intervention
strategies are appropriate only when the client agrees to these approaches
with a full awareness of methods and expected results.

Most professionally trained counselors, after beginning practice, find it
necessary to develop an eclecticism in their own theory and techniques.
This eclecticism occurs because a counselor may have to vary style and
techniques depending upon the client's problem, the personality characteristics of the client, and the setting in which the counselor works. Since
no one theory has yet proved sufficient, it is likely that counselors who
stick religiously to one approach may limit the kind of client problems
they will see.

My own theory is an eclectic one, but basically I consider myself a
phenomenological psychologist. I believe that humans have inner organizing structures (brain, nervous system, sensory organs) through which
they develop the capacity to determine purposes and to make choices in
life with considerable potential freedom from environmental control.
Further, humans, in constant interaction within their environment, have
the potential for changing their environment. I perceive intellectual and
emotional processes as having equal importance and believe that it is the
interaction of these processes that contributes to personality development
and lifestyle. Because of this interaction of intellect and emotion, the perception of reality is often a greater determinant of behavior than is reality
itself.

On the other hand, the client-centered notion that some natural tendency automatically unfolds into positive attitudes or behavior under favorable environmental conditions is too deterministic for me. Nor can I
accept the notion of some Gestaltists that ineffective interaction of individuals in the environment is almost always the result of the individual's
misperception of the environment or failure to take sufficient responsibil-

ity for his or her behavior. Some environmental barriers do exist. I further reject some of the extreme humanistic views that any intellectual or reasoning process, by its very nature, detracts from emotional experience. Finally, I do not find the antiscientific, antiresearch views of some existentialists productive. Instead, approaches different from traditional scientific designs need to be found.

Since I define counseling as a consideration of normal developmental conflicts, some characteristics of developmental counseling have proved compatible with my views. I find the conceptualization of developmental tasks that must be mastered at different life stages to be a reasonable and useful framework for counseling with people of all ages. Also, the importance given by developmental counselors to educational and career conflicts and choices is refreshing. And their use of vocational and personality inventories as measures for contributing to clients' self-understanding is consistent with a humanistic psychological view. However, some views of developmental counselors have led to practices inconsistent with my values. As I indicated earlier, some developmental counselors perceive society as being so restrictive that intervention in the lives of total populations is necessary to assure that everyone reaches maximum human effectiveness as defined by the counselor. Also, research into social systems and into models of human effectiveness has led to systems of human technology that are antithetical to a humanist's views about behavior.

Most behavioral counseling based upon operant conditioning has not been consistent with my counseling beliefs. The emphasis upon conditioning individuals to adapt to society or upon the counselor's manipulating the environment has seemed unsuitable and too narrow in scope for counseling. Instead, these approaches appear more useful for behavior requiring social management, such as juvenile delinquency, severe mental retardation, or schizophrenic reactions. The more recent trends in behavioral approaches that take into account cognitive, reasoning, and perceptual factors are closer to my views about the importance of clients' problem-solving characteristics. Nevertheless, I still give more credence to human inner processes in counseling than do behaviorists.

Projects and Activities

1. *Compare Rogers's later writings with his original client-centered theory, published in 1942. What are the similarities and differences?*
2. *Are human-technology systematic skills developed by Rogers's students (Truax and Carkhuff) or based on Rogers's helping relationship philosophically consistent with his early or present theoretical position? Give your rationale for your view.*
3. *Make a list of essential counselor characteristics described in the literature by various counselor experts. Do any characteristics appear to be universal?*

Carefully evaluate research on these characteristics. Does the research pertain to counseling as described by the professional associations?

4. What is your philosophical or theoretical leaning about the use of diagnosis in counseling? What are your views on the use of tests in the counseling process?

5. Interview counselors in a college, in a school, or in the community about how they arrived at their current views about counseling theories.

6. Read Rogers and Williamson's debates about the merits of a nondirective versus a directive approach in counseling. Compare these debates with those of Rogers and Skinner on phenomenology and behaviorism.

7. Interview a number of counselors who specialize in marriage and family counseling. Compare their theoretical backgrounds and the techniques each prefers to use in practice.

8. Some behavioral counselors, such as Thoresen and Mahoney, have tried to place some of the humanistic inner processes in a behavioristic framework. For example, they use terms such as self-control and self-discipline. Read their work and evaluate whether their views of human nature and reality are consistent with their techniques for self-monitoring.

9. Both social-learning theorists and phenomenologists agree that perception is an important dimension of behavior. How do they differ in their definitions of the process of perception and the way in which it relates to behavior or attitudes?

10. Compare an environmentalist with a humanist in terms of their definitions of counseling and their beliefs about the origin of values. How do these definitions and beliefs relate to their views about the impact of counselor values in the counseling process?

11. List techniques used by two different kinds of theorists—for example, Gestaltists and behaviorists. Determine differences in type and use of the techniques, and indicate how these differences tie in with philosophical views on human nature and reality.

12. Consider a counseling or therapy theory not discussed in this book, such as biofeedback, strategic therapy, or cognitive therapy. Try to evaluate this theory on the basis of the theorist's view of human nature and the relationship of this view to values, goals, and methods important to the theory. Does it fit an insight/action classification or a rational/affective one?

5

Individual Counseling in Secondary Schools

In this chapter I will briefly discuss the rationale for supporting individual counseling as a major function of secondary school counselors. Then, after a look at the need for such counseling, I will present a sample of secondary school students' counseling concerns that I have experienced in my own practice and in my supervision of counseling interns. Junior high schools, which usually include the seventh, eighth, and ninth grades and assign students different teachers for each subject, will not be discussed separately. The organization of junior high schools is similar to that of secondary high schools, and surveys have shown that their students' concerns are remarkably alike (Mezzano, 1971; Shertzer & Stone, 1980).

The Development of Counseling in Secondary Schools

There is a certain irony in the history of secondary school counseling. The first secondary school counselors were forerunners of the present-day counselors as defined by professional-counseling associations; these people functioned as the first professional group of counselors, serving primarily as vocational counselors from 1910 through the 1940s. The first professional standards for training were outlined for secondary school counseling. And these counselors constitute the largest group of professional counselors. Yet in spite of their deep-rooted, positive heritage in education and psychology, they have had a difficult time implementing counseling programs as described by their professional associations. As Aubrey (1972) and Warnath (1973b) have observed, too many secondary school counselors have become institutional agents of the administration.

Factors Affecting the Development of the Counselor's Role

F. W. Miller, Fruehling, and Lewis (1978) point out numerous internal and external factors that influence the counselor's role or that distort the counselor's role in a school system. Important internal factors include the expectations of administrators, teachers, parents, students, and counselors about appropriate counselor roles; salary concerns; and counselor/student ratios. External factors are professional organizations; accrediting agencies; counselor educators; and federal aid to counseling.

The Expectations of Administrators, Teachers, Students, and Parents.   In surveys school administrators have tended to refute counselor educators' views that counselors should be relieved of clerical or administrative duties. Administrators have viewed counselor/client confidentiality as inappropriate secrecy (Hart & Prince, 1970). They have also expected counselors to support and reinforce Establishment policies, help students follow school rules, and discourage students from questioning the prevailing system (Filbeck, 1965). Administrators have, however, tended to support vocational and educational advisement.

An attitude of some administrators that has not received sufficient attention in the literature is that counselors are not competent or are not appropriately trained. In a 1962 national-magazine article questioning the value of counseling, Brossard quoted a principal as saying that counselors are second-rate in training and in personality and that they are unable to establish closeness with students. Later, in 1970, Hart and Prince found that some administrators expressed doubt that counselors are competent to help students with personal problems.

Surveys of teacher expectations generally indicate that teachers have had mixed reactions to counselors and appropriate counselor duties. Since counselors often function as administrative aides, they are perceived by teachers as an essential arm of the administration and thus not an essential part of the teaching program (F. C. Lewis, 1972; Shertzer & Stone, 1976). There are some studies, however, that have shown teacher support for counselors' involvement in counseling (Kandor, Pulvino, & Stevic, 1971; Maser, 1971).

Students often perceive counselors as academic advisors, not as professional people who are there to help them with personal problems (Van Riper, 1971). When counselors handle class scheduling, attendance, and other administrative duties, students consider them quasi-administrators. This view probably cuts down on the numbers of students approaching counselors for help. Another general belief of students is that counselors serve college-bound students more than they do students who are not interested in or not inclined toward college.

A review of early surveys about parent attitudes toward the counselor's role shows that parents tended to perceive counselors predominantly as vocational and academic advisors (Dunlop, 1965). Later studies indicate that parents, more often than teachers or students, conceptualize the counselor's role as including personal counseling (Jacobs, Krogger, Lesar, & Redding, 1971; Worthington, 1972).

These discrepancies between professional role expectations and the expectations of others attest that secondary school counselors have not yet been able to convince these people of the importance of professional counseling with students. In some cases they have not been able to convince others that they are professionally equipped to handle counseling. As Van Riper (1971) indicates in discussing student perceptions of counselors, the counselor is what he or she does. Trotzer and Kassera (1971) believe that counselors have had difficulty in role definition because they do not have opportunities to perform appropriate counselor functions. Buckner (1975) asserts that counselors themselves do not understand their roles.

Economic Factors.   Secondary school counselors for many years have been tied to teacher certification and therefore have been dependent upon education associations rather than counselor professional associations for tenure security, salary raises, and other collective-bargaining issues. This relationship has helped shape the counselor's role in the direction considered desirable by administrators.

Alternative Counselor Roles

As indicated in Chapter 2, some counselors have reacted to the inappropriate assignment of counselors by recommending alternative primary roles to supplant that of direct counseling. Carroll (1973), Ivey and Alschuler (1973a), and Pine (1974) have all expressed legitimate concern about the failure of secondary school counseling programs. They recommend that counselors change their primary role from that of individual counseling to that of psychological educator. However, their contention that secondary school counseling has failed because it has been too involved in an outdated therapeutic model, too involved in the image of the private clinician, or too focused on a few problem students is not consistent with actual practice. On the contrary, overwhelming evidence exists in the literature that professional counseling has rarely been done in secondary schools (Arbuckle, 1976; Shertzer & Stone, 1976). Nor does their contention that counselors' role problems will be solved by changing their role to psychological education and consultation and by giving counseling over to teachers and student peers jibe with history. Arbuckle, in his debate with Ivey in the *Personnel and Guidance Journal* (1976) about the counselor as a psychological educator, indicates that the idea of teachers doing counseling is not revolutionary. He advocated that position in the 1940s and abandoned it as unworkable. Arbuckle's view coincides with my comments in Chapter 2 about the return of progressivism in counseling that had failed in the 1940s.

In one of the few arguments in the literature challenging psychological education as a primary function of counselors, Arbuckle questions the rationale for psychological educators. He perceives consultation in counseling as meaning that consultants become experts in counseling before they can consult with others or train others in this capacity. He also believes that this movement to permeate the curriculum with affective education is a move toward increasing social conformity to the educational system. Noting that counseling in schools has been atypical rather than typical, Arbuckle asks, "If counselors are going to give counseling away, just what is it they are giving away" (p. 430)?

The Need to Strengthen School Counselors Professionally

Shertzer and Stone (1976, 1980) believe that the reasons counselors function inappropriately as administrative aides or clerks are insufficient preparation to handle the role as defined by the professional associations and lack of professional strength to determine their role. They conclude:

> Homogeneity in regard to role and function will come when professional training becomes substantial, unified, and sequential. This kind of training would do much to generate a professional identity. It will come when school counseling becomes a career rather than a stepping-stone to administration or an escape from the classroom [Shertzer & Stone, 1976, p. 149].

Similarly, the position presented in the earlier chapters was that professional identity and professional unity are needed for all counselors if professional role definitions are to be fairly evaluated. Certainly, the role definitions of the APGA, the ASCA, and the ACES have not had sufficient opportunity to be tested in the schools. More important, the rationale for continuing to press for application of professional standards for secondary school counselors ultimately must go back to the student need for this type of service. This need, as the literature shows, does exist and is, in fact, growing in intensity. These standards do incorporate important contributions of Ivey and others to psychological-education activities and consultation.

Students' Need for Counseling

In the arguments for and against the secondary school counselor's role, insufficient attention has been given to expressed or implied needs for counseling. Yet the literature shows that experts on adolescence agree on troublesome areas for adolescents, that the results of polls about the concerns of secondary school students are consistent with the views of the experts, and that these concerns are those described in counselor role definitions as personal, social, vocational, and educational ones.

Hurlock (1973) portrays the adolescent as working through a transition period between childhood and adulthood and as experiencing physical and social changes while searching for emotional, social, and economic independence. Havighurst (1953) and Erikson (1968), in their classic works on developmental stages, include personal, social, sexual, and vocational direction as key factors in early and late adolescence. In a review of the literature, Shertzer and Stone (1976) indicate that most authorities on adolescence would agree with three generalizations about adolescence: problems in transition, concern about sexual identity, and struggles for economic, social, and emotional growth.

The results of surveys on adolescent concerns have followed a fairly consistent pattern throughout the past 30 years except that more recent surveys show more questions about sex and drugs (Shertzer & Stone, 1976). These results parallel the areas considered important in the APGA and ASCA counselor role definitions (see Appendix A). Mezzano (1971), for example, found that educational and vocational future most often rated first among the concerns of secondary school students in all grades. Other important areas were school problems, male/female relationships, home relationships, and problems centered on the self. In a 1975 survey by Redfering and Anderson, students rated "my future" as the first concern, followed by male/female relationships, personal appearance, money and job, health, social adjustment, and home and family relationships. In this study Redfering and Anderson compared counselor, counselor educator, and student perceptions of important student problems. Counselors and counselor educators rated self-concept and social adjustment as very important, whereas students zeroed in on more pragmatic concerns.

Alcohol and drug usage, concerns about pregnancy, birth-control measures, and family and personal crises related to the divorce or death of someone close are examples of other concerns of adolescents.

Sources of Referral

Counselors and counseling staffs will want to encourage students who believe they need counseling to ask for it on their own. However, teachers, administrators, and parents can be an important source of referral for counseling if they understand the nature of counseling and trust the competency and professional stature of the counseling staff. Counselors can visit classrooms, publicize their service, and otherwise make themselves visible to faculty and students. Suggestions on how and when to refer students can be given to teachers and administrators with an emphasis upon the freedom of students to choose whether they want counseling.

Counseling Problems of Secondary School Students

At this point I will describe how I would handle some specific concerns regarding vocational, personal, or social development that students will bring to secondary school counselors if they trust the counselors professionally and personally. In the following three chapters I will describe more briefly my counseling approach with similar problems of individuals in elementary school and in colleges and communities. The focus is on secondary school problems because counseling approaches for these can be generalized to problems in the other settings. Secondary school counselors have much in common with other school counselors because they all work in public or private schools, yet they resemble counselors in colleges and in the community in that they are working with students who are legally adults or soon will be. Also, at present there are more counselors in secondary schools than in all the other settings combined.

For a number of reasons, I decided to discuss short case studies rather than using transcripts or demonstrations of various counselor responses to a client comment. Brief transcripts show only a very small portion of a counselor/client interaction. Long but few transcripts emphasize dealing with only a very small sample of the problems that students present. Demonstrations of counselor responses focus on counselor interviewing techniques in a brief section of a counseling session. None of these approaches helps prospective counselors to see the dynamics of student concerns and to understand the reasoning behind counselors' proceeding in the manner they do as well as short case studies. Obviously, the short case study has limitations too. Only brief dynamics can be presented, which may give the appearance of superficiality. Nevertheless, the advantage of this approach outweighs this possible risk.

My approach in this chapter and in the following chapters is based upon my personal philosophy of counseling and upon the nature of the client's concerns, the client's personality, and my own personality characteristics. Readers should keep in mind that these discussions demonstrate how I would deal with these concerns and are not suggested as definitive or universal methods.

In evaluating the counselor's role, readers should ask themselves who would respond to these student concerns if counselors were tied up with administrative and clerical tasks. Readers should also note that teachers' training does not prepare them for this type of counseling. Nor would peers with simple interviewing and listening skills be competent to handle these concerns.

Vocational/Educational Problems: Exploration and Conflicts

General Comments.   Students in secondary school put top priority on vocational exploration and choice because they are getting close to the time when they must be financially independent. After high school approximately two-thirds will enter the labor market, so that interest in and concern about how they will make a living are realistic. The other one-third, who will be going to college or undergoing further training of some sort, must begin to consider the institutions to which they will be applying and the kind of training they wish to begin.

These decisions on immediate occupational exploration or advanced training or education beyond high school are more complicated than they were a few decades ago. In our society male students have been expected to be preoccupied with their life work because they have been perceived as the primary breadwinners. Until recently, relatively few women pursued careers. Women's liberation has helped to change this pattern. Many women are preparing themselves for suitable jobs whether they plan to marry or not. More complex choices about occupational roles of men and women and about their role in a family must be made. In addition, more occupational avenues are open to minority groups. These increased options can lead to more productive and satisfying lives. They can also lead to conflicts as new patterns replace old stereotypes. The opportunity for individuals to break out of safe but stifling cultural patterns often means more responsibility to make decisions and to take risks. The opportunity may involve upheaval in personal relationships if individuals select options that displease people close to them. Life can become more exciting but also more filled with anxiety. The complex and overcrowded labor market and the spiraling costs of college degrees pose further problems for high school students. Thus, counseling for vocational concerns is not a simple process of giving vocational tests and information and picking out the right occupation. It cannot be separated from other personal or interpersonal problems. Choice of occupation is part of total personality development and part of total lifestyle.

Questions about vocational or educational plans are presented by students in three general ways. They may ask for vocational exploration or vocational information. They may present a conflict between themselves and others over vocational choice or planning. They may see a counselor to resolve some self-conflict, confusion, or mixed motivation that they are experiencing regarding two or more occupational plans.

Counseling people with vocational concerns and questions has historically been associated with the use of vocational inventories and occupational information. The measures most often used are vocational-interest inventories, aptitude tests, and paper-and-pencil intelligence and personality measures. The most common inventories and tests used in high schools are the Kuder Preference Record (KPR), the Differential Aptitude Test (DAT), and the General Aptitude Test Battery (GATB). The Strong-Campbell Interest Inventory is sometimes given in the higher grades. A variety of group intelligence and personality inventories are used. The personality inventories are usually related to normal traits that might affect choice of occupation, such as sociability, flexibility, and degree of introversion or extroversion. Most recently, computerized testing programs have gained some popularity in high schools. They usually include an interest measure and a general-aptitude test.

I believe that vocational testing is not essential to successful vocational counseling in every instance. I extend a choice to clients on whether they believe vocational tests will be helpful but will express my opinion on whether testing will either enhance or inhibit the counseling process. If inventories or tests are decided upon, the client and I agree upon the type of inventories or tests. I then select specific ones. When I use tests, I do not consider them as predictors of success in a chosen occupation. No battery of tests has demonstrated sufficient validity to warrant that expectation. However, they can give information to me and to the client that can help in the client's decisions or planning.

Recently the federal government raised serious objections to vocational-interest measures and aptitude tests that have been developed or standardized so as to reinforce male and female educational or occupational stereotypes. The government, through the Education Amendments of 1972, refuses to grant monies to any school or agency that uses sex-biased tests. In addition, objections have been raised that tests developed to evaluate students' intelligence or achievement in schools show artificially low scores for lower socioeconomic groups, bilingual persons, and various ethnic groups because they have been standardized on middle-class White persons. Some states have banned the use of tests for evaluating minorities for this reason. Test makers have been trying to develop tests free of cultural biases. Counselors should be alert to the possibilities of bias.

Other background information from students' cumulative records concerning additional test data, performance in school, and extracurricular activities may also be helpful. However, I ascertain whether the data are pertinent to the counseling question before I decide to use any of the information. I also ask students whether they would like this step taken and share with them any information used.

Use of occupational data usually comes later in the counseling process. These data can be gained from occupational files, from interviews with workers in business and industry, and from computerized occupational-data systems. A specialist in career guidance would be helpful in more specific exploration about jobs and would be more directly involved if the client is considering job or apprenticeship placement or detailed information about colleges.

Exploration. In the following examples the major question of each student relates to career planning. Usually the students are asking for more information about themselves or about occupations in order to evaluate alternative possibilities. Personal conflict or conflict with others over the choice are not presented as part of the request for counseling (the presenting problem).

- *Client 1.* Arthur, a sophomore, pops his head in at your door and asks for an appointment. He is presently trying to work out his junior-year program. His grades are all good, and he likes all subjects. He says he wants to go to college but is not sure what career to consider. He would like to explore interests and aptitudes to get some ideas about vocational direction.

- *Client 2.* Andrea is a junior who tells you that her girlfriend suggested she stop in to see you. She has grades of "B" or better in all her subjects, but she particularly enjoys and does well in physics and mathematics. She is definitely going to college and has selected engineering as a major. Her parents are pleased with her choice. She says, "I'm just checking up—just touching all the bases to be sure I'm heading in the right direction."

- *Client 3.* Bill is perplexed. He is a freshman who is trying to decide whether to take a college preparatory curriculum or look for apprenticeships and attend a technical school. He enjoys drafting and machine shop. He had discussed the question with his industrial-arts teacher, who had given him some occupational information and recommended that Bill talk with you.

- *Client 4.* Ava, a senior, comes in for her first appointment looking and sounding dejected. She has been moping around the house, and her parents suggested that she talk with you. Ava wants very much to work with animals. She has for a long time thought about becoming a veterinarian. But she struggles with biology courses and with other science and math courses. She is much stronger in English and social studies. She tearfully asks, "Do I have to give up the idea of being a vet? If I do, what in the world would I change to?"

Attempts would be made in the interviews to help the students pull together what they already know about themselves that might contribute to their ultimate decision about alternative possibilities. Included would be their perceptions about themselves and the world of work, their values about work, and the lifestyle they imagine for themselves. Parents' perceptions about the student's vocational planning would be explored. The degree to which the parents support the student attitudinally and financially might be of importance.

After this, the advisability of gathering more information through use of tests and/or data in the cumulative record can be brought up. I would not introduce tests immediately or too quickly in order to minimize closing off important communication with the students about their feelings, attitudes, or values. Also, there is then less risk that the students will depend upon tests to give all the answers. Most important to me is that the initial counseling hours set up a relationship tone that will give most opportunity for the students' self-exploration and decision making.

Arthur appears most likely to be highly responsive to the idea of tests and, in fact, may ask for them. His question relates to a general vocational exploration, so that an interest inventory, a general-aptitude battery, and a measure of intellectual ability might be considered to supplement the exploratory interview. For Andrea, more specific testing might be used to compare her interests with those of engineers and to check on aptitudes that relate to engineering, such as spatial visualization, mechanical comprehension, and computational skills. Arthur might be directed to general, descriptive, occupational material. Andrea could explore specific occupational information on engineering specializations. If her interests seem to lean toward physical-science areas, she could expand her occupational exploration to physics, geology, and related areas.

I would probably not bring up tests and occupational material as quickly with Bill and Ava. I would prefer first to try to get Bill to express some of his ambivalences about life planning and lifestyle. Ava, I believe, needs an opportunity to air her feelings of uncertainty, frustration, or hopelessness about her poor performance in biology and other courses related to veterinary work. After these concerns have been dealt with, the decisions about tests and use of occupational information would follow as with Arthur and Andrea.

A counselor must be alert to the possibility that the student's request for counseling is covering over more complicated problems than the presenting problem reveals. These requests for vocational exploration, for example, might turn out to be secondary to personal conflicts or doubts or conflicts with others about the vocational choice or behavior and attitudes in general. Since vocational planning is part of total personality development and the choice of a career is one of the most important decisions people make in life, complications are liable to occur. However, counselors should not assume that all requests for vocational exploration are cover-ups for more significant problems in the individual's personal and social life and begin to probe for them. A request for vocational exploration can be, and often is, legitimate in itself. To minimize its importance or to assume that it must be converted to seemingly more important problems can rob students of a fruitful and necessary vocational exploration.

If conflict is expressed by students in the first interview that was not brought out in the request for counseling, I would spend time helping them clarify their own motivations, values, and interpersonal relationships before further explorations of occupations occurred.

Conflict with Others. In these situations the students' presenting concerns relate to conflicts with others that are inhibiting vocational exploration or choice.

- *Client 5.* Bob, a sophomore, makes an appointment with you at the suggestion of Bill (Client 3). Bill felt that you had helped him in concerns about his parents. Bob calls himself a drama freak. He is not only interested in acting but has demonstrated talent in play performances. He is thinking of directing and writing as well as acting. He is highly verbal, expressive, and articulate. His father is a highly successful pipeline contractor who wants Bob, his only child, to come into the business. He scoffs at drama as unrealistic and as an effeminate occupation. Bob's mother is quiet and unassuming but subtly supports Bob. His father refuses to support Bob in college if he persists in drama. Bob feels he is letting his father down. At the same time he wonders whether drama is a realistic choice economically.

- *Client 6.* Ben has been an average student. He is a senior and is bored with school. He has an opportunity to go to work immediately in a fairly well-paying nonskilled job, so he wants to drop out. His girlfriend is upset. She thinks he must get at least a high school diploma or get some skill training. The conflict has threatened to break up the relationship. His parents side with his girlfriend. They suggested that he see you so that you can talk some sense into him—that is, convince him to stay in school. He is willing to talk with you.

- *Client 7.* Catherine, a senior, is referred by her social-studies teacher. Catherine shared with her some of her concerns about her career. She is an excellent student who has a scholarship to an out-of-state college. She is thinking of law. Her boyfriend is registering at the local community college. He is distressed because she has decided to leave the state. He says she apparently does not care enough for him to change her plans. Catherine feels somewhat guilty and wonders whether her educational plans are selfish.

Such presenting questions are vocational ones complicated by interactions with or expectations of significant people in the students' lives. The students see you because they feel uncertain about how to cope with the differences between their expectations and the expectations of others. Often an impasse has been reached in the interpersonal relationships. Such an impasse may cause students to wonder about their vocational choice and about their capability to make decisions. In these instances vocational exploration is appropriate because each student is relating the conflict to value differences in occupational choice. Also, they are expressing some doubts about their vocational choice themselves. This exploration should be integrated with the personal concerns that the students are expressing about others. Thus, I probably would not begin considering vocational testing or appraisal until I explored the dependence/independence conflicts and ambivalences in the parent/adolescent relationships or in the relations with friends. Time would be spent in helping the students clarify their values and attitudes and those of parents and friends. In addition, their prevailing responses to parental or outside pressures would be discussed.

I assume that students ultimately have the responsibility to make choices and that a number of possibilities may occur. Through increased knowledge about self and occupations and relationships with others, Bob, Ben, and Catherine might become convinced that their occupational planning is right and might be successful in changing the minds of the dissenting persons. Through counseling, one or all three may reaffirm their choices so convincingly that others will withdraw objections.

It is also possible that modifications of the students' vocational expectancies arising out of counseling may contribute to modifications of the other persons' expectancies, so that a suitable compromise can be reached. Bob might continue with drama and work in the summers for his father to gain practical experience. Ben might look for a job that will develop skills leading toward an occupational goal. Also, if he decided not to return to school, he could gain the equivalent of a high school diploma by taking the Test of General Educational Development. Catherine's opportunities for compromise are fewer. The compromise might consist of an agreement that she and her boyfriend will visit on holidays to determine further whether they will continue their relationship. Perhaps her boyfriend could decide to go to a school closer to hers, since he would not lose a scholarship by changing schools.

Any of the clients may become convinced that his or her choice is correct, but the other person or persons may be so adamant that a break in the relationship is possible. For Bob, this could mean a break in the family relationship and withdrawal of economic support. For Catherine, the decision to persist in her action in spite of objections could mean the break-up of a love relationship. For Ben, the loss could be in both family and love relationships.

If an impasse began developing between student and family, I would discuss with the student the possibility of a conference including his or her parents. If the parents were willing, I would work with them and the student toward resolving the conflict in the same general way I had been working with the student alone. If the parents were not willing, I would continue to work with the student on handling his or her own needs and expectations in spite of opposition. In addition, the painful prospect of a break in the relationship must be faced if the impasse continues. If Catherine or Ben had a deep relationship with boyfriend or girlfriend, counseling could be extended to include this person under conditions similar to those used to involve parents. Certainly, if Catherine is considering a sustained relationship, any differences between her and her boyfriend over her professional-career development should be confronted.

One can see from these examples that preparation in family and premarital and marital counseling can be important to school counselors. Obviously, if any of these interactions proved to be more complex than could be handled in school because of time or facilities, the counselor should refer the student to a family-counseling agency, a community clinic, or a counselor in private practice.

Personal Conflict and Doubts. Students often come to counselors about vocational planning when they are experiencing a conflict between or confusion about alternative actions or attitudes. Strong interests and abilities in two or three areas become confusing especially if it appears that one choice excludes the others. In other situations personal values and goals seem at odds.

- *Client 8.* Dorothy, a freshman, is an excellent musician and an excellent math student. She seems quite self-sufficient and has good relationships with her family. She is planning her 4-year program and cannot fit in all the music and math she would like. She wonders whether preparing for a career demands that she give up one for the other. Also, math seems a much more practical career choice to her than music, but music is much more appealing.

- *Client 9.* Dan is referred by a local minister who knows of you. Dan, a senior, is expressing value conflicts related to occupations. He is a warm, outgoing person who enjoys working in social services. He is considering the ministry or YMCA work. However, he believes that he wants to make good money in a job. His lifestyle includes material rewards that he thinks social service will not give him. Yet business does not appeal to him. His mother is in banking, and his father is a social worker. They encourage him to make his own choice.

These questions relate to ambivalences or contradictory motivations or values. I would first explore with the students the alternatives they present, the various values and motivations each choice represents, and the reasons they are having difficulty in deciding which way to go. We would explore how much external pressures are influencing the situation and also consider whether these alternatives are truly mutually exclusive.

At some point Dorothy might profit from vocational-interest exploration and from opportunities to look into occupational information to determine whether music theory might combine both interests or whether a double major is possible. I would not move too quickly on testing for Dan. His direct expression of his conflict in values is an important step for him and one that should be followed up. His perception of his mother and father's values may be contributing to his confusion. I might, as counseling progressed, explore his vocational interests and/or use a personality inventory that includes some expression of his motivations compared to others in different occupational fields.

Personal Problems: Conflicts and Doubts or Confusion

General Comments. In these situations, students present problems about their attitudes and behavior that are causing inner conflicts, tensions, indecision, or confusion. Also, students may ask for help in gaining information or skills in order to change behaviors or attitudes they do not like in themselves.

Concerns about oneself relate to physical appearance, bodily changes, and increased urges and opportunities for independent action and sexual activities. In addition, there are increased opportunities and desires to imitate "adult behavior" by drinking, smoking pot, and trying drugs. The expected increase in independent action can be exciting but also can cause feelings of uncertainty and inadequacy in the adolescent. These ambivalences contribute at times to seemingly contradictory behavior in this age group. Also, engaging in activities that are taboo because of age restrictions or are illegal for anyone can become a daring exploit for adolescents. Participating in these activities is often accompanied by excitement and by fears of getting caught or getting hooked.

The central feature of the presenting problems in this section is that the students are expressing their own ambivalences or uncertainties or guilt about attitudes, feelings, or behavior. The students are asking for help in arriving at some self-imposed guidelines for their feelings, attitudes, or behaviors. They do not present their concerns as a result of interactions or conflicts with other specific persons or groups.

When students seek counseling or are referred for counseling with these types of problems, few devices are available to the counselor who has a strong appraisal orientation. Inventories related to how persons perceive their feelings, attitudes, values, or beliefs or to how they rate themselves on self-acceptance or self-esteem are the most appropriate measures. If one does use personality measures, the emphasis should be on inventories that are based on normal personality traits rather than on pathological behavior. The California Psychological Inventory (CPI), Personal Orientation Inventory (POI), Meyers-Briggs Type Indicator, Tennessee Self-Concept Scale, Junior and Senior High School Personality Questionnaire, and the Mooney Problem Check List are examples of appropriate inventories.

Conflict.   In these situations, students raise questions about their own attitudes and behaviors that are causing inner conflicts, tension, indecision, or immobility.

- *Client 10.* Edith, a senior, is referred by her parents. She is 2 months pregnant and unmarried. She cannot decide whether to keep the child, have an abortion, or give the child up for adoption. Marrying the father is not an alternative she will consider. She has discussed the options with her parents. They are distressed but are supportive of her. They believe that she must make the choice.

- *Client 11.* Earle is a quiet, highly responsible student. He is an active church member. He is having considerable difficulty reconciling his strong sexual desires and his religious beliefs. He feels guilty about masturbation and sexual fantasies. He is quite concerned that the interview be confidential. These feelings, he says, are considered sinful by the church.

- *Client 12.* Emily is graduating in a few months and is planning to go to an out-of-state college. She is the oldest child in a large, closely knit family. She thinks she should move away from the family, who are encouraging her to do so. However, she is apprehensive about being away from home and has experienced homesickness in the past. Also, she wonders how her mother will be able to handle the family without her help. She has complained about headaches during the year.

- *Client 13.* Ed, a junior, is an "A" student. He is bored with life and has decided to drop out of school. Parents and school officials have given permission. Now Ed is not sure that it is a wise move. He had expressed doubts to the vice-principal, who suggested he see you.

- *Client 14.* Ellen is upset with herself. She is an intense person who talks rapidly. She had seen you earlier in the year about scholarships. She has an impressive 3.9 average out of a possible 4.0. She describes herself as academically compulsive. She spends all of her spare time on her schoolwork. She wants to get into other activities but cannot shake her urgency about grades. She is sure that her grade-point average will drop if she engages in extracurricular activities. She has had continual headaches. She has seen her doctor, who calls them tension headaches. She says that her parents are concerned. She denies any pressure from them.

As with personal conflicts over vocational choices, in all these instances the students are confronting decisions and attitudes for which they must take considerable responsibility. The necessity for handling such adult decisions as abortion or sexual drives requires a move toward the independence essential for personal integration and effective social interaction.

Edith is aware of her options. The conflicting feelings and attitudes that are preventing her from making a decision need to be understood. The consequences of each choice need to be thoroughly explored in terms of both her beliefs and feelings and her hopes about a future lifestyle. Ambivalences in her parents' feelings may be affecting her choice, and a conference with them and Edith may be helpful. Once Edith has decided upon an option, I might refer her to a pregnancy-counseling center if a trained staff is available.

Earle's ambivalence about sex drives is a rather common problem for both male and female students with strong conservative beliefs. These instances may increase as public discussions about the naturalness of sexual feelings increase. I would proceed in exploring the guilt feelings about sex as I would do in any such situation. But, I would also ascertain how rigid the church's position is concerning masturbation and sexual fantasies and how strongly committed Earle is to the church. This information can be gained by encouraging Earle to discuss the church's teachings with his minister or by having him read the policies of the church carefully.

If Earle finds that the church is not as rigid as he thought, we could discuss further the naturalness of sexual and other feelings. If his church is strict but other local churches of the same denomination are more liberal, then he might decide to change churches. If Earle finds that his perception of the rigidity of the church is valid and if he maintains a strong commitment to that church, then the question of ethical practice develops. If I were to encourage him to disregard the teachings of his church, I could place him in further moral conflict. I must determine from Earle what it is he hopes to gain from counseling. If he has decided not to consider changing churches, then I can at best help him discover ways of handling his emotions in a manner that will not throttle him or be contrary to his beliefs. Earle might decide to try to change the viewpoint of the church if he considers that he is bound to follow the ruling even though he believes it unfair.

Emily presents a typical developmental task expected of adolescents. She needs to break away from dependence and the security of her home but is experiencing a typical conflict over doing so. After a considerable amount of college counseling, I can attest to the large number of freshmen who experience homesickness regardless of orientation and group sessions carried out in residence halls. If Emily works through some of her conflicting feelings in high school, she might be spared much disruption in her first semester in college.

Emily has had some security in being the oldest child and given considerable responsibility in a closely knit family. These security props will be gone. In addition, there may be mixed feelings upon the part of her mother about Emily's leaving, so that she may be getting contradictory comments from her mother about the advisability of going away to college. If it appears likely that ambivalences in her mother and/or father are contributing to Emily's concern, I might encourage some family counseling.

If Emily has particularly strong fears about independence, it is possible that she can enroll in a college close enough so that she can get home occasionally. With continued counseling at college, she might then transfer farther from home as she gains personal strength. In essence, a form of desensitization to separation would be set up.

I have a word of caution regarding Emily's headaches. A counselor might surmise that her headaches are related to tension. Nevertheless, I would insist upon a medical examination to determine whether the headaches have a physical base. I believe it a professional and ethical responsibility of counselors to determine whether physical symptoms have a medical base before they assume that the symptoms are psychologically based.

Ed is expressing doubts about whether to drop out of school. He will be bombarded with a great deal of advice about the advantages of staying in school. Most parents become apprehensive about the consequences of adolescents' not graduating from high school. Administrators, in addition to believing it unwise, have to consider the potential loss of state revenue if too many students are allowed to drop out of school. Counselors have to be careful that their own values do not influence the student to stay in school. My view is that the motivations and the factors at school or at home that have a bearing on dropping out should be carefully explored with the client. At times, dropping out of school can be more productive than drifting numbly through classes.

Our interviews may indicate that Ed's dissatisfaction is part of a malaise about life in general. If so, I would encourage him to talk about these feelings before deciding whether to drop out. An alternative school might be a possibility. If he is bored with schoolwork and believes that he would profit more from working for a time, his doubts about dropping out of school may arise from fears about whether he can find a job. In that case I would discuss these concerns and help him with methods of exploring the labor market.

Ellen is experiencing a drive that she believes she cannot control. Discussions may reveal a perfectionist attitude about academic work and a fear of making mistakes. Perhaps her compelling drive about grades is a defense against fears of social interactions. If so, she needs an opportunity to gain understanding that her reasons for her overconcern about grades relate to her feelings of uncertainty about herself and about her interactions with others. With a new perspective about her behavior, we can then move toward increasing her personal interests and her degree of social interaction.

Some behaviorally oriented counselors would respond to the complaints about headaches by presenting Emily or Ellen with some form of relaxation techniques in the first stages of counseling. Systematic desensitization (described in Chapter 4) or relaxation exercises or some form of biofeedback are examples of these techniques. My preference is to help the client confront fears and to gain perspective on the validity of these fears rather than moving too quickly to reduce tension through handling the symptom.

Value conflicts may be particularly acute in most of these situations, for counseling involves what society terms moral decisions. Counselors who have strong beliefs one way or the other about abortion, premarital sex, homosexuality, or fundamental religious beliefs may have difficulty permitting students to make their own decisions. As I have indicated, it is a counselor's professional responsibility to examine his or her values to be sure they are not unduly influencing a client's attitudes or actions. If they are, the counselor should refer the client to someone who can be more objective.

Doubts or Confusion.   The presenting problems of these clients focus either on uncertainty about behavior and attitudes or on expressed dissatisfaction with their everyday behavior or attitudes. In either case there is doubt or confusion about how to resolve their uncomfortable feelings.

• *Client 15.* Ernest speaks his mind freely. He says that he is the first one to volunteer answers in class and to offer opinions at meetings. He wonders whether he sounds off too much. He thinks that his enthusiasm sometimes ruffles others. He asks whether he should assert himself less.

- *Client 16.* Esther daydreams about success. But she procrastinates on assignments. Her mind wanders when she is studying. Her scholastic record is good. She may work extremely hard if a project interests her. She is not pleased with her behavior and wants to develop self-discipline.

- *Client 17.* Frank is restless. He wonders what life is all about. "Who am I? What's the purpose of it all?" he asks himself. School and life seem meaningless; courses do not make sense. He sees himself as alienated. He says that he has no religious convictions but is curious about religion.

- *Client 18.* Fran is a junior. Her academic record is good. She has been active in student government. She tells you that she is bored stiff with high school and with typical high school activities, such as football games and pep clubs. She feels a lack of intellectual stimulation from teachers and peers. She is interested in women's liberation and has professional interests that make her feel alienated from other students. She wants to complete her high school education in 3½ years instead of the usual 4 years so that she can begin college sooner. Her assertiveness gives the impression that she is very sure of herself, but she admits to feelings of uncertainty and loneliness.

In these examples the students are not presenting requests for specific changes in behavior. Rather, they are asking for an opportunity to understand their own behavior, motivations, and attitudes. All are expressing some uncertainty or uncomfortableness about their feelings or behavior. My tendency would be to resist setting specific goals in the first interviews. To arrange quickly for an assertiveness-training group for Ernest or a self-awareness group experience for Fran or Frank or a study-habits program based on reinforcement schedules for Esther might prove inhibiting. Also, students with the added pressure of meeting counselor demands may drop out of counseling.

Ernest needs to explore both the nature of his uncomfortable feelings when he is expressing himself in groups, and the reasons why these feelings arise. If our discussions indicate that he is dominating or stifling other group members, I would help him explore some of the reasons why he may be forcing group attention on himself. Then we could work on more constructive and appropriate ways for him to interact with the group. Suppose, however, our discussions indicate that often some members of the group are disturbed by his controversial comments. I would then help Ernest accept that although his comments may be pertinent and necessary to resolve a topic, confronting issues in an overly assertive manner may bring out defensiveness in others and may decrease his popularity within a group. Possibly he could decrease the degree of negative or defensive reaction in the group by improving the way in which he presents his controversial concerns. Perhaps he could learn to calm his militant tendencies while retaining his candid self-expression through role-playing in our interviews.

I find that counselor interns tend to move too quickly to help a person like Esther improve study habits, only to find that she cannot hold to schedules and that her mind wandering continues. I prefer to explore factors contributing to the discrepancies between what she says she wants and what she does. Questions about her daydreams and the differences between what she aspires to and what she believes herself capable of doing are important. Some confrontation about the reasons for her contradictory behaviors may occur fairly early in counseling, since she admits to her contradictions. Study habits then may become a pertinent topic of discussion.

Frank's presenting problem is often termed existential because he is concerned with broad questions about life or existence. If he is articulate, the interviews may involve a good deal of careful listening and reflecting by the counselor. However, if Frank has difficulty expressing himself, I would not hesitate to ask questions or make observations through which I could help him confront the source of his concerns. Religious questions or questions about life begin to surface as adolescents begin to question the beliefs or lack of beliefs of their parents and to ponder how adults have run the world in general.

Fran is attempting to develop her personal identity in what to her is a sterile environment. She should receive support for her desire and attempts to be independent and to develop herself professionally. Leaving school early sounds like a sensible possibility. It would permit more independence and place her in an environment in which she might be able to cultivate friends who accept and encourage her independence. If she left high school, I would like her to have an opportunity in counseling sessions to increase her self-assurance about asserting herself in spite of adverse criticism. I would not gloss over her feelings of loneliness. If she is to be different, she needs to be prepared for the possibility of future criticism and for the likelihood that she will end up with a few select friends rather than many. The type of friendships and social interactions she wants to work toward would be discussed.

Social Problems: Interpersonal Conflicts and Feelings of Social Inadequacy

General Comments. The presenting problems of students in these counseling requests or referrals focus on conflicts related to differences between individuals' needs or expectations and the needs or expectations of significant persons in their lives. Students may also indicate that they feel socially inept and request help in developing skills in interacting with others.

For counselors interested in testing appraisal, personality inventories with social-interaction scales might be used. Data from cumulative records are primarily useful in determining whether the patterns of behavior have persisted in the individual's interactions over the years. Also, one can gain some idea of whether the reactions have been to specific types of situations. If I believe that cumulative-record data will be useful, I recommend that we use it and then share the information with the student.

Interpersonal Conflicts. The adolescent, while searching for identity and working through dependence/independence relationships, can be expected to run into conflict at times with authority figures (teachers, parents, administrators). Social pressures upon the individual can also be generated by the groups or cliques that form in most high schools. Peer groups and cliques have varying expectations of conformity in particular behaviors. Engaging in these behaviors gains approval from these groups. Conflicts or anxiety can occur for the adolescent who decides to behave in a manner different from the peer group in general or different from any of the cliques. Independence can increase periods of loneliness as well as contribute to inner strength.

- *Client 19.* George stomps into your office between classes and asks to see you after school; he is angry at his social-studies teacher. George complains that the teacher picks on him, criticizes him, and is sarcastic. He claims that the teacher belittled him in front of the class by calling him a clown.

- *Client 20.* Glen is referred by his English teacher. Glen acts up in class. He and the teacher have talked about it, but the behavior persists. Glen and the teacher agree that Glen wants to stop the behavior.

- *Client 21.* Heather is an outgoing student fiercely expressing her need for independence. Her parents grounded her for 2 weeks because she came in late from a date. She believes that her parents are too strict and really are harsh in discipline. She argues with them. Her father storms around, and her mother ends up in tears.

- *Client 22.* Hugh is a school leader and a good student who is popular with both sexes. He is concerned because he and his girlfriend constantly clash. She is highly independent. She refuses to let him pay her way on dates and becomes annoyed if he opens doors for her or performs other traditional courtesies. He admires her independence yet feels irritated when she asserts herself. Hugh's friends are highly sociable, enjoy traditional male/female relationships, and see his girlfriend as an odd "women's libber."

When students bring conflicts with others to the attention of counselors, the counselors, I believe, should not perceive themselves as the advocate of the student in the disagreement. Nor are counselors arbiters, ombudsmen, or referees. Nor are they defenders of teachers, parents, or the Establishment. Rather, they function to help students express and clarify the conflict and explore both their own expectations, values, and feelings and the attitudes or values of those with whom they are in conflict. Then alternative actions and the consequences of these actions can be evaluated. Counselors can quickly lose effectiveness or become bloodied if they assume a stance of advocate one way or the other.

In the first example of friction between student and teacher, it would be easy to agree with the student if the teacher is known to be sarcastic with students. Or, if the teacher is your close friend and well liked by students, you might be tempted to defend the teacher. Rather than taking sides, the counselor should permit students like George to express anger and frustration and then assess the situation with the student.

A careful discussion of the specific behavior that George is complaining about as well as some analysis of how George himself behaves in class is important. George might then feel more capable of handling himself in class, or he might decide that a talk with the teacher about their interactions might help the teacher behave differently. If the teacher and George prefer a joint consultation with the counselor, the counselor should emphasize that he or she is not a referree. Rather, the counselor can help communication between student and teacher if they both desire it. Teachers and students are often surprised at the success of a direct discussion. If the relationship between the teacher and George is beyond reasonable discussion, all he can do is to drop out of the course, if that is possible, or learn to manage until the end of the quarter.

Glen's problem with the teacher starts out positively because the teacher has already shown interest in working through the problem. In this case, if Glen agrees that his behavior needs changing, I would work with him on specific ways of modifying his interaction with the teacher. Some counselors like to use behavioral contracts outlining the behavior change agreed upon. Rewards are given for changes accomplished. Formalized behavioral contracts have not proved satisfactory in my counseling. I prefer to set specific behavioral goals with the client and to work on specific understandings and skills to attain these goals. If goals are not met, the client and I determine whether the reason is the client's resistance to change or environmental factors that are inhibiting any change. Thus, even though Glen accepts responsibility for the difficulty with the teacher, I would want to determine whether the teacher's attitudes and behavior are contributing to Glen's continuing misbehavior in class. If so, a three-way conference would be suggested.

Some differences in my approach would occur if George and Glen indicate that they have had consistent problems with teachers and other authority figures rather than just experiencing isolated difficulty with one teacher. Then counseling would focus on the student's interactions with authority in general. Also, if the teacher has had difficulty with many students and has not been amenable to change over the years, I would help the student cope with the teacher's behavior and make sure that the student is not reinforcing the teacher's behavior.

Heather and Hugh are expressing value conflicts similar to the ones that arise in vocational conflicts, and I would proceed in the manner I described for them. Heather needs some help in learning how to confront her parents with her feelings of injustice. I might do some role-playing with her to aid her in explaining her feelings to her parents. Family counseling may be necessary, assuming her parents are willing. If they are unresponsive, I would help Heather arrive at standards of behavior that she can use when she is on her own legally.

Hugh is confronted with changing expectations in male and female development and relationships. He requires an opportunity to search out the reasons for his ambivalence about his girlfriend's independence when he puts a high premium on his own. He appears attracted to and yet bewildered by her attitudes. Another factor contributing to his confusion is the difference between her behavior and the behavior of the social group of which he feels a part. Searching out his attitudes about his present relationship with a female is important to his future attitudes toward and relationships with women and with social groups in general.

Feelings of Social Inadequacy.   Students at times express feelings of inadequacy about social awareness, social ease, or social skills. Teachers also may find that a student's behavior in the classroom or with them is immature or uncertain.

- *Client 23.* Ginger expresses concern about an inability to make friends, get dates, or feel part of her own peer group. People do not dislike her, she says. It is worse; they are indifferent. She describes herself as shy. She wants to learn to be more outgoing.

- *Client 24.* Howard finds it difficult to assert himself appropriately in social situations. He cannot make effective social overtures to females and feels awkward with both sexes. He tends to brag and to make up stories to build himself up.

- *Client 25.* Helen has difficulty speaking to adults. She gets tongue-tied with teachers, her parents' friends, and sales clerks. Helen has no difficulty with peers or with younger persons.

Students such as these are expressing a desire to change specific behaviors or attitudes. Because of this specificity, some counselors begin to engage in assertiveness training or other kinds of training in communication or relationships skills almost immediately. I prefer to talk with students about their perception of their social interactions to determine whether the problem lies more in lack of social skills or more in attitudes about oneself. If lack of skills is paramount, I would then proceed with some specific skill building through assertiveness training, role playing, or some other appropriate technique. These also are the type of concerns for which I have sometimes found homework assignments useful. Students can practice relatively safe interactions with others between counseling sessions. A significant part of this type of counseling is to prepare students to handle various types of responses from others when they begin to assert themselves or to act differently than they usually do. If the responses from others are not anticipated, students can have inhibitory or traumatic experiences when a close friend or an acquaintance responds aggressively to the new behavior.

If I believe that a student's concerns are more complicated than originally presented, I would continue personal and environmental exploration through interviews before starting any specific action. Ginger might be ready for training in specific skills. There is no evidence that she has developed behaviors that might be annoying to others. Howard might need to discuss his feelings of inferiority and Helen her fears about authority figures before attempting to pursue a plan of action. Group counseling might be useful for Ginger and Howard to gain practice with other members of their peer group who are experiencing similar concerns.

Antisocial Acts

In the situations discussed here, a student seeks out a counselor and reveals that he or she has been involved in or is contemplating an act that is either illegal or unethical—for example, shoplifting, destroying school property, taking drugs, plagiarizing, or cheating on an exam. The student not only admits the behavior but expresses concern and guilt about it. The student wants to get it off his or her chest and asks for help in stopping the behavior.

- *Client 26.* John tells you that he set a fire in the wastebasket in a lavatory. He was angry at the teachers and administrators because he felt that he was being treated unfairly. This was the first time he had set a fire. His own behavior scared him.

- *Client 27.* Jo is a quiet, somewhat withdrawn student who keeps to herself much of the time. Jo has difficulty talking about why she made the appointment. Finally she bursts out that she has shoplifted articles in downtown stores on a number of occasions and given them to friends as gifts.

- *Client 28.* Karl, while discussing difficulties in getting along with peers, tells you about a party he attended where he smoked pot and consumed considerable liquor He was hungover. He had driven home from the party but was so intoxicated that he had no recollection about the drive home. He does not want to drink or smoke pot but feels that he will lose his friends if he refuses.

- *Client 29.* Jim has been in a few times to discuss poor study habits. He received an "A" in a history course. You notice that he is uncomfortable. When you bring this up, he stammers that he got the "A" by cheating on the final. He admits that this was not the only time he has cheated.

These situations pose ethical dilemmas for counselors. John, Jo, and Karl have committed illegal acts. Setting fires can endanger others; stealing is taking property that belongs to others; and driving while drunk could lead to serious injury or death for the intoxicated person and/or other persons. Jim's cheating is an unethical act that can affect total grade distribution. An artificially high grade does not represent the true achievement of the cheating individual and may also cause other students to get a lower grade than they actually deserve. Yet these students have voluntarily come to the counselor to try to change the behavior. The counselor wants to help the students resolve the difficulties and change the behavior and still protect the public. In addition, the counselor wants to encourage students with similar problems to take steps on their own to get counseling help. If counselors were to involve parents or school and community authorities regarding all antisocial acts, students would be reluctant to reveal similar problems to the counselors. Thus, counselors must make professional decisions about whether they should involve parents or administrators or whether community mental-health professionals working with juveniles need to be consulted.

In none of these situations as I have described them would I involve parents, other authorities, or professionals. The behavior is not chronic, and the students are serious about getting help. I would commend them for recognizing the need for help and give them full opportunity to express their anxieties. I would make it clear that I cannot protect them from legal or disciplinary action if their behavior continues and is discovered while they are in counseling. However, I would explain that if parents and the authorities discovered the behavior, they would most likely be relieved that the student had already voluntarily sought help.

As counseling progressed, I would try to help each student explore the factors contributing to the antisocial behavior. There would be no attempt to condone or excuse the setting of a fire, the shoplifting, the excessive drinking, or the cheating on the basis of emotional factors. Rather, we would discuss reasons for John's inability to handle anger more productively, Jo's frantic efforts to buy friendship, Karl's desperation about peer acceptance, and Jim's urgency about grades. Often in these situations, counseling brings out evidence of poor family interactions that are contributing to the behavior. If so, I would recommend to the student that we inform his or her parents about the behavior and about our progress so far in counseling. If the student is willing and the parents are cooperative, counseling sessions with the family can be arranged. Students who admit to cheating sometimes want to let the specific teacher or teachers know about the cheating so that grade distribution can be adjusted if necessary. I would support and help students to take this step. I would, however, perceive this as part of the counseling process rather than as a "confession" that was intended to relieve guilt and to eliminate the belief that counseling is necessary.

If John and Jo expressed irresistible urges to set fires and steal, I would discuss with them the need to get more intensive help than I probably could give at the school. Also, since their behavior is potentially injurious to others, I would point out the need to contact parents and the school psychiatric consultant to arrange for more concentrated help. If Karl gave evidence of being an alcoholic or addicted to hard drugs, I would also recommend more intensive treatment for him. If the state law grants privileged communication to minors who are drug abusers and seek counseling, I would inform Karl of this law and ask him whether he wished to have his family involved. If not, he would be referred to a drug or alcohol treatment center for more evaluation and treatment.

In my experience, students with uncontrollable impulses who seek help voluntarily are relieved when the counselor can arrange for discussions with parents or others that can lead to appropriate treatment. It is not unusual for a decision to be made, after consultations, that the school counselor, if professionally trained, continue counseling with the student or with student and family. In that case the counselor could arrange for periodic meetings with the outside consultant.

Problems Involving Student Rights and Responsibilities

Students may seek out counselors because they object to school rules that they believe violate their civil rights. For example, a student may refuse to comply with dress codes or with school guidelines about appropriate topics for the school newspaper. Another student may circulate a petition against some administrative action. If the principal prohibits the circulation of the petition, the student may believe that his or her freedom of speech is being jeopardized. Another student may refuse to agree to have his or her locker or desk searched because he or she considers it an undue invasion of privacy. In these instances the administrator may threaten the students with suspension from school if they persist in their actions.

If students seek out a counselor because they are in this type of conflict with a principal, what is appropriate behavior for the counselor? I believe that counselors should help students know their rights and work out their own decisions on alternative actions and their consequences. Students should be helped to determine carefully whether their rights are being violated and, if so, whether they choose to resist the rules, even if resisting means suspension. It should be anticipated that counselors will be in the forefront of protecting individual rights and civil liberties. Nevertheless, I believe that the decision about which action to take must rest with the individual.

It is tempting for the counselor with strong civil-libertarian leanings to put pressure on the student to stick to his or her guns. And it is equally easy for the counselor who strongly identifies with Establishment procedures to cajole the student out of trouble-making behavior. Promoting thorough understanding by students of their rights, their reasons for conflict in pursuing alternative actions, and the consequences for their personal well-being if they do or do not assert themselves constitutes appropriate counseling.

In Chapter 9, ways in which counselors can work to change policies that inhibit student and teacher rights will be discussed as an important outreach activity of a counseling staff.

Crises

I define crisis-intervention counseling as pertaining to situations requiring immediate attention because an individual is seriously disoriented, depressed, or agitated. Crises can also occur when sudden, radical changes occur in an individual's life or environment. I do not consider the counseling examples I have been discussing up to now as crisis counseling. Crises require prompt action and often direct intervention to avoid the possibility of serious consequences or further deterioration. Prompt action is important in high schools. Approximately 25,000 suicides occur in the United States in one year with 4000 of these committed by adolescents. In the last 20 years adolescent suicide has increased by 250% (Mears & Gatchel, 1979). Indian and Black youths need particular attention since their suicide rates are much higher than the national youth suicide average (Gottesfeld, 1979).

In schools the counseling staff should be a first line of call when emergencies arise. Counselors who handle crises need to do what they can to assess the situation and take immediate action when necessary. Then a determination is needed on whether the counselor should continue to work with the student or refer him or her to someone else or to a community agency.

In crisis situations counseling-staff members should remain calm. They should talk with the student to determine whether the behavior shows disorientation caused by psychotic reactions or a drug reaction or whether the behavior results from a sudden, acute depression or confusion caused by some upsetting circumstance, such as a sudden death in the family, a sudden separation of the parents, pregnancy, or the breakup of a relationship.

If a student is so disoriented, depressed, or agitated as to be suicidal or dangerous to others, administrators need to know the seriousness of the problem, and the parent need to be informed. In instances in which a student is in a state of shock over a sudden death or breakup in the family, the counselor may need first to help the student get over the initial shock. Then the counselor may need to continue with some counseling sessions to help the student express grief, anger, or frustration and confront the reality of the event. In these situations psychiatric and psychological consultation should be available either from a consultant hired on a retainer by the school district or from a professional staff member at the community mental-health clinic. It is important that school counselors know and support resources in the community where a referral can be made or where consultation can be obtained.

Community mental-health clinics have recognized the need for quick action. In order for community programs to get federal funding, it is necessary to include facilities for handling crises on a 24-hour basis. Hot lines, crisis clinics, and 24-hour walk-in clinics have been developed in communities to meet that requirement. Counselors should be familiar with these facilities or help develop them in the community as part of their outreach activities.

Projects and Activities

1. *Interview a number of high school counseling staffs near you about their interest in and use of inventories, personality measures, and intelligence and aptitude tests.*

2. *Evaluate two computerized vocational-information systems developed for use with high school students. If possible, use a computerized program yourself to explore areas of interest to you.*

3. *Develop a list of agencies in the community that appear to you to be essential for the school system to have as resources. Then determine how many of these agencies actually exist in nearby communities.*

4. *Develop a policy statement about procedures for referring students to counselors on a voluntary basis. Include a rationale. Consider ways of involving teachers, parents, and students in the development of procedures. How does your rationale relate to the ASCA standards?*

5. *Make a survey of the literature or of adolescent students about their contemporary concerns. Are counselor preparation programs with which you are familiar geared to meet those needs?*

6. *This activity will require a tape recorder and another interested student who will team up with you for a series of role-playing counseling interviews. Role playing is widely used in the training of counselors. It is suggested here so that you can get a sense of its possible wide use in studying many different aspects of counseling as well as a feel for counseling. At this time I suggest that you use it simply to study the different types of counselor responses possible to a client's remarks. You and your fellow student should each take a few minutes to work out a possible counseling situation. Then present your concern (with the recorder playing) to the other person, who acts as the counselor. (You will reverse roles after completing your client role.) It is wise to role-play for at least 10 minutes and to make sure that the person playing the counselor*

makes several responses or comments. Then replay and review the tapes, and summarize what was said by the client and by the counselor. Classify the counselor's responses. Here are some suggested categories to use, but you will have to add others or at least a "miscellaneous" category to cover all possibilities:

a. **Probing** *for more facts and details by questioning.*
b. **Giving** *advice or telling the client what to do.*
c. **Judging** *or* **interpreting** *responses.*
d. Making responses that **facilitate** *the expression of the client's feelings. (See author's comments below.)*

7. *Role-play an interview with Catherine, Client 7, using first a female as the counselor and then a male. Discuss the reactions of the participants. Were differences felt by the participants or by observers when the counselor was a male and when the counselor was a female?*

8. *A counselor working with Bob, Client 5, might want to help him constructively assert himself with his father concerning the father's biases about drama. In small groups discuss how a counselor might go about this from a behaviorist view or from a Gestaltist view.*

9. *Explain how a client-centered counselor would handle the concerns of Arthur, Client 1, about vocational exploration.*

10. *Compare a client-centered approach with a developmental approach for working with the sexual concerns of Earle, Client 11.*

11. *Assume that you are applying for a job as a school counselor and that one of the members of the interview committee says: "I really don't know why we need counselors, since teachers should be able to handle any problem that comes along. What makes you feel that your services are really needed?" Write a response to the board member's remark. Take into consideration the types of problems discussed in this chapter. (See author's comments below.)*

Author's Comments

Activity 6.[1]   *The role-play activity is included to help the prospective counselor get a feeling for counseling and have experience in using one of the most common training devices, the tape recorder. As you and your partner reviewed the counselor responses on the tape and classified them, you very likely became aware of a variety of insights about how you responded. Probably one of the most common observations is that the responses during the interviews were most likely to be a series of questions and that these questions, in turn, very likely were worded in such a way as to seek more factual details about the situation. Also, the beginning counselor usually asks questions from his or her frame of reference rather than from the client's. In the early stages of counseling, it is far more productive in most cases to convey to the client your understanding of his or her concern from* his or her frame of reference than it is to ask a series of detailed, probing, factually oriented questions. Obviously, you cannot conduct a meaningful interview without the use of questions, but there are some noticeable differences between the style and type of questions of the beginning counselor and those of the experienced counselor. For example, beginners tend to ask closed questions (questions that can be answered with "yes" or "no"), while experienced counselors use more open questions (questions that allow the client to expand upon or explore the concern expressed). Another difference is that beginning counselors stress factual details, whereas experienced counselors explore, as appropriate, the affect, or feeling, areas. Novice counselors also tend to respond in ways that convey that they have or are seeking an "answer" for the client, while trained counselors are more likely to encourage clients to explore their own perceptions, attitudes, and solutions that would be appropriate and possible for them.

Activity 11.   A counselor should be aware of the role definitions of the national professional associations and of training standards for certification. Counseling, according to these standards, involves the training and expertise to handle the concerns of students in a nonevaluative atmosphere. Most teachers do not have the training required. Those teachers who do have neither the time nor the proper environment to develop appropriate counseling relationships. A good teacher must be a fair evaluator, must maintain classroom discipline to ensure a good learning environment, and must focus on teaching subject matter in a pleasant, organized atmosphere. Counselors are not evaluators or disciplinarians. They facilitate a good classroom learning environment by being able to work with students who because of personal concerns are not functioning well personally or academically in class.

6

Individual Counseling in Elementary Schools

The Development of Elementary School Counseling

Counseling in elementary schools started much later than in secondary schools (Tolbert, 1978). The first book on elementary school counseling was not published until the 1950s. The delay can be attributed to a number of factors. The early counseling movement was steeped in vocational placement, which is not appropriate for younger children. Also, it was widely believed that elementary school teachers should serve as counselors because they are with the same children throughout the day. Psychological work in elementary schools consisted primarily of diagnosis and placement of children with learning or emotional problems or of attention to children suffering from severe physical or emotional neglect by parents because of seriously disrupted home situations. School psychologists trained to handle diagnostic work were apt to concentrate on classroom behavior, and social workers prepared to intervene in difficult family/school relations were hired instead of counselors.

In 1964, the federal government moved to provide more elementary school counseling services through the National Defense Education Act, which authorized grants to school districts for developing elementary school counseling. In 1968, grants were authorized for training institutes for elementary school counselors (Shertzer & Stone, 1976). Such funding was previously available only for secondary school counseling. Since then, the number of elementary school counselors has increased rapidly. Although exact figures are lacking, it has been estimated that 10,000 elementary school counselors were employed in 1978 (Shertzer & Stone, 1980). Employment prospects for elementary school counselors appear favorable through the mid-1980s.

The Counselor's Role

Counselors preparing for elementary school positions have a more diffi-cult time defining their potential counseling populations than do coun-selors in secondary schools. Elementary schools usually include kinder-garten through the sixth grade. A review of the literature indicates that this organization is the most common one. However, there are separate middle schools, which usually consist of the sixth through the eighth grade. In this text middle schools will be considered similar to the upper grades in an elementary school because they are organized more like ele-mentary schools than junior high or secondary schools.

Whether one works in a K–4, K–6, or K–8 school, there is a much great-er difference in sophistication between beginning students and older ones than there is between freshmen and seniors in high school. A fresh-man and a senior are more alike in overall behavior and maturity than a 5-year-old and a 9-year-old, an 11-year-old, or a 13-year-old. Elementary school children in any of these age ranges vary much more in indepen-dence, motivations, judgments, and developmental tasks than do adoles-cents between 14 and 18 years of age.

Because of this large difference in the age and sophistication of elemen-tary school children, counselors serving this group require a wider reper-toire of theories and techniques than secondary school or college counsel-ors do. The theories and techniques used in direct counseling can be used with older elementary school children, but counselors may also use games, puppets, drawings, stories, or other play media, particularly with younger children, to help the children express themselves.

A number of experts on elementary school counseling (for example, Boy, 1972; Keat, 1974; Muro, 1970; Nelson, 1972) specify that the counsel-or's primary function is direct counseling. Keat states, "It is imperative that the counseling relationship, whether it be with children or important adults, retain its place at the core of the counselor's role" (p. 5). None of these authorities neglects the consultation, psychological-education, and guidance functions of the counselor but perceives them as important com-plements of the major focus of counseling. The ASCA's 1978 definition of the elementary school counselor's role includes direct counseling with students as a primary function. Consultation and coordination of guid-ance services are also considered important.

Other writers on elementary school counseling and guidance (for ex-ample, Dinkmeyer, 1973; Faust, 1968b; Lundquist & Chamley, 1971) argue that the counselor's role should be that of a consultant or psychological director, with most work done with significant adults in the child's life. Improving the communication skills, behavior, and attitudes of parents and teachers should take precedence over direct work with children. Some of these authors—Dinkmeyer and Faust, for example—see counsel-ing with children as a minor function and state that if direct work does occur, group counseling is preferable. Others, such as Lundquist and Chamley, perceive any direct work with children as an inefficient use of counselor time.

The term *child-behavior consultant* has been used during the past ten to fifteen years to describe a guidance specialist who does not work directly with children but spends his or her time instead consulting with or counseling parents, teachers, or administrators who influence the children's behavior. It is believed that the changed behavior of these adults will change the behavior of children without the necessity of directly counseling the children (Shaw, 1973). Although Shaw indicates some difficulty in trying to pinpoint the derivation of the term, he believes that it may have been generated by Gerald Caplan, a psychiatrist interested in preventative medicine. Shaw also points out that a series of studies funded by the Interprofessional Research Commission on Pupil Personnel Services (IRCOPPS) in 1968 indicated that consultation with significant adults did not result in changing children's behavior. Group counseling with adults did help to improve children's attendance and grades. The results, Shaw indicates, were inconclusive.

One of the arguments presented by this group and by others recommending a consultation emphasis in counseling is that elementary school children are too young to profit from direct counseling because they have difficulty in expressing themselves. Hawkins (1967) refuted this argument. In an analysis of elementary school counseling interviews, Hawkins found that both older and younger students were able to verbalize in the interviews, though the older ones of course showed more facility. Those who doubt this capability should read the transcripts of counseling interviews in texts written by experts on counseling children (Keat, 1974; Muro, 1970; Nelson, 1972).

Nelson argues that it is not enough to examine or change the environment of the child. The child has some degree of control over his or her environment. While recognizing that adults are important in the child's world, Nelson believes that counselors "cannot wisely exclude the child himself from the process that is designed to help him" (p. 43).

Most persons who engage in individual child counseling define the counseling process and relationship in terms similar to those used for adults. The components of a confidential, trust relationship between a professional counselor and a child needing help with normal conflicts or concerns are considered essential ingredients. This position is consistent with the ASCA definition of the elementary school counselor's role.

I concur with the writers who say that direct counseling should be a major focus of elementary school counseling and with Nelson's (1973) statement that direct counseling has not really been given a chance. He commented that "it hasn't been given a thoroughgoing trial yet, so how can we justify deserting it" (p. 88)? I concede that in kindergarten through the second grade more consultation may be necessary, but I still believe that direct interaction with these children is important.

Elementary school counselors tend to have closer and more frequent contact with teachers and parents than do high school, college, or community counselors. Young children are more dependent upon their parents and more under the jurisdiction of teachers than are older students. Also, elementary school children are in self-contained classrooms in the majority of school districts, so that more personal attention, personal interaction, intimacy, and conflict can exist between teachers and children than in other counselor settings. Nevertheless, the counselor's main role should be direct counseling with the children, even at early ages. Young children often have less difficulty in expressing emotions than do older children, teenagers, and adults. Adolescents and adults often have built up defenses that contribute to denial or misperceptions of emotions (Nelson, 1972). Counselors therefore need to spend time helping them restructure their understanding of their attitudes and emotions before action can be initiated for change. Because children are often more direct and less guarded in revealing their feelings about themselves or about their interactions with others, the opportunity to help them understand and label emotions and express themselves effectively is in some ways greater than with older persons. Children who are angry or resentful about parent or teacher expectations or about relations with peers and siblings need to become aware of the naturalness of these emotions in themselves and in others close to them. Healthy attitudes about such emotions, together with learning constructive ways of working through and expressing them, can help a child experience some inner consistency and harmony (Keat, 1974).

Free Choice and Confidentiality in Elementary School Counseling

As indicated in Chapter 3, it is vital that counselors, administrators, and teachers not overlook the importance of free choice, confidentiality, and the right to privacy for elementary school children in counseling. My experiences with children of this age, the experiences of counseling interns I have supervised in elementary schools, and my contacts with professionally trained elementary school counselors have demonstrated that attention to these factors can lead to children's developing positive attitudes about counselors.

When young children are offered the opportunities for free choice and confidentiality that are offered to older children and adults, their involvement in counseling and their sense of responsibility for their own behavior can increase. These conditions can also enhance the relationships of the teacher and the parents with the counselor and the child. Van Hoose (1968) found that in an elementary school counseling program emphasizing confidentiality, the number of students asking for counseling increased. Keith (1978) also found that educating children about the possibility of seeking counseling (self-referrals) led more students to ask for it. Keith believed that at least 50% of the students who sought counseling would not have been referred by teachers.

In an earlier article Biasco (1968) gave three suggestions for encouraging requests for counseling in elementary schools: the children must be made aware of the counseling service, the counselors must be highly visible and available, and the teachers must encourage students to seek counseling. Referrals by teachers, administrators, and parents that are non-coercive and that emphasize free choice can be encouraged by educating them about counseling services.

The concept of confidentiality with children is a crucial one in elementary school counseling. Van Hoose (1968), in discussing confidentiality in consulting with parents, says:

> The fact that the counselee is a child in no way gives the counselor the right to violate or betray confidences. In fact, since the child is almost defenseless, the counselor has an even greater responsibility to make certain that he does not provide the adults with a weapon which can be used against the child. The counselor cannot risk making secret deals with the parents and he cannot align himself with either faction in a conflict [pp. 135–136].

In 1978 Wagner conducted a survey of elementary school counselors' views on confidentiality with children. She sent a questionnaire to 347 randomly selected elementary school counselors in New York State and Pennsylvania. Of the responses 111 were usable. She found that 89% of the group believed in the importance of confidentiality but in practice showed ambivalence. The ambivalence increased as the age of the children decreased. Wagner recommends that the counselor's first obligation remain with the child. If a child does not want confidential information given to parents, the counselor should discuss the child's objections with the child to discover the reasons for the objections, what information is disputed, and possible consequences of giving out information. If the counselor believes that sharing information would be beneficial, this belief should be shared with the child, who can then contribute to a decision about talking with others.

If a teacher, administrator, or parent were to refer a child to me for counseling, I would inform the adult that I would like him or her to tell the child why the referral was made. Also, I would want to share with the child the reason given me for the referral and the nature of my discussion with the adult. I would let the adult know that I would encourage the child to continue working with me but would give the child the option of continuing counseling. I would inform both the adult and the child that any conferences held would be with the child's knowledge and consent. These steps would be intended to increase the child's trust in me and in the referring adult and to enhance the child's freedom to speak candidly. The process is not intended to increase secrecy or to reduce communication between adult and child. Rather, it is intended to open up honest and pertinent communication among all the parties.

Parents may be concerned about young children's seeing counselors on their own. If counselors meet with parents to discuss the value of such an approach, a great deal of resistance can be extinguished. Also, a counseling advisory committee composed of interested parents and teachers can be set up to help implement the policy. Finally, a letter emphasizing the voluntary nature of the counseling can be sent to parents at the beginning of the year. If parents object, they can have the opportunity to discuss their objections with a counselor.

Sources of Referral

Since elementary school teachers have the same children in class for all or most of the day for the entire school year, the teachers usually refer more students for counseling than secondary school teachers do. Elementary school teachers have the opportunity to observe children's lack of motivation or lack of ability to handle classwork. They can perceive children's uncertainties about themselves and/or unproductive interactions with others. They can sense when a child's home situation is not going well. These teachers are also more aware of a child's withdrawal and more affected by a child's nuisance behavior (constant fidgeting, consistently getting out of his or her seat at the wrong times, lying, or getting into fights). Stealing or other antisocial behavior can be observed more readily too.

Since elementary schools tend to be smaller than high schools, the principals and vice-principals have more intimate interactions with the children and the teachers. Therefore, elementary school administrators are more likely to refer children to counselors than are administrators in other schools.

If it becomes clear to children, even very young ones, that a counselor is available to them, they will begin to seek counseling on their own. Administrators, teachers, and parents should encourage them to do so by letting them know that they can talk to their counselor if something is bothering them. Often a student who has had a successful experience with a counselor will suggest that his or her friend see the counselor. It is also quite common for students to bring their friends with them to their counseling sessions because their friends need help.

Referrals also come from children and from teachers as counselors make themselves more visible to them through informal classroom visits and through helping teachers work through classroom units related to child development or mental health or teaching the units themselves. These types of activities will be discussed in Chapter 10.

Counselors should recognize that some students who are nonverbal or resentful or whose ethnic background is different from their own may be reluctant or unwilling to be referred by a teacher or to seek counseling themselves. Counselors must be visible to these students and approach them in a noncoercive way whenever possible (Van Hoose, Pietrofesa, & Carlson, 1973). A feeling of trust should be more likely to grow under these circumstances than it would through either indifference or attempts to cajole, persuade, or force the children into counseling.

When administrators, teachers, or parents refer a child to a counselor, they often expect the counselor to observe the child in the classroom. Presumably, the counselor will gain a more accurate picture of the child's behavior by watching his or her interactions with the teacher and with the other students. The child is not informed of the observation in order to maintain natural behavior.

I see little value in this strategy and a number of disadvantages. First, the ethical policies of confidentiality, free choice, and the right to privacy are being violated. Second, if counseling is designed to encourage self-development and self-control in behavior change, surreptitious observation is contrary to those goals. It sets a tone of external manipulation. Third, if a counselor makes a habit of observing in the classroom, the children will quickly pick up cues that the counselor is watching someone. A guessing game about who the "victim" is can follow. Finally, a teacher's awareness that the observation of a child includes the teacher/child relationship can subtly change his or her interactions with the child or with the class, so that the counselor may get an inaccurate perception of the usual class interaction.

If it appears that classroom observation might be helpful, it can be arranged after counseling has begun. With this approach the student and the counselor can discuss beforehand the need for observation or the reasons that it might be useful. Any information gained by observation can then be used by the counselor and the child in their counseling sessions and in their relationships with the teacher and the parents.

The Use of Play Media and Tests and Inventories

Play Media

Games, puppets, dolls, toys modeled after adult possessions (phones, trucks, cars), clay, paints, tools, and similar media are used in counseling sessions with children in the elementary grades. These media can serve various purposes, such as establishing contact with children through dolls, replicating reality with cars or phones, encouraging catharsis with hammering, building up self-concepts with puzzles, and working off aggressive drives with clay (Keat, 1974). Another form of play is mutual story telling, in which the counselor tells a story and then the child tells one.

Faust (1968b), Nelson (1972), and Waterland (1970) agree that play comes naturally to the child in developing social relationships, so that the use of play media facilitates communication between the counselor and the child. Counselors who use unstructured play expect more openness and spontaneity from children than might occur through verbal interaction alone.

Some writers make a distinction between play therapy used for the diagnosis of severely emotionally disturbed children and the play activity used in counseling. Nelson says that play therapy is designed to analyze children's behavior, whereas "counseling with play media is to facilitate spontaneous expression and communication by the child" (p. 200). Faust agrees that the "play process suggests more of an emphasis on the normal range of ineffective behavior of nearly all children than does play therapy" (p. 157).

Because young children have a high potential for expressing themselves with candor and can profit from expressing and identifying emotions directly, elementary school counselors should guard against overusing play media. Nelson (1972), a strong proponent of the appropriate use of play media, cautions that play activities may distract the child ready to deal directly with a problem and thus interfere with communication. Hawkins's (1967) finding, discussed earlier in the chapter, that children do have the capacity to verbalize in counseling should be kept in mind. Puppets, games, drawings, or story telling can be used when it is obvious that a youngster is having difficulty verbalizing his or her thoughts or feelings directly.

Tests and Inventories

Standardized tests measuring intellectual ability, achievement level, and reading ability are available to elementary school counselors for use in improving the student's self-understanding. These tests can be obtained from well-known test-publishing companies, such as the California Test Bureau, Science Research Associates, Harcourt Brace Jovanovich, and Columbia University's Teachers College Press.

Group personality or vocational-interest inventories are not used frequently in elementary schools. Standardizing these forms of measurement at early, formative ages has not proved fruitful. Nelson (1972) views standardized group personality tests as of dubious value and believes that personality-inventory check lists are more beneficial. Similar comments apply to vocational measures.

Keat (1974) gives a comprehensive overview of tests used with school children. He discusses three major individual intelligence tests, the Wechsler Intelligence Scale for Children (WISC), the Stanford-Binet, and the Wechsler Pre-School and Primary Scale of Intelligence (WPPSI). He also lists group intelligence and achievement tests, and group interest and personality inventories that can be useful for counseling children. Some of the commonly used tests are the California Short Form Test of Mental Ability (K–8), the Otis-Lennon Mental Ability Test (K–9), the Primary Mental Abilities Test (K–6), What I Like To Do (Grades 4–7), the California Test of Personality (K–8), and the Early School Personality Questionnaire (Grades 1–3).

Some elementary school counselors prefer to use individual personality measures that involve drawings made by the child, such as House-Tree-Person Test (H-T-P) (Buck, 1950). In some instances, counselors just ask children to draw what they please and then have them tell a story about the picture. Counselors may also ask children to draw a picture of their family.

An important distinction exists between testing done for the purpose of diagnosing learning or emotional disabilities to help parents, teachers, and administrators make administrative decisions about a child's education and testing done in counseling to help improve a child's self-understanding and educational experience. This distinction parallels the one between play therapy for diagnosis and play activity for helping the counseling process. Goldman (1971), an expert on the use of tests in counseling, differentiates noncounseling uses of tests from the appropriate use of tests in counseling. Noncounseling uses involve activities related to the administration of an institution. These activities include selection of individuals for an institution, placement of individuals within the institution, and development, adaptation, or revision of institutional practice for the benefit of a particular individual or for individuals in general. Counseling uses include gaining information to help decide upon the goal of the counseling process, gathering information to help the client make a decision, and exploring new areas of interest. In addition, tests and inventories may facilitate the interaction of counselor and client or may prepare the client for future counseling sessions.

The Counseling Needs of Elementary School Children

According to surveys of teachers, parents, and children, the counseling needs of elementary school students fall into categories similar to those for other settings. These categories are consistent with the general developmental tasks proposed for children of these ages. Van Hoose (1968) perceives elementary school counseling objectives as "aiding children in (1) appropriate academic achievement, (2) furthering normal social and emotional development, (3) developing self-understanding, (4) acquiring realistic self-concepts, and (5) developing self-knowledge relative to the world of work" (pp. 98–99). Most later writers on elementary school counseling use similar categories in describing the problems of children. For these reasons the categories of vocational/educational, personal, and social problems seem appropriate ones to use here.

The Presenting Problems of Elementary School Children

Vocational/Educational Problems: Exploration and Conflicts

Students are not likely to be referred for or to seek counseling on direct vocational planning in elementary school unless the school includes eight grades. However, in counseling sessions students may reveal attitudes about work, occupational values, or occupational stereotypes when they are discussing relationships with or expectations of their parents. These discussions may contribute to personal development and awareness of the multiple factors in career choice and thus help students toward more effective future vocational planning. As career-awareness programs increase, more younger children may show interest in discussing what the future may hold for them.

Some experts note that pressure on children about occupational choice is greater and more common than people generally realize. Dimick and Huff (1970) contend that elementary school children are often pushed by adults to specify what they are going to be when they grow up. Counselors in these cases need to reduce pressure to choose and encourage exploration of vocations instead. Indeed, in these situations, dealing with inappropriate pressure from parents may be more important than career exploration. Children may also be confused when parents express distaste for their own occupations or talk about occupations in terms of social status.

Educational interests and abilities in earlier stages of development contribute to the vocational direction that children may take later. Their expressed interests and performance may also lead to premature parental expectations about choice of an occupation. Further, it is at this stage of development that occupational stereotypes based on gender or on ethnic groups may develop. These stereotypes may cause conflict for the young female or male student showing interest in areas traditionally considered appropriate only for the other sex or may inhibit the young person from following natural inclinations in exploring vocational possibilities.

The concept that vocational development is a part of total personality development and of the development of the self-concept has implications for elementary school counseling. Exploring and understanding one's interests, aptitudes, and values are processes that start early in life, and they should receive attention in elementary school (Van Hoose, 1968).

Referrals for educational difficulties are usually more numerous than in secondary schools. Like vocational concerns, these problems are often tied in with personal values and attitudes and with interpersonal problems. Teachers tend to refer students who lack motivation to start or complete work assignments or who are not working up to their estimated ability. Children may seek out counselors and complain that they are bored with school or that they find the work too hard. Counselors can help students explore the reasons for difficulties with schoolwork. There may be undue pressure from teachers or parents over quality of academic performance. Conversely, teachers or parents may not be paying sufficient attention to the child's work. As in secondary school counseling, I would help the teacher and the student determine whether the child is being expected to do work above his or her ability. If so, the teacher can modify the expectations. If the educational difficulty looks severe or puzzling enough to require psychological assessment regarding placement in a special-education or learning-disability class, I would recommend referral to a school psychologist. If the home situation is contributing to lack of educational progress, some family counseling might prove fruitful. If the home situation involves severe neglect or confusion, a referral to a social worker is in order. If either of these referrals occurred, the counselor might still continue counseling with the student and/or the family. Also, the school psychologist or social worker and the counselor might work jointly with the student and the family.

- *Client 1.* Allison is a second-grader referred to you by her teacher because she is not working at the level her teacher believes she should. Allison has above-average ability to learn and superior scores on reading and standardized achievement tests. She is not failing, but she does not hand in assignments on time, is careless in her work, and generally acts bored. Allison comes to see you apparently willingly but looks disinterested during the first counseling session.

- *Client 2.* Brett, a fifth-grader, has asked the secretary for an appointment for counseling. When he comes in to see you, he tells you that he is having trouble with math and science units. He expresses little interest in them. His mother is a physicist and his father a biologist. Brett believes that they are disappointed because they would like him to carry on the scientific tradition. He prefers English, social sciences, and art.

- *Client 3.* You have been presenting a career-awareness unit in a fourth-grade class. Bess, a member of the class, has shown considerable interest in the class discussion. After class she asks whether she can make an appointment to see you to talk more about careers. When she comes for her appointment, she explains that she is confused about career options for women. You learn that her mother and father are currently experiencing some friction because her mother wants to train for a career while her father insists she stay at home until the children are older.

- *Client 4.* Billy is a second-grader who is referred by his teacher because he does not seem to be able to comprehend the reading assignments in class.

The teacher is dubious about his ability to learn second-grade material and wonders whether he belongs in a special-education class. He is new in the school district, and no records of intellectual capability or of achievement are available.

Allison has been referred by her teacher, so her motivation for counseling may not be very great. In this type of referral, I have found it profitable to clarify with the student why the referral was made, whether the student agrees with the teacher's appraisal, and whether the student believes that a problem exists. I would invite Allison to continue seeing me, but I would also tell her that she does not have to if she prefers not to do so. If she prefers not to continue with me, I would encourage her to see me whenever she thought the situation warranted it. If she decided to continue, then we could discuss her attitudes, feelings, and behavior in the classroom.

If Allison had difficulty expressing herself or discussing her interactions in class, I would probably use play media, such as free drawing or playing with puppets, as a means of helping her relax and of facilitating her communication with me. Her drawings or puppet play might give some clues to her feelings about herself and her interactions with others. If Allison talked freely, I would not use play media. In our discussions we could explore whether her reactions to class material and to the teacher stemmed from boredom or whether her behavior was a form of withdrawal because of fear of not meeting her standards or the standards of adults. In these discussions I would share with her what her achievement and ability testing indicated and get her reaction to those results. If more tests seemed advisable, I would arrange for them to be given or administer them myself.

Since her teacher had made the referral, I would suggest to Allison that the teacher might find it useful to get some feedback about our discussions. Allison and I could decide together on what we would and would not share with the teacher. We would also determine whether Allison or I or both of us would talk with the teacher.

In talking with Brett, it would be important to me to help him first explore whether his belief about his parents' expectations about science is accurate. This exploration could include encouraging Brett to talk with his parents about their aspirations for him. If this discussion indicated that Brett's parents would not be concerned if he did not follow scientific lines, the focus of my interviews with Brett would relate to his own expectations about himself. If, on the other hand, his parents are set on his going into science, I would determine with Brett whether it would be helpful for me to talk with his parents. If he agreed, I would suggest that he ask them to make an appointment with me. In the ensuing discussions with them and Brett, I would attempt to help his parents realize the importance of Brett's feeling free to explore his interests and abilities if he is to make productive choices at important points in his vocational and personal development.

Bess's reason for asking for counseling reflects a need for her to confront a potential conflict in her career and personal exploration and development. The impasse between her parents about her mother's career aspirations, if not resolved productively, could inhibit Bess's own career planning. However, counseling might enable her to recognize the importance of exploring her career options as part of her total personality development.

If her parents' conflict is severe enough to detract from Bess's personal development, the parents may need to be involved in the counseling. It would be beneficial if Bess could talk with her parents about her concern over their conflict and also suggest an interview with her counselor. Role-playing her interactions with her parents might be useful at this point. If the parental conflict seems severe enough that Bess's intercession might prove counterproductive, I would, with Bess's permission, call her parents about her concern.

If Bess's parents are willing, some family counseling might help them handle their conflict and its implications for Bess. If, after meeting with the parents, it appears that the marital discord is severe and goes beyond the career question or that divorce is a possibility, I would concentrate on getting them marriage counseling. But whether or not the parents received marital counseling, I would continue to work with Bess to help her explore the meaning of careers in an individual's life and the importance of her developing the ability to make productive choices for herself.

Billy has been referred by his teacher for a psychological evaluation that may convince his principal, teacher, and parents to place him in a special-education class. The referral, as it stands, is inappropriate. In my opinion, it should have been made to the district school psychologist after the teacher had consulted with the principal, who in turn had arranged for consultation with the parents. Because an administrative decision is anticipated, the school staff is obligated to get the parents' permission before the evaluation is done. The school psychologist is the learning specialist who is trained in this form of psychological evaluation.

Even though I disapprove of the referral, I would not immediately send Billy back to class. Instead, my first response to Billy would be to ask him if he knew why the teacher had referred him to see me and how he felt about seeing me. I would make sure that he realized the teacher was concerned about whether the classwork was too difficult for him and was interested in finding out if the situation could be improved. I would point out that an exploration might be helpful, particularly since he is new at the school and no previous records are available.

I would explain to Billy that I would not be the person who would work directly with the teacher and his parents to consider the level of schoolwork most comfortable to him. But I would assure him that I would be interested in helping in any way I could and would invite him to come to see me if he wanted to talk over what was going on. In this way, if Billy's parents received an administrative recommendation that Billy be placed in a special-education class or in a lower grade, I could serve as a resource to him and his parents while they were coping with the change. If, however, he proved to have the ability to remain in the same class, counseling might help him to reduce any anxiety he felt about classwork and, if necessary, to increase motivation toward assignments.

Before sending Billy back to class, I would tell him that I would talk to his teacher about our conference and suggest that she talk to him about her concerns and about what she would like to do to help him become more comfortable in school. During my conference with the teacher, I would recommend that she talk to the principal, parents, and school psychologist. I would also explain the ways in which I could be helpful to her and Billy. The inappropriate assignment of counselors to handle psychological evaluations of children for the administrator will be discussed more fully later in this chapter.

Personal Problems: Conflicts and Doubts or Confusion

Children experience feelings of loneliness, inadequacy, rejection, self-hate, and doubt similar to those experienced by adolescents and adults. Children also have doubts about their intellectual ability and worry about their classroom or playground behavior. Nelson (1972) begins his book on elementary school counseling by listing guidance needs encountered by all children and adults. His list includes a number of concerns that reflect feelings of personal inadequacy. Some of these are "No one listens to me, I wish I had more friends, I don't feel good about myself, I worry about things, I'm afraid of some things and I wish I weren't, some (or all) of this work is too hard (too easy) for me" (p. 1).

Children also express beliefs that they are dumb, unattractive, or worthless. Anger, disappointment, or bewilderment about themselves may be felt but not recognized or articulated. Counselors need to help children express, understand, and label these feelings and work toward more productive perceptions of themselves.

- *Client 5.* Doris, a second-grader, is referred by her teacher because she has difficulty in her interactions with other children. She is very sensitive to criticism and breaks into tears when students tease her or when the teacher corrects her work.

- *Client 6.* Dave, a third-grader, sees you in an assembly and runs over to ask whether he can come in to see you later in the day. When you see him, he tells you that he has been having bad dreams and that he gets stomach aches. His schoolwork is not going as well as he would like, and he is not making friends easily. His two older siblings have good academic records and seem socially secure. Dave describes himself as dumb.

- *Client 7.* Ellie is a 5-year-old kindergarten student. Her mother, Mrs. S., a single parent, calls you and asks you to talk with Ellie. Mrs. S. says that she phoned the principal, who referred her to you. Her daughter, she tells you, says she hates school. It is an effort to get Ellie to school in the morning. She cries and complains of headaches and stomach aches. At times she throws up her breakfast. Mrs. S. recently went through stormy divorce proceedings. She has custody of Ellie and two older children. She has just gotten a part-time job. She says that she is at her wit's end about Ellie.

Students with a pattern of behavior like that of Doris may readily agree to talk with a counselor because they want to do what they are asked and not risk disapproval. However, because they often have strong feelings of inadequacy, they may find it difficult to open up about their negative feelings or impulses. In these cases play media may be useful adjuncts to the interviews. At any rate, Doris needs a nonevaluative, trusting relationship in which she can express her doubts about herself and her apprehensions about others' opinions. She also needs to explore whether her expectations and/or the expectations of her parents are unrealistic.

Dave apparently is undergoing some depression and stress related to concerns about his capabilities and may be having some physical reactions to the pressure. However, as with any client expressing physical symptoms, I would recommend a medical checkup if he has not had one to determine whether there is any physical basis for the stomach aches.

Dave has initiated counseling and is open about his concerns, so the chances of helping him develop self-esteem and realistic aspirations for himself are favorable. He has shared his concerns with his parents, which should facilitate their involvement in counseling if that becomes necessary. In all probability, Dave's teacher can be useful in helping him learn more productive attitudes. Dave may want to discuss his counseling with his teacher or may prefer that the counselor make the initial contact with the teacher.

Ellie may have a moderate case of school phobia. In view of the recent stress at home, this reaction is not surprising. In situations like this one, the parent often unconsciously encourages or reinforces dependency, so it may be necessary to work with Ellie and her mother together.

Before seeing Ellie, I would ask her mother to discuss her concern with Ellie and to indicate that she has called me and would like me to talk with Ellie and herself. As stated earlier, a physical checkup would be expected unless Ellie has recently been examined by a physician.

Ellie's mother may need help in being firm and consistent in her expectation that Ellie will attend school. In addition, I would encourage Ellie to talk about some of her fears about school. Ellie's mother may find it productive to talk about the added pressures of being a single parent, any lingering emotional problems stemming from the divorce, and her aspirations in her job and personal life.

Social Problems: Interpersonal Conflicts and Feelings of Social Inadequacy

A significant portion of referrals in elementary school result from children's problems in interactions with teachers, with parents, and with peers. Teachers may refer children because a constant demand for attention or a constant need to correct or discipline them takes up an inordinate amount of teaching time. Friction may build up because of the distracting behavior of the child and/or the impatience of the teacher. Teachers may also be concerned by excessive shyness or may believe that a child's home situation is contributing to over-dependence, nuisance behavior, or underachievement. Physical fights and name calling are also common ways for children to handle their frustration and anger. If these behaviors become a child's predominant method of interaction, the teacher may refer the child to a counselor.

Parents may be concerned because they cannot control the child or because the child does not relate well to other children. Also, if a separation or divorce has occurred or is imminent, one or both parents may be worried over the effect this action might have upon the child.

Children may ask for counseling if they are unhappy or frustrated at school or at home. They may express anger at what they consider unfair expectations or discipline from parents or teachers. They may be unhappy over a recent or impending divorce or over constant friction between their parents. Sibling or peer interactions may not be going well.

- *Client 8.* Cal is a first-grader who is referred by his teacher because he has been having conflicts in class. He gets into fights with other children, interferes with other children's work, and pushes others when the teacher is not looking. The teacher has talked to his parents and has tried numerous ways of disciplining him but has not seen much improvement.

- *Client 9.* Carrie, a fifth-grader, comes to your office in tears. She has had a fight with her best friend. Now her friend is giving a party and has not invited her.

- *Client 10.* Christie, a third-grader, runs up to you in the hallway during recess and asks to see you sometime during the day. When you see her later, she exclaims that she is both angry at and afraid of her teacher. She says that her teacher picks on her and blames her for things she did not do. The teacher also yells at her and at the class, which upsets her.

- *Client 11.* Evie, a second-grader who is one of your current clients, leaves a note in the message envelope on your door asking to see you as soon as possible. When she arrives at your office, she has another second-grade student, Donna, in tow. Evie tells you that Donna is a new student in her class who is "homesick" for her former friends. Donna appears a bit abashed but volunteers that she is not happy at school and wishes she were "back home."

Cal is a typical referral by teachers in elementary school. In my first contact with Cal, I would try to determine how he perceives the referral and what he believes the purpose of counseling to be. I would indicate what behavior the teacher was concerned about and ask him whether he agreed with his teacher. During this first interview I would assure Cal that he was not being sent to me for disciplining or for a scolding but to talk about how things are going at school. I would do what I could to encourage Cal to continue seeing me but would let him know that he has the option of not having to continue.

If Cal agrees to work with me but is untalkative or belligerent, play media might be particularly useful. Drawing pictures, playing with puppets, or telling stories might help him express the anger or resentment that appears to be motivating his behavior. Getting to the source of his anger and helping him to label emotions and to express them more constructively would be the goals of counseling. If Cal and I arrived at some suggestions that might help the teacher reduce the amount of acting out or handle it productively, I would, with Cal's knowledge, share this information with the teacher, most likely with Cal present.

The counseling approach used with Carrie would depend on whether this type of rejection or difficulty is typical of Carrie's interactions with her peers. Peer friction occurs frequently with children this age and most often quickly disappears if adults do not complicate matters. If Carrie basically has good interpersonal relationships and this incident is simply a spat, I would listen sympathetically but not overreact. With some catharsis, Carrie would probably arrive at a suitable way of resolving the conflict and of mending fences. If she does not get invited to the party, I would help her handle her disappointment and anger and work with her on reestablishing her friendship.

If Carrie has had persistent problems with her peers, I would explore what in her behavior and attitudes and in the behavior and attitudes of her peers is contributing to friction. This type of exploration would require more counseling sessions than if the problem was of a temporary nature. Carrie might also profit from group counseling with students who are having problems similar to hers in their interactions with peers.

Christie presents a type of problem that requires diplomacy upon the part of the counselor as well as trust upon the part of teachers, students, and administrators in the counselor. If teachers perceive that counselors take the student's side in teacher/student conflicts, the staff as a whole may become resentful. If students perceive counselors as taking the teacher's side, they will be less likely to seek out counselors when friction occurs with teachers. It is much more productive if administrators, teachers, and students perceive the counselor's goal as helping to improve the relationship and communication between teachers and students. This problem becomes more difficult when a teacher tends to harass children. Then it may become necessary for the counselor to work with the teacher. If the teacher is not willing to consult with the counselor, the counselor may have to help the child learn strategies to minimize stress in that classroom.

In Christie's situation I would accept her feelings about the classroom interaction and work to help decrease the friction. If the teacher is approachable and Christie has the ego strength, I would encourage her to discuss her concerns with the teacher. Here role playing might prove useful. Other considerations might include whether Christie's behavior is contributing to the friction and, if so, how she might change her behavior to improve the interaction. If necessary, a conference with the teacher with Christie's participation might prove constructive.

When a counselor has worked well with a person, it is quite common for that person to refer friends. Youngsters in school often bring a student directly to the counselor, as Evie did. Donna is having a common reaction to new surroundings. It would be useful to encourage her to express some of her feelings of loss and to explore some of her apprehensions about the new situation. Perhaps she lacks social skills and needs some strategies for initiating new friendships and responding to overtures of friendship from others. However, if she has feelings of uncertainty or inadequacy sufficient to inhibit her development of social skills, time needs to be spent in helping her build self-esteem before social-skills development will be effective.

Crises

Crises occur for children through a disruption in the family, such as a severe illness, the death of a parent, a sudden separation and divorce or the threat of either, or the unexpected remarriage of a single parent. In severe and sudden family disruptions, the crisis may be even more frightening or traumatic to children than it would be to adolescents or adults because children are totally dependent upon their parents. Loss of a pet or loss of a close friend who suddenly moves away can also unduly disturb a child. At times children are confronted with a parent who does not have legal custody but suddenly shows up at the school and demands to see the child. If a counselor works in a K–8 school, traumatic reactions to drugs or alcohol or concerns about pregnancy may occur. As in any other counseling setting, elementary school counselors must have the background to alleviate immediate trauma and then decide whether to continue counseling or refer the student to an appropriate agency.

Antisocial Acts

Children's antisocial behavior includes stealing, defacing school property, truancy, breaking windows, cheating on tests, chronic lying, and physically hurting themselves or others. In the lower grades, throwing rocks at other children or at buildings or cars is a common problem. Drug or alcohol addiction may occur in the higher grades. Running away and refusing to go to school (school phobia) are other problems.

It is crucial that counselors do not handle the investigation or disciplining of children accused of antisocial behavior. As with counselors in high schools, colleges, and communities, the children must feel free to go to someone for help in dealing with antisocial impulses who is not bound to report them or expected to take disciplinary action. Counselors are not disciplinarians; they are meant to be available to help students who are engaging in inappropriate behavior to understand and try to change the behavior.

Family Counseling and Consultation

Elementary school children depend almost totally upon their parents and other significant adults for their economic, personal, and social welfare. Parents are held morally or legally responsible for the well-being of their children and for helping them develop behavior and attitudes that are not injurious to themselves or to others. Children have one teacher for all or most of the day because this arrangement is assumed to provide stability while they are away from their parents.

The close ties between parents and child give rise to closer home/school communication and to more family counseling and family consultation than goes on in other educational settings. In fact, in the area of family/child relationships, elementary school counselors resemble community counselors more than counselors in other educational settings.

Some counselors believe that the parents should always be involved when children are referred or ask for counseling because the parents exert such a strong influence upon the children. Goldenberg (1973) cautions that parental involvement may inhibit children's exploration of their emotions. My own practice, as well as that of counselor interns I have supervised, has been to decide whether family counseling is necessary to determine the timing of family interactions while counseling the child and to make sure that the child and the family are ready for communication. Family counseling will be discussed further in Chapter 9.

Examples of Elementary School Counseling in the Literature

The presenting problems of elementary school children and some procedures for counseling them are covered more amply in the literature than are the problems and procedures in secondary school, college, or community counseling. Because of the wealth of case studies in elementary school counseling, I will review some of the more representative ones as an addition to those I have presented based on my experience.

Keat (1974) briefly discusses a number of counseling theories and their application to working with children. He then provides a spectrum of counseling techniques used with individual children, including play media, relaxation exercises, and assertiveness training, and such behavioral techniques as modeling, role playing, and cognitive restructuring. He also demonstrates using the child as a consultant to help determine the direction and goals of the counseling sessions.

Keat then presents some examples with brief transcripts to show how to use these techniques. He helped an inhibited, withdrawn child assert himself more with his parents, peers, and teacher through judicious use of behavioral techniques. First, he encouraged the child to express some of his suppressed anger and to assert himself more in the counseling sessions. Then, through role playing, he had the child practice asserting himself with his father, who the boy believed did not do enough things with him. Finally, he was given homework that consisted of taking assertive action outside the counseling sessions.

Keat describes another situation in which a child with a barely noticeable cleft palate had become distressed because other children had been calling him Lippy or Bugs Bunny. Keat used an Ellis approach as a form of cognitive restructuring in which he helped the boy realize that he was unduly upset about the name calling because of his irrational belief about the magnitude of his physical disability.

Keat recommends using the child as a consultant to help determine the goals of counseling by asking what the child would like to change through counseling. One of my interns in elementary school counseling tried this approach with one of his third-grade clients when it became obvious to him and the child that consultation with the boy's parents could be profitable. When the intern learned that the parents were very hostile toward the school staff and had in the past refused to come to the school for conferences, he discussed this problem with the child. The child said that he would ask his parents to come in to see the intern. The parents responded willingly and were cooperative in the counseling sessions.

In another instance Keat used the technique of mutual story telling developed by Gardner (1971) to work with a child referred for stealing.

First, Keat asked the child to tell a story with a beginning, a middle, and an end. After she had done so, he told his own story. The child's story helped her express her conflicts and needs. Keat's story, based on the child's tale, helped her clarify some of her conflicts and develop more positive attitudes about herself.

Nelson (1972) also presents a brief examination of a variety of theories as they apply to elementary school counseling, including psychoanalysis, transactional analysis, reality therapy, behavior therapy, Gestalt theory, and existential theory. Nelson then indicates his leanings toward an existential approach and gives suggestions on using this theory with children. He also advocates the use of behavioral approaches in some work with children. He provides some breakdown of the structure of counseling interviews and gives examples on how to initiate an interview, provide structure in the interview, and terminate the counseling relationship. Some examples of appropriate listening and responding techniques are also offered. Brief presentations of counseling interactions deal with such problems as parental pressure to behave in a certain way, sibling conflict, peer friction, academic difficulties, fighting, and expectations that one be a model child.

Van Hoose (1968) approaches the counseling of individual children from a developmental point of view. He describes the developmental process and indicates the developmental tasks expected of children from 6 to 12 years of age. He sees the counselor's major responsibility as helping children develop wholesome attitudes about themselves, achieve personal independence, learn to interact with peers, and develop concepts for everyday living. Van Hoose then discusses his work with a third-grader who was having trouble with his peers and with a sixth-grader who was having academic difficulties. In both these instances the interview was a major tool in counseling. The third-grader was helped to understand his own feelings about and reactions to other children, and the sixth-grader learned to understand his concerns and to select alternative ways of resolving them.

Muro (1970) presents a transcript of one of his practicum students working with a child referred for aggressive behavior in the classroom and on the playground. The student used a Glasser reality-therapy approach in this counseling session. In this approach the clients are expected to be responsible for their own behavior at a level consistent with their age and maturity. A critical evaluation of the session notes that the emphasis was not upon discussing classroom or playground difficulty itself but on helping the child explore his own values and make judgments about his own behavior. Responsibility for change was expected of the child.

It is often asked whether primary school children profit from direct counseling. Meeks (1968) is enthusiastic about its possibilities. She briefly discusses a first-grader who had expressed concern to a counselor about not having any friends. She also verifies that children refer other children to a counselor after they have had an effective relationship with the counselor. She provides an example of a second-grader who brought a friend to the counselor because he knew the counselor could help his friend.

The Interaction of Counselors with Other School Specialists

A Comparison of Counselors with School Psychologists and Social Workers

Many school counselors, school psychologists, and social workers find it hard to differentiate their primary functions for either themselves or administrators. Role definitions prepared by each group often seem almost identical in types of duties performed. Typically, these functions include "counseling, appraisal and consultation with children, teachers, parents, other school personnel and various members of the community" (Arbuckle, 1967, p. 534). Because of this confusion, many of these professionals see themselves as rivals rather than as unique specialists who work cooperatively in a coordinated program. The difficulty in differentiating the roles of counselors, school psychologists, and social workers is particularly acute in elementary schools because more psychologists and social workers are hired at this level than at the secondary level.

I have proposed a role differentiation based upon the different psychological needs of students, school personnel, and parents expressed over the years. These different needs have led to the development of different psychological specialists uniquely trained to be primarily responsible for these different needs (Nugent, 1973). My contention is that school psychologists and social workers should be primarily responsible for involuntary referrals, in which some administrative action is expected. Counselors should handle the voluntary referrals, in which the student can choose whether to have counseling, and in which administrative involvement is not anticipated.

In some situations the child's behavior is so disruptive or debilitating, learning problems are so acute, or the home situation is so poor that intervention becomes necessary. In these cases the child no longer has the option of refusing help, and the problem goes beyond the purview of the teacher. The child either does not recognize the problem or does not respond to ordinary attempts to help. Also, in comparison to counseling referrals, the individuals referring the student expect some administrative action or recommendation to evolve from the intervention and evaluation.

Psychologists and social workers came to be hired in schools because of administrators' requests for psychological and social intervention. These specialists' training is geared to these types of referrals. A school psychologist should be the primary resource when behavior or learning difficulties arise in the classroom that require administrative psychological intervention and consultation. After assessing the situation through conferences with the child, teacher, and parents, the psychologist may make specific recommendations about treatment—for example, placement in a special class or development of a special learning program. A social worker, by virtue of background and training, should have unique responsibility when family interactions are poor or school/home relationships are so unproductive that intervention is considered necessary for the child to function in school. Changes in the home environment may result from the social worker's interaction with the family.

When school psychologists and social workers function as administrative consultants for school districts, counselors can work with students with normal developmental concerns. Recognition of such needs developed only recently in the schools, and counselors are uniquely prepared to work with these needs. These concerns can be handled by giving the students a choice and by making the counseling service available and attractive to them.

If the role distinctions are clearer, more appropriate referrals can be expected among these three kinds of psychologically oriented specialists. In some situations a counselor can help the teacher, the student, or the parents determine whether the problem is severe enough to warrant a consultation between the teacher or the parents and the school psychologist or social worker. Also, if a counselor accepts an initial referral and finds that an evaluation for administrative action may be necessary, he or she can refer the student and the parents or teacher to the principal, who can then decide whether a referral to the school psychologist or social worker seems necessary. If the school psychologist or social worker, after an evaluation, believes that the child needs counseling, a referral can be made. At times a counselor may work with the child and the other professionals with the parents. Finally, cross-referrals between counselors and school nurses, speech therapists, or reading consultants can occur more easily because the unique contribution of each of the other specialists has been spelled out more clearly.

The Counselor as Part of a Team of Specialists

Some writers on elementary school counseling (for example, Faust, 1968b; Keat, 1974) advocate a team approach to working with children's problems. These authors assume that each specialist has developed unique skills for working with children and that pooling these special skills will benefit the children. This system usually includes a meeting of the psychologist, social worker, counselor, nurse, teacher, and principal, who try to determine how severe the problem is and what can be done to alleviate it. Decisions are made about grade placement, involvement of the parents, possibilities of further evaluation, advisability of referral to an agency, and development of educational plans tailored to the individual.

This approach has been used for a number of years and obviously has the advantage of specialists' sharing expertise for the welfare of the child. Counselors have been used in a number of ways. Often they are expected to coordinate the information and lead the discussion. At times they are expected to handle the evaluation and screening. I am in favor of counselors' being involved with any or all other staff members to help children, but I have serious reservations about a counselor's assuming responsibility for diagnosis and evaluation in a team conference. These reservations apply to all problems needing this type of evaluation, but they apply even more if the student being evaluated in the conference is a current or former client. In this case the ethical problem of confidentiality arises. In states in which privileged communication has been granted the client and/or the client's parents, the problem becomes a legal one. In addition, if the counselor coordinates these sessions and handles evaluation, teachers, parents, and, most important, students will begin to perceive the counselor as an arm of the administration.

This team approach has increased in scope since the passage of PL 94–142 in 1975. This legislation, called the Education for All Handicapped Children Act, establishes the right of all children to a free, appropriate public education regardless of how seriously they are handicapped. The act affects professional-counseling programs at all levels in the public schools, and I will discuss it further in the last chapter, which deals with implementing counseling programs. At this point the main concern is that the act requires a team child-study process similar to the team conference procedure discussed above to determine whether the child is handicapped. If the child is handicapped, an Individual Education Plan (IEP) must be developed by members of the team and carried out by the school staff. If elementary school counselors become overly involved in the assessment procedures and the development of learning packages or in the monitoring or coordinating of conferences, they may be acting in violation of ethical and legal codes of confidentiality. Also, counselors may well end up neglecting important counselor functions.

Another problem is that elementary school counselors may not have had the course work and supervised internships necessary for handling diagnostic work of an administrative or institutional nature. The activities expected are much more similar to those of the school psychologist, whose training in testing for learning disabilities is extensive.

Counselors must guard against being assigned as psychometrician aides for school psychologists who become too burdened with the demands placed upon them by PL 94–142. Rather, more school psychologists should be employed to handle the diagnostic and evaluative work. This plan frees counselors for counseling and the supplementary functions involved in a counseling program, such as consultation, psychological education, and social-change activities.

Elementary School Counselors and Community Agencies

All school counselors should develop close ties with community mental-health and counseling agencies. In particular, elementary school counselors need to be aware of the resources available for family and marriage counseling when problems of this sort come to their attention and prove to be beyond the scope of the services the school can offer. Also, when a child demonstrates serious emotional difficulties or when a severe crisis leaves a child with lingering emotional problems, a referral for outside counseling may be in order.

Projects and Activities

1. *Interview elementary school counselors, psychologists, and social workers who are working in the same school district. How does each group perceive its unique responsibilities? How well do the various specialists work together?*
2. *An elementary school counselor is asked to be a member of a team for evaluating whether a student has a learning disability. Other team members include the school psychologist, the social worker, the teacher, and the principal. The student happens to be one of her clients. Considering professional-role definitions and ethical concerns about confidentiality, how should she respond? (See author's comments below.)*
3. *Read rationales for classroom observation of potential clients by elementary school counselors. Compare these rationales with the view that such observation can hinder the development of trusting counseling relationships. Discuss these arguments as they relate to minors' right to privacy.*
4. *A teacher tells a counselor that she wants to talk to him about a student in her class who is in counseling. The counselor explains that he wants to get permission from the student in order to preserve confidentiality. Later the principal tells the counselor that the teacher is upset because he acted as though she could not be trusted. Consider how this situation could be handled so as to preserve confidentiality and yet not antagonize the teacher. (See author's comments below.)*
5. *Assume that a new counselor is meeting with a group of teachers to discuss her role and to suggest guidelines for referral. A teacher tells the counselor that he is confused about referral for children who are creating minor discipline problems. He asks the counselor when to refer a student to the principal*

and when to refer one to her. Write a response clarifying referrals. (See author's comments below.)

6. *Suppose that Doris (Client 5) has a teacher whom you believe is hypercritical without her being aware of it. How might you involve the teacher in order to improve the classroom environment for Doris and the other students in the class? (See author's comments below.)*

7. *A 7-year-old child is in counseling. A parent who does not have legal custody or visiting rights comes to the counselor's office, demands to see the child, and wants to know what he has been doing with the child. How does the counselor respond? (See author's comments below.)*

8. *Invite an elementary school counselor and a counselor working with children in a community agency to talk with your group about the types of children's concerns with which they work. Ask them to discuss their use of play media.*

9. *You are asked to talk at a PTA meeting about your role as a counselor. Outline what you believe would be important considerations to include. Compare your ideas with the ASCA's role definition.*

10. *Compose a memo that could be sent to parents at the beginning of the academic year that defines your role and duties. Write the memo in such a way as to include confidentiality and freedom of choice as important components in counseling.*

11. *A third-grader asks you for counseling because he does not like school and does not have any friends. His parents object to his seeing you. The child shows up at your door. How would you handle this situation? (See author's comments below.)*

Author's Comments

Activity 2. *The counselor should explain her ethical responsibility to the student. The development of the trusting, nonevaluative relationship necessary for counseling can be impeded if she gives out information obtained in confidence in counseling and if she assumes an evaluative function leading to an administrative decision. The APGA code of ethics covers these points in Section B and Section B12. If the counselor believes that she can be helpful to the student by working with the team, she can indicate this belief to the student with her reasons for this belief. She should be sure that this interaction will not interfere with the counseling relationship. If such action is taken, the student should be aware of what the counselor is sharing. The team must be willing for the counselor to share with the student her interactions with the team. This procedure is consistent with my belief that keeping children informed about and involved in psychological processes is not only ethically sound but therapeutically more effective.*

Activity 4. *The counselor should commend the teacher for her interest in the child. Then he should explain to the teacher that it is vitally important to let the child know that the teacher believes it will be helpful to talk to the counselor. This* *can be done by the teacher's indicating to the child that she is interested in talking to the counselor and giving her reasons for wanting to talk to him. Or the counselor could tell the child that the teacher is interested and ask the child whether a conference between teacher and counselor would be helpful. All three should agree on what information will be shared. The counselor should emphasize to the teacher the importance of the child's maintaining trust in both the counselor and the teacher. If the child is reluctant to involve the teacher, the counselor can discuss this reluctance with the child and explain to the teacher that it might be best for the teacher to communicate directly with the student about her interest and concerns.*

Activity 5.   *The counselor should recommend that a referral to the counselor is in order if the teacher and the student agree that the referral is for the purpose of the student's exploring the behavior and trying to improve teacher/student interaction. If the teacher has reached a point where he wants disciplinary or administrative action, the student should be sent to the administrator. In the counseling referral the student has a choice; in the administrative referral the student has no choice. The administrator may talk with the student, may take disciplinary action, or may confer with teacher and student. The administrator may also refer the student to the counselor to discuss the classroom situation with a view of trying to improve it. The principal's referral should be a voluntary one; that is, disciplinary action is not contingent upon whether the student agrees to see a counselor.*

Activity 6.   *With Doris's awareness and involvement, you might arrange a conference with Doris's teacher and ask her how she perceives their interaction and what difficulties she is having in responding to Doris. Suggestions can be made on how to respond more effectively to Doris's behavior and how to approach her differently. If the teacher is not responsive, you must concentrate on helping Doris gain insights, more self-acceptance, and more effective behaviors, so that she will respond less defensively to personal criticism or to criticism of others important to her.*

Activity 7.   *The counselor should indicate to the parent that there are legal questions involved in seeing the child that require that he talk with the principal, who is the legal administrative head of the school. Under no circumstances should the counselor get into a discussion about his counseling with the student.*

Activity 11.   *I would see the student because he asked to see me himself. First, I would ascertain that he does not have a severe emotional problem or a severe learning disability that might require a referral to an outside agency or might suggest an administrative evaluation. If either condition exists, I would indicate to the child the necessity of getting parental involvement and the need for possible referral. If he is expressing a normal concern about himself, his relationships, or his academic progress, I would ask him whether he is aware of his parents' objections and whether he has told his parents about his desire to continue seeing me. If he* *has not, I would strongly recommend that he do so and that he try to get his parents in for a conference with both of us about the process of counseling. Most parents, if they are aware that their child has asked for counseling and that no administrative action is necessary, would withdraw their objections. If the parents persisted in their objections and the child persisted in coming in to see me, I would feel it a professional obligation to see the child. The parent consultation would include exploring the rights and responsibilities of minors and of adults. I would inform the administrator of my decision and have legal counsel available to explore the rights and responsibilities of minors and of parents. Note the difference when a child is seen involuntarily or for an administrative evaluation, as typically happens with school psychologists or social workers. Then I firmly believe that the parents must be informed and give their consent. In some states this is a legal requirement. I support that requirement.*

7

Individual Counseling in Colleges

The Development of College Counseling

In the early 1900s the social and economic factors that led to the development of vocationally oriented counseling in secondary schools did not significantly influence college counseling services. Student personnel work consisted of advisement, educational guidance, and admissions services, with very little emphasis on vocational concerns (Tolbert, 1978). Since relatively few students attended college and most of those who did were academically oriented and since colleges offered strong liberal-arts rather than vocationally related curriculums, there seemed to be little need for vocational guidance.

In the 1930s and 1940s, college attendance increased, as did interest in preparation for occupations. The University of Minnesota, under people like Williamson, developed a college counseling center based upon vocational and educational needs of students. Personal concerns of students were not ignored but were not a major focus. This program was very similar to programs considered necessary in secondary schools. Williamson's 1950 book, *Counseling Adolescents,* could apply to either setting. Under this plan counseling centers were considered an essential part of student personnel services, much like counseling in public schools developed as a part of guidance services. In 1946 the Veterans Administration decisions to fund training programs for doctoral programs in counseling psychology and to subsidize vocational counseling for veterans of World War II spurred the development of college counseling centers like Williamson's throughout the United States.

Two trends in the 1950s broadened the base of counseling centers to include more recognition of students' social and personal concerns. Super (1953) and others began to describe vocational development as part of total personality development, and Rogers (1951) severely criticized the diagnosis and assessment emphasis in counseling. The idea that vocational development is an intrinsic part of total personality development and that vocational choice often is an implementation of the self-concept encouraged some counseling-center staffs to consider conflicts about vocational planning and choice as personal conflicts. In some centers this attitude was combined with Rogers's emphasis upon personal growth, so that a variety of vocational, educational, personal, and social concerns of students were handled. In other centers Rogers's influence was so great that testing, assessment, diagnosis, and vocational counseling and any approaches besides the client-centered one were virtually ignored. In these centers, counseling for self-actualization took over. Some centers became indistinguishable from mental-health clinics using Rogers's approach.

The Confusion between Counseling and Student Personnel Work

During the late 1960s and the early 1970s, it became evident at annual national meetings of counseling-center directors that their staffs were experiencing confusion over professional identity and the major purpose of counseling centers. Some of the confusion resulted from the extremely different philosophical views of Williamson and Rogers about counseling. But further complications occurred when budgets for student services were severely cut and demands for accountability of student services arose from administrators. Not only was the necessity for counseling services questioned, but all of the work of student personnel workers came under fire. Not only counselors questioned their professional identity; so did student personnel administrators.

The confusion over professional identities in both groups was heightened as a strong trend toward a human-development model began to influence student personnel administrative work and training. Through this model student personnel workers began to perceive themselves as psychological educators. This view of student personnel work was fostered not only by a reaction to real or threatened budget cuts but also by a move away from outdated surrogate-parent roles of deans of students and associate deans of students. In the early 1960s many colleges were still requiring women to live on campus. Deans of students, deans of men, deans of women, and directors of residence halls were functioning as fair, friendly, on-campus parents involved in disciplining students, watching over their morals, and developing their social lives. When the legal-majority age dropped from 21 to 18 and when the social upheaval of the 1960s led to student desire for autonomy, the parental role of student personnel administrators became obsolete. As a result of these factors, a tug-of-war developed between counseling-center staffs and student personnel administrators over who was responsible for offering counseling.

Some student personnel workers began to describe student personnel work in terms of a human-development model in response to the social changes. This approach is characterized as "the application of human development concepts in postsecondary settings so that everyone involved can master increasingly complex developmental tasks, achieve self-direction and become interdependent" (T. K. Miller & Prince, 1976, p. 3). The term *student affairs* was used for the major administrative subdivision of student personnel services. Student-affairs workers were staff members who carried out counseling, advisement, encouragement of personal growth, and the like. The title of student development educator was coined to describe a faculty member or an administrator interested or engaged in the student-affairs profession. This student-affairs professional "purposefully works to bring about the growth of all engaged in higher education" (T. K. Miller & Prince, 1976, p. 3).

People supporting this model of student services advocated the organization of student-development or student-life centers that would be staffed by professional counselors, deans, and other student personnel administrators. The major purpose would be to help students' personal growth. Counseling in these centers would be primarily a psychological-education activity in which fairly simple universal relationships and communication skills would be taught to students, faculty, and staff.

As indicated earlier, some counselors who were center directors such as Morrill, Ivey, and Oetting (1968), urged directors to organize counseling centers based on a psychological-education model of student affairs. In this system student personnel administrators and the counseling-center staff would function together in a student-development or student-life center as educators for the personal growth of students and faculty. All staff members would be engaged in training students, faculty, and other college staffs to counsel, to improve the psychological climate in classrooms, and to improve communication throughout the campus. A major argument presented against most existing counseling centers was that they were based on a clinical model and neglected outreach activities.

The Reaction of the Counseling Profession

These attempts to incorporate counseling centers into personal-growth centers increased the unrest and confusion among counseling-center directors and in counseling psychology. In response to the confusion, Kirk, Free, Johnson, Michel, Roston, Warman, and other counseling-center directors developed Guidelines for University and College Counseling Centers. These guidelines were based upon input from counseling-center directors throughout the United States, were agreed upon at a national meeting of counseling-center directors in 1970, and were published in *American Psychologist* in June 1971. The guidelines reaffirmed counseling as the primary function of counselors and included numerous activities, such as consultation, group activities, and psychological education, as important additional functions.

Some directors of college counseling centers were not satisfied with these guidelines and strongly urged that counseling centers take a new direction toward either the psychological-education models mentioned earlier or social engineering. Warnath (1971, 1973a) was a most persistent and highly vocal critic of counseling centers. A director himself, he asserted that professional associations representing college counseling centers lacked the professional leadership, power, or motivation to help counseling-center staffs in their struggle against unreasonable administrative demands. Emphasizing that some college counseling centers were fighting for existence or were being dismantled, Warnath argued that counseling centers had to face reality and change directions. He believed that the scientific-practitioner model, the medical model, and the vocational-testing model were at the core of the difficulties. Advocating a need to be accountable to administrator and students, he recommended that counseling-center staffs leave their cloistered offices, become social engineers, and engage in outreach activities designed to change the institutions for the betterment of students.

In a book of readings that Warnath edited, *New Directions for College Counselors* (1973a), consultation, psychological education, and systems training were recommended as primary roles for counselors. Again, these suggestions for college counselors were remarkably like those for counselors in the public schools.

Note that Warnath was expressing strong criticism of professional associations for not backing up counseling-center directors in handling administrators' demands. At the same time he was criticizing the counselor role as too narrow. His solution was to change the role radically to that of an agent of social change deeply involved in educating the college community. Although his ideas were similar to those of student personnel workers, they were not identical. He perceived counseling as a specialized skill but was pushing for a change in emphasis rather than simplifying counseling into skills acquisition.

Counseling-Center Activities, 1960–1970

In retrospect, Warnath's criticism that professional associations were not giving necessary leadership or strength to counseling-center staffs was legitimate. In fact, this lack has continually proved to be a key factor preventing counselors from clarifying and asserting a strong, productive professional identity.

However, he was inaccurate in two other contentions. One was that counseling-center staffs were confining themselves to their offices, and the second was that counseling-center problems essentially would dissolve if the centers would engage in outreach functions. Surveys of counseling-center activities taken from the early 1960s to the early 1970s, at the time Warnath was writing, indicate that most centers had given up their earlier preoccupation with individual counseling and were actively engaged in consultation, training, and psychological education. Yet they were still having problems. The core of the difficulty lay in their not presenting a unique professional identity with backing from the professional associations.

In 1965, data collected in a national survey of 461 college counseling centers (Nugent & Pareis, 1968) showed that counseling-center staffs, in addition to offering individual counseling, were offering faculty consultation (88%), academic advisement (71%), reading and study skills (67%), testing and consultation with administrators (67%), research on counseling (54%), group counseling (50%), and training for graduate students (33%). Unfortunately, the survey did not include questions about training and consultation for residence aides, which were being carried out on some campuses. Gallagher and Demos (1970) indicate that in the late 1950s consultation for residence halls was being offered by counseling centers in San Jose, California, and Denver. In 1962 at Western Washington University, the residence director and I, as counseling-center director, initiated training and supervision for residence aides. In addition, staff counselors served as consultants to various residence halls, did some direct counseling with students in the dorms, and handled crisis interventions.

These activities are similar to those Clark (1970) found in a survey of counseling centers at 50 colleges with an enrollment of more than 10,000. Gallagher and Demos, describing the activities of a number of college counseling centers on the West Coast, indicated that a composite of counseling-center brochures in 1970 included individual and group counseling—specifically, personal, social, vocational, educational, marriage, and family counseling. Ten other services were also listed: testing, foreign-student affairs, coordination of foreign study, veterans' affairs, professional development and in-service training, counseling internships, coordination of academic advisement, freshmen seminars, consultation service, and research.

Ironically, Warnath (1971) sharply criticized counseling-center staffs for holing up in their offices, yet he at the same time presented data refuting that contention: David Mills's 1970 survey of data from the College Counseling Center Data Bank at the University of Maryland was included in the index of Warnath's book. This survey showed that only 10% of 204 centers were not involved in outreach activities. The outreach projects specified by these centers included a myriad of activities centering on consultation with faculty and staff; residence-hall consultation; paraprofessional training; the establishment of crisis-center hot lines; the teaching of communication skills to various campus constituents; the direction of groups for women and couples and drug, alcohol, and for persons with sex concerns; and work with minorities.

The Need to Reaffirm a Unique Professional Identity

The historical perspective demonstrates that college counseling centers have responded to various pressures in psychology and education in trying to define their role. Some of these psychological and educational trends have been positive, as can be seen in the increased outreach and group activities. However, history also shows that these pressures have kept the profession in turmoil and have had some deleterious effects. The 1977 issue of *The Counseling Psychologist* entitled *Professional Identity* demonstrates that counseling psychologists are torn between the psychological-education thrust of student personnel administration and the thrust to become licensed for private practice on an equal basis with clinical psychologists.

Counseling-center directors and staffs need to specify the unique contribution they make to a college community. It is crucial for them to examine the common elements in the APGA (1974) description of postsecondary counselors, Kirk and her colleagues' 1971 Guidelines for University and College Counseling Services, and the APA's Division 17 Standards for Providers of Counseling Psychological Services (1979) and to articulate the special skills that distinguish them from clinical psychologists, student personnel administrators, and psychological educators involved in teacher training.

A key factor in determining professional identity is to clarify students' needs for professional counseling and the ways in which these needs differ from the needs of students served by student personnel workers or clinical and psychiatric services. Then counseling staffs need to be sure that students and staff have an accurate perception of the counseling-center services through appropriate publicizing of the services.

An excellent resource for college counseling centers is *A Handbook and Guide for the College and University Counseling Center* (Schoenberg, 1978). This handbook contains articles by directors of college and university counseling centers and by college and university counselors. The articles cover the history and philosophy of college counseling, the structure and organization of college counseling centers, and descriptions of formal and informal counseling programs. Also included are activities important to the development and operation of a successful counseling center such as the training function of a center, referral and case management, and university relations. In general, the guide presents a comprehensive, balanced approach that is consistent with many of the ideas in this book.

Students' Expressed Needs for Counseling

The literature on college counseling shows that the counseling needs of students have not been surveyed sufficiently, nor have the opinions of students about counseling centers been surveyed with any consistency (A. R. Benedict, Apsler, & Morrison, 1977). The surveys that have been done on student needs have consistently shown that students express needs for counseling about personal, social, vocational, and educational conflicts or concerns. These needs persist in spite of the admonitions that counseling is antiquated, old fashioned, and ineffective.

Kramer, Berger, and Miller (1974) found in a survey of undergraduates and graduates at Cornell University that the two most pervasive areas of student concern were vocational problems and personal unhappiness. In a survey of student counseling needs at the Charles River campus of Boston University, a campus of 22,000 students, 76% of the 228 respondents indicated that they needed help with one or more problems. More than 85% said that the center should provide help with any type of personal problem, 52% indicated that vocational counseling should be available, and 47% checked educational counseling. It is likely that some students considered vocational and educational conflicts as personal ones (A. R. Benedict et al., 1977).

Students' Perception of a Counseling Center

The Boston study just described included student perceptions of the counseling services as well as counseling needs. The investigators found that student needs closely matched the services offered by the counseling center but that many students did not realize that these services were available. An important finding was that 96% of the respondents believed that a counseling center offering necessary services is essential for a college campus. Students said that a counseling center is necessary because "students cannot always turn to peers or faculty with problems" and "only specially trained counselors can best handle student problems" (A. R. Benedict et al., 1977, p. 112). The authors concluded that the center had failed to project its image adequately to students. They recommended that appropriate information be channeled to students.

Sources of Referrals for Counseling

Counseling-center staffs try to encourage students to ask for counseling, but they should also educate faculty members, administrators, and service and dormitory personnel about the extent of their services, In addition, guidelines on when and how to refer students should be developed by the counseling staff for use by members of the other college staffs.

Faculty members who are interested in students and who have small enough classes to get to know students will respond much as public school teachers do if they understand the services and trust the counseling-center staff. They will refer students having academic difficulties or showing signs of emotional blocking or emotional distress. They will also consult with the counseling-center staff about students they believe need help.

Administrators and administrative committees, such as scholastic standing and student disciplinary committees, may see the counseling center as a resource for students having problems in studying or in controlling antisocial impulses. Counseling in these cases should still be perceived as voluntary. For example, staying in school should not be dependent upon getting counseling. Rather, after an administrative decision is made based upon academic progress or personal behavior, counseling can be recommended to the student.

Directors of residence halls and their aides can contribute greatly to the success of a counseling center. If they trust and respect the counseling staff, they will be an excellent source for referral of on-campus students. Other student-affairs administrative staff are also potentially a good source for referral. Since these groups are particularly interested in the personal and social development of the student, they are likely to refer students who are struggling with vocational, personal, or interpersonal concerns. Also, cross-referrals between the counseling center and other offices, such as the placement bureau or the financial-aid office, can be productive.

Finally, as the counseling center develops appropriate outreach activities in psychological education and consults with women's groups, minority workshops, and the like, referrals from these groups can be anticipated.

The Presenting Problems of College Students

General Comments

As one might anticipate from the survey of college students' needs, the presenting problems of college students parallel those encountered in high schools. They, too, center around vocational/educational, personal, and social decisions that can cause self-doubt or confusion. Like high school students, college students are in an educational setting with requirements they must fulfill to graduate and policies they must agree to follow in order to remain in school. They differ from high school students in that almost all of them are of legal age, so that they are primarily responsible for their behavior rather than sharing responsibility with their parents. They differ also in that they are not legally compelled to attend school. Another factor is that their flexible schedules permit easier access to the counseling center.

Ironically, although they are legally adults, many college students are in a more ambiguous dependence/independence situation than are high school students. Quite a number are still bound to their parents because of the need for financial aid to handle the high costs of education. Their ability to get federal loans is dependent upon their parents' income, but they are ultimately responsible for paying back these loans and the interest on them after graduation. If they work, their jobs usually involve menial tasks at odd hours and the possibility that they will jeopardize their grade-point average. Thus, significant numbers of college students remain in a state of suspended immaturity and dependence compared to noncollege persons their own age who find jobs, begin careers, and have a steady income.

It is true that college students have more choice of instructors than in high school and that the instructors are not usually involved in disciplinary measures. However, a poor relationship with a certain instructor can hinder or prevent a student's acceptance into a specialized professional curriculum. Similarly, poor grades in a particular course can have a significant effect upon acceptance into graduate school.

Since most college students are of legal age and since some of them are married, have families, or have started college later than most freshmen do, some presenting problems resemble those of clients in community counseling. Concerns about marriage problems, career change, aging parents, and child care are likely to crop up. These problems may show up more often in 2-year, community colleges because the average age of the students is higher than in 4-year colleges.

Because of the similarity of college and community presenting problems to high school concerns, I will discuss the short case studies more briefly in this chapter and the next. The briefer discussion may also permit some more advanced readers to speculate on how they would tackle some of these problems in ways different from those presented here.

As with the student problems presented in Chapter 5, I would feel free to use tests and inventories to help clients explore their interests and abilities, but I would keep in mind the potential sex and cultural biases of some tests.

The inventories and tests used most frequently by counseling staffs over the years have been the Strong Vocational Interest Blank (now the Strong-Campbell Interest Inventory), the Minnesota Multiphasic Personality Inventory (MMPI), and the Wechsler Adult Intelligence Scale (WAIS). Other measures used with some frequency are the Kuder Preference Record, the Edwards Personal Preference Schedule, the Bennett Mechanical Comprehension Test, and the Minnesota Spatial Relations Test. Group intelligence tests, such as the Otis Quick-Scoring Mental Ability Test, and the Cooperative School and College Ability Tests (SCAT) are also used in some centers. As one might anticipate, counseling staffs and individual staff members tend to select groups of tests and inventories that they collectively and/or personally find useful.

Vocational/Educational Concerns

In the 1960s, during the student activism and the push for alternative life-styles, there was less student interest in exploring more traditional vocational choices or in attaining high grade-point averages. Some counseling centers, swept up in the cries for personal growth and social action, neglected vocational counseling or began to perceive the vocational concerns of students as secondary ones. Currently, vocational concerns and academic success appear to be foremost in the minds of students. Many view the shrinking labor market and the overcrowded professions with dismay and even feelings of panic. Jobs are not readily available upon graduation, and professional-school entrance requirements have become stiffer.

Like high school students, college students request counseling for vocational and educational concerns or decisions because they need more information about themselves or about occupations or because they have conflicts with others over their plans or because they have doubts about educational or career directions.

More refined decisions about careers are expected in colleges than in secondary schools. In most colleges, students are forced to select a major. Also, some students are concerned about entrance into graduate school. Some students may have difficulty deciding which vocational interest to pursue because they have two or more interests that appear to conflict. Other students may be at a complete loss over an appropriate major. Or parents may try to influence a son or daughter to select a particular major whether or not the student has any interest or ability in that direction.

An increasing group of potential clients are women who have raised families and have decided to return to school after many years at home. They often express confusion about career choice and doubts about their ability to handle academic work. Some must also face the anxiety of a husband who is ambivalent about his wife striking out on her own.

Educational problems may often be of more concern to college students than they are to public school students. College students pay fees toward their education, and, unlike most public school students, they can and do flunk out. Requests for counseling and referrals from faculty members and deans of students can be expected regarding poor scholastic standing. Students may also want to discuss the advisability of dropping out of school.

In these cases, the student may be in the wrong major, may be unsuited for college, or may be working too many hours in order to earn enough money to stay there. On the other hand, students may lack motivation because they see no purpose in attending school. Or some personal concerns may be interfering with academic progress.

A relatively frequent educational concern of students is getting a mental block on tests, on math assignments, in speeches before a class, and in writing English themes or term papers. These blocks are often a result of anxiety reactions, which are common in high school as well.

- *Client 1.* Janet, who is 32, requests counseling because she is concerned about her academic progress and about her vocational goals. She has returned to college after 13 years of marriage and is a sophomore. Her children are 11 and 9 years old. Her husband is a busy executive in a local advertising agency. Janet says that he supports her attending college but is too busy to give much help at home. Janet finds schoolwork stimulating but overwhelming, particularly since she must make arrangements for child care and assume the major responsibility for the home. She also is not sure what career she wants. Law school and environmental science are two possibilities. Janet looks anxious and fatigued.

- *Client 2.* Neil, a freshman, is taking a math course required for graduation. He was referred to the counseling center by his math teacher. Neil tells you that he does well in his homework assignments but blanks out on tests. He studies hard, but as soon as the test is handed out, he becomes immobilized. The math teacher is sympathetic and believes that Neil understands his work but has no option but to fail him on tests.

- *Client 3.* Jay, a senior in psychology, has an "A" average. He wants to do graduate work in psychology and obtain a doctorate in clinical psychology. However, he has been rejected by every graduate school to which he has applied. He feels depressed and uncertain of himself.

- *Client 4.* Roberta is a sophomore who has to declare a major. She describes herself as having a wide range of interests with excellent grades in all of her subjects. She is motivated to work but has only vague notions about possible vocations. She feels restless, somewhat anxious, and uncertain about the future.

- *Client 5.* Wilma will be graduating in June with a degree in philosophy. She had planned to go on to graduate work in philosophy but finds that impossible financially. She wants to find employment but has no idea of what she is interested in or is capable of handling. She had registered at the placement bureau and was referred to the counseling center.

- *Client 6.* Stuart will be graduating in June with a degree in electrical engineering. He makes an appointment for vocational counseling. He says that he is happy with electrical engineering but is having trouble finding a job. He wants to stay in the area.

Janet has to come to grips with the amount of responsibility she is taking for the management of the family and the household before productive exploration of her career plans can occur. Any residual guilt feelings about leaving her children or any doubts about her academic ability that may be contributing to her anxiety must be worked through. The degree to which her husband is willing and able to share responsibility for the home and children and the degree to which she has, so far, been able to accept his help need discussion. Perhaps some joint counseling is necessary. When these factors are clarified, then the areas of law and environmental science can be explored from the standpoint of how her interests, abilities, and values relate to either field or to other fields. Interest inventories, personality inventories, and any other appropriate testing may be used if considered necessary. If she appears to need environmental support for her plans, I would encourage her to seek out women's groups on campus that would be supportive.

Neil's problem presents a common type of academic concern. These blockages occur most frequently in math, speech, and English classes, but they can happen in almost any testing situation. I would help Neil explore some of the reasons why he becomes so anxious that he cannot complete a math test successfully. He obviously is capable of understanding math concepts, since he does well on homework assignments. Thus the immobilization may represent an unreasonable anxiety about the consequences of failing, may be part of an underlying belief that he needs to be superior or perfect in all his work, or may be a fear conditioned by poor teaching in earlier math experiences. If Neil responds well to discussions about the source of his fear and about his overreaction to it, his anxiety may be reduced sufficiently for him to perform better on tests.

Some counselors might use Wolpe's (1973) desensitization techniques with Neil. I will discuss Wolpe's procedures more fully later in this chapter (see Case 10, Al's phobia). At this point, it is sufficient to say that Neil would be taught to relax systematically and then to visualize an increasing hierarchy of anxiety-provoking situations. Through imagining himself relaxed in the tension-producing situation, Neil will presumably learn to relax during the actual test-taking experience.

Jay is confronting something common for many students—graduate work in a highly crowded field or in programs that stringently limit enrollment. He needs help in maintaining perspective about his own ability and worth. I would explore with him his procedures in applying for various programs and his selection of schools and would also recommend that he consider fields related to clinical psychology. This reexamination of career goals might require vocational and academic appraisal as well as exploration of the counseling-center occupational-resource library.

Roberta's need for exploration of vocations was covered in case studies in Chapter 5. Roberta might need to survey various fields through discussions and appraisal of her interests, abilities, and personality characteristics, as well as reviewing some occupational material.

The presenting problems of Wilma and Stuart demonstrate the difference between the services of a placement office and a counseling center, as well as the importance of cross-referrals between the two agencies. Wilma needs to survey thoroughly her own attributes and the attributes of jobs in order to get some direction in job seeking. Then a referral to the placement bureau would be appropriate for information and help in specific job seeking and placement. Stuart has made a vocational choice with which he is apparently happy. The placement-bureau staff has the expertise and the listings to help him find a job. There he could get help in developing a résumé, practicing job-interviewing skills, tracking down companies with possible openings, and evaluating which companies offer the most promise for advancement.

It should be clear that the vocational concerns of Janet, Jay, and Roberta fall within the province of the counseling center, not the placement bureau. Conflicts or anxieties related to vocational planning or choice need to be worked through rather than exploring possible jobs or methods of finding one.

Personal Concerns

In addition to personal concerns about vocational choice, college students have continuing questions about traditional social mores, sexual patterns, and lifestyles. Some students begin to explore new religions or philosophical beliefs. As students move away from the immediate jurisdiction of their parents, there is less activity based upon rebellion against adults and more exploration of new behaviors based upon curiosity. Students may request counseling because they have mixed feelings about these new alternatives in behavior.

Self-doubt and uncertainties about managing one's life are more frequent than in high school. Homesickness can occur early in the freshman year. If severe, it can lead to dropping out of school if professional-counseling help is not available. Students may become restless if they believe that they are floundering in school while other people their own age are successfully employed. Anxieties may also increase for college students as they near graduation and have to leave the security of school to enter the work world.

Questions and concerns about homosexuality, lesbianism, and bisexuality are more frequently raised by college students than by high school students. College students will seek out counseling if they trust counselors and believe that counselors will recognize their right to their own sexual preferences regardless of the counselors' orientation.

- *Client 7.* Vivian is a 20-year-old junior who has found herself feeling attracted to women. She has dated men and has had some intimate heterosexual relationships, which have been pleasant. She has had no relationship with women sexually. In a discussion with members of the campus Gay Liberation group, it was suggested that she seek counseling because of her ambivalence. Her preoccupation with her sexual concerns is interfering with schoolwork.

- *Client 8.* Georgia is a 20-year-old junior who describes herself as lacking motivation and self-discipline. She has not been attending classes regularly and has been sleeping in past her first class. Neither college nor social life is stimulating. She has done well academically but is beginning to have trouble in some of her courses. She attended a women's consciousness-raising psychological-education group jointly sponsored by the student-affairs office and the counseling center. Her apathy induced leaders of the group to refer her for counseling.

- *Client 9.* Donald, a sophomore, complains of restlessness and feelings of depression. His schoolwork has been going well, and he claims that he is satisfied with his major field of journalism. He expresses pessimism about the future of humanity. Concerns about dishonest politicians, the threat of nuclear power, and the possibility of war make him feel depressed and hopeless about the future.

- *Client 10.* Al says that he has a phobia about going to a dentist. He has been told that further neglect of his teeth may lead to serious gum problems. He makes appointments and then manages to talk himself out of going.

- *Client 11.* Gina is a freshman referred by a residence aide. Gina is experiencing severe homesickness. She feels nauseous, has periods of crying, and has missed classes. She has been thinking of dropping out of school. She has phoned her parents, who have tried to convince her to work it out on campus.

- *Client 12.* Pete is a 26-year-old student who has been experiencing anxiety attacks. He had attended college several years ago and had dropped out because of emotional problems. He was later involuntarily hospitalized for 6 months. Upon his release it was recommended that he reenroll in college. He is taking prescribed tranquilizers and sees a psychiatrist once a month.

When students come to the counseling center expressing concerns about homosexuality, it is essential that the counselor clarify the nature of the presenting problem. Some students have already decided upon and openly admitted a preference for homosexuality. These students may want help in handling the bewilderment or resentment of their immediate families. Other students may admit their homosexuality to themselves but want to discuss their reluctance or fears about informing their parents or friends. Other clients may be hassled on a job and fear that the job is in jeopardy. Still others, like Vivian, may be expressing uncertainty about their sexual identity.

Vivian is expressing a need to clarify her sexual identity in a nonjudgmental, neutral atmosphere. A client-centered approach might be productive in helping her sort out her feelings, attitudes, values, and the reasons for her ambivalence.

Depression seems to be the keynote of the counseling requests of Georgia and Donald. Handling depressed clients has recently received a great deal of attention from counselors and other mental-health professionals.

Workshops based upon behaviorally oriented theory have proposed confronting depressed clients with the degree of reality of their concern to change negative reinforcers to positive ones and to spur the depressed person into action.

Georgia obviously has been withdrawing from the demands of school and social interaction. There are two positive notes, however. She attended a group activity, and she has agreed to come in for counseling. I would help her search for and articulate any fears or uncertainties she has about herself academically, personally, and socially that may be contributing to her withdrawal. At the same time, I would help her to take further action in gradually increasing degrees to increase her academic input and social interaction. If it seems that dropping out of college is a wise choice, I would make sure that this move was not a further withdrawal. Rather, her plans for life outside college would have to be discussed realistically.

Donald needs an opportunity to talk about his doubts and uncertainties. His questions could be termed existential in that recognizing his own responsibilities for productive choices and actions could help him develop his own meaning and purpose in life.

Wolpe's desensitization techniques, discussed earlier for working with Neil's math blockage, are used by quite a few counselors to help a client like Al rid himself of an unreasonable fear. In Al's case, a counselor using this approach would help him develop a list of situations that elicit varying degrees of anxiety related to keeping a dental appointment. Al and his counselor would work together to rank these situations in a hierarchy of severity of anxiety, with Al's highest anxiety presumably being that of having his teeth worked on in a dentist's chair. Al would then be taught to relax various muscles progressively until he is capable of relaxing himself fully in a few minutes. Next Al would be taught to visualize increasingly anxious situations while relaxed until he was able to visualize himself in a dentist chair and remain calm. While following the desensitization through imagined actions, Al would be encouraged to take actual steps toward seeing the dentist.

While working with Al or anyone presenting a phobia, it is important for the counselor to spend time with the client assessing whether the fear is the central problem, how disabling the fear has become, and whether the fear of dentists has generalized to other similar situations. Also, the counselor must be aware that some clients do not respond readily to the idea of relaxation. In fact, some clients' presenting anxiety may increase if they perceive relaxation as a giving up of control to the counselor. In cases in which the fear has generalized considerably or in which the clients are resistant to relaxation, the counselor must try other ways of working with clients presenting themselves as phobic.

In my experience, specific phobic reactions are not common. I usually treat the presenting problem as I would any other expression of anxiety. Al's fear might have risen from unhappy experiences with dentists earlier in his life, or may result from fears he has modeled from attitudes and actions of parents or other significant adults in his life. It may also be a fear that is part of a more generalized pattern of withdrawal from unpleasant or difficult situations, such as asserting himself when he believes someone is taking advantage of him, when he takes a course he finds difficult, or when he attempts a new or unfamiliar activity.

If the fear does focus specifically on dental work, I would help Al look at the genesis of the fear. When the situation became clearer, I would ask him to be more specific about his fears of dentistry. What did he believe would happen to him in the dentist's chair? Where did he get these ideas? How realistic were these beliefs? What were the consequences of not having dental work done? Next I would suggest he take actions that would gradually lead up to making and keeping a dental appointment. These actions might consist of visiting and talking to the dentist when the appointment is made, to discuss, beforehand, his fears and concerns. Talking about dentists with a friend who is not afraid of dentists might be helpful as long as the client does not then perceive himself as inferior to the friend. Role-playing a telephone call to the dentist for an appointment or actually visiting the dentist might also be productive.

If Al's phobia appears to represent a more generalized reaction to fearful or unpleasant situations, more time would be spent in counseling and exploring the reasons for this pattern of behavior before confronting Al with the immediate question of a dental appointment. The attitudes and actions used to reduce the dental fear could then be used to reduce or minimize withdrawal in other specific unpleasant situations.

In Chapter 5 I discussed Emily, who was expressing anxieties about leaving home to go to college. Gina represents the next step in the sequence of students' struggling with dependency needs. A counselor should work closely with Gina to help reassure her and to help her stay in school. Gina might require more than one counseling session a week for a while. I would find it important to discuss concerns about being able to handle the work, feelings of inability to make friends, guilt about leaving her family, and any other uncertainties that might be contributing to her anxiety. Also, I would determine with her whether any specific uncomfortable situations are adding to her unhappiness, such as an uncooperative roommate, an intimidating professor, or an overload of classes. In most cases, with support for the student, homesickness wanes. Then one must consider whether further counseling is needed regarding dependency. In homesickness, cooperation between student-hall personnel and counseling-center staff, with due regard for confidentiality, can be a plus for the student's ultimate resolution of the problem.

Pete exemplifies a number of students who have had a serious emotional trauma who return to a college campus. At times, support and reassurance in the first month or so are all that is needed; that is, one makes sure that medication is taken, that the students do not overload themselves, and that they do not feel excessively lonely. Some students require more help when they become anxious about being anxious or when symptoms of withdrawal or depression recur as pressures build.

Interpersonal Conflicts and Concerns

Students in dormitories frequently seek counseling because of friction with a roommate. Students must learn to handle different values, different lifestyles, and different sexual attitudes of roommates. Also, they must learn appropriate ways of asserting themselves if a roommate behaves in an inconsiderate way or takes unfair advantage of them.

Premarriage, marriage, or couple counseling (couples living together but not married) occurs fairly frequently. Couple problems become difficult when a breakup occurs, particularly when only one partner wants to end the relationship. Since both people are on campus, it is hard for them to avoid seeing each other. Also, they must often contend with the reaction of friends or acquaintances who are curious about the breakup and/or want to help them resolve their problems.

In many colleges the majority of the students do not live at home. Nevertheless, a considerable amount of college counseling relates to parent/student relationships. Problems over financial dependence and filial responsibility are frequent. Parents may subtly or directly threaten to withdraw financial support for college or to disown students if they behave in a way that displeases them. This displeasure can be over anything from choice of a mate, choice of friends, or choice of a career to drinking habits or general living. At times college students worry about the emotional stability of a parent. For instance, some students worry that a parent may have a nervous breakdown or a heart attack if they persist in certain behaviors.

Counselors must help students to decide upon their own behavior and to confront their parents appropriately over their differences. This confrontation may be frightening and painful, but if it is handled correctly, it can lead to a more mature relationship between student and parents. In some situations, as I discussed in Chapter 5, students must be prepared for the possibility of rejection by their parents if the parents are adamant.

- *Client 13.* Bev, a freshman, is having problems with her roommate. She describes her roommate as being almost the opposite of her. Unlike Bev, her roommate is friendly, sociable, and ingratiating. She is also untidy, keeps odd hours, and brings in friends at all hours without checking with Bev. Bev expresses fondness for her roommate and wishes that she could have the dates and social contact of her friend. However, she also feels resentful about her roommate's inconsiderateness but cannot express it directly. Her residence director referred her for counseling.

- *Client 14.* Sue is a 26-year-old graduate student who has been living with Fred, a social worker, for the past 3 years. Neither has been previously married. Their relationship has been stormy, with a great deal of verbal haranguing on both parts. But they also have had close comradery and close, satisfying physical intimacy. Recently, in some of their heated arguments, Fred has become violent and struck Sue. Later he becomes very contrite. Both are concerned about his loss of control over himself.

- *Client 15.* Matt has been having difficulty in a required course in his major field. He has an excellent grade-point average but finds that there is friction between himself and a professor in one course. Matt's midterm was below average. Matt believes that the exam was unfair. Other students, Matt claims, have the same feeling. He describes the professor as belligerent, arrogant, and biased. His motivation to work on assignments is low. The counseling staff has received similar complaints from other students. This professor is the only person teaching the course.

- *Client 16.* Bert is a 26-year-old graduate student living with his mother in an apartment off the campus. His mother is in her early sixties. She cooks for him, cleans house, and waits up for him when he dates. Bert wants to move out on his own. When he brings this up with his mother, she expresses concern about being able to take care of herself. She and Bert have lived together since his father's death 10 years before. Bert feels frustrated and guilty.

Roommate problems often result from a student's inability or reluctance to assert himself or herself with a roommate. In Bev's case this lack of assertion is compounded by ambivalent feelings. The counselor would want to help her confront her roommate in a constructive manner but also explore with her some implicit concerns about her own social behavior. Assertiveness training might be appropriate. Gestaltists might focus on her ambivalence as contradictory behavior and confront her with her responsibility to confront her roommate if she expects change. I would want to explore with her some of her implicit concerns about her own social behavior. She may need help in developing social skills other than assertion.

In those situations in which communication between roommates appears to be at an impasse, the student may decide to move rather than attempt a difficult adjustment. Counselors should be aware of whether residence halls are set up to match students with similar habits, interests, and values. If so, as counseling progresses, the counselor can refer a student to another residence hall if that plan seems appropriate.

Examples of marriage or couple counseling will be discussed in the next chapter. Here the key factor in counseling with Sue and Fred is the problem of the battered woman. Since both are willing to confront the problem, the prognosis is somewhat favorable. The relationship as presented shows a great deal of ambivalence, which needs to be worked out. The reasons for excessive quarreling need to be aired. Sue needs to clarify at what point she will refuse to maintain the living arrangement if Fred continues to have difficulty controlling his use of physical force. Fred needs help in developing ways to express anger or frustration without resorting to force.

A behaviorist would look to behaviors in both clients that might be reinforcing violent arguments and resultant physical force and work toward extinguishing these behaviors and shaping new ones.

Matt's difficulty with a professor resembles student problems at all levels of education. The counselor needs to clarify with Matt what he hopes to gain from counseling. The question focuses on whether Matt wants to develop some attitudes and skills in interacting with the professor or whether he wants to register some form of administrative complaint. If his major goal is learning how to develop constructive emotional responses in his interaction with the professor, then counseling is in order. A number of possibilities exist. Matt could confront the professor with his concerns in a constructive manner if it appears that there is any likelihood of the professor's responding in a positive, nonpunitive way. Role-playing might be used to help Matt practice the proposed interview. Also, the counselor might explore why the professor has had such a deleterious effect upon Matt's motivation that he has fallen into a self-destructive pattern. Since no alternative exists for changing courses or professors, ways of coping with this situation and similar situations could be discussed.

If Matt wants to register an administrative complaint about the professor's behavior, the procedure for doing so can be clarified. This procedure usually involves the student's talking with the head of the department. The counselor should not intervene in these situations. If a counseling center were to report information about a professor's behavior to the authorities, the faculty would begin to perceive the center as an evaluative agency monitoring the faculty. Also, the counselor might be called as a witness by the administrator if the professor's and the student's accounts of behavior differ considerably. However, the counselor should make sure that the student is aware of his or her rights and knows the procedure for reporting the behavior and the procedure for appealing to higher authorities if no satisfaction is gained from the department head.

Bert has a dependence/independence problem. He needs help in developing the strength to confront his mother with the importance of his developing his own life and of her developing her own. Guilt feelings must be explored. As Bert gains strength, he might investigate some of the programs available for men and women his mother's age. If his mother continues to express anxiety about Bert's deserting her and her inability to take care of herself, counseling might be suggested. Joint sessions with Bert and his mother might also be profitable.

Antisocial Acts

College students request or are referred for counseling about antisocial, aberrant, or illegal acts and impulses similar to those of students in public schools and of persons in the community. Shoplifting, drug or alcohol abuse, sexual aberrations, and similar actions occur in all the settings in which counselors work. Cheating on exams, creating havoc in a dormitory or in some other college building, harassing teachers, and stealing exams or exam questions are representative of actions indigenous to an educational setting.

Since students who ask for counseling are attempting to get help, the conditions of confidentiality remain the same as those discussed in Chapter 5. No report goes to the dean of students' office or to the office of the vice-president for student affairs.

At times these problems surface in dormitories or come to the attention of one of the deans in the student-affairs office. The administrator may feel obligated to report the behavior or to take disciplinary action and then recommend that the individual receive counseling. Or the administrator may decide to refer the person for counseling without taking disciplinary action or without reporting the incident to the local police or to a disciplinary committee on campus. In these cases it is very important that the counselor let the student know that he or she cannot be protected from legal proceedings or disciplinary action if the illegal or inappropriate behavior continues.

From a legal standpoint the student, as an adult, potentially can receive more severe penalties than a juvenile in public schools. If the counselor is licensed by the state, privileged communication exists, so that the counselor can decline to testify about illegal situations without the consent of the client.

Students ask for help or are referred because of sexual aberrations, such as exhibitionism and voyeurism, more often than in high schools and in the community. One reason is that housing arrangements are more conducive to these incidents' occurring. Another is that most residence-hall personnel feel comfortable about referring students with these problems for counseling. Counseling usually consists of first helping these students to understand their behavior, to confront feelings of sexual inadequacy or hostility toward women. Then the counselor can help them develop the skills to interact directly with women socially and sexually. Generally, people with this type of behavior problem respond well to counseling.

Crises

Crises arising out of suicide threats or attempts are fairly frequent. Statistically (Mathesen, 1975), college students have a very high suicide rate compared to the general population. It is true that the difference in rates may be inflated because more accurate records of college suicides are kept in colleges than in the general community. Nevertheless, they occur in sufficient numbers that counseling staffs must be prepared to handle these situations. Anxiety reactions requiring immediate counseling or acute psychotic reactions requiring possible hospitalization or drug therapy are common on college campuses. Students away from the security of home and lifelong friends may give way under academic pressures, the need to make independent decisions, traumatic breaks in relationships, or the death of a relative or friend.

In these situations it is imperative that the individual be seen immediately. Then it can be determined whether a referral to psychiatric facilities or psychiatric consultation is needed regarding medication or hospitalization. In larger universities, particularly those with medical facilities, health services with a psychiatric staff and/or mental-health clinics staffed with psychiatrists, clinical psychologists, and social workers are also part of student services. In these situations, referrals and cross-referrals can and should be worked out between these services and the counseling center. In most colleges the counseling center is the only major resource, so that referral to a community agency or continuing with a client on a support basis with psychiatric consultation may be involved.

Cooperative emergency policies and procedures must be developed among the counseling-center staff, student personnel administrators, and residence-hall personnel, particularly if the counseling center is the main mental-health resource. Emergency situations occur frequently in residence halls. Immediate intervention is required, and in some cases a determination must be made about whether the crisis is of short duration or whether the student appears too incapacitated to continue in school. Further decisions may be necessary about hospitalization, drug therapy, and notification of the student's family. Immediate intervention can be provided by the counseling–center staff, with continued counseling if the crisis is a temporary one. If the counselor believes that the student needs hospitalization and/or believes that the family should be informed, the student personnel officer in charge should take the necessary steps and notify the family.

Since many counseling centers have waiting lists, it is important that emergency procedures be set up to handle the individual who comes into the center or is brought to the center in a severely distraught or despondent condition. Counseling centers should either have a person serving as an emergency admitter or assign counselors emergency hours throughout the day and night.

Counseling Interns

College counseling centers are potentially the most efficient setting for giving interns individual counseling experience. College students' schedules are flexible, and counseling experience is available under professionally trained supervisors. Interns can be gradually introduced to more difficult counseling problems and can have opportunities of profiting from close supervision by the counseling staff.

Close interaction and cooperation are required among the psychology department, the school of education, and the counseling center in the training of doctoral and master's-degree persons in psychological counseling. The counseling staff ideally should be involved in the training of counseling interns beyond supervision. Their expertise in group counseling, career education, assessment and appraisal procedures, counseling techniques and theories, and behavior dynamics can add richness to a counselor training program that may be lacking if no instructors are actually involved in counseling.

Projects and Activities

1. *A counselor in a college counseling center receives a visit from a roommate of one of her clients. The roommate tells the counselor that he is concerned that the client is not leveling with the counselor about his real problem. He offers to give background information about his friend that he believes will be helpful. How should the counselor respond? (See author's comments below.)*
2. *Discuss the unique responsibilities of a college counseling center and a college placement office in career planning and career choice for students. Consider how the two agencies can work together for the benefit of the students. Can you envision a similar plan for persons not in college?*
3. *The director of a college counseling center notes that the proportion of minority students seeking counseling is significantly lower than that of the student body as a whole. What steps can the director take to be sure that minority students needing help will receive it?*
4. *Referrals from faculty and other professionals on campus are encouraged by directors of counseling centers. Some faculty members who have referred students to the center call and ask whether the students have shown up and what has happened. What should a counselor do in these instances? (See author's comments below.)*
5. *An official of a government agency telephones the director of a college counseling center and asks whether a certain student has had counseling. If the student has, the official wants an evaluation of the student regarding security risks. How should the director respond in a manner consistent with professional standards? (See author's comments below.)*
6. *A residence director refers a student to a counselor. The student, who is under age, has been drinking in the dorm. The student is willing to receive counseling. After a few sessions the residence director calls and tells the counselor that the student is still drinking and wonders what to do. How might the counselor respond? (See author's comments below.)*
7. *A student who is a residence aide calls the counseling center and explains that one of the students on his floor appears to be in a serious emotional state. The student has not left his room for days, is incoherent, and seems to be experiencing hallucinations. The college has no psychiatrist on the staff, and the health center offers predominantly first-aid treatment. How should the counseling-center staff respond? (See author's comments below.)*
8. *What justification can one make for having counseling for normal develop-*

mental conflicts in a college setting and not having a similar service for the community?

9. *What are some of the differences among the type of occupational information that would be useful in a college counseling center, a high school counseling center, and a community counseling center?*

10. *Either through interviews or through exploring the literature, compare the purposes of a university or college counseling center with those of a university or college mental-health clinic.*

Author's Comments

Activity 1.   *The counselor should indicate that she sympathizes with the roommate's interest in and concern about the client but cannot talk about him without his approval. The counselor should suggest to the roommate that he let his friend know about his interest and concern and ask whether it is all right for him to talk with the counselor. The counselor could also suggest that she let the client know of his friend's interest and discuss whether a conference would be agreeable. If the friend describes behaviors indicating that the client is in imminent danger of hurting himself or others, it would be necessary to assess the situation with the friend and decide whether intervention is necessary.*

Activity 4.   *In cases in which a faculty member has referred a student directly to the center, I suggest in the first interview that the student let the referral person know that he or she has followed through. I also tell the client that the person is interested and might call as a follow-up. I would ask the client to indicate what he or she would suggest the receptionist or I do if a call comes in from the faculty member. If the student agrees that I can talk with the referral person, then we would discuss what information I should share. If the student prefers that I not talk with the faculty member, I would then suggest to that person that the student prefers to be contacted directly.*

Activity 5.   *The director should refuse to give any information to the agency, including whether the student has had counseling. If the student has signed a form indicating that he or she has had counseling and agrees to information's being shared, the counselor should try, if possible, to get in touch with the former client and discuss what is to be shared. Some college counseling centers have a policy of not giving any information out or of not writing any recommendations. This policy is based on the belief that there is often some coercion involved on application forms regarding previous counseling. The student must indicate whether he or she has had counseling or therapy and must agree to have the counseling agency contacted if he or she is to be considered for the job.*

Activity 6.   *The counselor should tell the residence director that he or she should take the same action that would be taken with any other student breaking* rules. Counseling does not negate disciplinary action. The counselor can help the client explore the reasons for the continued breaking of rules and recognize and handle the consequences of the continued behavior.

Activity 7. In these cases the counseling-center staff has an obligation to handle the immediate crisis and to determine how serious the behavior is. If the behavior looks as though medication or hospitalization should be involved or if the student appears dangerous to himself or others, the counselor should take appropriate steps to get medication or hospitalization. If the behavior is serious enough to warrant retention for psychiatric observation for possible commitment, the parents of the student should be informed. This is an administrative action that should be handled through the office of the vice-president of student affairs after consultation with the member of the counseling-center staff.

8

Individual Counseling
in the Community

The Development of Community Counseling

Numerous counseling programs outside an educational setting are beginning to flourish in communities. In Chapters 1 and 2, I discussed how these counseling services emerged from a growing acceptance by the general public and by psychological workers that normally functioning persons in a community need and can profit from counseling. I also noted the influence of counseling theories and techniques appropriate for normal conflicts that were developed by humanistic psychologists, human-development professionals, and behaviorists.

Although the counseling needs of the public are apparent and counseling groups have begun to develop services in communities, serious obstacles still face professional organizations and professionally trained persons attempting to initiate and maintain counseling programs. These barriers result from entrenched historical attitudes of federal, state, and local funding agencies that it is only feasible economically to support services developed for seriously emotionally disturbed persons and that it is most sound to offer such services in a medical, mental-illness model. Funding agencies and legislators subscribe to the notion that persons experiencing difficulties within the normal sphere of conflicts and anxieties should be able to handle these problems themselves or be served predominantly by volunteers, aides, or paraprofessionals at no or little cost.

These funding agencies need to become aware of the economic losses that communities incur when persons stymied by everyday problems or situational distress become unproductive workers, inadequate parents, apathetic citizens, or rebellious youths. A brief look at the history of community mental-health services and their relationship to the development of effective counseling programs may help to demonstrate the importance of gaining economic support for counseling.

The Development of Community Clinics

The first psychiatric clinic was started in Chicago in 1908 by William Healy, a psychoanalytically trained psychiatrist. He chose the name Juvenile Psychopathic Institute because the services were designed to work with juvenile delinquents. The funding for the clinic was provided by a philanthropic source concerned about the juvenile crime rate (Levy, 1971). This clinic and others like it were staffed through the next few decades by a psychiatrist to do primarily therapy, a social worker to work predominantly with home problems, and a psychologist to do mostly testing. Treatment was predominantly in a modified psychoanalytic mode.

The first psychological clinic was developed by Lightner Witmer in 1896 at the University of Pennsylvania primarily to diagnose and treat children with learning and behavioral problems. This service was used by school personnel when their children were experiencing academic, behavioral, or social problems. Other universities opened similar clinics. From these clinics the profession called clinical psychology emerged. Later these influences led to the development of school psychologists, who tried to assess and treat children's learning and behavior problems. The idea of counseling students or families was not entertained by these staffs.

In the 1920s continued concern about problem children brought about funding for the Child Guidance Demonstration Clinics. These clinics used Healy's clinic as a model. However, there was a broadening of interest from juvenile delinquency to more general problems (Levy, 1971).

The focus on work with children and families continued into the 1940s and 1950s, but gradually services expanded to include emotionally disturbed adults. Psychotic and postpsychotic patients were not seen at clinics in large numbers because most psychotics ended up in mental hospitals for a long if not permanent stay.

The Comprehensive Community Mental Health Act

The Kennedy Comprehensive Community Mental Health Act, passed by Congress in 1963, provided the funds for an ambitious program aimed at treating all degrees of mental illness in the community. Under this act, persons with a psychotic reaction who would previously have left the community for hospitalization were to be hospitalized and treated in local facilities. Other treatment facilities in the program included outpatient clinics and halfway houses for transitional care. In addition, crises clinics and hot lines were proposed to handle emergencies.

As Randolph (1978) points out, the Kennedy Community Mental

Health Act of 1963 and subsequent revisions were designed to include "treatment for normal people with a broad range of problems, as well as development of prevention programs" (p. 244). However, in practice the community centers have had to zero in on severely emotionally disturbed, psychotic, or postpsychotic persons and persons with marginal adjustment. Psychological counseling, which could have become a part of the total service, was not included in these programs.

This neglect of counseling occurred partially because the need to make psychological counseling available to the general public had not been fully recognized. But an even greater deterrent was insufficient funding. The intention of the act was to decrease federal funding progressively each year, so that state and local funding could take over. However, sufficient federal monies were not available from the beginning of the comprehensive program and became even more inadequate as state legislatures cut back on funds after they assumed financial responsibility for the program.

Additional burdens were heaped on communities when large state mental hospitals began using psychotropic medication, which dramatically reduced the need for long-term hospitalization. This move increased the number of persons in the community requiring the services of the community mental-health program for rehabilitation and for monitoring of medication. In some states large state mental hospitals were closed prematurely without adequate funding for increased facilities and staff in the community.

Crisis clinics, hot lines to handle emergencies, and halfway houses to help patients make the transition from hospitalization to normal functioning were started on shoestring budgets with inadequate staffs often run by well-intentioned, overworked, and untrained volunteers. This money crunch left little for working with people's normal conflicts and concerns.

The Concentration of Counselors in Educational Settings

Professional associations representing counselors tended to contribute to this community emphasis on mental illness because of their own preoccupation with developing standards and training programs for persons with normal conflicts in educational settings. Pallone (1977) surveyed the placement of counselors over the past 20 years. He concluded that the vast majority of counseling psychologists worked in educational settings. Only 1.9% reported that they were working in hospitals or clinics. Until the American Mental Health Counselors Association joined the APGA recently, only a very small percentage of APGA counselors worked in the community.

Counselors in private practice have not been adequately surveyed, but estimates are that there have been very few during the past few decades.

Yamamoto found in 1963 that only 5% of counseling psychologists who were members of the APA's Division 17 were in private practice. In a 1976 study of job placement of doctorate counseling psychologists from both APA-approved and non-APA-approved training programs, only 4.5% of both groups specified that they were in private practice (Banikiotes, 1977).

A number of professional problems contributed to this dearth of community counseling. As I indicated earlier, many states would license only clinical psychologists or counseling psychologists with a degree from a psychology department. Thus, counseling psychologists with a degree from an education department would be in violation of the state law if they practiced psychology privately. Also, persons with a master's degree in counseling had no strong professional associations to help them work toward licensing such as social workers with a master's degree have in some states. The APA would not accept master's-degree persons as full members and has been unequivocally opposed to licensing for this group. Until recently the APGA was not very much involved in community counseling or in licensing. Community counselors could join the AMHCA, but this group had not gained sufficient membership to make a significant impact nationally.

Trends toward Increased Counseling in Communities

The change in attitude about counseling for normal concerns began to surface in the late 1960s. Shapiro, Maholick, Brewer, and Robertson (1968) described this change in discussing how a mental-health clinic in Georgia expanded its traditional emphasis on mental illness to include mental-health counseling for normal conflicts. The clinic started with nonpatient volunteers. The staff found that only a small percentage of the volunteers had severe personal problems. But the staff observed:

> Very few of these "normal" people were in the state of bubbling peace and tranquility which is sometimes mistakenly equated with mental health. Rich or poor, the typical volunteer we met was facing mild or moderate conflicts and stress in the conduct of his life. . . . Professionally, we would have dismissed them because they lacked the specific kinds of psychopathology that would cause them to seek our help, yet a sizeable proportion of them were struggling with problems of marriage, career, children, fears of the future, self-doubts, and others [p. 11].

The need to upgrade and expand vocational-counseling and placement-counseling services and facilities was expressed by Gellman and Murov in 1973. In the same year Sinick wrote about changing roles, changing settings, and changing clientele for rehabilitation counselors. Sinick believed that persons with emotional disturbances, persons with drug or alcohol problems, and other disabled or disadvantaged persons were becoming client populations for rehabilitation counselors. Because of this trend, he said, rehabilitation counselors would have to view clients as insufficiently self-actualized persons. He supported certification of rehabilitation counselors and accreditation of preparation programs.

In separate articles in 1975, Schlossberg and Salisbury discussed the growing opportunities for counselors in working with older persons. Salisbury criticized counselor preparation programs as not including sufficient crisis work or skill development in this area. Blake (1975) was more optimistic in that he saw interest increasing in this work. Considering that the over-50 population is increasing rapidly, the importance of including training and experience in gerontology is obvious.

Tolbert in 1978 indicated that opportunities were increasing for placement of counselors in correctional institutions or with probation and parole services and that counselors could be employed in halfway houses and work-release programs. F. W. Miller, Fruehling, and Lewis (1978) believe that the roles of correctional counselors should be similar to those of counselors in other settings. Correctional counselors have to work hard to maintain prisoners' or parolees' free choice in accepting counseling, as well as confidentiality and their right to privacy. The distinction must be made clear between probation officers, who have administrative and supervisory relationships with prisoners or parolees, and counselors, who should not be involved in evaluation, discipline, or decisions about parole. Brodsky (1974) believes that counselors must make sure that prisoners' rights are protected. In October 1974 the *Personnel and Guidance Journal* published a feature section about correctional counseling edited by Dye and Gluckstern. Also, a new division of the APGA designated as the Public Offender Counselor Association was formed in December 1974.

Business and industry were slow in recognizing the need for counseling services to help increase the morale and productivity of employees (Kunze, 1973). However, interest has recently increased in both counseling and consultation services (D. S. Benedict, 1973; Emener, 1975). In particular, employees with an alcohol problem are of prime concern to businessmen because of its effect upon productivity.

Marriage and family counselors have been working in the community for some time. A few states now license marriage counselors. Most of these persons are social workers with a master's degree or psychologists with a doctorate. Individuals with a doctorate or a master's degree in counseling are beginning to offer counseling services in communities through either nonprofit private corporations or private practice. Problems brought to these counselors include marital concerns, parent/child conflicts, adolescent problems, and conflicts with families.

Some churches have set up counseling centers for parishioners staffed by ministers who have had counseling training or by trained counselors. These centers usually cater to the emotional needs of their parishioners but may also serve other members of the community (Jones, 1970). Marriage and family conflict and work with teenagers usually take precedence (Shertzer & Stone, 1976).

Most recently, community mental-health clinics have begun to recognize the need for counseling services. For example, the names of a number of clinics in Washington State have been changed to include the word *counseling*. Also, persons who have had training or experience in working with a range of vocational, educational, personal, and social concerns are being hired more frequently. Banikiotes (1977) found that the number of counseling psychologists working in clinics in 1976 was almost 20% of the graduates of APA-approved programs. Tolbert (1978) sums up these trends with this comment: "Community agencies and services offer a wide variety of occupational opportunities for counselors. . . . Counselors work in community mental-health agencies, family-service agencies, crisis-intervention centers, halfway houses, drug-counseling centers, and a host of programs set up for special populations, such as minorities, the disadvantaged, and the unemployed" (p. 300).

Tolbert also points out that the push for licensing and for professional identification with counselor associations appears to be a response to the opportunities for counselors to work in community agencies or to handle private practice. Further, there is a growing feeling of responsibility on the part of counselor professional associations for monitoring the quality of services offered in the community under the guise of counseling.

The cooperative efforts of the APGA and Division 17 to work for the licensing of doctorate counseling psychologists on an equal footing with clinical psychologists indicates a growing awareness that counseling psychologists are needed to do counseling outside educational settings. This move also reflects a belief that persons with training and experience in counseling for normal conflicts or problems should be handling counseling. The APGA move toward national licensing reflects similar ideas for master's-degree counselors. The affiliation of the AMHCA with the APGA, the recent national counselor certification procedures established by this group, and the licensing laws for counselors in Virginia, Arkansas, and Alabama further document this trend.

Counseling Needs in the Community

The counseling needs of persons in the community have not been thoroughly surveyed. However, attention to these needs has increased at professional-association meetings and in the literature. Both the APGA and the APA's Division 17 offer workshops and symposiums about problems and growth processes throughout the individual's life span. Workshops about career change, death and dying, gerontology, and retirement concerns are examples of program offerings. Similarly, entire issues of leading professional-counseling journals have been devoted to counseling needs throughout one's life span. The special needs of minorities and of women in the community have also been covered. Sheehy's *Passages*, a 1976 best seller, presented for the general public the theme that humans face anxieties, concerns, or crises throughout their lives and that they are capable of continued growth as they pass from one life stage to another. A brief overview of some of the articles published in journals should show the extent of the need for community counseling.

Counseling Needs in Midlife and Old Age

In November 1976 a special issue of the *Personnel and Guidance Journal* was published entitled *Counseling over the Life Span*, with Sinick as guest editor. A number of articles surveying general problems of midlife and of old age were included. The counseling needs of the dying, the terminally ill, and the bereaved and of older women and aging members of minorities were also covered. I will discuss the articles in this special issue that come under the general headings "Is there Life beyond Adolescence?" and "Can Second Careers Come First?" They seem to cover the majority of concerns of these age groups.

Kimmel (1976) outlines three stages in adult lives in which counseling may be necessary: late parenthood, dealing with aging parents, and dealing with bereavement. He discusses how parents may feel guilty or have conflicts if their children do not become successful or happy adults or do not develop values or lifestyles compatible with their own. Or parents may feel lonely and rejected when their children leave and make their own lives. Kimmel points out that it is anxiety provoking for adults to perceive parents who have been their model and bridge to the future become aged, incapacitated, or senile. The adults must handle their emotional reactions to their parents' deterioration and also face the inevitability of their own aging and deterioration. In addition to these emotional reactions is the practical problem of how best to care for incapacitated parents. Kimmel also describes the problems of loneliness and helplessness that can occur when a partner in a long-term marriage dies.

Kimmel presents a perceptive picture of late parenthood and of the handling of aged parents. I would add that the children of anxious parents may also have problems of guilt about not measuring up to their parents' expectations. Their problems of breaking away from an oversolicitous parent may need attention. Also, the dilemmas and the emotional reactions of the aging parent must be considered. Many fiercely refuse to face loss of strength or independence; others collapse prematurely. Some feel like an unwanted burden and experience feelings of rejection. They may also need an opportunity to talk about their new status as "senior citizens."

Rappoport (1976), Heddesheimer (1976), and Entine (1976) discuss the counseling needs of persons in midlife from different viewpoints. Rappoport points out the increasing divorce rate among the middle aged and the increasing efforts of individuals to find a second career. He observes that a sex reversal may occur at midlife. Men looking ahead to retirement may reduce their attention to work and begin to refocus on home life. Women may show increasing interest in channeling their energies outside the home when the children leave. These reversals can lead to conflicts and friction in the marriage. In his article Entine includes the counseling needs of women exploring careers, of unemployed and retiring persons, and of workers whose jobs become obsolete because of technological change. Heddesheimer emphasizes the multiplicity and complexity of motives involved in changes of career that can contribute to the need for counseling. She also examines pressures from the environment related to family, job, or societal change and the desire to obtain more satisfying work.

In the same year the above articles were published, Schlossberg and Entine served as guest editors for a full issue of *The Counseling Psychologist* titled *Counseling Adults*. This issue was reprinted in its entirety in a paperback by Brooks/Cole Publishing Company in 1977. The articles are divided into four sections, each presenting a different perspective on counseling adults in a developmental framework. The first section covers theories about male midlife crisis, stages of development of men in the age range of 18 to 45, the importance of intimate relationships for middle-aged men and women, the effect of unanticipated stress throughout the life cycle (such as the death of a child), and the achievement patterns of adults. In the second section the need for counseling services is emphasized, a developmental-counseling approach is presented, and the problem of age bias is discussed. These articles are followed by examples of existing and emerging counselor training programs in section three. The issue closes in section four with a series of minireviews by Sinick of books on midlife published since 1971. The authors in this issue agree that life does not end at 40, that crises, concerns, and decisions continue to confront persons in midlife. These authors also believe that people of this age group can change behavior and attitudes to increase the richness in their lives.

In response to a growing recognition of the counseling needs of the aged, the APGA in 1979 published a training syllabus called *Counseling the Aged* under the editorship of Ganikos. The syllabus contains 11 modules covering theoretical views about aging, the needs of the aged for counseling, and recommendations for curriculum changes in counselor education on counseling the aged. The editors feel that the knowledge and skills for counseling the general population apply to older populations as well. However, they believe that additional course work must be added if counselors are to understand the needs of older people and the effects of aging upon behavior. Physiological changes, common health problems, crises of older persons (retirement, where they will live), and concerns about death and dying are thoroughly reviewed.

The Counseling Needs of Women

The counseling needs of women were presented in three issues of *The Counseling Psychologist* in 1973, 1976, and 1979. The first two issues, edited by Harmon, Birk, Fitzgerald, and Tanney, were published together in a paperback by Brooks/Cole Publishing Company in 1978. The third issue was guest-edited by Hill, Birk, Blimline, Leonard, Hoffman, and Tanney. These three issues provide an ongoing, thorough overview of the needs of women for counseling and the need for changes in attitudes, theories, and practice in the counseling profession to meet these needs.

In the first issue counseling theories and practice are examined as they relate to women, with particular attention to the deficiencies in prevailing theories when they are applied to women. For example, problems of counseling bias with women, sexual bias in personality and counseling theories, and inadequacy of the counseling literature about occupational choice and about the development and behavior of women require attention. The second issue includes counseling women with special problems, such as the rape victim, the mastectomy patient, and the divorced or widowed woman. Also covered are some theoretical approaches to counseling women and the importance of helping Black women develop their strengths. The third issue presents continued discussion of potential bias and principles of counseling with women. This issue also contains short articles about counseling with specific subgroups of women with a variety of concerns throughout the life span.

The Counseling Needs of Minorities

Specific discussions of the counseling needs of minorities in the community have appeared infrequently in the literature. Most authors of articles about counseling minorities discuss the overall counseling concerns of minorities, whether they be in public schools, colleges, or communities.

The training syllabus for counseling the aged does recognize the special needs of elderly non-Whites and the difficulties in getting counseling services to them. In a special section Solomon discusses problems and concerns of Black, Hispanic-American, and Indian elderly people. He comments that the outlook for counseling services for the elderly is problematical at best but that "the outlook is particularly dismal for elderly members of ethnic and cultural minority groups" (p. 157). Elderly people's counseling needs revolve around feelings of worthlessness, rejection, isolation, and loneliness, deterioration in physical health, and worries about financial deficiencies. Problems in attaining counseling services include multiple discrimination (age and minority status), language problems, and insufficient numbers of minority counselors. Vontress in 1976 wrote about counseling middle-aged and aged members of minority groups and the potential barriers that exist if the counselor is White, young, or unable to speak the client's language fluently. These barriers may result in termination of counseling before the needs of the elderly person have even been determined.

The Counseling Needs of Late Adolescents and Young Adults

This trend toward working with adult counseling problems in midlife and later life is one that I endorse heartily. However, attention must also be given to the needs of many adolescents and young adults who are not in school and who are at important decision and conflict points in their lives. Only one-third of high school students go on to college, where counseling is usually part of student services. Thus, after 18 the great majority of adolescents and young adults have no professional-counseling services available to them for exploring careers or handling choices, confusion, and conflicts regarding personal development and social interaction. These young people, just entering the labor market, developing more permanent relationships with the opposite sex, searching for personal values, handling friction in love or marriage relationships, and developing social interaction, need the services of professionally trained counselors. Premarital counseling, couple counseling, marriage counseling, family counseling, and counseling for concerns about sexual adequacy are important needs for this age group in addition to the kinds of counseling needs discussed in Chapters 5 and 7.

Persons in their middle twenties and early thirties are confronted with the establishment of a career, the start of a family, marriage relationships, the rearing of young children, the handling of teenagers, the establishment of more permanent social relationships, and the maintenance of personal development and personal creativity. All of these can present problems for which counseling is needed.

Community Counseling with Teenagers and Children

One would hope that counseling services in elementary and secondary schools will continue to improve professionally, so that most counseling with teenagers and children can be done there. There is no doubt in my mind that the counseling of children and teenagers will move into the community if professional counseling does not flourish in the schools.

However, even if counseling services in schools were to handle counseling effectively, community counseling centers still would be used by teenagers if the facility was conveniently placed, the counseling staff was trusted, and the teenagers had an accurate perception of the services offered. Some teenagers might prefer using a community counseling service because privacy becomes easier to manage and because the hours for appointments may be more flexible. In particular, community counseling centers could be useful in the summer when the schools are closed.

Similarly, parents might prefer to use a neighborhood counseling service if one were available. They could receive help in their interactions with their children, or they might request help if a child was having difficulty in his or her interactions with peers or with his or her teacher. Unlike the situation in elementary schools, requests for counseling would not be anticipated from young children. Nevertheless, counseling should still involve agreement of the child and should not consist of diagnostic or screening procedures to help the school and the parents make administrative decisions. If these services are offered, they should be done by a separate diagnostic unit and by a different professional than the person who might be counseling with the child.

Sources of Referral

If professional-counseling services are offered in the community, referrals can be expected from physicians, lawyers, school staff, employment agencies, rehabilitation officers, and supervisors in business and industry. Information and referral agencies, such as birth-control centers and drug referral services, will also refer people. However, as always, the best source for referrals will be present and former clients.

Counseling Problems in the Community

Concerns of Later Adulthood: Vocational, Personal, and Social

Vocational Concerns.

- *Client 1.* Jan, 38, has been referred to the community counseling clinic by a friend. She has two children in school and has expressed interest in trying to develop a career. She had 1½ years of college and worked for 2 years as a cashier in a department store before marriage. She is considering college or vocational training. Her husband is supportive but ambivalent. She expresses ambivalence also. She is anxious about her ability to do well in school and is uneasy about whether she is being fair to the children.

- *Client 2.* John, 52, is referred to the counseling clinic by his supervisor in the company at which he works. He is a robust-looking person who has worked as a repairer of heavy equipment. He has suffered a heart attack and has been told that he cannot continue in his present job. He is quite shaken by this experience. His concerns have affected his relationship with his wife and family. He expresses a strong need to be employed.

In both situations these individuals have to make a career choice or career change complicated by factors related to this decision that arouse some anxiety and apprehension. The counselor must have the professional capacity to help Jan and John make decisions about career planning and must also possess the background to help them confront and work through personal uncertainties about their capacities to handle new demands in life.

Jan may need some recognition that her anxious feelings about getting training and her ambivalences about her responsibility for her own growth and for her family's welfare are not unusual. She is contemplating a significant change in lifestyle that will take some cooperative effort from the whole family. Some joint interviews with Jan and her husband may help reduce the ambiguities in their attitudes about Jan's future plans. Jan may also need to explore whether or not some of her uneasiness about the children results from her beliefs about what society expects from her as a mother and wife.

As these attitudes are being clarified, the exploration about her vocational choice can proceed. Her interests and abilities as they relate to vocational fields can be discussed. If necessary, vocational-interest inventories and general-aptitude or scholastic-aptitude tests might be decided upon, much as one would do in a college or high school setting. As career planning begins to solidify, more specific discussions about child care, sharing household duties, getting time for completing assignments, and other necessary adjustments in lifestyle may be helpful.

I believe it important that a counselor, in working with a client like Jan, resist the temptation to downplay her anxieties and urge her to go into a career. The anxieties must be confronted and resolved, with the decision remaining with the client.

In working with John, I would expect to have a medical report about the extent of his physical incapacity due to his heart attack and some estimate of the amount of physical labor he can handle. This information would be obtained with John's written consent and would be shared with him. Then I would explore his own perception of his incapacity and his feelings of anxiety or even anger about his decrease in physical strength. A realistic assessment of his physical capacities and his acceptance of this assessment would be important factors in helping him reduce some of his apprehension. In addition, any fears he has about coping with new job-training demands should be explored.

The effect of his physical incapacity and his attitudes upon his family relationship also may be included. Whether any family apprehensions are contributing to his anxiety needs to be considered. Also, one might find that fears about another heart attack are interfering with sexual activity between John and his wife. If family communications appear to have broken down, family counseling may be helpful, assuming John and other family members are willing. If family counseling proves unnecessary or not feasible, then counseling with John about his interactions with his family may be fruitful.

As counseling progresses, the types of work that John might find suited to his interests and abilities and to his physical capacities can be explored. If interviews do not sufficiently bring out vocational interests and aptitudes, an appropriate interest inventory and aptitude test might be arranged. A General Aptitude Test Battery (GATB) administered by state employment agencies may give pertinent data to use in making a choice. Information about jobs or on-the-job training can be gained from the state employment agency. If suitable jobs are available in the company for which he has been working, the adjustment may be easier. In any event, some continued interviews may be helpful as he starts a new job. The state vocational-rehabilitation agency can be very useful in helping gain appropriate job placement or job training.

Personal Concerns.

- *Client 3.* Fran, a 45-year-old widow, is referred by her physician. She is a registered nurse who enjoys her work. Having just gone back to work, she expresses doubts about her ability to make decisions. She expresses feelings of loneliness and of loss of purpose and personal identity. Her husband died suddenly 2 years ago, and her two children have left home. She has doubts about how good a parent she has been. Neither child finished college, and her daughter recently went through a trying divorce. Fran has very little female or male companionship. She feels uncomfortable with the few married couples she and her husband knew.

- *Client 4.* Fred, who is 67, makes an appointment because of feelings of restlessness, boredom, and mild depression. He retired after a highly active career as a salesman. He had not made any plans for retirement. He expresses general malaise and a recent sharp decrease in sexual potency. His wife, 55, is employed at a travel agency. She enjoys her job and has a great deal of contact with people. He states that he is happy about her job but also feels some resentment about her constant activity.

Fran has been left on her own after a prolonged, protected life in her marriage. New demands include performing adequately on the job, handling all the business details related to the home, and developing new relationships with males and females. The central problem expressed is her overall feelings of inadequacy about coping with these new expectations and new social roles. Doubts about herself as a capable person have cropped up in all areas of living.

In counseling Fran needs to explore her attitudes and beliefs about herself in order to gain more confidence and self-esteem. Fears about approaching new situations need to be recognized. The uncertainties and ambiguities about establishing and developing relationships with males need to be examined. Her expectations and the expectations of potential new male friends about sexual interaction may need clarification. The effect of her single status upon former and new friendships with females also may be important to consider. If necessary, some help in social interactions could be given through role playing or through suggested activities that would give her practice in social interactions. These activities would come after some assurance that her confidence has improved sufficiently for her to profit from the experiences. Fran's chances of gaining confidence are enhanced by the fact that she is employed as a nurse and likes her job.

Fran also needs to explore the reasons for her uncomfortable feelings about her children's lives. As she gains more understanding of herself, her expectations and feelings of responsibility for her children may become appropriate and reasonable.

Fred has made an appointment for counseling on his own. I perceive this decision as a first positive step toward improving attitudes. He needs an opportunity to express his feelings of loss of identity and loss of purpose in life that seem to occur at retirement. He also requires an opportunity to develop attitudes and strategies to help him build a revised lifestyle that will include sufficient activity to help him gain self-respect. He can explore how to use the talents, attitudes, and experiences that contributed to his success as a businessman to develop activities that will give him personal satisfaction and that will gain him some social recognition, such as involvement in community service. Finally, he needs to confront his new involvement in the home, for his wife is now the breadwinner. Then he might more fully support her constructive activity, and she might better understand his confusion and help him work through his resentment and uncertainties.

Interpersonal Conflicts and Concerns.

- *Client 5.* Margaret and Lou, a couple in their early forties, have been married 24 years. They have been discussing the possibility of divorce. Because of their ambivalences, their attorney recommended they seek marriage counseling. They have three children, none of whom is at home. All are successfully launched in life. Since the children left, they have noticed an increase in tension between themselves. Both feel irritation and some boredom. Margaret comes in for the first interview. She is willing to receive counseling. Her husband is reluctant. She is not sure that he can be convinced to come in for counseling.

- *Client 6.* Helen and Joe, a couple in their forties, have been referred by a visiting nurse. Helen's mother is in her seventies. She has been living by herself since her husband died 6 years before. She is beginning to develop some signs of physical deterioration and senility. The couple sense that she can no longer take care of herself. Helen is considering taking her mother into their home. Her husband believes that a retirement home or a nursing home would be better. There has been friction over the years with his mother-in-law. Also, he asserts that throughout their marriage Helen has consistently gotten upset or suffered severe headaches when she and her mother were together. Helen works full time as a librarian, at times including evenings and weekends.

If Lou decides not to come in for counseling and Margaret remains willing to do so, I would continue with Margaret on an individual basis. Although her problems with her marriage would obviously be an initial focal point of our discussion, I would not consider these sessions marriage counseling. Rather, I reserve the term *marriage counseling* for counseling with both parties.

The object of counseling with Margaret would be to help her understand her own feelings and develop her strengths whether she remained with her husband or not. The degree to which Margaret was preoccupied with her children as they grew up should be discussed to determine whether she limited her own personal development in the process. She may need to cultivate new or dormant interests or hobbies and consider whether she might profit from developing some career interests. The extent of Lou's involvement with the family over the years bears some scrutiny. Perhaps he has perceived Margaret as predominantly the mother of his children and not as a friend and mate.

If Lou agrees to counseling after Margaret has had some counseling sessions, the possibility of productive marriage counseling increases. The goal of marriage or couple counseling is for the couple to arrive at a decision about whether or not to maintain the relationship. In counseling this decision is assumed to result from working through the problem emotionally and intellectually. In most marriage counseling one expects that the marriage will become stronger. But some marriage or couple counseling can be considered successful when the couple decide that a divorce or separation would be more constructive.

The first decision to be made with Margaret and Lou is whether one counselor should see both of them, whether co-counselors should see them together, or whether a different counselor should work with each partner. I have found that seeing a couple together is usually most productive. I can help a couple improve communication by recognizing, expressing, and working through painful emotions or experiences. Also, at times, I have worked with a female co-counselor in marriage counseling when either husband or wife was resentful or suspicious of a counselor of the opposite sex. Less often, I have counseled one partner in the marriage while another counselor worked with the other partner. This approach can be particularly useful when it appears that the marriage is basically strong but that each partner may need help with personal concerns that may in turn further strengthen the marriage. In these instances, any communication between counselors should be carried out with the knowledge and consent of both clients. Also, the reason for and the information gained in the counselor interchange should be shared with both partners.

In the case of Margaret and Lou, I would prefer counseling them myself unless Margaret expressed concern about seeing a male counselor. Their presenting problem centers on changes in their relationship resulting in part from the children's absence. Essentially, they have to explore whether they can build a new relationship based upon a more direct and more intimate interaction than they had when their relationship with the children served as a buffer. An increase in intimacy, which could lead to a richer marriage, may require that both work through possible feelings of discomfort or apprehension about the demands of a close relationship. They may need to discover how a mutually satisfactory relationship can be maintained that will decrease rather than increase dependence upon each other and that will be neither boring nor stifling.

The problem confronting Helen and Joe represents a growing concern in our culture as older persons live longer. The custom of an extended family, in which the grandparents live with the immediate family, has decreased. No longer is this practice viewed as being the only natural way of helping older persons. Alternative plans, such as retirement homes for physically and mentally sound persons and nursing homes for those older persons needing physical care, have been established. These alternative plans allow a variety of choices, but they also can cause confusion or conflict, as Helen and Joe's situation demonstrates.

I would help Helen and Joe carefully explore the advantages and disadvantages of the various alternative plans. These discussions of alternatives must be done in conjunction with encouraging Helen to express fully her guilt feelings and to explore some of the reasons for this guilt. Joe's emotional reactions must be explored. Also, his recognition of the consistent friction with his mother-in-law and his observation that his wife becomes tense in interactions with her mother cannot be ignored.

Other factors besides these emotional considerations are important. We would need to determine how much personal care Helen's mother needs, the types of facilities available in retirement and nursing homes, and the facilities available at Helen and Joe's home. An estimate of how much time Helen could spend caring for her mother and still hold her job would be essential. I believe that it would be important not to attempt to persuade them in one direction or another, for they must live with the consequences of their decision.

Concerns of Late Adolescents and Young Adults: Vocational, Personal, and Social

Vocational Concerns.

- *Client 7.* Maggie is 18 and divorced. She dropped out of school to get married when she became pregnant. She lost her baby in childbirth. After that her marriage deteriorated. She has been working part time as a waitress and has been on and off welfare. She is discouraged about her life so far. She is worried about her recent weight increase. She considers herself ugly and worthless. She is looking for a full-time job or for appropriate training.

- *Client 8.* Michael, who is 25 and single, is referred by the state employment office. Mike is a chemist who has held seven different jobs in the past 3 years. He is bright, energetic, and sardonic. He says that he has yet to find a good boss. He has either been fired or has left jobs because of friction with supervisors. He is not sure that chemistry is the right profession. He has started to drink heavily.

Personal Concerns.

- *Client 9.* Maura is a 29-year-old highly successful lawyer. She is single and lives alone. She is a leader in the community. Her major concern relates to her uncertainties about what she wants for her future. She has male friends and enjoys their company but is reluctant to become involved in a long-term relationship. Yet, she says, she would like children and admits to feeling lonely at times.

- *Client 10.* Nina, 19, makes an appointment for counseling because of her inability to handle her grief over the loss of her mother and father in an automobile accident 6 months before. She has frequent crying spells and is finding it difficult to handle her job as a clerk in a bank.

Interpersonal Conflicts and Concerns.

- *Client 11.* Matt, a 19-year-old, reveals that he has recently recognized and accepted his homosexuality. However, he is having difficulty confronting his parents and friends about his sexual preference. He is an only child. His parents are looking forward to his marriage and to future grandchildren.

- *Client 12.* Nick, a 22-year-old police officer, indicates that he is having difficulty relating to women. After a number of interviews, he relates his concerns about his sexual adequacy. He has problems with potency and premature ejaculation, so that he has not had a satisfactory sexual relationship. He is an athlete, fisherman, and a hunter and in general presents the traditional picture of masculinity.

I would use counseling procedures similar to those I outlined earlier to help these clients work through their developmental conflicts. I would pay attention to Michael's obvious problem with authority and his tendency to withdraw from difficult situations by losing jobs or drinking. The question of whether Matt has authority problems or whether he has ambivalences about or difficulties accepting homosexuality might be raised. The feelings of inadequacy stifling Maggie and Nick might need to be confronted before their presenting problems could be resolved. Maura could profit from a careful look at how she could balance her needs for independence with her needs for companionship and productive relationships with others. Nina's unrelenting grief might be a sign of unresolved guilt feelings about her relationship with her parents before their death or a sign of unresolved dependency.

Crisis Counseling

Community counselors, like counselors in schools and colleges, must be prepared to handle crises. They must have the knowledge, skill, and experience to know how to handle the immediate presenting emergency, take any immediate action required to help a person through the trauma, and then decide whether they should continue the relationship or refer the individual to another professional or another agency.

Historically, community emergencies have been severe stress or emotional reactions resulting from attempted or contemplated suicide, severe immobilizing depression, psychotic reactions, or a sudden, traumatic emotional experience, such as the loss or death of a loved one. In the past decade severe drug reactions have become more common. More recently, crisis problems in other situations have been recognized, such as battered wives, rape victims, child abuse, and juvenile runaways.

Calhoun, Selby, and King (1976) discuss crisis problems in the general population. Their handbook covers adolescent conflict, sexual dysfunctions, abortion, rape, divorce, illness, and death and dying. J. Lewis and Lewis (1977) define a crisis as "intense, immediate and short lived" (p. 107). They emphasize the need for immediate help in accessible settings in the community. They recommend having counseling services available in the community to handle some of these problems before crises arise. Similarly, counseling services should be accessible after the immediate crises are handled. According to Mann (1978), studies show that "crisis intervention does appear to be effective in preventing hospitalization for adults and evidence from other studies suggests it may be for children as well" (p. 91).

In some communities crisis centers and counseling services have been established that are staffed by persons specially trained and specially interested in each of these areas. A counseling-center staff should include persons knowledgeable about these areas and also maintain close liaison with other agencies.

Antisocial Acts

Community counselors will also get their share of clients who request counseling to help them handle impulses, attitudes, and behaviors that they consider immoral or unethical or behaviors that are illegal. Also, referrals from probation officers and juvenile courts are likely to occur. Shoplifting and aberrant sexual behaviors, such as exhibitionism, voyeurism, obscene phone calls, and transvestism, are examples of some of the problems that may come to the attention of counselors.

Alcohol and Drug Problems

Counseling services for persons with alcohol or drug problems from young adolescence through old age should be available and coordinated with community alcohol and drug referral and treatment centers. Persons may come into a counseling service specifically for help with alcohol or drugs, or the problem may emerge during counseling a client who originally presented a different problem. Also, the family of an alcoholic who refuses to recognize his or her alcoholism can profit from counseling.

Community counseling staffs must determine when they can handle a particular problem and when a referral to an agency specializing in the treatment of chronic or severe alcohol or drug problems is necessary.

Licensed Counselors in Private Practice

The APGA's licensing proposal mentioned earlier recommends state licensing for both master's-degree and doctorate persons in professional counseling for the purpose of private practice. A number of states now license counselors.

Assuming this licensing continues, people with the kinds of concerns discussed here will have professionally trained counselors available if they are not in school and prefer not to go to clinics. Presently, normal developmental conflicts and concerns are not emphasized in the training or practice of clinical psychologists and psychiatrists. These concerns are handled, if at all, by walk-in clinics staffed with paraprofessionals and volunteers. Mandatory psychological intervention, evaluation for probation offices, decisions about commitment to mental institutions, home intervention, work with neurotic or psychotic disorders, the handling of children, and the like can be the focus of clinical psychologists and psychiatrists.

Projects and Activities

1. *Survey your community to determine what resources are available for counseling individuals with normal development concerns who are not in schools or in college.*
2. *Explore various community agencies in your vicinity from the standpoint of training. What percentage of the staff members is professionally trained? How much in-service training is given? How much dependence is there on volunteers? What is the specific training of various professionals?*
3. *Select several problems presented in this text. Visit a number of community counseling agencies and read their brochures and other publicizing materials. Does the information indicate that the agencies are prepared to handle the types of concerns discussed in this book?*

4. *Interview a number of probation officers in your community. Do they perceive any bind in trying to counsel their parolees while maintaining jurisdiction over them? Do the officers have resources to whom they can refer clients?*

5. *What resources are available in the community for counseling elderly persons? Do these services appear satisfactory? How are they funded? What improvements would you make?*

6. *Survey community minority groups and their attitudes about and use of mental-health facilities. Are minorities represented on the staffs of various agencies?*

7. *Visit your county or regional community mental-health clinic. Ask the director if you can obtain an organizational chart of services offered under the community comprehensive mental-health program in your area. Explore which needs are being met and which are being neglected. Try to determine reasons for the selection of services.*

9

Secondary Functions of Counselors

Although some disagreement exists, professional counselors generally believe that counseling staffs should spend a majority of their time in their primary function of direct counseling. The American School Counselor Association in presenting guidelines for implementing its policy for secondary school counselors indicated, "The school counselor should devote no less than 50 percent of his assigned time in counseling with individuals or small groups" (Loughary, Stripling & Fitzgerald, 1965). Ohlsen believed similar expectations existed in 1974. After studying data collected from college and university counseling centers for the College Center Data Bank in 1976, Cass and Lindeman (1978) comment, "It seems evident that the vast majority of most counselors' time is being spent in individual and group counseling and psychotherapy" (p. 288).

The remaining time is divided among secondary functions. These secondary functions include group counseling, family counseling, and various types of educationally oriented outreach programs, such as consultation, psychological-education programs, and informational services. In college and community counseling, marriage and couple counseling are other expected services. Overall, these supplementary functions are very similar, whether a counselor works in a public school, in a college, or in the community.

All the counselors on a staff should be expected to do individual counseling. Secondary duties can be shared proportionally depending upon the counselors' interests and backgrounds. In fact, a counseling staff can increase its flexibility and versatility by hiring staff members with different interests and/or backgrounds in secondary functions. For example, one counselor may enjoy coordinating group counseling or group activities, while another may prefer to develop a library of vocational and educational resources. Students enrolled in small schools or colleges staffed with one counselor are often deprived of the richness of these secondary services. One counselor would find it difficult to handle them all.

Group Counseling

Decisions about the Use of Group Counseling

Most experts agree that group counseling differs from group guidance (Belkin, 1975; Gazda, 1971). In group counseling, as in individual counseling, each individual is presenting specific concerns that he or she is trying to resolve. In group guidance, members are requesting educational and informational activities to help them grow personally or vocationally or to improve social understanding and skills. The term *group therapy* generally refers to extensive, relatively long-term treatment for serious emotional problems (Tolbert, 1978).

Encounter, personal-growth, and sensitivity-training groups are sometimes confused with group counseling. These activities originated as psychological ways to train people in personal and social awareness and skills. Thus, I will discuss these group experiences under psychological-education activities.

Group counseling appears most appropriate when individuals perceive that a central factor contributing to their discomfort or confusion is their inability to function effectively or express themselves effectively in social situations. Sometimes group counseling may be useful when a group of persons individually express very similar concerns about themselves or about interpersonal relationships. Here the sharing of similar concerns can be helpful in testing the legitimacy of their feelings and may permit members to express appropriate anger or resentment toward other persons more freely. In addition, pooling ideas of how to cope with the mutual concerns may be profitable.

Group counseling does not seem appropriate when individuals are confronting highly personal or private conflicts within themselves or with others close to them that they do not wish to share with other people. Nor do I consider groups effective for persons who express very strong fears about social interactions. In either case, a group may be an inhibiting factor, at least in the individual's first contacts with the counselor. Groups might also be unprofitable for students who have demonstrated behaviors or expressed feelings of overdependence upon the opinion of others. A group experience might reinforce dependency needs or a tendency to overconformity. After individual counseling is used to reduce the amount of fear, anxiety, or dependency, group counseling might be recommended.

I do not decide upon group counseling in order to use my time more efficiently or in order to reduce a waiting list. In my experience, group counseling does not permit counselors to see more clients. Often some members of a group may want or need individual counseling. Also, each session of group counseling usually lasts longer than a session with an individual, and the group usually needs to be maintained throughout a quarter or a term.

Some persons believe that group counseling is inherently more effective than individual counseling because it is carried on in a social system similar to real life. Actually, group-counseling social systems are by no means a prototype of social living. They are structured social interactions designed for all members to contribute to helping each individual understand and come to grips with his or her own personal concern.

The Characteristics of Group Counseling

There is general agreement that the optimal size for group counseling is six persons, with a range of from four to 12 (Shertzer & Stone, 1980). In my experience productive interactions become difficult if the group has more than ten members.

I have found that grouping students with similar concerns is more effective than placing students in groups regardless of their reasons for requesting counseling. In a group with dissimilar problems, the advantage of mutual sharing of concerns is lost, and communication and rapport can become artificial.

Some counselors prefer to have a co-leader and share the responsibility for groups. I prefer to do group counseling by myself. My reasoning is that individual members of groups are trying to make decisions or to resolve confusions or conflicts rather than attempting more generally to develop their potential or their social skills. I use the interactions and communications of group members to help each person arrive at the understanding necessary to make a personal decision or obtain the necessary skills to take productive action. Two counselors' assuming leadership could inhibit communication between group members and between a counselor and the group. On the other hand, these limitations do not seem to hold for me when I work with psychological-education groups. In these situations co-leading has appeared useful and effective.

The Ethics of Group Counseling

The choice of joining a group should ultimately be the client's. Concerns about confidentiality have been expressed about groups. I have not found this a problem in working with groups. I set guidelines with the group on my responsibility for confidentiality and then explore with group members their responsibilities. Corey (1977) believes that confidentiality fostered and continually reinforced by a counselor becomes part of the total group experience.

Attempts by a group counselor or by a group to force or persuade a group member to behave in a manner the group feels desirable are a much bigger potential ethical problem in groups than is confidentiality. Consistent with professional-counseling ethics, each member in group counseling has the right and the obligation to make the ultimate decision about participating in particular behaviors in the group.

Examples of Counseling Groups

In secondary and middle schools and in colleges, groups can be developed when students are concerned about vocational/educational or personal/social feelings and interactions. In the vocational/educational area, group counseling for those considering dropping out of school or for those confused about their future occupational aims can be useful. Students who are expressing feelings of restlessness or ambivalence about their behavior or life goals in general can profit from exploring these concerns with individuals with similar problems. Counseling groups may consist of students who are having problems with their parents over their attitudes or behavior or whose communication with their parents is poor. Similarly, students having difficulties with peer relationships with the same or opposite sex might resolve these difficulties through group interaction.

In elementary schools, groups will most likely develop around children's interactions with peers, problems in motivation to do schoolwork, friction with teachers or parents, low self-esteem, or generally unproductive classroom behavior.

Community counseling services are most likely to include, in addition to the above, group counseling related to job dissatisfaction, anxieties about changing jobs or retiring, feelings of loneliness or isolation, concerns of women and men over changing roles and values, reevaluation of lifestyle, and concerns about death and dying.

Family, Marriage, and Couple Counseling

Family counseling may be carried out in schools when the behavior of the family is interfering with the child's or the adolescent's behavior. When the family problem focuses on serious friction between mother and father, with separation or divorce a possibility, then marriage counseling is in order. Marriage counseling is not normally considered appropriate for public school counseling. The reasoning of school boards and administrators is that counseling should be confined to student problems or a family situation in which the child is directly involved. Nevertheless, counselors should be free to consult with parents about the need for marriage counseling and to help direct them to community agencies for counseling. Frequently when parents are having marriage counseling or decide upon a separation or divorce, the student may want counseling from a school counselor.

In colleges family counseling is rarer, since most students are of legal age and are frequently not living at home. Marriage counseling and counseling for couples living together occur with some frequency in colleges.

Counseling centers in communities and counselors in private practice may see a higher proportion of persons desiring family counseling and marriage and couple counseling than occurs in public schools and colleges. Some clinics refuse to see a child or an adolescent unless the parents agree to engage in family counseling. This policy may be appropriate when the clinic is handling severe emotional disturbance or child abuse. With counseling for normal concerns or conflicts, I prefer to function as I do in schools and see the young person first. Then, if necessary, I would involve the family. Young adults deciding whether to marry or start a family, which involves embarking on a more permanent relationship with another person, may request family or marriage counseling.

As I discussed in Chapter 8, it is important that both parties agree to counseling when marital or couple counseling is requested. The couple may see one counselor together, with some individual sessions included. They may see two counselors jointly or two different counselors who consult with each other and give feedback to each person. If two counselors are seen jointly, it is often wise to have a male and a female counselor share counseling sessions to minimize sex bias. My preference is to see a couple together, with some individual sessions if necessary. Also, co-counseling with a female counselor has proved highly satisfactory with some couples.

If a counselor sees a couple individually and then in joint sessions, the counselor and both clients should agree on the amount and type of information that will be shared from the individual sessions. Otherwise, each partner may become anxious or suspicious about the exchanges going on in the individual sessions. Also, the counselor may promise complete confidentiality in an individual session and then learn of factors that are highly pertinent to the marriage problems that are not then open to discussion in the joint sessions. Similar precautions are necessary when two counselors are seeing the couple separately. Interchange of insights and information is important, since a major goal of marriage counseling is to improve communication.

If one person agrees to marital counseling and the other refuses, then individual counseling is involved rather than marriage counseling. Also, if each party sees a different counselor about their marriage with no interchange between counselors or no joint sessions, then each person is receiving individual counseling. It should be noted that successful marriage counseling may end up in a decision to separate or divorce if both agree that this is the wiser plan.

Outreach: The Guidance Activities of Counselors

The Characteristics of Professional-Counseling Outreach

Outreach functions are important educational and informational activities that complement individual counseling. Outreach programs have always been an essential part of effective counseling programs. The recent proliferation of theories, techniques, and systems of personal and social skills has increased the number of outreach activities that are suitable for counselors. Categorization has become more difficult, especially when some of the activities are inconsistent with counselor training or goals. I have found the following five categories helpful when trying to set up or evaluate the outreach activities of a staff: consultation, psychological education, informational and appraisal services, social-change activities, and liaison with other community agencies and other specialists. Outreach activities are equally important components of counseling programs in public schools, colleges, and communities.

A major purpose of counselor outreach activities is to broaden the knowledge and skills of individuals in personal, social, and vocational development. Another major purpose is to improve the school or community environment, so that this learning will be encouraged and enhanced.

Effective counselor outreach activities, as defined here, have the following characteristics: (1) They supplement but do not attempt to replace individual counseling. (2) They are within the expertise of the counseling staff. (3) They are subject to the same professional and ethical considerations (for example, free choice, confidentiality) as in individual and group counseling. (4) They do not inhibit the possibility of developing effective counseling relationships with students desiring counseling or of developing appropriate expectations of students, staff, or parents regarding counseling services. (5) They do not require each counselor to have equal preparation or interest in all activities.

In my experience, contrary to popular opinion, effective and appropriate outreach activities do not decrease overall requests for counseling. Instead, they tend to increase them. As a counseling-center staff becomes better known and more trusted, a greater number of persons may ask for counseling or be referred by other persons. Whereas more educational and informational services may help some persons reduce their need for counseling, the services may awaken in others the need for counseling. If teachers become more effective in communication, relationship, and behavioral skills, they not only improve the classroom climate but also become more cognizant of students' need for professional counseling. Thus, overall, outreach activities may prevent the development of some problems, but they may also spark the recognition of a need for counseling, which in itself can prevent more serious conflict.

In outreach the counseling staff should be considered the resource rather than individual counselors. Then it is possible for counselors to emphasize outreach functions most suited to their interests, backgrounds, and experience. In small school districts, colleges, or clinics, consultants from outside agencies may have to be used. In larger districts, colleges, or clinics, consultants from other agencies can be used if no staff member has had professional training in a particular area.

I do not use one systematic set of consultation procedures or helping skills for outreach activities. The procedures and skills used are philosophically consistent with the phenomenological developmental view of human nature that is basic to my individual counseling. Also, I am eclectic in my counseling-outreach practice in my choice of techniques because of the varied personalities, needs, and activities involved in outreach.

Consultant Functions of Counselors

The Definition of a Consultant. Counselors as consultants are viewed as professional persons who can be looked to for expert help in specific areas related to their counselor training. If fully prepared, they are specialists in behavior dynamics, personal and interpersonal relationships, occupational knowledge, appraisal information, and communication skills.

Consultation in counseling should not be confused with supervision in counseling. Consultation involves offering an expert opinion to other persons about handling their own or others' behavior in a particular situation. Supervision primarily involves direct responsibility for training counseling students or beginning counselors and overseeing and evaluating their performance.

When teachers seek me out for consultation about a student, I prefer to discuss the situation without identifying the student if that is possible. Students' right to privacy is maintained in this way. Also, this attitude makes it easier for teachers to generalize from the specific behavior of one student to similar behaviors of other students.

This approach has proved feasible and effective in my college counseling experience because anonymity is fairly easy to maintain. In larger high schools this approach also can be arranged fairly simply. However, in small schools the preservation of anonymity becomes more difficult. In particular, this policy is difficult to carry out in elementary schools with a small, intimate staff and a small number of students. Nevertheless, I recommend that in initial contact with teachers, the names of students should be of secondary importance unless it is determined that the identity of the individual is necessary for productive discussion.

Consultation with Teachers about Individual Students or about Interactions with a Class.   Teachers request a consultation when they have concerns about their interactions with individual students, about class dynamics, or parent conferences. At times the consultation pertains to whether a referral is in order and, if so, to whom the student should be referred. Teachers also ask for consultation when they have personal concerns interfering with their job performance. College faculty make similar requests of college counseling centers with the exception that parent conferences are infrequent.

If the counseling staff is well trained and respected by the teaching staff, consultation requests by teachers will be frequent. Teachers may be concerned about the behavior or attitudes of a student toward the teacher or toward the class in general. They may also be uncomfortable about their own reaction to a particular student. They may question the appropriateness of a student's interaction with peers. Or they may be concerned about a student's poor self-image. Teachers may want to understand better what is going on in their interaction with a student, what they might do to help, and whether a referral is necessary.

- *Teacher A.* Ms. A tells the counselor that she is concerned about a student who does no work in her English-composition class. He scores high on standardized intelligence and achievement tests but is presently doing "D" work because he does not hand in papers. He is polite, presents no discipline problems, and consistently promises to improve. She has persuaded and cajoled the student to no avail. Ms. A, a young, energetic, first-year teacher, has begun to feel frustrated and annoyed. Her negative feelings toward the student bother her.

- *Teacher B.* Mr. B is a high school teacher just out of college. He looks and dresses like the average student. He perceives himself as a friend of the students and goes out of his way to show personal interest. A sophomore has responded with a crush on him. She finds all kinds of excuses to see him. She stares dreamily at him in class. There have been some harmless, prank phone calls to his home. He is convinced that she made the calls.

- *Teacher C.* Mr. C, a sixth-grade teacher, complains about two disruptive students in his class. They talk out loud, answer insolently at times, and in general demonstrate rudeness and disrespect. The class laughs and becomes restless when these students act up. When one or the other or both are absent, the class works smoothly. He has had similar difficulties before. He prefers trying to change his behavior rather than sending the students to the administrator for disciplinary action.

- *Teacher D.* Ms. D, a college teacher, has good trust relationships in her physics class. A student confides that she thinks she is pregnant. Another confesses that he has tried hard drugs and is worried about it. Still another student shares deep concerns about his alcoholic parents. Ms. D wants to maintain openness with her students but feels overwhelmed and ill equipped to handle the students' problems.

All the above teachers are expressing different concerns about interaction with individual students. Ms. A wants help with an underachieving student and with her reactions to the student. Mr. B is wondering how to handle a sticky relationship that may be a result of his general attitudes toward adolescents. Mr. C is struggling with particular student behavior that he finds difficult to handle. Ms. D is expressing concern about over-involvement with problems of students.

I first determine with the teacher what he or she is hoping to attain through consultation. Next we explore what the teacher has or has not done so far to resolve the problem. Then we can discuss further suggestions for improvement. If the teacher has not made sufficient attempts to talk his or her concerns over with the student, I usually offer suggestions on how best to approach the student. Role playing might be useful for a teacher who is particularly hesitant to interact with students.

Ms. A might be pressuring the underachiever, who may be resisting because of fear of failure or because of unreasonable, perfectionist attitudes. In either case, consistent encouragement to live up to an academic potential of which he is uncertain may lead to further withdrawal. Perhaps helping the student set smaller, achievable, sequential goals for a paper would be more productive.

Mr. B may need to confront the student with her behavior in a kind but firm manner. He might also search out whether he is subtly contributing to the uncomfortable relationship through his own behavior of trying to be "one of the boys."

Mr. C can be shown the importance of setting limits with disruptive students and given guidelines on how to stick with the limits. Concurrently he could explore with the students how he and they can work to reduce the instances of disruptive behavior. He can be encouraged to confront students with their behavior and to set up some agreement or contract about what is acceptable classroom behavior. If the students are responsive, a joint consultation with the counselor can be arranged as long as the counselor is not perceived as an umpire. In addition, Mr. C can explore with the counselor why he is having difficulty with this particular type of behavior whereas he generally copes well in classroom management.

Ms. D can be given a perspective on differentiating between the "caring"-teacher role and the professional-counselor role. If she continually responds to students so as to invite unrestrained self-revelation, she should not be surprised that the students expect her to function as a professional counselor. Ms. D has apparently become aware that mere disclosure does not lead to the resolution of problems. Thus, she can be given guidelines on how to listen to a student with a problem, how to determine with the student whether she can handle the problem, and how to refer the student to a counselor when it appears necessary. Teacher D, then, can continue to be a resource for students who wish to bring up problems, but she also can be a bridge to professional counselors when that help is necessary.

- *Teacher E.* Ms. E, visibly upset, approaches a counselor in the coffee room. She asks whether he has time to talk with her about some students. The counselor suggests taking some coffee to his office, where they can talk in confidence. Two of her students confided to her that a number of class members believe Ms. E is sarcastic and puts some kids down. Students otherwise like her interactions in class. This perception by students is a surprise to her. Putting students down is the last thing she wants to do. She has thought that her remarks were humorous.

- *Teacher F.* Mr. F drops into the counselor's office and sits down heavily. He appears to be a highly perceptive teacher but a little unsure of himself. He is being evaluated for tenure. His administrator, after visiting Mr. F's class, tells him that he is well organized but somewhat distant with students. The administrator recommends that Mr. F be more outgoing, spontaneous, and friendly—characteristics of the administrator's behavior. Mr. F senses some need to open up more to students but cannot see himself emulating the effervescent administrator.

Both teachers are expressing concerns related specifically to classroom behavior. In situations like these, sometimes teachers want simply to unburden themselves. At other times they are hoping to get specific help. It is important that counselors clarify the teachers' expectations.

Ms. E has some apparent strengths. Students generally like her. Two students felt secure enough with her to tell her about the complaints. She seems willing to try to improve. Her problem lies in not having recognized the behavior bothering students. Ms. E has a number of alternatives. She can ask these students to let her know specifically when she makes remarks that sound like put-downs. Or she can indicate to the class that this behavior was brought to her attention and that some discussion might help. In either of these approaches, she can monitor her own behavior. In addition, some further consultation with Ms. E could be held to help her determine whether she has some implicit feelings of resentment toward students that need to be confronted.

Mr. F's acceptance of the administrator's criticism and his desire to improve his behavior are favorable. He also recognizes that trying to change his behavior by modeling it on the behavior of an individual with different personality characteristics can be fruitless. Some discussions about the reasons for his uncertainty about his professional ability and some suggestions on how to capitalize on his sensitivity to student needs may lead to more natural opening up with students.

Consultation with Teachers about Personal Concerns.   Teachers sometimes bring personal concerns to counselors. For example, a teacher may be experiencing marital problems with threats of divorce being bandied about. Another teacher may be experiencing depression or general anxiety. Or a counselor may notice that a teacher is unusually distracted or jumpy in his or her interactions with students and staff. In these types of situations, a counseling staff can be helpful to teachers as consultants rather than as counselors. Counseling fellow teachers is not considered good professional practice. The counselor and teacher may find it difficult to disengage their social and/or business interactions from the counseling relationship. Establishing a relationship necessary for effective counseling would be difficult.

On the other hand, consultation between a counselor and a fellow teacher may be valuable. In consultation the teacher and counselor can evaluate the seriousness of the problem and can discuss whether counseling help is needed. These consultations may go on for two or three sessions in the form of preparation for counseling or psychotherapy. For example, apprehension about seeking help may have to be handled. Or a joint consultation with a couple contemplating marriage counseling may be needed to discuss the importance of both parties' being involved. If counseling is decided upon, the counselor can refer the teacher to a professional person whom the counselor respects.

Consultation with Administrators.   Administrators are often faced with conflicting demands and pressures from students, parents, and teachers concerning student behavior and school policy, student rights and responsibilities, and teacher or parent rights and responsibilities. Difficult interactions with parents or with individual teachers or groups of teachers may plague the administrator. A gap between curricular offerings and student needs may occur. Testing programs, appropriate use of school records, and changes in laws about administrative and student interactions are also areas in which school administrators may want consultation.

The counseling staff can offer information and guidelines about potential consequences of certain administrative actions upon the student body or the teaching staff. Counselors can also use their expertise on school-wide testing and use of records to make sure that policies about these are in line with the rights and responsibilities of students and adults.

Guidelines on handling interactions between parents and teachers also can be discussed. However, I prefer that counselors and administrators not discuss a specific teacher's interaction with students or proficiency in teaching. This sort of evaluative interview can raise ethical dilemmas for counselors who are inviting referrals from teachers. If a teacher and an administrator request a joint consultation with a counselor about their interaction, a consultation may be useful as long as there are no evaluative overtones. When an administrator is concerned about a severely disturbed teacher whose safety or the safety of others is involved, a consultation is in order. The following are some examples of appropriate counselor/administrator consultations.

- *Administrator A.* A department head asks for a consultation about a faculty member who is very depressed and who has mentioned suicide. The faculty member has asked that the information be kept confidential but has also been reluctant to seek professional help. The department head is worried about the teacher, the students in the teacher's class, and her own responsibility for the welfare of the teacher.

- *Administrator B.* The principal of an elementary school is concerned because he believes that cumulative records have become practically useless. He says that teachers stopped putting meaningful data in the records when Congress passed the Buckley amendment requiring that parents see student records on demand. He has felt reluctant to include negative data in the records but also believes that good cumulative records are for the students' benefit.

- *Administrator C.* The principal of a high school asks for consultation because she is considering revamping the curriculum to meet the students' needs more effectively. The town has changed from a suburban residential area to a semiindustrial one during the 10 years since the last curriculum overhaul. She wonders whether the students' vocational aims are being served.

I would try to get Administrator A to recognize that the teacher in question is placing an undue burden upon her by sharing suicidal thoughts and then rejecting the idea of professional help. I would recommend that she indicate to the teacher that she cannot in good conscience keep this information in confidence unless the teacher seeks help. I would offer to see the teacher and help to arrange appropriate treatment. If the teacher refused any help, I would suggest that the administrator, with the teacher's knowledge, notify the teacher's family and arrange sick leave.

A consultation with Administrator B could aid him in resolving the dilemma about records productively. It could be shown that appropriate application of the Buckley amendment could improve the quality of records and give the type of feedback to students for which the records were originally intended. The administrator could instruct teachers to use specific behavior descriptions in cumulative records. For example, "John does not hand in any assignments on time" is much more meaningful than "John is lazy" or "John wastes his time." Also, teachers should be sure that parents and children are aware of comments that are included in the cumulative record, whether they be positive or negative ones. In this way there are no surprises if parents ask for access to the records. Administrator B could be encouraged to use the cumulative records in the same way. If parents refuse to agree to a psychological evaluation of their child when a learning disability is suspected, the refusal should be noted in the record and the parents asked to sign in the record that they have rejected the idea. When records become accurate, open indicators of students' progress and of parental attitudes, they become more useful in continuing guidance.

A counseling staff can help a principal like Administrator C improve the curriculum by giving some general feedback about student requests for courses and some ideas about what students do after graduation. Also, the counseling staff can offer to do a survey of students about their curriculum needs and a follow-up study of graduates of the school.

Consultation with Parents.   Parents may request consultation about their child's or adolescent's behavior when the student is not having counseling. It is not only ethical but also good professional practice to tell these parents that it would be best to let the student know that a consultation has been requested and the reason for the consultation. If the student has serious objections, the parents may need to resolve these objections before seeing the counselor. The counselor might also talk with the student about his or her objections to the conference, which in itself might help communication between parents and child. The rationale here is that, if one starts effective communication processes right away based upon the right to privacy and upon confidentiality, the possibility of the student's perceiving intrigue between adults is reduced, and a counseling relationship or family counseling might arise out of the consultation.

At the time a request for consultation is made, the counselor should determine whether the parents should be consulting with a school psychologist, school social worker, or administrator rather than with a counselor. The same principles apply to parental requests as to teacher requests. Administrive psychological evaluation or administrative decisions requested by parents are not the province of the counselor, as I have indicated throughout the book, nor are referrals for disciplinary action.

Consultation by Community Counselors.   As communities develop counseling services in clinics and in private practice for normal developmental concerns or conflicts, it should be expected that some of the clientele will be children and adolescents and their families. Thus, the type of consultations with teachers, administrators, and parents that I have described for school counselors may also occur if such consultations are encouraged. In addition, school counselors will have doctorate community counselors available as consultants.

Increased numbers of doctorate counseling psychologists should be available to employment offices, Social Security disability departments, vocational-rehabilitation services, and Veterans Administration offices. In these situations, counseling psychologists with expertise in vocational counseling can be used to help determine appropriate career opportunities or training for individuals in the community who are puzzled about career choice. Counseling psychologists can also help determine whether disabled persons who can no longer continue in their current jobs can find more appropriate careers or training consistent with their interests and abilities.

Psychological-Education Activities

Five types of psychological-education activities are representative of present practices in counseling. Briefly, they are (1) teaching psychological courses, (2) helping teachers broaden subject matter to include personal relevance to students, (3) helping teachers evaluate humanistic systems of education, (4) training others to improve their communication and relationship skills, and (5) training counselor aides.

There is one essential characteristic that must be mentioned if these activities are to remain consistent with the prevailing standards of the professional associations representing counseling. In carrying out these training and educational experiences, it is important that counselors maintain voluntary involvement and avoid the types of social or personal intervention that violate the right to privacy. Since counselors are not primarily concerned with disruptive or pathological behavior or with behavior requiring social management, psychological intervention without the consent of the individual is unethical according to counseling philosophy.

This policy does not mean that counselors should not publicize their willingness to offer these activities. A counseling staff can issue notices, publish newsletters, or post bulletins about their willingness to involve themselves in these types of outreach.

Teaching Psychological Courses in Public Schools, Colleges, and Communities. Counselors have the background to teach courses in vocational, personal, and social areas. Professional counselors can offer elective, nongraded courses in public schools, in colleges, and in the community. They can teach specific units in a particular class in conjunction with the regular instructor, or they may be invited into classrooms to cover certain topics within their area of expertise. Community colleges, extension divisions of colleges and universities, and extended day programs at colleges are major resources for community counselors to offer evening courses of this type.

Courses or units dealing with factors involved in career awareness, personal development, and social interactions are pertinent. Also pertinent are teaching units related to such social issues as race relations, cultural differences, mental-health issues, the changing roles of men and women, sex and marriage, family relationships, and individual rights and responsibilities. Opportunities to discuss factors contributing to the development of values and to decisions about values can be important as well.

These courses should be offered by counselors with a particular interest in teaching; they should not be expected duties of all counselors. Moreover, in all of these situations, counselors and teachers must be cautious that persons being educated in personal and social development are not being influenced to develop specific personal beliefs or social attitudes of the instructor or of the institution. Also, this sort of education for personal development should be perceived as expanding a curriculum rather than substituting for professional counseling.

Supplementing Classroom Subject Matter.   Counselors can also be of assistance to teachers at all levels who want to broaden academic subject matter to make it personally relevant to students. Stanford and Roark (1974) give examples of personalizing units of study in government, war, geology, physics, poetry, and arithmetic. They advocate using "you" questions for increasing relevance. In a unit on arithmetic, for example, mail-order catalogues might be examined and shipping and insurance costs computed. Then "you" questions would be asked regarding how important material things are to each student and how each would decide what to buy. Counselors can also be used as resource persons in such classes as social studies, health, home economics, physical education, and English literature, all of which are conducive to discussions on value systems, communication, lifestyles, and the like.

Requests for counselors to supplement the academic work of teachers are most frequent in elementary schools. These requests will increase as administrators increasingly demand that teachers become responsible for the personal development of students. As these demands escalate, counseling staffs should reaffirm that they should not be primarily responsible for training teachers in affective curriculums or in human relationships. Instead, teachers should be encouraged to put pressure on teacher training institutions to offer this training as part of their program.

Evaluating Humanistic Systems and Programs with Teachers.   Humanistic-education corporations, often run by psychological educators, advertise their particular systems as best fitting a school's needs for humanistic education. The numerous choices available can be bewildering to teachers trying to augment their intellectual subject matter with an appropriate affective curriculum. The counseling staff probably can best serve the teaching staff by helping them evaluate the suitability of these programs for their classrooms. Then, if the program appears suitable, a counselor can serve as a resource person to the instructor and as a referral resource when necessary. Simpson and Gray's (1976) book, which includes a comprehensive bibliography on humanistic education, is a valuable resource for counselors doing this kind of work with teachers.

The following considerations are offered as guidelines for determining the appropriateness of various humanistic programs and systems in education. (1) Are the participants truly permitted to choose whether they want to be involved in a particular class exercise? (2) Are the rights to privacy of the participants and of their families protected by limiting the expectations of unrestrained expression of personal feelings? (3) Are safeguards included so that the participants' attitudes are not shaped according to some predetermined values or moral beliefs? (4) Are the discussions or exercises of such a nature that they do not provoke psychological or emotional reactions that the instructors are not professionally prepared to handle? (5) Are games or units regarding self-disclosure designed to protect individuals from indulging in intimate revelations that may subsequently lead to psychological distress? (6) Are there precautions to make sure that the program does not foster superficial resolutions of student problems or lead to superficial or hypocritical relationships among class members? Some examples of evaluating these programs with teachers should illustrate applications of some of the guidelines.

Simon (1970) developed the concept of sensitizing modules by which students could meaningfully interact with their environment outside school. This concept has some basic merit. Some activities in which students interact with community agencies appear appropriate. For example, a student visits a courtroom as an observer, keeps a list of the cases brought before the judge, and notes how each case was handled. Or a student requests an opportunity to ride in a patrol car with an officer during the officer's normal tour of duty and notes the types of problems that the officer had to handle in one evening.

Kirschenbaum (1970) recommends a sensitivity module for an elementary school class that seems productive. He suggests that the class explore their own city to discover parts new to them when they are studying a unit on world exploration. These activities, designed to get students to become active in their community, do not violate rights to privacy or impinge on the value choice or the emotional privacy of the individual or the class.

On the other hand, there are sensitivity modules discussed by Simon and Kirschenbaum about which I have serious reservations. In setting up experiences especially for middle-class students, Simon (1970) recommends the following: "Wear old clothes and sit in the waiting room of the State Employment Office. Listen, observe, talk to the people sitting next to you. Read the announcements on the bulletin board, etc. Try to overhear an interview if possible" (p. 29). In another module the student is to go to a waiting room of a maternity ward and try to determine through conversations which of the patients are charity cases and which are not. Kirschenbaum recommends that students pretend they are having trouble getting a landlord to do some repairs in an apartment and that they call city hall to register a complaint.

Dressing up in old clothes in order to mingle with other people, attempting to overhear a private interview, or striking up a conversation to determine the social or economic status of another person constitutes invasion of privacy. Calling city hall on a pretense can reinforce deceptive behavior rather than the type of direct action intended in these activities. Such activities are useful, I believe, when students investigate community agencies in a straightforward manner. For example, Kirschenbaum himself offers an alternative to the pretended complaint about the landlord that seems to me to be more suitable. He suggests that students find a neighbor who is having a problem of this sort and offer to help.

Programs have been developed commercially called self-disclosure activities in which persons are encouraged or taught to reveal intimate personal feelings, attitudes, or experiences to a class or group. Care is required when using self-disclosure activities, for there are definite psychological risks in these types of programs. Invasion of privacy is inherent if all students are required to participate. If involvement is voluntary, the risk of teachers' evoking psychological or emotional reactions that they are not prepared to handle is great if the exercises are used inappropriately. Discussions built around one's general attitudes about oneself and others or discussions about how it feels to try to break into a new group can be useful. Also, one's attitudes toward or experiences with discrimination, one's views about male/female roles, or some sharing about future occupational or life plans or hopes can be productive. On the other hand, the teacher is on shaky ground when the topics include revealing secret problems or worries to a class or writing autobiographies to be mimeographed and read by all class members.

Stanford and Roark (1974) describe a self-disclosure activity for teachers that I believe is professionally questionable. All class members are instructed to write down, in as much detail as possible, a secret problem or worry that is disturbing them. It is recommended that the students camouflage their handwriting and keep the problems anonymous by not using their names or the names of other persons. The problems are then distributed at random. The students take turns reading the problem and telling how they would feel if they had that problem. If a student gets his or her own problem, the student is not to let the others know and is to proceed as though it were another person's problem.

This type of activity is based upon the assumption that the greater the self-disclosure, the better a person's mental health will become. In my experience quite the contrary can occur. Unrestrained self-revelation in a group can lead to psychological distress. Also, the artificial anonymity in this particular exercise can contribute to even further emotional trauma.

When individuals reveal a secret worry or problem in detail in public, latent, distressing emotional reactions may be aroused. These reactions may occur after the person mulls over what he or she has revealed and considers the reaction of the group. Students may also begin guessing games about who has what problem. Highly sensitive students may become upset when they sense that other students have figured out their problem, or they may get feelings of paranoia, believing that the whole class or student body knows of their secret problem. Other students may not put down the "real" secret problem and may develop anxiety because they believed it too terrible to reveal. On the other hand, some students may receive superficial feedback about a problem that strengthens ineffective defenses and offers temporary, nonproductive reduction of anxiety.

Counselors can help teachers evaluate appropriate uses of other popular humanistic-education programs, such as values clarification, moral-education exercises, Duso kits, and magic circles. Shaver and Strong (1976) express some reservations about the indiscriminate use of programs in values clarification and moral education that are worthwhile reading. For example, they criticize Raths and Simon, the originators of values clarification, for demonstrating insufficient concern about which values a teacher should choose to probe. They also present an example of how an exercise in values clarification can lead to psychological trauma if the privacy of an individual student is not protected. Their recommendation is that teachers differentiate between public and private values and then emphasize public ones—for example, emphasize attitudes about racial discrimination rather than attitudes about private sexual behavior. I concur and further recommend that teachers emphasize classroom interactions rather than initiating discussions about students' private lives or family interactions. This approach tends to make the classroom unit more relevant and to increase good communications in class. These conditions can lead to a more productive classroom environment.

Building Personal and Social Skills.   The major methods of building personal and social skills are through workshops and group experiences. Workshops and educational group experiences differ from the instructional units just discussed in that they are usually short-term, do not involve academic credit, and are less structured than a classroom activity.

A counseling staff can survey students, staff, or members of a community about the type of workshops or group experiences they would like. Workshops or groups can be offered by the counseling-staff members who have the appropriate background, or the counseling staff can arrange for outside consultants to run an activity when no staff member has the expertise in that particular area.

Workshops on vocational development, decision-making processes, women and careers, job-seeking skills, assertiveness training, self-esteem building, communication skills, parental skills, or similar developmental areas can be offered. Communitywide workshops can also be formed. Leaders of local or regional ethnic groups, for example, can be invited to the school or community to discuss means of improving communication and the understanding of differing value systems. Or a workshop on the use and abuse of alcohol or drugs might be developed by the local alcohol referral center. The staff of a birth-control clinic could also be invited to present their function in the community.

It is important that skill workshops be based upon the needs expressed by the population being served rather than upon the belief of a counselor or counseling staff that everyone needs training in some important universal skill. Thus, if all groups were offered assertiveness training or values clarification or skills in listening to others, regardless of request, one can legitimately wonder whether the counselor is pushing one system of skills rather than tailoring these experiences to concerns specifically expressed by different groups.

Encounter, personal-growth, and sensitivity groups, as discussed in Chapter 4 and as indicated earlier in this chapter, are designed to train people in personal and interpersonal skills. Lakin (1972) makes a useful distinction about these training groups. The distinction is whether the emphasis is upon improving social interaction or upon increasing personal development. The first type he calls interactional awareness and the second expanded experiencing. Although either type of group experience may improve both social and personal development, Lakin believes that most groups focus primarily on one.

Groups intended to develop communication and social-interaction skills, sometimes called sensitivity-training or organizational-development groups, are very similar to workshops in social skills. They differ in that there is less structured leadership and less emphasis on developing particular social skills. These groups, whose members learn to develop their own system of democratic processes, their own leadership, and their own methods of developing social cooperation, are quite acceptable in schools and in colleges. They can be used to help student-government groups function more equitably. They can be developed to help improve student/faculty interactions. They are also applicable to community agencies and to businesses.

Personal-growth groups and encounter groups, which are formed to increase self-awareness, raise consciousness, and the like, are less like workshops than are the sensitivity groups. The group is expected to serve as a means for each individual to develop emotionally, which usually entails expressing feelings very openly. Encounter groups are often more intense and even less structured than personal-growth groups. Most school officials are highly dubious about using personal-growth groups in public schools and even more negative about encounter groups. There is considerable justification for their reservations about these groups on the basis of how they were used in the late 1960s and early 1970s. Then intense encounter and personal-growth groups were in vogue, often led by untrained persons. These untrained leaders tended to do no screening of group members and tended to encourage intense emotional interactions or intimate self-disclosure without having the ability to provide emotional safeguards or backup counseling. As a counseling director, I became aware of a number of individuals who were emotionally traumatized by this indiscriminate use of groups.

Current interest is in less intense or intimate experiences centered on raising the self-esteem or self-awareness of various groups, such as homemakers, minority groups, and persons in midlife. If the leaders are professionally trained counselors who do screen group members and who are alert to the persons who might need counseling, personal-growth groups can be appropriate in schools as well as in the community.

Training Counselor Aides.   In-service training is a function of counselors when they are developing paraprofessionals in counseling. These paraprofessionals are called paracounselors or, preferably, counselor aides. Paraprofessionals should be differentiated from volunteers in that they receive specific training from a professional to perform specific auxiliary duties related to the professional's duties. Also, paraprofessionals should be differentiated on the basis of which professional group has trained them. Thus, paramedics should have a different set of skills than do counselor aides, and social-worker aides' skills should not be identical to those of counselor aides.

Counselor aides can also be trained in skills at different levels. Some individuals can be trained to help collect and give out materials in information-resource rooms. They might function in the same capacity as do student aides in libraries. Other counselor aides might receive some basic interviewing skills and be used to staff referral and information desks. Still others might be trained to score simple paper-and-pencil tests used in counseling interviews.

Some counselor aides can be trained for somewhat higher skill levels. For example, in colleges, students are often hired as aides in the residence halls to act as resource persons for the students. Through in-service training with professional counselors at the counseling center, these students can learn to listen and attend to students' problems as they arise in the dorms. Then, through close consultation with a counselor, decisions about whether to refer students can be made. These consultations follow the same principles outlined for teacher consultations. Different levels of counselor aides can be developed as the aides gain more experience.

Groups of special counselor aides can be developed in schools, colleges, and communities with large minority groups. If large groups of Indians, Blacks, or Chicano students are part of a particular institution or community, a counseling staff should initiate counselor-aide training for members of these groups who show an inclination toward and interest in this work. These aides can be a resource for counseling staffs and, most important, a bridge between the minority students and their families and the counseling staff.

Counselor aides can also be helpful to professionals when they are trained to handle information and referrals for a specific community service, such as drug or alcohol referral centers or pregnancy-counseling centers. In these more complex counselor-aide positions, skills acquisition must go beyond such interviewing techniques as listening and knowing how to ask questions. Knowing how to avoid becoming overly involved in a person's problems and knowing when and how to refer an individual to a professional are crucial additional skills.

Counselors have a professional and ethical responsibility to select counselor aides carefully, to supervise closely, and to indicate the limitations they have because of limited training. The counseling profession has the obligation to develop different levels of counselor-aide training that involve gradually increasing responsibility and remuneration. All of these experiences should be designed in a ladder form that relates to further training. In this way these experiences become an excellent training ground for future professional counselors, can increase counselor-aide commitment to the total program, and can decrease the tremendous turnover of counselor aides in the middle of a developing program.

Information and Appraisal Services

The counseling staff's expertise in vocational and educational planning and in skills for personal and social growth makes the counseling center a logical and central place for organization and dissemination of information in these areas. In addition, individual staff members can become resource persons for guidance activities that involve the teaching and administrative staff. The counseling staff can also be a bridge for staff and students to other community agencies. They can arrange for seminars and for workshops for teachers, students, and administrators led by specialists from community agencies.

Resource Rooms.   The counseling-staff resource room should contain material describing general and specific occupations, local and national trends, local outlets for jobs, apprenticeship opportunities, opportunities for women, affirmative-action guidelines, and characteristics of various occupational fields. Books and pamphlets about the importance of work and its relationship to personal development and to personal and social values can be included. Occupational materials lend themselves to computer storage and retrieval. Computer-based exploration systems should be housed in the resource room.

Educational materials should include up-to-date catalogues of the state's higher educational institutions and professional schools and catalogues of representative colleges throughout the country. College-scholarship and financial-aid materials should be on file and readily accessible.

Books and pamphlets about drugs and alcohol, birth control, sex and marriage, race relations, environmental and social issues, and civil rights are examples of information related to personal and social development that can be made available in the resource room. Pamphlets from national and regional mental-health committees and agencies can be included. Information about the legal responsibilities and rights of individuals is also appropriate to keep on file.

A very important function of the resource room would be to have on file the names and phone numbers of all the community agencies in the city or county. Procedures for contacting agencies about birth control, legal aid, alcohol, drugs, family counseling, or marital counseling should be included. In addition, the names of licensed or certified counselors and psychologists and psychiatrists in the surrounding area should be available.

Another important service of the resource room would be to have guidelines available on how to evaluate the various group experiences offered in the community. The qualifications of the group leader and the safeguards against potential psychological trauma are important for students and their families to consider before joining a group.

Teacher Adviser Programs. Some schools and colleges have developed advisement systems in which faculty are involved in helping students in programming. Teachers are assigned about 20 students to advise. Programs are developed and approved in individual and group sessions. I have found systems of advisement more productive if a counselor serves as a resource person for a particular group of faculty advisers. If the programming for a particular student is confused because the student has inner conflicts or environmental pressures that are different from his or her needs, the teacher can consult with the counselor or refer the student for counseling. The vocational-counseling problems I presented in an earlier chapter are examples of conflicts that might be expressed directly or indirectly. In addition, students may bring other personal concerns into their interactions with their advisers that can be handled in a similar manner.

If teacher adviser programs are developed, counselors can offer in-service training on interviewing and referral skills. They can also make available data on college requirements, technical-school requirements, and job requirements.

Counselors as a Resource in Appraisal and Testing. The term *appraisal* is used frequently in counseling to describe the use of tests and background data to help clients gain more information about themselves upon which to base a decision. In outreach appraisal, counselors help teachers and administrators to use tests, cumulative records, anecdotal records, and other appraisal data in a legal, ethical, and constructive manner. Guidelines on the type of data to be accumulated, the purpose of keeping records, and the sharing of data can be presented. For example, counselors should alert administrators to any testing program or tests that discriminate on the basis of sex, race, or socioeconomic status.

It is not advisable for counseling centers in schools or colleges to be responsible for coordinating and administering schoolwide testing programs or college-entrance tests. A testing officer should be responsible for the selection of and the procedures for administering these tests. Maintaining a difference between the counseling staff and the testing staff keeps the counseling staff from being perceived as an evaluative service. This problem is particularly acute at the college level, where a considerable variety of testing and evaluation goes on.

During my administration of a college counseling center, I insisted upon separation of the counseling center from the testing center. This policy was based upon the reasoning that a counseling center that does evaluation for the institution has a different image for students and faculty than a counseling center that does not. For example, some counseling centers grade exams, run faculty evaluations, and administer admissions tests. The results are then funneled back to faculty and administrators. These functions, I believe, can arouse confusion about the purpose of a counseling center and can raise questions about counselor confidentiality.

However, the counseling staff can be a resource for the schoolwide testing program in other ways. The counselors can evaluate the need for and value of schoolwide tests. They can offer the opportunity for students to get the results of tests individually or in groups. If tests on vocational interests and aptitudes are given to all students, the counseling staff can interpret the results of these tests to students in informal vocational-guidance group sessions.

Career Education.   The APGA and Division 17 of the APA agree that vocational exploration and decisions fall within the expertise of professionally trained counselors. Thus, when the Career Education Incentive Act was passed in 1978, the question of appropriate involvement in career education received attention.

School career-education models have received most attention. They include career-awareness programs at elementary school levels, career exploration in junior high school, and career preparation in senior high school (Herr, 1974). The major curricular activities focus on using a project approach that includes discussing factors about the environment and the self that influence ultimate occupational choice, expanding academic courses to include factors related to occupations, and making sure that students develop the basic skills to handle a job. For high school seniors, training in writing job applications, preparing résumés, and undergoing job interviews is included.

In colleges, courses on job orientation, vocational planning, and influences on vocational choice can be carried out jointly by the counseling-center staff and the placement bureau. In addition, career workshops to handle special concerns of women and minority groups can be developed by the counseling-center staff in cooperation with women's groups and the office of minority affairs. Community colleges, in particular, could supplement career-education programs developed in high schools.

Community counseling centers need to develop career-education programs to supplement vocational counseling in order to help the career-change person, the displaced homemaker, and the school dropout as well as the individual exploring career choices. Workshops and group guidance activities related to career information and job seeking can be carried out jointly with college counseling and placement staffs or with employment-security offices, rehabilitation services, or businesses or industries. Career-education programs have been rare in the community but are growing. Waters, in a 1974 APGA monograph entitled *A Comprehensive View of Career Development* wrote: "Clearly career guidance can't stop at the college level. Adults in increasing numbers are changing careers, and all evidence seems to indicate that trend will accelerate" (p. 54).

These views are consistent with Shertzer and Stone's (1976) comments about counselor involvement in career education. They say, "Counselors at every educational level and in noneducational settings are viewed as professionals whose active involvement is required if career education programs are to realize their promise" (p. 345). The APGA expects counselors to give leadership in accumulating and disseminating occupational information, in curriculum revision, in liaison activities with communities, and in coordinating need surveys and follow-up activities.

I believe that counselors should follow the APGA's conception of counselor leadership in career education, for it emphasizes that counselors should serve as resource persons and consultants rather than as persons totally responsible for the program. Total immersion in career education might mean neglect of counseling and other consultation or guidance activities. A career-guidance specialist at the school or college or in a community agency would be a sensible choice to coordinate much of the program.

Counselors can also contribute by making sure that sexism and racism in occupational materials are eliminated. They should make sure that students at all levels as well as clients in the community are not pushed to premature occupational choices. Helping teachers and administrators discover and evaluate commercial career-education programs or kits can be another counselor contribution. On this last point, Hansen (1974), in the APGA monograph just mentioned, presented 14 conceptual and operational career-education models at all levels of education.

Social-Change Activities

In some ways, most outreach programs are social-change activities in that they attempt to educate significant persons in an institution or a community so as to improve general mental health for all persons. But counsel-

staffs can also take the initiative by making specific suggestions and ing specific actions to change the social environment. There are three general ways in which counseling staffs can make an impact on the social environment: (1) They can help individuals or groups in an institution or a community become aware of a need for changes in policy, in curricular offerings, or in services. (2) They can help individuals or groups in an institution or a community become aware of their right to work for change and learn procedures by which they can attempt to make changes. (3) The counseling staff or individual members of the staff can express directly a need for a specific change in policies, curricular offerings, services, or organizational procedures.

In discussing individual counseling, I pointed out how counselors can help clients become their own agents of social change whenever possible. In outreach social-change activities, the same principle of encouraging people to try to make changes themselves seems sound.

Awareness of a need for change can come through workshops in which policies and procedures can be discussed and recommendations for change made to the appropriate administrator. Sexual or racial discrimination or stereotyping related to curriculums, student activities in school, standardized tests, or jobs in the community is one area that has received attention recently. Appropriate policies on student rights and responsibilities and the rights of minors in general have also become topics requiring clarification. Policies on the education of pregnant high school girls are important to examine. The need for information in high schools on pregnancy and the use of contraceptives is another example of topics needing discussion in schools and in communities.

It is important to let people know that they will not always be successful in making changes and that they may come out of the interactions with authorities somewhat bruised. Nevertheless, students or other individuals who decide to try to make changes should be given help. They can be shown how to proceed in a fair and firm manner that will give the best possibility of convincing the persons in charge that a change is necessary. Support for students should come from the counseling staff, but there should not be persuasion or pressure to convince them that they should take action. This decision and the consequences of the decision are the responsibility of the students. The rest of this section provides some examples of social-change activities from my own experience.

An example of helping an individual make a change in an institution occurred in a nearby high school. A female junior student became aware that there was no women's swim team at her high school. She talked with me and expressed her concern that this condition deprived her and other female students of engaging in swim competition. She wanted to take action herself. We decided that the first step should be for her to talk with the principal. The principal responded positively but did not indicate that he personally would take action. He suggested that she talk to the superintendent of schools. When she called the superintendent, he recommended that the question be brought before the board of education. The student presented her rationale to the board, who then decided to hire a swim coach for the female students in midseason. This action took some persistence but went fairly smoothly.

The same student had more difficulty when she attempted to get the athletic director of the same district to include women's sports on a wallet-size schedule of men's sports to be handed out to the general public. The director gave evasive responses and numerous rationalizations about why the change could not be made and continuously delayed a decision. The student needed support to persist with this legitimate request. She continued to make appointments and phone calls. After a year of continuous pressure, the change was made in line with the affirmative-action regulations. In situations like these, if the student is unsuccessful, the counseling staff should make attempts to get changes made.

Another example of joint efforts by counselors and students to effect change occurred as follows. At a college where I worked before the Buckley Amendment guaranteed college students access to their records, a group of students consulted me about misuse of students' personal records. All women students were required to live in dorms for the first 2 years of college. These students' social and personal dormitory behavior was rated by residence directors or student residence aides without the knowledge of the students. To make matters worse, some faculty members who were asked to write recommendations for graduating students used these ratings in the personal records, particularly when they did not know the student well. The administrator was reluctant to accept the students' recommendation that the practice be stopped because he felt that the intent was to help students improve their behavior. The students and I developed a rationale against the practice, and after a number of meetings with the administrator, the policy was changed.

One more example demonstrates how an educational institution and a community agency can work together for change. A number of years ago, when I was director of a college counseling center, a group of students asked me whether the college administration would be receptive to having a birth-control resource center on campus. I was aware that the administrators at that time might be cool to the idea of a center specifically for students. I was also aware that the public-health officer in the community was eager to get pregnancy counseling started in the community. I therefore recommended that the students aim at a broad-based community center by talking with the public-health officer and then approaching the college administrators. Through the joint efforts of college and community, a center was developed.

An example of helping individuals or groups become aware of their right to ask for change was given to me by a teacher in one of my classes. Her middle school class complained regularly about the luncheon menu.

The counselor suggested to the teacher that the class invite the cook to hear their complaints and to talk about procedures in the cafeteria. The cook listened to the criticisms and explained some of the financial and staff limitations that were contributing to the problem. She did, however, become aware of some changes she could make, and the relationship of the students with the cafeteria staff improved as well as the menu.

When a counseling-center staff has respect for administrators, the instructional staff, and the community in general, it is usually successful in having its suggestions for social change carried out. The counseling staff tends to be more successful if it starts with the assumption that the administrators may be following an unfair or ineffective policy because they do not have all the facts rather than assuming that the administrators have ulterior motives. In this way social change becomes an educative process rather than a pitched battle.

Liaison with Other Community Agencies and Specialists

By maintaining good professional relationships with other community agencies and specialists, the counseling center can expand its service to clients. Referrals to these agencies and specialists can then be made with a minimum of delay or red tape.

In addition, joint outreach programs in such areas as drug education, sexual behavior, and career problems at various stages of development can be arranged through communitywide workshops or seminars. School counselors will also have a varied group of consultants available for use in the schools. When school, college, and community counseling staffs make these efforts, a truly comprehensive community mental-health program becomes a real possibility.

Projects and Activities

1. *A counselor receives a call from a parent who is concerned that her son is going with the wrong crowd. The student is not and has not been a client of the counselor. The parent asks the counselor to call in her son to set him straight. She requests that the counselor not tell her son that she called. How should the counselor respond? (See author's comments.)*

2. *Develop an educational and informational program focusing upon the culture and customs of a minority group in your locality or in a locality in which you might like to work. How could you involve leaders and other members of the group in the development of the program?*

3. *Consider how one might use peer advisers and counselor aides in a counseling program in a manner consistent with APGA and ASCA professional standards and ethical guidelines. What types of in-service training and supervision would be appropriate?*

4. *Select two psychological-education programs that have been proposed in the literature for counselors to use in educational institutions and/or in the community. Evaluate these programs on the basis of theoretical orientation, consideration of rights to privacy, protection against psychological harm, and appropriateness to age level.*

5. *A school district decides that regardless of the reasons for absences, students will not receive credit for a course if they miss ten class sessions. A counseling staff believes that this policy does not distinguish students who cut from those who are legitimately ill. What procedures should be followed to question the policy and elicit change? (See author's comments.)*

6. *Discuss how a birth-control agency and a counseling-center staff in a school, college, or community center could develop a cooperative educational program that would appeal to both females and males.*

7. *Select and organize a list of books, pamphlets, and films about drug education, sex education, careers, and self-help. Consider the criteria you would use in selecting the material.*

8. *Compare definitions of group counseling, personal-growth groups, encounter groups, and T-groups from your reading. I believe that growth, encounter, and T-groups are psychological-education activities rather than professional counseling. On the basis of your reading and the definition of counseling proposed by professional associations, do you agree with this distinction?*

9. *Develop a list of social-change activities that a counseling-center staff in a community could work to accomplish and still not violate individuals' rights to privacy.*

Author's Comments

Activity 1. *The counselor should acknowledge the mother's interest in the welfare of her son. He should also express willingness to work with her son if the son is agreeable. However, he should be adamant that the son be aware of his mother's concern and of her desire for him to talk over their differences with a counselor. It should be made clear that the counselor will try to help both of them to communicate about their differences over choice of friends and to improve communication in other interactions but will not try to determine who are or are not suitable friends for the son.*

Activity 5. *The counseling-center staff should express their concern as a group and request a rationale for the policy. A counterrationale should be presented to the administrators. If the counseling center has an advisory committee composed of parents, faculty, and students, this group's input would be essential.*

10

Implementing Professional-Counseling Programs

In this chapter, ideas on how to implement counseling programs consistent with professional standards will be discussed. Suggestions will be offered on the organization and administration of counseling programs consistent with the role definitions and the training and ethical standards of the APGA, the ASCA, and the APA's Division 17. Then some common barriers that confront counselors in trying to develop a program in the field will be discussed, followed by some suggestions on how to overcome them.

General Administrative Organization

Public Schools

There is considerable agreement in the literature that school counseling services should be housed in each public school building in a district whenever possible. This arrangement permits convenient or immediate interaction of students, teachers, and parents with counselors.

A head counselor or director of counseling should be appointed to administer the program (G. E. Hill, 1974; Johnson, Busacker, & Bowman, 1961). This person should have had more training and experience than the rest of the staff, since duties will include coordinating and facilitating staff policies, supervising new counselors and counseling interns, and handling budget and personnel matters. In addition, the head counselor should act as a consultant to other counselors when particularly difficult problems or crises arise. Even if the staff consists of two persons, it is wise to have one person designated as responsible for the coordination of the counseling program. Sufficient secretarial and clerical help should be available to the director and to the counseling staff.

The counseling staff, under the direction of the head counselor, is responsible to the building principal for carrying out the program. However, Hill makes the important point that the counseling staff should also be responsible to a person in the school-district office in charge of psychological counseling or psychological services throughout the district. Continued professional development of counseling programs requires interaction of the counseling staff with a professional worker in the central office who is aware of and will support counselor professional expectations and standards. A relationship of counseling staffs to building principals helps assure that the programs are carried out and coordinated with the total school program. An administrative relationship to the district office helps to assure that the quantity and quality of counseling will not be left to the whim of a building principal.

Advisory committees composed of parents, teachers, students, and counselors can be of immeasurable help to a head counselor and his or her staff. These groups can help the staff in developing and implementing policies and in publicizing the nature of the counseling program.

Colleges and Universities

In a national survey of 461 college counseling centers (Nugent & Pareis, 1968), it was found that 58% of the counseling centers were organized under the dean of students, with most of this group combined with testing services for the college. Other counseling centers were completely independent (15%) or under the academic dean (9%). Some counseling services were tied to academic units in psychology or to a psychiatric clinic. In the most usual arrangement, counseling services were considered one part of student services, such as the housing, financial-aid, placement, residence-hall, and administrative offices of associate deans of students.

In Chapter 7 I discussed the move of some college counseling directors and student personnel administrators to consolidate counseling centers with other student services under one umbrella called a student-development center. A counterrecommendation was presented in the 1970 Guidelines for University and College Counseling Services that counseling centers be an "administratively autonomous unit," with the additional recommendation that "The Director of the Counseling Service should be administratively responsible to the President or one of his direct representatives" (Kirk, Johnson, Redfield, Free, Michel, Roston, & Warman, 1971, p. 586).

The rationale behind this organizational recommendation that counseling centers not be tied to either student services or academic departments is based upon the recognition that professional counselors are not administrators, as are student personnel workers, and that they are primarily service oriented rather than training and research oriented, as are academic units. Almost all student personnel administrators are involved in administrative decisions about the status of students, whereas counselors are defined professionally and ethically as persons who should not be involved in administrative relationships. These differences can cause confusion about appropriate roles of professional counselors, which in turn may lead to friction between counseling-staff members and student-affairs administrators. The first obligation of academic-department members is instruction and research. The overuse of a counseling center for research in human behavior would interfere with service to students. Under an autonomous administrative organization with a unique service defined, it is possible for counseling staffs to have effective interactions with student-services administrators, members of academic departments, and the staffs of health services and psychiatric clinics.

Whatever the administrative pattern, no records of counseling appointments or of information gained in counseling should be available to anyone, including the vice-president of student affairs, without the student's consent. The exceptions, as in public schools, apply to those situations in which students may harm themselves or others.

Traditionally under student services, college counseling centers have been combined with college testing services (Nugent & Pareis, 1968). This combination has distinct disadvantages for counseling-center directors who want to develop policies consistent with professional standards on nonevaluative relationships and confidentiality. A counseling center in which students are administered tests for screening applicants for graduate school, for example, can soon be perceived as an administrative evaluation agency. Similar perceptions can arise when a counseling-center staff is responsible for scoring faculty evaluations or for administering student evaluations of faculty. A center that hires a psychometrician to administer tests needed for counseling and that functions separately from a testing bureau avoids this professional and ethical dilemma.

Community Counseling

A wide variety of counseling services have developed only recently in communities throughout the United States (Tolbert, 1978). Many of these services have cropped up as a result of immediate needs or have been dependent upon special financing through federal, state, or local programs. This haphazard growth has contributed to disjointed organizational systems in which services are isolated from one another or have different governing boards battling one another for federal, state, or local funding.

As discussed in Chapter 8, some recent efforts have been made to incorporate professional counseling into existing mental-health services or to initiate some counseling services to supplement existing ones. Some community mental-health directors are beginning to recognize the need to add professional counselors to their staffs to supplement the work of clinical psychologists, social workers, and psychiatrists. In addition, some clinics offer in-service training, consultations, and referral services for various counseling services in the area.

Private counseling centers and nonprofit counseling organizations are being developed with a primary emphasis upon personal, social, or vocational concerns of individuals, upon marriage and family counseling, and upon career change. In addition, these centers serve as referral services for other agencies. This type of center, located in regional districts or in neighborhoods, fits the pattern advanced by professional-counseling associations, for individual, group, marriage, and family counseling would be readily accessible to anyone who desired them.

When professional counselors are working in a counseling and psychiatric service, they must be responsible to the clinic director, who in turn should be responsible to a mental-health coordinating board. As community counseling clinics devoted primarily to persons with normal developmental conflicts are established, an organizational structure similar to that of college counseling centers may apply. The counseling-center staff would need a director with more experience or training than other staff members to coordinate budgetary, personnel, and program policies. If the counseling center is a public agency rather than a private one, the director would need to be responsible to some central mental-health administrative board that coordinates budgeting and programs for all mental-health agencies in that area. In addition, like other community agencies, a board of directors can help the director and staff set policies, handle personnel matters, and develop programs.

Counseling Facilities

Soundproof offices, group rooms, seminar rooms, and offices for graduate interns are essential for carrying out confidential individual and group counseling and counselor training in all settings. Resource rooms containing occupational material and material on personal and social development should be located in the counseling complex. A room for administration of tests used in counseling should be available (Kirk et al., 1971; Loughary, Stripling, & Fitzgerald, 1965; Nelson, 1972). Resource rooms in community counseling centers should have material similar to that in school and college centers but should also have material for persons considering or requiring a career change, contemplating late entry into school or the labor market, or looking for part-time occupations after retirement.

Authorities at all levels of education agree that the counseling-center complex should be away from the administrative offices (G. E. Hill, 1974; Kirk et al., 1972; Nelson, 1972). In public schools this separation permits faculty, administrators, and counselors to make distinctions between referrals or contacts related to administrative decisions and referrals for counseling. In college settings an office complex separate from a student-services complex and from psychological or educational training clinics provides the atmosphere of nonevaluation, free choice, and confidentiality essential for counseling programs. There are some advantages in having the placement office and the counseling center in close proximity because of the mutual interest in careers. Occupational-resource rooms could be jointly staffed, and cross-referrals could become more prevalent.

Counseling Staff

Public Schools

In a counseling program consistent with professional standards, the staff members would be expected to hold a minimum of a master's degree in counseling. Academic background would include behavior dynamics, human growth and development, personality organization, vocational counseling and career awareness, standardized tests, individual, group, and family counseling, and supervised internships (ACES standards). Awareness of the cultural values of various ethnic and minority groups is also important (Belkin, 1975). Teacher certification or experience would not be required, but supervised internships in schools would be expected (Nugent, 1966). Elementary school counselors would be expected to have particular exposure to theories and techniques used in working with young children and their families (Keat, 1974; Nelson, 1972).

Colleges and Universities

A significant proportion of counselors in college and university counseling centers are expected to have a doctorate degree. In the survey mentioned earlier, 50% of all college counselors had a doctorate. There are a number of reasons for this expectation. Counselors are likely to be engaged in the supervision and training of counselor interns in doctorate and master's-degree programs. Requests for consultation with government agencies, such as those handling vocational rehabilitation, and with public schools occur frequently. Since students usually live away from home, college counselors have to be prepared to work with a wider range of student problems and to intervene in emotional crises more often than do public school counselors. These demands are even greater when the college is located in a rural area with limited mental-health facilities or when the college has no or limited psychiatric services. Research on counseling processes and outcomes is also expected of counseling staffs in colleges. A proportion of persons with a master's degree who can focus on direct service and some outreach and less on training and research helps the service reach more students sooner.

In spite of having to handle more complex emotional problems and crises, the primary emphasis, as described in professional standards, should remain on normal developmental concerns. Therefore, college counselors need the training and experience required of counseling psychologists to work with vocational and other concerns in personal and social development. If clinical psychologists and social workers are hired, they may require in-service training in counseling people with career concerns or conflicts in other areas of development. If standards are to be upheld and students protected from malpractice, all counselors in college counseling centers should be licensed if a state licensing law exists. The notion that only counselors in private practice need licensing is illogical.

Community Counseling

A community counseling program consistent with professional standards would include professionally trained counselors at the doctorate and master's-degree levels. If they are employed at a central mental-health clinic, their training in normal developmental conflicts and their expertise about vocational concerns would supplement the services of clinical psychologists and social workers. These latter professionals are trained to work with more severely disturbed persons and with families with persons requiring management of behavior, such as juvenile delinquents, mental retardates, or persons with character disorders.

When counseling centers function as separate units in a total mental-health program, the staffs will most likely be composed of doctorate and master's-degree counselors. The staffs should be licensed if the state has passed licensing regulations. Doctorate counselors generally will be expected to work with more difficult clients, supervise interns, consult with other agencies, and conduct research and evaluation. Generally, master's-degree counselors will be expected to handle more direct counseling and be involved in outreach programs.

A balance of male and female counselors and members of various ethnic groups can give breadth and depth to a counseling service in any setting. Since no one counseling theory has proved universally workable, staff members with differing theoretical views add richness to the staff and to continued professional growth.

Counselor/Staff/Student Ratios

In order for a counseling staff to have time for individual and group counseling and necessary outreach activities, a minimum of one counselor per 250 students is recommended by the ASCA for secondary schools. The recommended ratio for elementary schools is about one counselor per 500–600 students. The rationale for the great difference in the ratios is that teachers in self-contained classrooms can handle a lot of the personal interactions that counselors are responsible for in high schools. Also, some administrators point out that the lack of scheduling and programming in elementary schools reduces the need for counselors. However, if one looks carefully at elementary school counseling programs, this ratio appears to be based upon unsound arguments. Teachers with effective personal interactions with students tend to refer more students than do insensitive ones. These teachers do not tend to emulate counselors. Also, the increased amount of family and teacher consultation adds to counseling-staff loads. Thus, one counselor for 250 students in elementary schools seems logical. Shertzer and Stone in 1976 indicated that the trend in elementary schools was one counselor for 250 to 300 students.

This recommended minimal ratio of students to counselors is sufficient only if other psychological and educational specialists and community mental-health resources are available to students and only if sufficient secretarial help is available to counselors. In secondary schools, for example, a counseling staff should welcome a dean of students to handle admissions, registration procedures, and student activities. A career-guidance specialist to develop work/study programs, placement procedures, and information on local occupations would be helpful. At all levels, well-prepared school psychologists are essential to handle requests from administrators, teachers, and parents for administrative psychological evaluations and educational planning regarding the learning and behavioral problems of students (Nugent, 1973). School social workers can be valuable specialists for responding to requests for assessment or treatment of school/home concerns, particularly if one suspects child abuse or neglect. Finally, school nurses can contribute much needed services, especially when health problems relate to a student's emotional concerns, personal development, or academic progress.

The ratio most frequently recommended by college counseling-center directors is one counselor to 750–1000 students. As in public schools, this ratio is minimally sufficient only if other necessary psychological and personnel services are available to students. Adequate psychiatric services in the student-health service or in the community reduce the number of crises, cases of severe emotional stress, and psychological-maintenance functions that the counseling staff must handle. Minority-affairs offices and sex, drug, and alcohol information and referral services also reduce the pressure on the counseling center to provide such information. Study-habits courses may reduce the extent to which the counseling-center staff assumes direct responsibility for necessary remedial services.

The ratio of psychological or professional counselors needed for the general population has not been determined. Again, the amount of additional services available in a total community mental-health program will be an important determinant of the number needed. For example, if crisis clinics, hot lines, centers for rape victims, drug and alcohol referral centers, and programs for minorities are available, the number of staff members in a counseling center may be fewer.

Visiting nurses are an invaluable service in the community, especially when emotional problems relate to illness, retirement, aging, terminal illness, or death and dying. A counseling-center staff should maintain close liaison with the visiting nurses, so that necessary cross-referrals, consultations, conferences, or joint treatment can be arranged.

Professional Growth

When counselors complete their internships, they are actually just beginning professional training. Continual exposure to new theories, techniques, and strategies is required for counselors to continue professional growth. Regular staff meetings, psychiatric and psychological consultation, workshops, and further course work are means of continuing professional growth.

Regular staff meetings to discuss staff policies and procedures, to present cases, to discuss clients with difficult counseling problems, and to upgrade counseling skills can be very profitable experiences for individual staff members. Through these meetings, counselors can expand their repertoire of techniques and strategies for working with clients.

Psychiatric consultation and referral should be available to the staff for emergencies, and psychological consultation should be available on a regular basis. Since counselors may see clients who are having a severe emotional crisis or may see students who require psychotropic medication, access to a psychiatrist can be useful. Similarly, the director should have access to legal consultation in cases that involve confusion about the legal rights of minors, parents, or professionals.

Consultation with a doctorate counseling psychologist can be another form of professional growth for the counseling staff. In contrast to psychiatric consultation, this psychological consultation is directed more specifically to questions concerning techniques used with clients with normal conflicts. In addition, situations involving ethical binds can be explored. Finally, counselors need to be given time and encouragement to attend workshops and to take courses in order to maintain the professional level essential in counseling.

These professional-growth experiences are carried out more often in college and community centers than they are in public schools. Case conferences are usually a weekly occurrence. Money is budgeted, and staff members are encouraged to attend workshops.

I have seen very few instances of regular staff meetings of public school counselors in which counseling cases are presented. Also, public school counselors are woefully lacking in psychological consultation about persons they are counseling. Neither is sufficient psychiatric consultation available when emergencies arise or when severely emotionally disturbed children come to the attention of counselors. Nor are workshops or continued training requested or required of school counselors. School counselors should insist that time be given for weekly staff meetings and that money be set aside for consultation services related specially to counseling services. The group itself should require some form of continued professional growth. School counselors must keep in step with other professional counselors in continued professional growth. Otherwise, they may find themselves relegated to administrative personnel and guidance functions, with professional counseling given over to community centers.

Barriers to Implementing Professional Programs

As the history of counseling indicates, professional counselors have had continuous problems in trying to implement professional standards even though they have been one of the most active groups in defining their role and developing ethical guidelines. It should be clear that professional counselors will be able to improve their professional strength if they unify and insist upon these standards' being followed. Licensing, which protects the public, may then become a reality, with monitoring of the professional members done by the professional association itself. Educating legislatures, funding agencies, and administrators about the importance of counseling would then be easier.

Also, the profession could consistently evaluate standards when necessary. One of the biggest problems in the counseling profession has been the tendency of some members of counselor professional associations to promote new ideas about roles, training, or ethics that are contrary to the prevailing standards. Consistent evaluation of standards with an eye to necessary change is essential, but a profession cannot survive if some members operate as though these guidelines did not exist.

In addition to general professional barriers, counselors have more immediate hurdles to overcome as they attempt to develop professional programs on the job itself. In schools, counselors continue to be assigned administrative duties, are asked to handle attendance problems, are given the job of evaluating and screening students for administrative decision making, are asked to reveal confidential information and accept involuntary referrals, and are often housed in an administrative complex. In colleges similar administrative assignments occur, and similar ethical considerations may be involved, though with less frequency than in public schools. Community counselors may be asked to train volunteers or paraprofessionals or other persons under the Comprehensive Employment and Training Act (CETA) to do counseling at what is assumed to be a professional level. Counselors in community work may also be expected to evaluate and make administrative decisions about the degree of mental or physical illness of persons in the community. In all settings, pressures to be accountable for counseling services exist.

Avoiding Assignment to Inappropriate and Unethical Duties

Junior and senior high school counselors typically get bogged down in assignments that can interfere with the development of effective counseling relationships. These assignments include such clerical tasks as scheduling, which waste counseling time, or such administrative duties as disciplining or attendance checking, which may inhibit the student body from seeking counseling (Nugent, 1969). Elementary school counselors have been assigned evaluative and screening duties for students with behavior problems or learning disabilities, and they may be expected to function as the administrator when the administrator leaves the building. At all levels, counselors are asked to serve as substitute teachers when teachers are unable to take their classes.

More recently, with the passage of the Education for All Handicapped Children Act (PL 94–142), mentioned briefly in Chapter 6, counselors at all public school levels are being pulled into screening students for possible learning disabilities and developing an Individual Education Plan (IEP) for each handicapped child. Humes (1978), in discussing the implications for school counselors, points out that counselors may be expected to develop the IEP, be responsible for monitoring the progress of the child, plan extracurricular activities, or manage record keeping, all of which are not primary or even secondary functions of counselors according to professional standards.

In colleges there have been fewer such problems. However, in 1972 Warnath warned that college counselors were giving in to pressure from administrators and were beginning to take over administrative duties that were alienating students from the counseling center. If counseling-center staffs continue to do selective testing or collegewide testing or if they accept mandatory referrals from scholastic-standing committees or deans, these administrative duties will continue to interfere with counseling functions.

It is too early to tell how much misassignment of counselors occurs or might occur in the community, since many of the programs are just being launched. However, if counselors are expected, for example, to handle psychodiagnostic work for juvenile courts as a primary function, the assignment would be inappropriate and reduce counselors' time for normal concerns.

Reasons for Inappropriate Assignments

Administrators assign counselors to inappropriate tasks for a number of reasons. Sometimes administrators are not aware of what counseling services offer because counselors have not educated them. Sometimes these inappropriate duties arise because the administrative budget is tight and the assignments are economically expeditious. In some instances these duties are assigned because administrators, particularly in public schools, believe that counseling services are an unnecessary frill or hogwash or that counseling of a personal nature is not a pertinent activity in an educational setting.

In any case, counselors must take the initiative to make sure that their duties conform as closely as possible to professional standards. It appears wise to start with the idea that some administrators are not aware of the importance of effective counseling services and that it is up to the counseling staff to educate them. It is well to remember that administrators have a number of problems. They often operate under limited budgets, are often understaffed, and frequently must contend with unrealistic expectations from the public, from governing boards, and from funding agencies. Also, they have administrative tasks that must be done if the institution or agency is to function adequately. For these reasons they may respond to counselors' confusion about their role, to counselors' inability to offer a convincing rationale for counseling, or to poorly trained counselors by deciding what counselors' functions should be. Counselors who are well prepared, who have a rationale for their unique service, and who have backing from professional organizations can educate administrators and make changes (Nugent, 1962). Then, in an economic crunch they are less likely to be the first group to be cut.

Educating People about Counseling

It is important, then, to acquaint administrators with the general role descriptions published by the counselor professional associations and to develop a specific counselor role based upon these standards for the school district, college, or community agency. If all the counselors in a school district, college, or community can develop a rationale such as the one presented in Chapter 3, a well-documented definition can be presented to the administrator, governing board, or funding agency. This presentation of role can include the reasons that confidential or voluntary conditions are imperative in counseling referrals. Also, it should be made clear that placing counselors in the position of having to make administrative decisions will confuse clients, place counselors in ethical dilemmas, and reduce the number of voluntary referrals.

The development of an accurate, colorful brochure describing the counseling program can be another strategy for acquainting administrators, potential referral sources, and potential clients with the voluntary, confidential nature of the counseling service. The brochure can include descriptions of the counselor role and can enumerate the various services offered. Staff members can be listed with their photographs, together with typical problems brought to the center by typical clients.

College counseling centers and community agencies usually distribute this type of brochure. Some elementary school counseling services have begun to print brochures using the comic-strip character Snoopy as a key figure. Secondary school counseling staffs, in my experience, have seldom used brochures. They might well consider this method of publicizing their services.

In schools, class visits, talks to student-body officers, or articles in the school paper about counseling bring the services to the attention of the students, teachers, and parents. College counseling staffs can give talks or offer workshops to various student groups on campus and to interested faculty. They might also invite deans and department heads to meetings or to brown-bag lunches to acquaint these persons with the staff, facilities, and services. In the community, workshops or talks to various agencies, including service clubs, can help acquaint the public with the unique nature of counseling services.

The Use of Advisory Committees

Another useful strategy for implementing a counseling program used by some counseling staffs is the organization of an advisory committee that meets regularly to discuss policies and the program. In educational settings these committees usually are composed of faculty members, students, and a member of the student-services staff. Parents are essential members of this type of committee in public schools. In communities interested citizens usually comprise the committee. This type of committee forces a counseling staff to look at and justify its policies and practices. The committee also can become a strong lever for implementing practices and policies that the staff develops.

Professional Agreement about Policies

Regularly scheduled meetings of counselors throughout the school district or within a college or a community should be arranged. In these meetings, policies and problems related to counselor functioning can be aired and recommendations made to resolve the problems. Also, meetings among counselors from various settings to discuss mutual goals, needs, and problems can help develop the professional unity and strength necessary for counselors to determine how they should function.

It is wise for counselors to take the initiative in clarifying the distinctions between their primary functions and those of other psychological specialists and in determining ways of interacting effectively with them for the benefit of potential clients. For example, joint meetings of school counselors, psychologists, and social workers can be arranged to discuss the unique contributions of each profession. Using their role definitions and rationale, counselors can argue against becoming psychometric or psychological aides in diagnostic screening of students. In colleges, directors of counseling centers can spell out the unique functions counselors have that differentiate them from deans of students or placement officers.

Handling Continued Administrative Resistance

If administrators persist in assigning counselors inappropriate tasks, counseling staffs can try other strategies. Staffs can keep logs of their activities and specify whether they fall into appropriate or inappropriate categories. When inappropriate duties go beyond reasonable expectations, counselors can indicate to administrators what counseling services are not being offered because of the time spent on these other activities.

If counselors in a high school find themselves spending an inordinate amount of time scheduling classes or making schedule changes, the staff should determine how much it is costing the district to use counselors for this job compared to using clerks. A high school counseling staff with which I worked did a cost estimate of this type, and it became the determining factor in a decision to turn class scheduling over to clerks.

If a counselor is required to be involved in diagnostic work and has had the training to do so, another counselor should handle counseling of any person evaluated, so as to keep the counseling relationship consistent with ethical standards. Any counselor doing diagnostic work, however, should persist in trying to be relieved of this responsibility because he or she might be seen as an arm of the administration.

When counselors continue to be given assignments that prevent them from doing counseling or that place them in ethical dilemmas, the staff should write a memo to the appropriate administrators and boards specifying their objections, the reasons for their objections, and the parts of the counseling program that are suffering because of these conditions. Obviously, if highly unethical conditions persist, the counseling staff may have to look for other positions.

The Use of Professional Associations

Because these professional problems exist, particularly in schools, it is essential that strong regional and local counselor professional associations be on hand to give aid and support to the counselor caught in a professional or ethical dilemma. Professional associations should have committees for giving counselors advice, support, or legal aid when necessary. Also, the associations should be willing to send representatives to meet with the administrators to try to convince them of needed change. If necessary, the associations should take steps to make changes through legislative action or through the state department of instruction. For example, if school principals are not required to take a course in guidance, some professional pressure should be placed upon the state department of instruction to correct that oversight. As titular heads of counseling and guidance programs, principals should be required to take at least an introductory guidance course.

An important note on relationships with administrators should be reiterated. Above all, a counseling staff's most important first step is to educate administrators about counseling. A wise administrator convinced of the value of counseling will be likely to give support.

Avoiding Ethically Inappropriate Expectations of Referral Sources

Involuntary Referrals

Counselors should strive for and encourage free choice in referrals. This policy is sometimes difficult to maintain consistently in practice, particularly in public schools. Some teachers will continue to send students to counselors whether the students are willing or not. These forced referrals are of three types. First, referrals come from well-intentioned teachers who believe that students need counseling whether they want it or not. Second, referrals come from angry or frustrated teachers burdened with unruly students. These teachers may want the counselor to reprimand or discipline the students for disruptive classroom behavior. Third, referrals for psychological evaluation come from teachers concerned about the educational progress or home situations of students. These students should be referred to a school psychologist or social worker.

In all situations a counselor should see the student and clarify his or her role with the student. If the referral involves some coercion, the counselor should express willingness to work with the student but make it clear that continuing the interviews is up to the student. If the student decides not to continue, the counselor should encourage the student to come in at a future date if the need arises.

In cases of inappropriate teacher referrals for disciplinary action or psychological evaluation, the counselor should talk with the student, clarify the counselor role, and find out how the student perceives the referral (Nugent, 1969). Then arrangements can be made to see the teacher about appropriate referrals and procedures for referral. If a teacher expects disciplinary measures or reprimands from a counselor, the counselor should indicate the need for the teacher and student to work out this administrative action with the appropriate administrator. The counseling staff should be available to work with the student if the student agrees to counseling after discipline by the teacher or administrator. If counselors are asked to perform a psychological evaluation of a student for grade-placement purposes or for diagnosis of a learning disability or a behavior problem, the counseling staff should clarify that these administrative evaluations should be referred to a school psychologist. Similarly, referrals requesting assessment of a student's home situation should go to a school social worker or a visiting nurse.

The condition of free choice about counseling referrals should also apply to college programs if these programs are to be consistent with professional standards. For example, students with scholastic or behavior problems should not be retained in school on the condition that they receive counseling. Counseling should be recommended but not required. If a student is referred inappropriately, the procedures just described should be followed here as well. The opportunity for voluntary counseling should remain open.

If community counseling centers are established in neighborhoods to supplement regional mental-health clinics, it would be inconsistent with current counselor professional standards to accept mandatory referrals or referrals that will involve administrative decisions. Court referrals in which probation is contingent upon counseling are inappropriate according to counselor ethical standards. So are requests for intellectual or psychological evaluations from courts for the purpose of determining eligibility for probation or for determining whether a person should be involuntarily committed to a mental institution. Referrals from social agencies requesting psychological evaluations to determine individuals' eligibility for benefits or for training also fall into the inappropriate category. These activities should be the province of the community mental-health clinic or consultants in private practice. Otherwise, the unique value of counselors' working with normal developmental concerns can be lost. The notions of free choice and confidentiality will not become hallmarks of the service. If professional counseling services become an official part of the community mental-health clinic, then the director of the clinic should be certain that a professional who evaluates an individual for an administrative decision not be assigned as a counselor to that individual. Obviously, these recommendations for an agency to separate counseling and evaluation do not preclude professional counselors from carrying out psychological evaluations within their expertise in private practice.

Confidentiality and Communication

Counselors express considerable concern and discomfort about maintaining confidentiality in individual counseling when parents, teachers, or administrators or other professionals in the community ask for information about a client. Counselors sense antagonism from some of these persons if they express the need for confidentiality. Parents and school staffs may feel that counselors are being unnecessarily secretive and are not treating them as responsible parents or professional persons. I have developed some guidelines that I believe preserve confidentiality and yet increase opportunities for productive interaction with parents and teaching staff when necessary. In addition, I have found that this approach can help increase communication between clients and parents and between clients and teachers or administrators.

Parents' Requests for Information.   If parents call a counselor about a daughter or son who is a client, I recommend that the parents let the student know they want to talk to me and what the nature of the contact will be. If the parents find this request too difficult, I suggest that I let the student know that they are interested in talking with me and what it is they want to talk about. Most students willingly agree to consultations when they are aware of the reason. Often they are involved in the consultation. If the student does not want me to meet with the parents, the student and I discuss the reasons he or she feels so strongly about it. I would probably suggest that the student present his or her objections directly to the parents. At times I recommend a three-way conference with the student and the parents to discuss their difficulties in communication. In most instances this procedure leads to an opening of communication between student and parents.

Counselors should avoid getting into intrigues with parents, which can hamper counseling. These intrigues result from secret contacts between the counselor and the parents. With these contacts it is often difficult for the counselor to remember what information was obtained from the parents and what information came from the student. The counseling relationship can thus become guarded. In addition, parents are not held to the same notions of confidentiality as counselors. Parents may reveal their interactions with the counselor in a heated moment of argument with the student. Trust in the counselor will be in jeopardy not only with that student but with the student body as a whole.

Another aspect of confidentiality should be clarified with parents. If a student agrees to counseling contact with the parents, this contact will not be shared with administrators or teachers without the parents' consent. This guarantee helps parents understand the importance of confidentiality in counseling.

Teachers' or Administrators' Requests for Information.   I follow very similar procedures for confidentiality when teachers or administrators request information about a client whom they have not referred. As with parents, I have found that student communication with teachers and administrators often improves. Also, teachers appreciate the notion of confidentiality if they know that their contacts with counselors will not be shared with administrators without their consent.

I anticipate that teachers or administrators who refer a student may want some sort of feedback on whether the student came in for counseling and what they can do to help. So, in the first interview, I indicate to the student that the teacher or administrator who was interested enough to make the referral will probably want some follow-up. The student and I discuss what information might be useful to that person and what information does not need to be shared. Throughout the counseling session, it is agreed that the student will be aware of any contacts between me and the other person and that no sharing of information will occur if the student objects.

I have found absolutely no advantage and many disadvantages to discussing information gained in counseling without the clients' informed consent. Few clients object to discussions if they are aware that they are occurring and know what is being shared. Functioning in this manner with parents, teachers, administrators, and clients' friends can lead to feelings of trust on the part of all concerned.

Requests for Information by Referral Sources or Other Professionals. Cooperation between counselors and other psychological workers in other agencies or in private practice becomes important when cross-referrals occur or when a person seen by one professional begins to receive help from another professional. However, there seems to be some belief that the principles of confidentiality can be waived in these instances because all interested parties are professionals. Some professional counselors find it awkward to emphasize the importance of confidentiality when speaking with a professional in another agency. Nevertheless, it is crucial that confidentiality be maintained. No information should be shared without the written consent of the client. The exceptions are clients deemed by a professional to be in imminent danger of harming themselves or others.

Requests for Information by Other Agencies. Information about a client for security checks or other matters should not be given to governmental agencies such as the CIA or the FBI unless the client expressly requests it. Similarly, high school counselors should not be expected to give recommendations about clients or any other students to prospective employers or to colleges without written permission from the students.

Consultation between Counselors and Other Psychological Specialists. Counselors should not idly share information about clients with other counselors or with other psychological specialists. This behavior is unprofessional and unethical. However, if a counselor wants some professional help in how best to help a client, it is professionally permissible and ethically sound to consult with another psychological worker. In these instances the name of the client is not disclosed unless it is absolutely necessary.

Referrals to Other Agencies or Professionals. A counseling-center staff cannot expect to be able to handle all requests for help that come to its attention. Policies about the types of problems and concerns the staff is professionally trained to handle and permitted to handle by the hiring or funding institution or agency need to be clearly spelled out. In this way, a decision about the appropriateness of the request can more easily be determined by a receptionist, an intake interviewer, or a counselor in the initial interview.

Policies must also be clear about referral procedures for individuals who come to the center presenting an inappropriate request for service, or for clients who require a referral after starting counseling to supplement or replace counseling at the center. Further, a center staff should develop a list of agencies and professionals who they know meet the standards of their profession to whom they can refer persons when necessary. The counseling-center staff should set up procedures for referrals with these other professionals that permit ethical communication about the client. For example, a signed statement by the client giving permission to share certain information with the referral source permits constructive sharing of information without violating confidentiality or privacy rights of the client.

Mills (1978) divided college counseling-center referrals among those individuals needing psychiatric hospitalization or medication, those needing information on noncounseling matters such as housing, financial aid or job placement, and those requiring longer-term treatment than the counseling center is permitted to do. School counselors' and community counselors' referral needs can be categorized along similar lines. In addition, referrals for information about birth-control methods, sex information, drug and alcohol information, welfare assistance, or health services are sometimes necessary.

When a referral is necessary, the counseling-center staff should tell the person why a referral is so important and recommend whom that individual should see. Counselors should be aware that a person coming for help or who has been referred to them for help may find the need for another referral discouraging. This attitude may occur particularly if the initial venture to the counseling center took considerable effort. In these cases, the counselor should then help the individual regain motivation and ease the person to the new source. If the counselor finds it necessary to refer a disturbed client whom he or she has seen for some time, it may take a number of counseling sessions to accomplish a successful referral. Clarifying the reasons for referral may diminish the chance of individuals perceiving themselves as rejected by the counselor or as hopeless and too difficult to handle.

Isolated Counselors

In some very small school districts, small colleges, or lightly populated communities, the counseling staff may consist of one counselor. Often this person is not only the sole counselor but also the only individual with any psychological background.

In contrast to counselors on a larger staff, these isolated counselors miss the opportunities for professional growth that result from sharing experiences, ideas, and concerns with other professional counselors. As the sole individuals with a psychological background, they may be expected to perform tasks that are outside their expertise and that should be handled by other psychological and educational specialists. Also, they may be expected to take over duties inappropriate to their role, which may prevent or interfere with the development of appropriate counseling relationships. Legal as well as ethical concerns arise when counselors take on psychological tasks different from or beyond their professional preparation. Professional and ethical dilemmas trouble counselors when they are asked to perform administrative tasks that interfere with carrying out the counseling duties for which they were trained.

Counselors working alone in small settings with limited budgets are quite vulnerable to administrative pressure to become jacks of all trades. Thus, it is imperative that these counselors educate administrators about appropriate counselor functioning and that they work with administrators to fashion as effective a counseling program as possible on a limited budget.

Suppose, for example, that a school principal expects a counselor to administer screening tests for possible placement of students in special classes. This function is rightfully that of a school psychologist. Suppose, in addition, that the principal needs help on administrative duties and assigns the counselor as a half-time vice-principal. Both assignments pose professional dilemmas for the counselor in that these evaluative and administrative duties interfere with or prohibit the development of counseling relationships. Further, a legal question of malpractice may exist if the counselor administers and evaluates tests without having the appropriate background. In this case the counselor can recommend that the school district contract the services of a school psychologist from a regional district office or a larger school district. Also, the principal could be encouraged to confront the school board and the general public with his or her need for administrative help.

Similar procedures are recommended if a counselor in a small college is expected to do the impossible task of handling all the student administrative functions, such as registration, admissions, financial aid, placement, discipline, and student activities. A counselor in these circumstances must convince the administrator that a dean of students, even on a part-time basis, may well be worth the extra salary in terms of the efficiency and quality of student services.

Isolated counselors must seek ways of meeting with other professional counselors for the purpose of developing the professional strength necessary to prevent gross misuse of their time and to enhance their professional expertise. Insights and strategies gained from other professionals may help them dismantle some of the barriers interfering with effective organization and administration of their counseling programs. Approaches and techniques in counseling can also be shared.

Regularly scheduled meetings with other counselors in nearby school districts, colleges, or community agencies need to have the support of the administrators. Not only should administrators give counselors time off from their regular duties to attend these meetings, but they should attend these meetings themselves at times to discuss budget problems and ways of developing programs that least compromise the professional counselor.

Ideally, consultant services for sole counselors or for small, isolated staffs should be available from the state superintendent of instruction's office. These consultations could be scheduled on a regular basis. Also, universities and professional associations could set up reasonably priced consultation services and in-service training specially geared to the problems of small school districts, colleges, and community agencies. In the long run these activities will strengthen the entire counseling profession and ensure as well that persons in small communities have professional-counseling services available.

Projects and Activities

1. *Compare how you would organize a counseling program if you were the only counselor in a secondary school with 300 students to how you would design a program for a large urban school. Assume your administrator agrees, in both situations, that you follow the recommendations of the APGA and the ASCA.*
2. *You are on a committee to design a counseling-center complex for a school or college. Draw up plans or write a description of how you would develop the facility. Include the placement of the complex, types of rooms, conference space, and so on. Suppose that your administrator wants the center adjacent to the administrative offices. Write an argument against this recommendation based upon professional standards.*
3. *Interview professional counselors in public schools and the staffs of various community mental-health agencies. With due regard for confidentiality, are communication lines open and appropriate referrals made between schools and other agencies? What recommendations would you make for improvement?*
4. *Are counseling programs in schools, colleges, and agencies in your community alert to the unique problems of minority groups? What is included in staffing or in outreach programs to indicate recognition of minority concerns?*
5. *Visit a regional community mental-health clinic. Find out how the major clinic relates to other mental-health services in the community. What is the total community mental-health organizational plan? What are the proportions of psychiatrists, social workers, clinical psychologists, and counseling psychologists on the staff? How is the total program funded?*
6. *Consider how you would organize an advisory committee for a counseling staff*

in a school, a college, or a community agency. What would be the duties of the committee? What representation would you include? What would be the relationship of the advisory committee to the director of the service?

7. *Interview the director of a mental-health clinic about sources of funding for the agency. Are the types of services offered influenced by the sources of income (for example, psychological evaluation for probation offices, third-party payments)? How does the type of funding relate to confidential, voluntary counseling?*

Appendixes

Appendix A. Definitions of the Counselor's Role

PRIMARY* AND SECONDARY† ROLES AND FUNCTIONS

¹Secondary Schools

*"Counselors believe that most students given the experience of an accepting, non-evaluating relationship, will make intelligent decisions . . . school counseling functions as a continuous process to assist students by identifying and meeting their needs in educational, vocational and personal-social domains" (p. 228).

"Counseling assists students in developing decision-making competence and in formulating future plans. The school counselor is the person on the staff who has special training in assessing the specific needs of each student and for planning an appropriate guidance program in the educational, vocational and personal-social domains" (p. 229).

†"Although personal counseling is a major function of the guidance staff, other responsibilities and involvements include, but are not limited to, staff consultation, parental assistance, student self-appraisal, educational-vocational information and planning, referral to allied community agencies, and public relations" (p. 228).

²Middle/Junior High

*"In serving as a facilitator of self-development the middle/junior high school counselor should provide an individual counseling environment for all students to help them gain understanding of themselves and find an identity" (p. 203).

†"To improve the educational climate and foster personal and social development of the counselee, it is incumbent upon the counselor to share his expertise with teachers. Through individual conferences, case conferences, inservice training, and as an integral part of the team, the counselor can assist the staff in becoming increasingly aware of and sensitive to the needs of the early adolescent" (pp. 203–204). Also included are counselors serving as consultants to parents and as coordinators to other community agencies. In addition, counselors have a special responsibility in career development and group activities designed for greater self-development of students.

³Elementary

*The elementary school counselor works . . . "to enable each child to arrive at an identity and learn to make choices and decisions. . . . Elementary school counselors, because of their specialized training, provide service and leadership in this area . . ." (p. 200).
Objectives of counseling and guidance include that children should be able to discuss their interests and skills, define role with family and others, develop a positive self-image, be able to resolve conflicts with others, fantasize future life roles and understand interrelationships of people and the world of work.

†"The teacher plays the primary role in working with children and the counselor aids the teacher in making education more meaningful to each child with the implementation of an appropriate guidance and counseling program" (p. 200). Counselors help teachers, administrators and parents to understand a child's self concept, to relate constructively to the child, and to provide experiences for children to learn decision-making skills.

⁴Post-secondary

*"The primary role of post-secondary counselors is to assist individual students in acquiring information and developing attitudes, insights, and understanding about themselves and their environment, which are necessary for optimal growth and development. This is usually accomplished through the counseling relationships, either individually or in groups" (p. 387).

---

¹American Personnel and Guidance Association. The role of the secondary school counselor. *The School Counselor*, 1977, 24, 228–234.

²American Personnel and Guidance Association. The unique role of the middle/junior high school counselor. *Elementary School Guidance and Counseling*, 1978, 12, 203–205.

³American Personnel and Guidance Association. The unique role of the elementary school counselor. *Elementary School Guidance and Counseling*, 1978, 12, 200–202.

⁴American Personnel and Guidance Association. The role and function of post-secondary counseling. *The School Counselor*, 1974, 21, 387–390.

Appendix A. (Continued)

"Post-secondary counselors work with students in educational, career, and personal-social counseling" (p. 387).

†". . . also include consultation with teachers, administrators, and other significant adults" (p. 387). Also includes orientation; institutional and professional research; testing; consultation with other institutions, agencies, and businesses; supervision of counseling interns; psychological education; group guidance; and help with curriculum development.

⁵Division 17, The Counseling Psychologist (1968)

*"As his job title indicates, the counseling psychologist's primary tool is *counseling*" (p. 3). "Provides individual and group guidance and counseling services . . . to assist individuals in achieving more effective personal, social, educational, and vocational development and achievement" (p. 1).
". . . counseling psychologists attach particular importance to the role of education and work in a person's life" (p. 6).

†*College*: Consultation to significant others, orientation, institutional and professional research, consultation for residence-hall programs, supervision of counseling interns, in-service training, counselor education, and curriculum revision.
Other agencies: Secondary functions are presented in narrative form. Includes consulting with significant others and helping to change the environment.

⁶Division 17, Standards for Providers of Counseling Psychological Services (1979)*

*Counseling psychological services "are intended to help persons acquire or alter personal-social skills, improve adaptability to changing life demands, enhance environmental coping skills, and develop a variety of problem-solving and decision-making capabilities. These services are used by individuals, couples and families in populations of all age groups to cope with problems in connection with education, career choice, work, sex, marriage, family, other social relations, health, aging, and handicapping conditions of a social or physical nature" (p. 5). Services include assessment, evaluation, diagnosis, individual and group counseling, professional consultation, program development, supervision, and evaluation.

†Consultation, program development, training, supervision of counseling psychologists, and educational activities are included.

⁷AMHCA Certification Standards
*"A *Certified Professional Counselor*: is a counselor certified as having the competency to assist individuals or groups in achieving optimal mental health through personal and social development and adjustment in order to prevent the debilitating effects of certain somatic, emotional, and intra- and/or inter-personal disorders. . . . *Counseling*: is the process of assisting individuals or groups, through a helping relationship, to achieve optimal mental health . . ." (p. 24).

†Not specifically spelled out, although qualifications of applicants for examination include supervisory skills, consultation, research, and preventative mental-health skills.

---

⁵American Psychological Association, Division of Counseling Psychology, Jordaan, J. (Ed.). *The Counseling Psychologist*. New York: Columbia Teachers College Press, 1968.
⁶American Psychological Association, Committee on Standards for Providers of Psychological Services. *Standards for providers of counseling psychological services*, Draft 9, Final Proposal, September 18, 1979.
*These standards are still evolving. Primary and secondary functions are not clearly delineated. Assessment, evaluation, diagnosis, and counseling activities appear to be considered major functions with other functions related to these.
⁷American Mental Health Counselors Association, American Mental Health Counselors Association Certification Committee. The Board of Certified Professional Counselors procedures. *American Mental Health Counselors Association Journal*, 1979, *1*, 23–38.

Appendix B. Comparison of Training Standards for Professional Counselors and Counseling Psychologists

	[1] *Standards for the Preparation of Counselors and Other Personnel Services Specialists* (1973) [2] "ACES Guidelines for Doctoral Preparation in Counselor Education" (1978)	[3] Division 17, *The Counseling Psychologist* (1968)	[4] Division 17, *Standards for Providers of Counseling Psychological Services* (1979)*
Differences in Master's and Doctoral Training	The 1973 standards constitute entry preparation for counselors, usually taking 2 years. Doctoral guidelines are based upon the entry guidelines. Doctoral programs usually take a minimum of 4 academic years, including the entry program and 1 year of internship. Doctoral programs require a strong background in behavioral sciences and advanced competencies in counseling, consulting, research, and supervision. Doctoral programs require more intensive supervised experiences. Doctoral programs prepare leaders and counselor educators in counseling.	Master's-degree programs of 1 or 2 years prepare students for beginning and intermediate positions. Doctoral programs prepare students for more responsible, less supervised positions and require more advanced clinical skills and research competence.	*"Providers of counseling psychological services . . .* subsumes two categories of providers of counseling psychological services. These are a) professional counseling psychologists, and b) all other persons who offer counseling psychological services under the supervision of a counseling psychologist. . . . Professional counseling psychologists have a doctoral degree from an organized, sequential, counseling psychology program in a regionally accredited university or professional school. . . . Master's level providers may be referred to as psychological associates or psychological assistants. Other providers may be designated by the use of the adjective 'psychological' preceding the noun, e.g., 'psychological technician,' 'psychological aide'" (pp. 4–5).
Core of Counseling Knowledge, Competencies, and Skills	Includes normal and abnormal behavior, personality theory, learning theory, and human growth and development.	Includes personality organization and developmental psychology, personality and learning theory, abnormal psychology, and psychology of adjustment.	"The professional counseling psychologist acquires doctoral education and training experience as defined by the institution offering the program. Only counseling psychologists, i.e., those who meet these education and training requirements, have minimum professional qualifications to provide unsupervised counseling psychological services" (p. 4). *"Professional psychologists who wish to qualify as counseling psychologists meet the same requirements with respect to subject matter and professional skills that apply to doctoral education and training in counseling psychology"* (p. 9).

[1]American Personnel and Guidance Association, Association for Counselor Education and Supervision, Commission on Standards and Accreditation. Standards for the preparation of counselors and other personnel service specialists. *Personnel and Guidance Journal*, 1977, *55*, 596–601.

[2]American Personnel and Guidance Association, Association for Counselor Education and Supervision. ACES guidelines for doctoral preparation in counselor education. *Counselor Education and Supervision*, 1978, *17*, 163–166.

Appendix B. (Continued)

	[1](1) *Standards for the Preparation of Counselors and Other Personnel Services Specialists* (1973) [2](2) "ACES Guidelines for Doctoral Preparation in Counselor Education" (1978)	[3]*Division 17, The Counseling Psychologist* (1968)	[4]*Division 17, Standards for Providers of Counseling Psychological Services* (1979)*
Counseling Theories and Techniques	Counseling theories, appraisal of individuals, individual and group testing, case-study approaches, group counseling, consultation theory, data gathering	Counseling theories, group counseling, psychological tests, diagnostic procedures, consultation skills	
Social Environment	Social change, subcultures, ethnic groups, women's roles, use of leisure time	Social-class structure, culture and personalities, socioeconomic factors, development of community resources	
Career Development	Vocational-choice theory, relationship between career choice and lifestyle, occupational-information sources, career-decision processes, career-development techniques	Structure of world of work, occupational trends, sociology of work, sources of educational and occupational information, vocational rehabilitation	
Research Competence	Statistics, research design, development and execution of research proposals, development and evaluation of program objectives (master's), doctoral research seminars	Review and analysis of research literature, measurement and evaluation, statistics, experimental design, doctoral research project	
Professional Orientation	Codes of ethics, legal considerations, role identity, goals of professional organizations	Professional ethics, relationships with other professions	
Supervised Practicum and Internships	Practicum: Laboratory experiences and role playing, listening to tapes, testing, preparing cases, observing professional counselors; supervised interactions with individuals and groups seeking service (usually done in campus clinic) Internship (postpracticum experience providing on-the-job experience): Supervision by supervisor in setting in which student wishes to work. Paid internships recommended. Increasing amounts for doctorate	Carefully graded supervision in campus clinic and in actual work setting. Usually 1 year of full-time, paid, supervised internship is expected	

[3]American Psychological Association, Division of Counseling Psychology, Jordaan, J. (Ed.). *The Counseling Psychologist.* New York: Columbia Teachers College Press, 1968.

[4]American Psychological Association, Division of Counseling Psychology, Committee on Standards for Providers of Psychological Services. *Standards for providers of counseling psychological services*, Draft 9, Final Proposal, September 18, 1979.

*In Draft 8, November 1978, course requirements paralleling those of the ACES and Division 17's 1968 pamphlet were included. These were not included in the September 1979 draft.

Appendix B. (Continued)

	[1](1) *Standards for the Preparation of Counselors and Other Personnel Services Specialists* (1973) [2](2) "ACES Guidelines for Doctoral Preparation in Counselor Education" (1978)	[3]Division 17, *The Counseling Psychologist* (1968)	[4]Division 17, *Standards for Providers of Counseling Psychological Services* (1979)*
Specialized Skills for Specific Professional Settings	Specialized knowledge and skills needed to work in a specific professional setting	Orientation to settings in which counseling psychologists work	
Accrediting Procedures	ACES Committee on Credentialing in effect July 1, 1978. Eight members (five from each region, three at large). Accreditation subcommittees in each of five regions chaired by the national representative from the region's voluntary program accreditation as of July 1, 1978. Manual for program evaluation being prepared.	Programs evaluated by the APA Education and Training Committee, which appoints members to visit site and make recommendations on accreditation (for doctoral program only)	Not specified. Presumably will be the APA Education and Training Committee if standards are approved

Ethical Standards of Psychologists [1]

Climaxing nine years of work by several task forces and the Committee on Scientific and Professional Ethics and Conduct (CSPEC), draft #11 of the Ethical Standards of Psychologists went to the Council of Representatives at its January 28-30, 1977 meeting. A number of changes were made in the document by Council, resulting in draft #12, which was adopted on January 30th as printed below.

Because the Council could not agree on several sections of Principle 5 (Confidentiality), the final action was to approve the final revised draft with the exception of this principle. The old principle (formerly Principle 6 in the Ethical Standards as printed in the 1975 *Biographical Directory*) will hold until a revision has been adopted by Council.

Council comments and suggestions applicable to this section are now being solicited by CSPEC. Council also directed the Committee to take into account the forthcoming report of the Task Force on Privacy and Confidentiality, as well as upcoming federal regulations covering similar matters. APA members having specific wording changes to suggest may send them to Brenda Gurel, Secretary, CSPEC, APA, 1200 Seventeenth Street, N.W., Washington, D.C. 20036.

PREAMBLE

Psychologists [1,2] respect the dignity and worth of the individual and honor the preservation and protection of fundamental human rights. They are committed to increasing knowledge of human behavior and of people's understanding of themselves and others and to the utilization of such knowledge for the promotion of human welfare. While pursuing these endeavors, they make every effort to protect the welfare of those who seek their services or of any human being or animal that may be the object of study. They use their skills only for purposes consistent with these values and do not knowingly permit their misuse by others. While demanding for themselves freedom of inquiry and communication, psychologists accept the responsibility this freedom requires: competence,

---

[1] Approved by the Council of Representatives, January 30, 1977. Reprinted from the APA "Monitor," March 1977.

[2] A student of psychology who assumes the role of a psychologist shall be considered a psychologist for the purpose of this code of ethics.

objectivity in the application of skills and concern for the best interests of clients, colleagues, and society in general. In the pursuit of these ideals, psychologists subscribe to principles in the following areas: 1. Responsibility, 2. Competence, 3. Moral and Legal Standards, 4. Public Statements, 5. Confidentiality, 6. Welfare of the Consumer, 7. Professional Relationships, 8. Utilization of Assessment Techniques, and 9. Pursuit of Research Activities.

PRINCIPLE 1. RESPONSIBILITY

In their commitment to the understanding of human behavior, psychologists value objectivity and integrity, and in providing services they maintain the highest standards of their profession. They accept responsibility for the consequences of their work and make every effort to insure that their services are used appropriately.

a. As scientists, psychologists accept the ultimate responsibility for selecting appropriate areas and methods most relevant to these areas. They plan their research in ways to minimize the possibility that their findings will be misleading. They provide thorough discussion of the limitations of their data and alternative hypotheses, especially where their work touches on social policy or might be construed to the detriment of persons in specific age, sex, ethnic, socioeconomic or other social groups. In publishing reports of their work, they never suppress disconfirming data. Psychologists take credit only for the work they have actually done.

Psychologists clarify in advance with all appropriate persons or agencies the expectations for sharing and utilizing research data. They avoid dual relationships which may limit objectivity, whether political or monetary, so that interference with data, human participants, and milieu is kept to a minimum.

b. As employees of an institution or agency, psychologists have the responsibility of remaining alert to and attempting to moderate institutional pressures that may distort reports of psychological findings or impede their proper use.

c. As members of governmental or other organizational bodies, psychologists remain accountable as individuals to the highest standards of their profession.

---

d. As teachers, psychologists recognize their primary obligation to help others acquire knowledge and skill. They maintain high standards of scholarship and objectivity by presenting psychological information fully and accurately.

e. As practitioners, psychologists know that they bear a heavy social responsibility because their recommendations and professional actions may alter the lives of others. They are alert to personal, social, organizational, financial, or political situations or pressures that might lead to misuse of their influence.

f. Psychologists provide adequate and timely evaluations to employees, trainees, students, and others whose work they supervise.

decisions involving individuals or policies based on test results have an understanding of psychological or educational measurement, validation problems and other test research.

e. Psychologists recognize that their effectiveness depends in part upon their ability to maintain effective interpersonal relations, and that aberrations on their part may interfere with their abilities. They refrain from undertaking any activity in which their personal problems are likely to lead to inadequate professional services or harm to a client; or, if engaged in such activity when they become aware of their personal problems, they seek competent professional assistance to determine whether they should suspend, terminate or limit the scope of their professional and/or scientific activities.

PRINCIPLE 2.
COMPETENCE

The maintenance of high standards of professional competence is a responsibility shared by all psychologists in the interest of the public and the profession as a whole. Psychologists recognize the boundaries of their competence and the limitations of their techniques and only provide services, use techniques, or offer opinions as professionals that meet recognized standards. Psychologists maintain knowledge of current scientific and professional information related to the services they render.

a. Psychologists accurately represent their competence, education, training and experience. Psychologists claim as evidence of professional qualifications only those degrees obtained from institutions acceptable under the Bylaws and Rules of Council of the American Psychological Association.

b. As teachers, psychologists perform their duties on the basis of careful preparation so that their instruction is accurate, current and scholarly.

c. Psychologists recognize the need for continuing education and are open to new procedures and changes in expectations and values over time. They recognize differences among people, such as those that may be associated with age, sex, socioeconomic, and ethnic backgrounds. Where relevant, they obtain training, experience, or counsel to assure competent service or research relating to such persons.

d. Psychologists with the responsibility for

PRINCIPLE 3.
MORAL AND LEGAL STANDARDS

Psychologists' moral, ethical and legal standards of behavior are a personal matter to the same degree as they are for any other citizen, except as these may compromise the fulfillment of their professional responsibilities, or reduce the trust in psychology or psychologists held by the general public. Regarding their own behavior, psychologists should be aware of the prevailing community standards and of the possible impact upon the quality of professional services provided by their conformity to or deviation from these standards. Psychologists are also aware of the possible impact of their public behavior upon the ability of colleagues to perform their professional duties.

a. Psychologists as teachers are aware of the diverse backgrounds of students and, when dealing with topics that may give offense, treat the material objectively and present it in a manner for which the student is prepared.

b. As employees, psychologists refuse to participate in practices inconsistent with legal, moral and ethical standards regarding the treatment of employees or of the public. For example, psychologists will not condone practices that are inhumane or that result in illegal or otherwise unjustifiable discrimination on the basis of race, age, sex, religion, or national origin in hiring, promotion, or training.

c. In providing psychological services,

psychologists avoid any action that will violate or diminish the legal and civil rights of clients or of others who may be affected by their actions.

As practitioners, psychologists remain abreast of relevant federal, state, local, and agency regulations and Association standards of practice concerning the conduct of their practice. They are concerned with developing such legal and quasi-legal regulations as best serve the public interest and in changing such existing regulations as are not beneficial to the interests of the public and the profession.

d. As researchers, psychologists remain abreast of relevant federal and state regulations concerning the conduct of research with human participants or animals.

PRINCIPLE 4.
PUBLIC STATEMENTS

Public statements, announcements of services, and promotional activities of psychologists serve the purpose of providing sufficient information to aid the consumer public in making informed judgments and choices. Psychologists represent accurately and objectively their professional qualifications, affiliations, and functions, as well as those of the institutions or organizations with which they or the statements may be associated. In public statements providing psychological information or professional opinions or providing information about the availability of psychological products and services, psychologists take full account of the limits and uncertainties of present psychological knowledge and techniques.

a. When announcing professional services, psychologists limit the information to: name, highest academic degree conferred, date and type of certification or licensure, Diplomate status, address, telephone number, office hours, and, at the individual practitioner's discretion, an appropriate brief listing of the types of psychological services offered, and fee information. Such statements are descriptive of services provided but not evaluative as to their quality or uniqueness. They do not contain testimonials by quotation or by implication. They do not claim uniqueness of skills or methods unless determined by acceptable and public scientific evidence.

b. In announcing the availability of psychological services or products, psychologists do not display any affiliations with an organization in a manner that falsely implies the sponsorship or certification of that organization. In particular and for example, psychologists do not offer APA membership or fellowship as evidence of qualification. They do not name their employer or professional associations unless the services are in fact to be provided by or under the responsible, direct supervision and continuing control of such organizations or agencies.

c. Announcements of, "personal growth groups" give a clear statement of purpose and the nature of the experiences to be provided. The education, training and experience of the psychologists are appropriately specified.

d. Psychologists associated with the development or promotion of psychological devices, books, or other products offered for commercial sale make every effort to insure that announcements and advertisements are presented in a professional, scientifically acceptable, and factually informative manner.

e. Psychologists do not participate for personal gain in commercial announcements recommending to the general public the purchase or use or any proprietary or single-source product or service.

f. Psychologists who interpret the science of psychology or the services of psychologists to the general public accept the obligation to present the material fairly and accurately, avoiding misrepresentation through sensationalism, exaggeration or superficiality. Psychologists are guided by the primary obligation to aid the public in forming their own informed judgments, opinions and choices.

g. As teachers, psychologists insure that statements in catalogs and course outlines are accurate and sufficient, particularly in terms of subject matter to be covered, bases for evaluating progress, and nature of course experiences. Announcements or brochures describing workshops, seminars, or other educational programs accurately represent intended audience and eligibility requirements, educational objectives, and nature of the material to be covered, as well as the education, training and experience of the psychologists presenting the programs, and any fees involved. Public announcements soliciting subjects for research, and in which clinical services or other professional services are offered as an inducement, make clear the nature of the services as well as the costs and other obligations to be accepted by the human participants of the research.

h. Psychologists accept the obligation to correct others who may represent the psychologist's professional qualifications or associations with products or services in a manner incompatible with these guidelines.

i. Psychological services for the purpose of diagnosis, treatment or personal advice are provided only in the context of a professional relationship, and are not given by means of public lectures or demonstrations, newspaper or magazine articles, radio or television programs, mail, or similar media.

PRINCIPLE 5.
CONFIDENTIALITY

Safeguarding information about an individual that has been obtained by the psychologist in the course of his teaching, practice, or investigation is a primary obligation of the psychologist. Such information is not communicated to others unless certain important conditions are not met.

a. Information received in confidence is revealed only after most careful deliberation and when there is clear and imminent danger to an individual or to society, and then only to appropriate professional workers or public authorities.

b. Information obtained in clinical or consulting relationships, or evaluative data concerning children, students, employees, and others are discussed only for professional purposes and only with persons clearly concerned with the case. Written and oral reports should present only data germane to the purposes of the evaluation and every effort should be made to avoid undue invasion of privacy.

c. Clinical and other materials are used in classroom teaching and writing only when the identity of the persons involved is adequately disguised.

d. The confidentiality of professional communications about individuals is maintained. Only when the originator and other persons involved give their express permission is a confidential professional communication shown to the individual concerned. The psychologist is responsible for informing the client of the limits of the confidentiality.

e. Only after explicit permission has been granted is the identity of research subjects published. When data have been published without permission for identification, the psychologist assumes responsibility for adequately disguising their sources.

f. The psychologist makes provisions for the maintenance of confidentiality in the prevention and ultimate disposition of confidential records.

PRINCIPLE 6.
WELFARE OF THE CONSUMER

Psychologists respect the integrity and protect the welfare of the people and groups with whom they work. When there is a conflict of interest between the client and the psychologist's employing institution, psychologists clarify the nature and direction of their loyalties and responsibilities and keep all parties informed of their commitments. Psychologists fully inform consumers as to the purpose and nature of an evaluative, treatment, educational or training procedure, and they freely acknowledge that clients, students, or participants in research have freedom of choice with regard to participation.

a. Psychologists are continually cognizant of their own needs and of their inherently powerful position *vis a vis* clients, in order to avoid exploiting their trust and dependency. Psychologists make every effort to avoid dual relationships with clients and/or relationships which might impair their professional judgment or increase the risk of client exploitation. Examples of such dual relationships include treating employees, supervisees, close friends or relatives. Sexual intimacies with clients are unethical.

b. Where demands of an organization on psychologists go beyond reasonable conditions of employment, psychologists recognize possible conflicts of interest that may arise. When such conflicts occur, psychologists clarify the nature of the conflict and inform all parties of the nature and direction of the loyalties and responsibilities involved.

c. When acting as a supervisor, trainer, researcher, or employer, psychologists accord informed choice, confidentiality, due process, and protection from physical and mental harm to their subordinates in such relationships.

d. Financial arrangements in professional practice are in accord with professional standards that safeguard the best interests of the client and that are clearly understood by the client in advance of billing. Psychologists are responsible for assisting clients in finding needed services in those instances where payment of the usual fee would be a hardship. No commission, rebate, or other form of remuneration may be given or received for referral of clients for professional services, whether by an individual or by an agency. Psychologists willingly contribute a portion of their services to work for which they receive little or no financial return.

e. The psychologist attempts to terminate a clinical or consulting relationship when it is reasonably clear that the consumer is not benefiting from it. Psychologists who find that their services are being used by employers in a way that is not beneficial to the participants or to employees who may be affected, or to significant others, have the responsibility to make their observations known to the responsible persons and to propose modification or termination of the engagement.

PRINCIPLE 7. PROFESSIONAL RELATIONSHIPS

Psychologists act with due regard for the needs, special competencies and obligations of their colleagues in psychology and other professions. Psychologists respect the prerogatives and obligations of the institutions or organizations with which they are associated.

a. Psychologists understand the areas of competence of related professions, and make full use of all the professional, technical, and administrative resources that best serve the interests of consumers. The absence of formal relationships with other professional workers does not relieve psychologists from the responsibility of securing for their clients the best possible professional service nor does it relieve them from the exercise of foresight, diligence, and tact in obtaining the complementary or alternative assistance needed by clients.

b. Psychologists know and take into account the traditions and practices of other professional groups with which they work and cooperate fully with members of such groups. If a consumer is receiving services from another professional, psychologists do not offer their services directly to the consumer without first informing the professional person already involved so that the risk of confusion and conflict for the consumer can be avoided.

c. Psychologists who employ or supervise other professionals or professionals in training accept the obligation to facilitate their further professional development by providing suitable working conditions, consultation, and experience opportunities.

d. As employees of organizations providing psychological services, or as independent psychologists serving clients in an organizational context, psychologists seek to support the integrity, reputation and proprietary rights of the host organization. When it is judged necessary in a client's interest to question the organization's programs or policies, psychologists attempt to effect change by constructive action within the organization before disclosing confidential information acquired in their professional roles.

e. In the pursuit of research, psychologists give sponsoring agencies, host institutions, and publication channels the same respect and opportunity for giving informed consent that they accord to individual research participants. They are aware of their obligation to future research workers and insure that host institutions are given adequate information about the research and proper acknowledgement of their contributions.

f. Publication credit is assigned to all those who have contributed to a publication in proportion to their contribution. Major contributions of a professional character made by several persons to a common project are recognized by joint authorship, with the experimenter or author who made the principal contribution identified and listed first. Minor contributions of a professional character, extensive clerical or similar nonprofessional assistance, and other minor contributions are acknowledged in footnotes or in an introductory statement. Acknowledgement through specific citations is made for unpublished as well as published material that has directly influenced the research or writing. A psychologist who compiles and edits material of others for publication publishes the material in the name of the originating group, if any, and with his/her own name appearing as chairperson or editor. All contributors are to be acknowledged and named.

g. When a psychologist violates ethical standards, psychologists who know first-hand of such activities should, if possible, attempt to rectify the situation. Failing an informal solution, psychologists bring such unethical activities to the attention of the appropriate local, state, and/or national committee on professional ethics, standards, and practices.

h. Members of the Association cooperate with duly constituted committees of the Association, in particular and for example, the Committee on Scientific and Professional Ethics and Conduct, and the Committee on Professional Standards Review, by responding to inquiries promptly and completely. Members taking longer than 30 days to respond to such inquiries shall have the burden of demonstrating that they acted with "reasonable promptness." Members also have a similar responsibility to respond with reasonable promptness to inquiries from duly constituted state association ethics committees and professional standards review committees.

PRINCIPLE 8. UTILIZATION OF ASSESSMENT TECHNIQUES

In the development, publication, and utilization of psychological assessment techniques, psychologists observe relevant APA standards. Persons examined have the right to know the results, the interpretations made, and, where appropriate, the original data on which final judgments were based. Test users avoid imparting unnecessary information which would compromise test security, but they provide requested information that explains the basis for decisions that may adversely affect that person or that person's dependents.

a. The client has the right to have and the psychologist has the responsibility to provide explanations of the nature and the purposes of the test and the test results in language that the client can understand, unless, as in some employment or school settings, there is an explicit exception to this right agreed upon in advance. When the explanations are to be provided by others, the psychologist establishes procedures for providing adequate explanations.

b. When a test is published or otherwise made available for operational use, it is accompanied by a manual (or other published or readily available information) that fully describes the development of the test, the rationale, and evidence of validity and reliability. The test manual explicitly states the purposes and applications for which the test is recommended and identifies special qualifications required to administer the test and to interpret it properly. Test manuals provide complete information regarding the characteristics of the normative population.

c. In reporting test results, psychologists indicate any reservations regarding validity or reliability resulting from testing circumstances or inappropriateness of the test norms for the person tested. Psychologists strive to insure that the test results and their interpretations are not misused by others.

d. Psychologists accept responsibility for removing from clients' files test score information that has become obsolete, lest such information be misused or misconstrued to the disadvantage of the person tested.

e. Psychologists offering test scoring and interpretation services are able to demonstrate that the validity of the programs and procedures used in arriving at interpretations are based on appropriate evidence. The public offering of an automated test interpretation service is considered as a professional-to-professional consultation. The psychologist makes every effort to avoid misuse of test reports.

PRINCIPLE 9. PURSUIT OF RESEARCH ACTIVITIES

The decision to undertake research should rest upon a considered judgment by the individual psychologist about how best to contribute to psychological science and to human welfare. Psychologists carry out their investigations with respect for the people who participate and with concern for their dignity and welfare.

a. In planning a study the investigator has the responsibility to make a careful evaluation of its ethical acceptability, taking into account the following additional principles for research with human beings. To the extent that this appraisal, weighing scientific and humane values, suggests a compromise of any principle, the investigator incurs an increasingly serious obligation to seek ethical advice and to observe stringent safeguards to protect the rights of the human research participants.

b. Responsibility for the establishment and maintenance of acceptable ethical practice in research always remains with the individual investigator. The investigator is also responsible for the ethical treatment of research participants by collaborators, assistants, students, and employees, all of whom, however, incur parallel obligations.

c. Ethical practice requires the investigator to inform the participant of all features of the research that might reasonably be expected to influence willingness to participate, and to explain all other aspects of the research about which the participant inquires. Failure to make full disclosure imposes additional force to the investigator's abiding responsibility to protect the welfare and dignity of the research participant.

d. Openness and honesty are essential characteristics of the relationship between investigator and research participant. When the methodological requirements of a study necessitate concealment or deception, the investigator is required to insure as soon as possible the participant's understanding of the reasons for this action and of a sufficient justification for the procedures employed.

e. Ethical practice requires the investigator to respect the individual's freedom to decline to participate in or withdraw from research. The obligation to protect this freedom requires special vigilance when the investigator is in a position of power over the participant, as, for example, when the participant is a student, client, employee, or otherwise is in a dual relationship with the investigator.

f. Ethically acceptable research begins with the establishment of a clear and fair agreement between the investigator and the research participant that clarifies the responsibilities of each. The investigator has the obligation to honor all promises and commitments included in that agreement.

g. The ethical investigator protects participants from physical and mental discomfort, harm, and danger. If a risk of such consequences exists, the investigator is required to inform the participant of that fact, secure consent before proceeding, and take all possible measures to minimize distress. A research procedure must not be used if it is likely to cause serious or lasting harm to a participant.

h. After the data are collected, the investigator provides the participant with information about the nature of the study and to remove any misconceptions that may have arisen. Where scientific or human values justify delaying or withholding information, the investigator acquires a special responsibility to assure that there are no damaging consequences for the participant.

i. When research procedures may result in undesirable consequences for the individual participant, the investigator has the responsibility to detect and remove or correct these consequences, including, where relevant, long-term after effects.

j. Information obtained about the individual research participants during the course of an investigation is confidential unless otherwise agreed in advance. When the possibility exists that others may obtain access to such information, this possibility, together with the plans for protecting confidentiality, be explained to the participants as part of the procedure for obtaining informed consent.

k. A psychologist using animals in research adheres to the provisions of the Rules Regarding Animals, drawn up by the Committee on Precautions and Standards in Animal Experimentation and adopted by the American Psychological Association.

l. Investigations of human participants using drugs should be conducted only in such settings as clinics, hospitals, or research facilities maintaining appropriate safeguards for the participants.

REFERENCES

Psychologists are responsible for knowing about and acting in accord with the standards and positions of the APA, as represented in such official documents as the following:

American Association of University Professors. Statement on Principles on Academic Freedom and Tenure. *Policy Documents & Report*, 1977, 1-4.

American Psychological Association. *Guidelines for Psychologists for the Use of Drugs in Research*. Washington, D.C.: Author, 1971.

American Psychological Association. *Principles for the Care and Use of Animals*. Washington, D.C.: Author, 1971.

American Psychological Association. Guidelines for conditions of employment of psychologists. *American Psychologist*, 1972, *27*, 331-334.

American Psychological Association. Guidelines for psychologists conducting growth groups. *American Psychologist*, 1973, *28*, 933.

American Psychological Association. *Ethical Principles in the Conduct of Research with Human Participants*. Washington, D.C.: Author, 1973.

American Psychological Association. *Standards for Educational and Psychological Tests*. Washington, D.C.: Author, 1974.

American Psychological Association. *Standards for Providers of Psychological Services*. Washington, D.C.: Author, 1977.

Committee on Scientific and Professional Ethics and Conduct. Guidelines for telephone directory listings. *American Psychologist*, 1969, 24, 70-71.

ASCA Code of Ethics

1. Responsibilities of the school counselor stem from these basic premises and basic tenets in the counseling process.
   A. Each person has the right to dignity as a human being
      1. without regard to race, sex, religion, color, socio-economic status
      2. without regard to the nature and results of behavior, beliefs and inherent characteristics.
   B. Each person has the right to individual self-development.
   C. Each person has the right to self-direction and responsibility for making decisions.
   D. The school counselor, equipped with professional competency, an understanding of the behavioral sciences and philosophical orientation to school and community, performs a unique, distinctive and highly specialized service within the context of the education purpose and structure of the school system. Performance of this rests upon acquired techniques and informed judgment which is an integral part of counseling. Punitive action is not a part of the counseling process. The school counselor shall use these skills in endeavoring constantly to insure that the counselee has the afore-mentioned rights and a reasonable amount of the counselor's time.
   E. The ethical conduct of the school counselors will be consistent with the state regulations.
   F. The school counselor may share information gained in the counseling process for essential consultation with those appropriate persons specifically concerned with the counselee. Confidential information may be released only with consent of the individual except when required by court order.

I. Principal responsibilities of the school counselor to PUPILS

   A. The school counselor
      1. has a principal obligation and loyalty to respect each person as an unique individual and to encourage that which permits individual growth and development.
      2. must not impose consciously his attitudes and values on the coun-

From "Code of Ethics," *The School Counselor*, 1973, 21, 137–140. Reprinted by permission of the American School Counselor Association.

selee though he is not obligated to keep his attitudes and values from being known.

3. should respect at all times the confidences of the counselee; should the counselee's condition be such as to endanger the health, welfare, and/or safety of self or others, the counselor is expected to report this fact to an appropriate responsible person.

4. shall be knowledgeable about the strengths and limitations of tests; will share and interpret test information with the counselee in an accurate, objective and understandable manner to assist the counselee in self-evaluation.

5. shall assist the counselee in understanding the counseling process in order to insure that the persons counseled understand how information obtained in conferences with the counselor may be used.

II. *Principal responsibilities of the School Counselor to PARENTS*

A. The school counselor
   1. shall work with parents so as to enhance the development of the counselee
   2. shall treat information received from the parents of a counselee in a confidential manner.
   3. shall share, communicate and interpret pertinent data, and the counselee's academic progress with his parents.
   4. shall share information about the counselee only with those persons properly authorized to receive this information.

III. *Principal responsibilities of the School Counselor to FACULTY, ADMINISTRATION AND COLLEAGUES*

A. The school counselor
   1. shall use discretion, within legal limits and requirements of the state in releasing personal information about a counselee to maintain the confidences of the counselee.
   2. shall contribute pertinent data to cumulative records and make it accessible to professional staff (except personal factors and problems which are highly confidential in nature).
   3. shall cooperate with colleagues by making available as soon as possible requested reports which are accurate, objective, meaningful and concise.
   4. shall cooperate with other pupil personnel workers by sharing information and/or obtaining recommendations which would benefit the counselee.
   5. may share confidential information when working with the same counselee, with the counselee's knowledge and permission.
   6. must maintain confidentiality even though others may have the same knowledge.

7. shall maintain high professional integrity regarding fellow workers when assisting in problem areas related to actions, attitudes and competencies of faculty or colleagues.

IV. *Principal responsibilities of the School Counselor to SCHOOL AND COMMUNITY*

    A. The school counselor
        1. shall support and protect the educational program against any infringement which indicates that it is not to the best interest of the counselee or program.
        2. must assume responsibility in delineating his role and function, in developing educational procedure and program, and in assisting administration to assess accountability.
        3. shall recommend to the administration any curricular changes necessary in meeting valid educational needs in the community.
        4. shall work cooperatively with agencies, organizations and individuals in school and community which are interested in welfare of youth.
        5. shall, with appropriate release, supply accurate information according to his professional judgment to community agencies, places of employment and institutions of higher learning.
        6. should be knowledgeable on policies, laws, and regulations as they relate to the community, and use educational facilities accordingly.
        7. shall maintain open communication lines in all areas pertinent to the best interest of counselees.
        8. shall not accept remuneration beyond contractual salary for counseling any pupil within the school district. The counselor shall not promote or direct counselees into counseling or educational programs which would result in remuneration to the counselor.
        9. shall delineate in advance his responsibilities in case of any confrontation and have an agreement which is supported by the administration and the bargaining agency.

V. *Principal responsibilities of the School Counselor to SELF*

    A. The school counselor
        1. should continue to grow professionally by
            a. attending professional meetings
            b. actively participating in professional organizations
            c. being involved in research
            d. keeping abreast of changes and new trends in the profession and showing a willingness to accept those which have proved to be effective.
        2. should be aware of and function within the boundaries of his professional competency.
        3. should see that his role is defined in mutual agreement among the employer, students to be served, and the counselor. Furthermore,

this role should be continuously clarified to students, staff, parents and community.

VI. Principal responsibilities of the School Counselor to the PROFESSION

A. The school counselor
1. should be cognizant of the developments in his profession and be an active contributing participant in his professional association—local, state and national.
2. shall conduct himself in a responsible manner and participate in developing policies concerning guidance.
3. should do research which will contribute to professional and personal growth as well as determine professional effectiveness.
4. shall under no circumstances undertake any group encounter or sensitivity sessions, unless he has sufficient professional training.
5. shall, in addition to being aware of unprofessional practices, also be accountable for taking appropriate action to eliminate these practices.

Accepted by the ASCA Governing Board in October 1972.

APGA
ETHICAL STANDARDS

Adopted by the Board of Directors

1974

Preamble

The American Personnel and Guidance Association is an educational, scientific, and professional organization whose members are dedicated to the enhancement of the worth, dignity, potential, and uniqueness of each individual and thus to the service of society.

The Association recognizes that the role definitions and work settings of its members include a wide variety of academic disciplines, levels of academic preparation, and agency services. This diversity reflects the breadth of the Association's interest and influence. It also poses challenging complexities in efforts to set standards for the performance of members, desired requisite preparation or practice, and supporting social, legal, and ethical controls.

The specification of ethical standards enables the Association to clarify to present and future members and to those served by members the nature of ethical responsibilities held in common by its members.

The existence of such standards serves to stimulate greater concern by members for their own professional functioning and for the conduct of fellow professionals such as counselors, guidance and student personnel workers, and others in the helping professions. As the ethical code of the Association, this document establishes principles which define the ethical behavior of Association members.

Section A: General

1. The member influences the development of the profession by continuous efforts to improve professional practices, teaching, services, and research. Professional growth is continuous throughout the member's career and is exemplified by the development of a philosophy that explains why and how a member functions in the helping relationship. Members are expected to gather data on their effectiveness and to be guided by the findings.

2. The member has a responsibility both to the individual who is served and to the institution within which the service is performed. The acceptance of employment in an institution implies that the member is in substantial agreement with the general policies and principles of the institution. Therefore the professional activities of the member are also in accord with the objectives of the institution. If, despite concerted efforts, the member cannot reach agreement with the employer as to acceptable standards of conduct that allow for changes in institutional policy conducive to the positive growth and development of counselees, then terminating the affiliation should be seriously considered.

3. Ethical behavior among professional associates, members and nonmembers, is expected at all times. When information is possessed which raises serious doubt as to the ethical behavior of professional colleagues, whether Association members or not, the member is obligated to take action to attempt to rectify such a condition. Such action shall utilize the institution's channels first and then utilize procedures established by the state, division, or Association.

The member can take action in a variety of ways: conferring with the individual in question, gathering further information as to the allegation, conferring with local or national ethics committees, and so forth.

4. The member must not seek self-enhancement through expressing evaluations or comparisons that are damaging to others.

5. The member neither claims nor implies professional qualifications exceeding those possessed and is responsible for correcting any misrepresentations of these qualifications by others.

6. In establishing fees for professional services, members should take into consideration the fees charged by other professions delivering comparable services, as well as the ability of the counselee to pay. Members are willing to provide some services for which they receive little or no financial remuneration, or remuneration in food, lodging, and materials. When fees include charges for items other than professional services, that portion of the total which is for the professional services should be clearly indicated.

7. When members provide information to the public or to subordinates, peers, or supervisors, they have a clear responsibility to ensure that the content is accurate, unbiased, and consists of objective, factual data.

8. The member shall make a careful distinction between the offering of counseling services as opposed to public information services. Counseling may be offered only in the context of a reciprocal or face-to-face relationship. Information services may be offered through the media.

9. With regard to professional employment, members are expected to accept only positions that they are prepared to assume and then to comply with established practices of the particular type of employment setting in which they are employed in order to ensure the continuity of services.

Section B: Counselor-Counselee Relationship

This section refers to practices involving individual and/or group counseling relationships, and it is not intended to be applicable to practices involving administrative relationships.

To the extent that the counselee's choice of action is not imminently self- or other-destructive, the counselee must retain freedom of choice. When the counselee does not have full autonomy for reasons of age, mental incompetency, criminal incarceration, or similar legal restrictions, the member may have to work with others who exercise significant control and direction over the counselee. Under these circumstances the member must apprise counselees of restrictions that may limit their freedom of choice.

1. The member's *primary* obligation is to respect the integrity and promote the welfare of the counselee(s), whether the counselee(s) is (are) assisted individually or in a group relationship. In a group setting, the member-leader is also responsible for protecting individuals from physical and/or psychological trauma resulting from interaction within the group.

2. The counseling relationship and information resulting therefrom must be kept confidential, consistent with the obligations of the member as a professional person. In a group counseling setting the member is expected to set a norm of confidentiality regarding all group participants' disclosures.

3. If an individual is already in a counseling/therapy relationship with another professional person, the member does not begin a counseling relationship without first contacting and receiving the approval of that other professional. If the member discovers that the counselee is in another counseling/therapy relationship after the counseling relationship begins, the member is obligated to gain the consent of the other professional or terminate the relationship, unless the counselee elects to terminate the other relationship.

4. When the counselee's condition indicates that there is clear and imminent danger to the counselee or others, the member is expected to take direct personal action or to inform responsible authorities. Consultation with other professionals should be utilized where possible. Direct interventions, especially the assumption of responsibility for the counselee, should be taken only after careful deliberation. The counselee should be involved in the resumption of responsibility for his actions as quickly as possible.

5. Records of the counseling relationship including interview notes, test data, correspondence, tape recordings, and other documents are to be considered professional information for use in counseling, and they are not part of the public or official records of the institution or agency in which the counselor is employed. Revelation to others of counseling material should occur only upon the express consent of the counselee.

6. Use of data derived from a counseling relationship for purposes of counselor training or research shall be confined to content that can be sufficiently disguised to ensure full protection of the identity of the counselee involved.

7. Counselees shall be informed of the conditions under which they may receive counseling assistance at or before the time when the counseling relationship is entered. This is particularly so when conditions exist of which the counselee would be unaware. In individual and group situations, particularly those oriented to self-understanding or growth, the member-leader is obligated to make clear the purposes, goals, techniques, rules of procedure, and limitations that may affect the continuance of the relationship.

8. The member has the responsibility to screen prospective group participants, especially when the emphasis is on self-understanding and growth through self-disclosure. The member should maintain an awareness of the group participants compatibility throughout the life of the group.

9. The member reserves the right to consult with any other professionally competent person about a counselee. In choosing a consultant, the member avoids placing the consultant in a conflict of interest situation that would preclude the consultant's being a proper party to the member's efforts to help the counselee.

10. If the member is unable to be of professional assistance to the counselee, the member avoids initiating the counseling relationship or the member terminates it. In either event, the member is obligated to refer the counselee to an appropriate specialist. (It is incumbent upon the member to be knowledgeable about referral resources so that a satisfactory referral can be initiated.) In the event the counselee declines the suggested referral, the member is not obligated to continue the relationship.

11. When the member learns from counseling relationships of conditions that are likely to harm others, the member should report *the condition* to the responsible authority. This should be done in such a manner as to conceal the identity of the counselee.

12. When the member has other relationships, particularly of an administrative, supervisory, and/or evaluative nature, with an individual seeking counseling services, the member should not serve as the counselor but should refer the individual to another professional. Only in instances where such an alternative is unavailable and where the individual's condition definitely warrants counseling intervention should the member enter into and/or maintain a counseling relationship.

13. All experimental methods of treatments must be clearly indicated to prospective recipients, and safety precautions are to be adhered to by the member.

14. When the member is engaged in short-term group treatment/training programs, e.g., marathons and other encounter-type or growth groups, the member ensures that there is professional assistance available during and following the group experience.

15. Should the member be engaged in a work setting that calls for any variation from the above statements, the member is obligated to consult with other professionals whenever possible to consider justifiable alternatives. The variations that may be necessary should be clearly communicated to other professionals and prospective counselees.

Section C: Measurement and Evaluation

The primary purpose of educational and psychological testing is to provide descriptive measures that are objective and interpretable in either comparative or absolute terms. The member must recognize the need to interpret the statements that follow as applying to the whole range of appraisal techniques including test and nontest data. Test results constitute only one of a variety of pertinent sources of information for personnel, guidance, and counseling decisions.

1. It is the member's responsibility to provide adequate orientation or information to the examinee(s) prior to and following the test administration so that the results of testing may be placed in proper perspective with other relevant factors. In so doing, the member must recognize the effects of socioeconomic, ethnic, and cultural factors on test scores. It is the member's professional responsibility to use additional unvalidated information cautiously in modifying interpretation of the test results.

2. In selecting tests for use in a given situation or with a particular counselee, the member must consider carefully the specific validity, reliability, and appropriateness of the test(s). "General" validity, reliability, and the like may be questioned legally as well as ethically when tests are used for vocational and educational selection, placement, or counseling.

3. When making any statements to the public about tests and testing, the member is expected to give accurate information and to avoid false claims or misconceptions. Special efforts are often required to avoid unwarranted connotations of such terms as IQ and grade equivalent scores.

4. Different tests demand different levels of competence for administration, scoring, and interpretation. Members have a responsibility to recognize the limits of their competence and to perform only those functions for which they are prepared.

5. Tests should be administered under the same conditions that were established in their standardization. When tests are not administered under standard conditions or when unusual behavior or irregularities occur during the testing session, those conditions should be noted and the results designated as invalid or of questionable validity. Unsupervised or inadequately supervised test-taking, such as the use of tests through the mails, is considered unethical. On the other hand, the use of instruments that are so designed or standardized to be self-administered and self-scored, such as interest inventories, is to be encouraged.

6. The meaningfulness of test results used in personnel, guidance, and counseling functions generally depends on the examinee's unfamiliarity with the specific items on the test. Any prior coaching or dissemination of the test materials can invalidate test results. Therefore, test security is one of the professional obligations of the member. Conditions that produce most favorable test results should be made known to the examinee.

7. The purpose of testing and the explicit use of the results should be made known to the examinee prior to testing. The counselor has a responsibility to ensure that instrument limitations are not exceeded and that periodic review and/or retesting are made to prevent counseling stereotyping.

8. The examinee's welfare and explicit prior understanding should be the criteria for determining the recipients of the test results. The member is obligated to see that adequate interpretation accompanies any release of individual or group test data. The interpretation of test data should be related to the examinee's particular concerns.

9. The member is expected to be cautious when interpreting the results of research instruments possessing insufficient technical data. The specific purposes for the use of such instruments must be stated explicitly to examinees.

10. The member must proceed with extreme caution when attempting to evaluate and interpret the performance of minority group members or other persons who are not represented in the norm group on which the instrument was standardized.

11. The member is obligated to guard against the appropriation, reproduction, or modifications of published tests or parts thereof without the express permission and adequate recognition of the original author or publisher.

12. Regarding the preparation, publication, and distribution of tests, reference should be made to:

a. *Standards for Educational and Psychological Tests and Manuals*, revised edition, 1973, published by the American Psychological Association on behalf of itself, the American Educational Research Association, and the National Council on Measurement in Education.

b. "The Responsible Use of Tests: A Position Paper of AMEG, APGA, and NCME," published in *Measurement and Evaluation in Guidance* Vol. 5, No. 2, July 1972, pp. 385–388.

Section D: Research and Publication

1. Current American Psychological Association guidelines on research with human subjects shall be adhered to (*Ethical Principles in the Conduct of Research with Human Participants*. Washington, D.C.: American Psychological Association, Inc., 1973).

2. In planning any research activity dealing with human subjects, the member is expected to be aware of and responsive to all pertinent ethical principles and to ensure that the research problem, design, and execution are in full compliance with them.

3. Responsibility for ethical research practice lies with the principal researcher, while others involved in the research activities share ethical obligation and full responsibility for their own actions.

4. In research with human subjects, researchers are responsible for their subjects' welfare throughout the experiment, and they must take all reasonable precautions to avoid causing injurious psychological, physical, or social effects on their subjects.

5. It is expected that all research subjects be informed of the purpose of the study except when withholding information or providing misinformation to them is essential to the investigation. In such research, the member is responsible for corrective action as soon as possible following the research.

6. Participation in research is expected to be voluntary. Involuntary participation is appropriate only when it can be demonstrated that participation will have no harmful effects on subjects.

7. When reporting research results, explicit mention must be made of all variables and conditions known to the investigator that might affect the outcome of the investigation or the interpretation of the data.

8. The member is responsible for conducting and reporting investigations in a manner that minimizes the possibility that results will be misleading.

9. The member has an obligation to make available sufficient original research data to qualified others who may wish to replicate the study.

10. When supplying data, aiding in the research of another person, reporting research results, or in making original data available, due care must be taken to disguise the identity of the subjects in the absence of specific authorization from such subjects to do otherwise.

11. When conducting and reporting research, the member is expected to be familiar with and to give recognition to previous work on the topic, as well as to observe all copyright laws and follow the principle of giving full credit to all to whom credit is due.

12. The member has the obligation to give due credit through joint authorship, acknowledgement, footnote statements, or other appropriate means to those who have contributed significantly to the research, in accordance with such contributions.

13. The member is expected to communicate to other members the results of any research judged to be of professional or scientific value. Results reflecting unfavorably on institutions, programs, services, or vested interests should not be withheld for such reasons.

14. If members agree to cooperate with another individual in research and/or publication, they incur an obligation to cooperate as promised in terms of punctuality of performance and with full regard to the completeness and accuracy of the information provided.

Section E: Consulting and Private Practice

Consulting refers to a voluntary relationship between a professional helper and help-needing social unit (industry, business, school, college, etc.) in which the consultant is attempting to give help to the client in the solution of some current or potential problem. When "client" is used in this section it refers to an individual, group, or organization served by the consultant. (This definition of "consulting" is adapted from "Dimensions of the Consultant's Job" by Ronald Lippitt, *Journal of Social Issues*, Vol. 15, No. 2, 1959.)

1. Members who act as consultants must have a high degree of self-awareness of their own values and needs in entering helping relationships that involve change in social units.

2. There should be understanding and agreement between consultant and client as to the task, the directions or goals, and the function of the consultant.

3. Members are expected to accept only those consulting roles for which they possess or have access to the necessary skills and resources for giving the kind of help that is needed.

4. The consulting relationship is defined as being one in which the client's adaptability and growth toward self-direction are encouraged and cultivated. For this reason, the consultant is obligated to maintain consistently the role of a consultant and to avoid becoming a decision maker for the client.

5. In announcing one's availability for professional services as a consultant, the member follows professional rather than commercial standards in describing services with accuracy, dignity, and caution.

6. For private practice in testing, counseling, or consulting, all ethical principles defined in this document are pertinent. In addition, any individual, agency, or institution offering educational, personal, or vocational counseling should meet the standards of the International Association of Counseling Services, Inc.

7. The member is expected to refuse a private fee or other remuneration for consultation with persons who are entitled to these services through the member's employing institution or agency. The policies of a particular agency may make explicit provisions for private practice with agency counselees by members of its staff. In such instances, the counselees must be apprised of other options open to them should they seek private counseling services.

8. It is unethical to use one's institutional affiliation to recruit counselees for one's private practice.

Section F: Personnel Administration

It is recognized that most members are employed in public or quasi-public institutions. The functioning of a member within an institution must contribute to the goals of the institution and vice versa if either is to accomplish their respective goals or objectives. It is therefore essential that the member and the institution function in ways to: (a) make the institution's goals explicit and public; (b) make the member's contribution to institutional goals specific; and (c) foster mutual accountability for goal achievement.

To accomplish these objectives it is recognized that the member and the employer must share responsibilities in the formulation and implementation of personnel policies.

1. Members should define and describe the parameters and levels of their professional competency.

2. Members should establish interpersonal relations and working agreements with supervisors and subordinates regarding counseling or clinical relationships, confidentiality, distinction between public and private material, maintenance and dissemination of recorded information, work load, and accountability. Working agreements in each instance should be specified and made known to those concerned.

3. Members are responsible for alerting their employers to conditions that may be potentially disruptive or damaging.

4. Members are responsible for informing

employers of conditions that may limit their effectiveness.

5. Members are expected to submit regularly to review and evaluation.

6. Members are responsible for inservice development of self and/or staff.

7. Members are responsible for informing their staff of goals and programs.

8. Members are responsible for providing personnel practices that guarantee and enhance the rights and welfare of each recipient of their service.

9. Members are expected to select competent persons and assign responsibilities compatible with their skills and experiences.

Section G: Preparation Standards

Members who are responsible for training others should be guided by the preparation standards of the Association and relevant division(s). The member who functions in the capacity of trainer assumes unique ethical responsibilities that frequently go beyond that of the member who does not function in a training capacity. These ethical responsibilities are outlined as follows:

1. Members are expected to orient trainees to program expectations, basic skills development, and employment prospects prior to admission to the program.

2. Members in charge of training are expected to establish programs that integrate academic study and supervised practice.

3. Members are expected to establish a program directed toward developing the trainees' skills, knowledge, and self-understanding, stated whenever possible in competency or performance terms.

4. Members are expected to identify the level of competency of their trainees. These levels of competency should accommodate the paraprofessional as well as the professional.

5. Members, through continual trainee evaluation and appraisal, are expected to be aware of the personal limitations of the trainee that might impede future performance. The trainer has the responsibility of not only assisting the trainee in securing remedial assistance, but also screening from the program those trainees who are unable to provide competent services.

6. Members are expected to provide a program that includes training in research commensurate with levels of role functioning. Paraprofessional and technician-level personnel should be trained as consumers of research. In addition, these personnel should learn how to evaluate their own and their program effectiveness. Advanced graduate training, especially at the doctoral level, should include preparation for original research by the member.

7. Members are expected to make trainees aware of the ethical responsibilities and standards of the profession.

8. Training programs are expected to encourage trainees to value the ideals of service to individuals and to society. In this regard, direct financial remuneration or lack thereof should not influence the quality of service rendered. Monetary considerations should not be allowed to overshadow professional and humanitarian needs.

9. Members responsible for training are expected to be skilled as teachers and practitioners.

10. Members are expected to present thoroughly varied theoretical positions so that trainees may make comparisons and have the opportunity to select a position.

11. Members are obligated to develop clear policies within their training institution regarding field placement and the roles of the trainee and the trainer in such placements.

12. Members are expected to ensure that forms of training focusing on self-understanding or growth are voluntary, or if required as part of the training program, are made known to prospective trainees prior to entering the program. When the training program offers a growth experience with an emphasis on self-disclosure or other relatively intimate or personal involvement, the member should have no administrative, supervisory, or evaluative authority regarding the participant.

13. Members are obligated to conduct a training program in keeping with the most current guidelines of the American Personnel and Guidance Association and its various divisions.

References

Adler, A. *Understanding human nature.* New York: Premier, 1959.

Allport, G. Psychological models for guidance. *Harvard Educational Review,* 1962, *32,* 373–381.

Alschuler, A. *Developing achievement motivation in adolescents: Education for human growth.* Englewood Cliffs, N.J.: Educational Technology Publications, 1973.

American Mental Health Counselors Association, American Mental Health Counselors Association Certification Committee. The Board of Certified Professional Counselors procedures. *American Mental Health Counselors Association Journal,* 1979, *1,* 23–38.

American Personnel and Guidance Association, American Personnel and Guidance Association Licensure Commission. *Licensure Commission action packet.* Washington, D.C.: Author, 1977.

American Personnel and Guidance Association, American Personnel and Guidance Association Licensure Network Licensure Committee. *Licensure Committee action packet.* Washington, D.C.: Author, 1980.

American Personnel and Guidance Association, Association for Counselor Education and Supervision, Commission on Standards and Accreditation. Standards for the preparation of counselors and other personnel services specialists. *Personnel and Guidance Journal,* 1977, *55,* 596–601.

American Personnel and Guidance Association, Association for Counselor Education and Supervision. ACES guidelines for doctoral education. *Counselor Education and Supervision,* 1978, *17,* 163–166.

American Personnel and Guidance Association. New board to certify, and APGA registry committee meets. *APGA Guidepost,* March 1, 1979, pp. 1–12. (a)

American Personnel and Guidance Association. Sweeney elected. *APGA Guidepost,* March 15, 1979, pp. 1–12. (b)

American Personnel and Guidance Association. Arkansas to license counselors. *APGA Guidepost,* June 14, 1979, pp. 1–12. (c)

American Personnel and Guidance Association. ASGW proposes 'group' guidelines. *APGA Guidepost,* October 25, 1979, pp. 1–12. (d)

American Personnel and Guidance Association. Louise Forsyth wins. *APGA Guidepost,* February 21, 1980, pp. 1–12.

American Psychological Association, Board of Directors. Guidelines for psychologists conducting growth groups. *American Psychologist,* 1973, *82,* 933.

American Psychological Association, Committee on Standards for Providers of Psychological Services. *Standards for providers of counseling psychological services,* Draft 8, November 1978.

American Psychological Association, Committee on Standards for Providers of Psychological Services. *Standards for providers of counseling psychological services,* Draft 9, Final Proposal, September 18, 1979.

American Psychological Association, Division of Counseling Psychology. *Division of Counseling Psychology Newsletter,* February 22, 1977, pp. 1–8.

American Psychological Association, Division of Counseling Psychology, Jordaan, J. (Ed.). *The Counseling Psychologist.* New York: Columbia Teachers College Press, 1968.

American Psychological Association. Guidelines for psychologists conducting growth groups. *American Psychologist*, 1973, *82*, 933.

American Psychological Association. Professional identity. *The Counseling Psychologist*, 1977, 7, 9–94.

American School Counselor Association. The role and function of post-secondary counseling. *The School Counselor*, 1974, *21*, 387–390.

American School Counselor Association. The role of the secondary school counselor. *The School Counselor*, 1977, *24*, 228–234.

American School Counselor Association. The unique role of the elementary school counselor. *Elementary School Guidance and Counseling*, 1978, *12*, 200–202. (a)

American School Counselor Association. The unique role of the middle/junior high school counselor. *Elementary School Guidance and Counseling*, 1978, *12*, 203–205. (b)

Arbuckle, D. S. Counselor, social worker, psychologist: Let's ecumenicalize. *Personnel and Guidance Journal*, 1967, *45*, 532–538.

Arbuckle, D. S. *Counseling and psychotherapy: An existential humanistic view* (3rd ed.). Boston: Allyn and Bacon, 1975.

Arbuckle, D. S. The school counselor: Voice of society? *Personnel and Guidance Journal*, 1976, *54*, 427–430.

Asher, J. K. The coming exclusion of counselors from the mental health care system. *American Mental Health Counselors Association Journal*, 1979, *1*, 53–60.

Association for Counselor Education and Supervision. ACES guidelines for doctoral preparation in counselor education. *Counselor Education and Supervision*, 1978, *17*, 163–166.

Aubrey, R. F. And never the twain shall meet: Counselor training and school realities. *The School Counselor* 1972, *20*, 16–24.

Bandura, A., & Walters, R. H. *Social learning and personality development*. New York: Holt, Rinehart & Winston, 1963.

Bangs, A. J. Privilege and the counseling profession. *Personnel and Guidance Journal*, 1971, *50*, 270–275.

Banikiotes, P. G. The training of counseling psychologists. *The Counseling Psychologist*, 1977, 7, 23–26.

Barclay, J. R. *Counseling and philosophy: A theoretical exposition*. Boston: Houghton Mifflin, 1968.

Barclay, J. R. *Foundations of counseling strategies*. New York: Wiley, 1971.

Belkin, G. S. *Practical counseling in the schools*. Dubuque, Iowa: William C. Brown, 1975.

Benedict, A. R., Apsler, R., & Morrison, S. Student views of their counseling needs and counseling services. *Journal of College Student Personnel*, 1977, *18*, 110–114.

Benedict, D. S. A generalist counselor in industry. *Personnel and Guidance Journal*, 1973, *51*, 717–722.

Berenson, B. G., & Carkhuff, R. (Eds.). *Sources of gain in counseling and psychotherapy*. New York: Holt, Rinehart & Winston, 1967.

Berne, E. *Transactional analysis in psychotherapy*. New York: Grove Press, 1961.

Bestor, A. E. *Educational wastelands: The retreat from learning in our public schools*. Urbana: University of Illinois Press, 1953.

Biasco, F. Encouraging self-referrals in the elementary school. *The School Counselor*, 1968, *16*, 99–102.

Birk, J. M., & Tanney, M. F. (Guest Eds.). *The Counseling Psychologist, Counseling Women II*, 1976, 6.

Blake, R. Counseling in gerontology. *Personnel and Guidance Journal*, 1975, *53*, 733–737.

Blimline, C. A., & Birk, J. M. A note of impatience. *The Counseling Psychologist*, 1979, *8*, 48–49.

Blocher, D. H. *Developmental counseling*. New York: Ronald Press, 1966.

Blocher, D. H. *Developmental counseling* (2nd ed.). New York: Ronald Press, 1974.

Bordin, E. S. Diagnosis in counseling and psychotherapy. *Educational and Psychological Measurement*, 1946, *6*, 169–184.

Boy, A. V. The elementary school counselor's role dilemma. *The School Counselor*, 1972, *19*, 167–172.

Boy, A. V., & Pine, G. J. Needed: A rededication to the counselor's primary commitment. *Personnel and Guidance Journal*, 1979, *57*, 527–528.

Brammer, L. M. Counseling theory. In *The encyclopedia of education* (Vol. 2). New York: Macmillan, 1971.

Brammer, L. M., & Allmon, D. Training packages. *Personnel and Guidance Journal*, 1977, *55*, 612–618.

Brammer, L. M., & Shostrom, E. L. *Therapeutic psychology* (3rd ed.). Englewood Cliffs, N.J.: Prentice-Hall, 1977.

Brewer, J. M. *Education as Guidance: An examination of the possibilities of curriculum in terms of life activities, in elementary and secondary school, and colleges*. New York: Macmillan, 1932.

Brewer, J. M. *History of vocational guidance*. New York: Harper & Row, 1942.

Brodsky, S. L. Personal commitment: Challenge for change. *Personnel and Guidance Journal*, 1974, *53*, 163–165.

Brossard, C. Teenager without a job. *Look*, 1962, *26*, p. 33.

Brown, W. F. Effectiveness of paraprofessionals: The evidence. *Personnel and Guidance Journal*, 1974, *53*, 257–263.

Brown, W. F., Wehe, N. O., & Zunker, V. G. Effectiveness of student-to-student counseling on the academic adjustment of potential college dropouts. *Journal of Educational Psychology*, 1971, *62*, 285–289.

Buck, J. N. *House-tree-person test*. Beverly Hills, Calif.: Western Psychological Services, 1950.

Buckner, E. T. Accountable to whom? The counselor's dilemma. *Measurement and Evaluation in Guidance*, 1975, *8*, 187–192.

Calhoun, L. G., Selby, J. W., & King, H. E. *Dealing with crises*. Englewood Cliffs, N.J.: Prentice-Hall, 1976.

Calia, V. F. Systematic human relations training: Appraisal and status. *Counselor Education and Supervision*, 1974, *14*, 85–94.

Callis, R. Diagnostic classification as a research tool. *Journal of Counseling Psychology*, 1965, *12*, 238–243.

Callis, R. (Ed.). *Ethical standards casebook*. Washington, D.C.: American Personnel and Guidance Association, 1976.

Campbell, R. E. Counselor personality and background and his interview subrole behavior. *Journal of Counseling Psychology*, 1962, *9*, 329–334.

Carkhuff, R. R. Differential functioning of lay and professional helpers. *Journal of Counseling Psychology*, 1968, *15*, 117–126.

Carkhuff, R. R. The development of systematic human resource models. *The Counseling Psychologist*, 1972, *3*, 4–11. (a)

Carkhuff, R. R. New directions in training for the helping professions: Toward a technology for human and community resource development. *The Counseling Psychologist*, 1972, *3*, 12–30. (b)

Carkhuff, R. R., & Berenson, B. G. *Beyond counseling and therapy* (2nd ed.). New York: Holt, Rinehart & Winston, 1977.

Carroll, M. R. The regeneration of guidance. *The School Counselor*, 1973, *20*, 355–360.

Cass, W. A., & Lindeman, J. C. Trends and directions. In B. M. Schoenberg (Ed.), *A handbook and guide for the college and university counseling center*. Westport, Conn.: Greenwood Press, 1978.

Clark, D. D. Current emphasis and characteristics of counseling centers in universities of over 10,000 enrollment. In P. J. Gallagher & G. D. Demos (Eds.), *The counseling center in higher education*. Springfield, Ill.: Charles C Thomas, 1970.

Cook, D. R. (Ed.). *Guidance for education in revolution*. Boston: Allyn and Bacon, 1971.

Corey, G. *Theory and practice of counseling and psychotherapy*. Monterey, Calif.: Brooks/Cole, 1977.

Cottingham, H. F., & Swanson, C. D. Recent licensure developments: Implications for counselor educators. *Counselor Education and Supervision*, 1976, 16, 84–97.

Cremin, L. A. *The transformation of the school: Progressivism in American education (1876–1957)*. New York: Random House, 1961.

Dewey, J. *The sources of a science of education*. New York: Liveright, 1929.

Dimick, K. M., & Huff, V. E. *Child counseling*. Dubuque, Iowa: William C. Brown, 1970.

Dinkmeyer, D. Developmental counseling in the elementary school. *Personnel and Guidance Journal*, 1966, 45, 262–266.

Dinkmeyer, D. A developmental model for counseling-consulting. *Elementary School Guidance and Counseling*, 1971, 6, 81–85.

Dinkmeyer, D. Elementary school counseling: Prospects and potentials. *Personnel and Guidance Journal*, 1973, 52, 171–174.

Dinkmeyer, D. *Systematic training for effective parenting*. Circle Pines, Minn.: American Guidance Service, 1976.

Dollard, J., & Miller, N. E. *Personality and psychotherapy: An analysis in terms of learning, thinking, and culture*. New York: McGraw-Hill, 1950.

Dreikurs, R. The Adlerian approach to therapy. In M. I. Stein (Ed.), *Contemporary psychotherapies*. New York: Free Press, 1961.

Dreikurs, R. *Social equality: The challenge of today*. Chicago: Henry Regnery, 1971.

Dunlop, R. S. Professional educators, parents, and students assess the counselor's role. *Personnel and Guidance Journal*, 1965, 43, 1024–1028.

Dunlop, R. S. Counselor competence: Some proposals in search of advocacy. *Personnel and Guidance Journal*, 1968, 46, 655–660. (a)

Dunlop, R. S. *Professional problems in school counseling practice*. Scranton, Pa.: International Textbook, 1968. (b)

Dunlop, R. S. Counseling as a profession: Toward occupational maturity. *Focus on Guidance*. Denver: Love, 1969.

Dunlop, R. S. The counselor: Educator, psychologist or something unique? In search of a professional home base. *Focus on Guidance*. Denver: Love, 1971.

Dye, L. L., & Gluckstern, N. B. Counselors in corrections: Surveying the scene. *Personnel and Guidance Journal*, 1974, 53, 128–129.

Egan, G. *The skilled helper: A model for systematic helping and interpersonal relating*. Monterey, Calif.: Brooks/Cole, 1975.

Ellis, A. *Humanistic psychotherapy: The rational-emotive approach*. New York: Julian Press, 1973.

Emener, W. G., Jr. Counselor education applied to industry. *Counselor Education and Supervision*, 1975, 15, 72–76.

Entine, A. D. Mid-life counseling: Prognosis and potential. *Personnel and Guidance Journal*, 1976, 55, 112–114.

Erikson, E. H. *Identity, youth, and crisis*. New York: Norton, 1968.

Eysenck, H. J. The effects of psychotherapy: An evaluation. *Journal of Consulting Psychology*, 1952, 16, 319–324.

Faust, V. *History of elementary school counseling: Overview and critique. With a chronological bibliography from 1924*. Boston: Houghton Mifflin, 1968. (a)

Faust, V. *The counselor-consultant in the elementary school*. Boston: Houghton Mifflin, 1968. (b)

Filbeck, R. W. Perceptions of appropriateness of counselor behavior: A comparison of counselors and principals. *Personnel and Guidance Journal*, 1965, *43*, 891–896.

Gallagher, P. J., & Demos, G. D. *The counseling center in higher education*. Springfield, Ill.: Charles C Thomas, 1970.

Ganikos, M. (Ed.). *Counseling the aged: A training syllabus for educators*. Washington, D.C.: American Personnel and Guidance Association, 1979.

Gardner, R. A. *Therapeutic communication with children: The mutual storytelling technique*. New York: Science House, 1971.

Gazda, G. M. *Group counseling: A developmental approach*. Boston: Allyn and Bacon, 1971.

Gazda, G. M. (Ed.). *Basic approaches to group psychotherapy and group counseling* (2nd ed.). Springfield, Ill.: Charles C Thomas, 1975.

Gazda, G. M. (Ed.). *Theories and methods of group counseling in the schools* (2nd ed.). Springfield, Ill.: Charles C Thomas, 1976.

Gellman, W., & Murov, H. The broad role of the community agency counselor. *Personnel and Guidance Journal*, 1973, *52*, 157–159.

Gilmore, S. K. *The counselor-in-training*. New York: Appleton-Century-Crofts, 1973.

Goldenberg, H. *Contemporary clinical psychology*. Monterey, Calif.: Brooks/Cole, 1973.

Goldman, L. Privilege or privacy: 1. *Personnel and Guidance Journal*, 1969, *48*, 88.

Goldman, L. *Using tests in counseling* (2nd ed.). New York: Goodyear Publishing, 1971.

Gordon, T. *Parent effectiveness training*. New York: Peter H. Wyden, 1970.

Gottesfeld, H. *Abnormal psychology. A community mental health perspective*. Chicago: Science Research Associates, 1979.

Gruver, G. G. College students as therapeutic agents. *Psychological Bulletin*, 1971, *76*, 111–127.

Hall, C. S. *A primer of Freudian psychology*. Cleveland: World Publishing, 1954.

Hansen, L. S. Guidance-based models for potentially effective career education programs. In G. Walz, R. L. Smith, & L. Benjamin (Eds.), *A comprehensive view of career development*. Washington, D.C.: American Personnel and Guidance Association, 1974.

Haraway, M. Training counselors. *The Counseling Psychologist, Counseling Women III*, 1979, *8*, 8–9.

Harmon, L. W., Birk, J. M., Fitzgerald, L. E., & Tanney, M. F. (Eds.). *Counseling women*. Monterey, Calif.: Brooks/Cole, 1978.

Harmon, L. W., & Fitzgerald, L. E. Counseling women. *The Counseling Psychologist, Counseling Women I*, 1973, *4*.

Hart, D. H., & Prince, D. J. Role conflict for school counselors: Training versus job demands. *Personnel and Guidance Journal*, 1970, *48*, 374–380.

Havighurst, R. J. *Human development and education*. New York: Longman, Green, 1953.

Hawkins, S. The content of elementary counseling interviews. *Elementary School Guidance and Counseling*, 1967, *2*, 114–120.

Heddesheimer, J. Multiple motivations for mid-career changes. *Personnel and Guidance Journal*, 1976, *55*, 109–111.

Henderson, G. (Ed.). *Understanding and counseling ethnic minorities*. Springfield, Ill.: Charles C Thomas, 1979.

Herr, E. L. Manpower policies, vocational guidance and career development. In E. L. Herr (Ed.), *Vocational guidance and human development*. Boston: Houghton Mifflin, 1974.

Hill, C. E., Birk, J. M., Blimline, C. A., Leonard, M. M., Hoffman, M. A., & Tanney, M. F. (Guest Eds.). *The Counseling Psychologist, Counseling Women III*, 1979, *8*.

Hill, G. E. *Management and improvement of guidance* (2nd ed.). Englewood Cliffs, N.J.: Prentice-Hall, 1974.

Hitt, W. Two models of man. In G. B. Bishop & W. F. Hill (Eds.), *Dimensions of psychology*. Philadelphia: Lippincott, 1972.

Hoffman, A. M. Paraprofessional effectiveness. *Personnel and Guidance Journal*, 1976, *54*, 494–497.

Humes, C. W., II. School counselors and PL 94-142. *The School Counselor*, 1978, *25*, 192–195.

Hurlock, E. B. *Adolescent development* (4th ed.). New York: McGraw-Hill, 1973.

Hurst, J. C. The role of skills dissemination in counseling psychology. *The Counseling Psychologist*, 1977, *7*, 61–64.

Ivey, A. E. The Association for Human Development: A revitalized APGA. *Personnel and Guidance Journal*, 1970, *48*, 528–532.

Ivey, A. E. *Microcounseling: Innovations in interviewing training*. Springfield, Ill.: Charles C Thomas, 1971.

Ivey, A. E. Counseling psychology: Toward an action orientation. *Division 17 Counseling Psychology Newsletter*, December 1979, *1*, 1–2.

Ivey, A. E., & Alschuler, A. S. An introduction to the field. *Personnel and Guidance Journal*, 1973, *51*, 591–597. (a)

Ivey, A. E., & Alschuler, A. S. Psychological education is. . . . *Personnel and Guidance Journal*, 1973, *51*, 588–589. (b)

Ivey, A. E., & Authier, J. *Microcounseling: Innovations in interviewing, counseling, psychotherapy and psychoeducation* (2nd ed.). Springfield, Ill.: Charles C Thomas, 1978.

Ivey, A. E., & Simek-Downing, L. *Counseling and psychotherapy. Skills, theories, and practice*. Englewood Cliffs, N.J.: Prentice-Hall, 1980.

Jacobs, M., Krogger, A. H., Lesar, D. J., & Redding, A. J. Parent perceptions of the role of the counselor in the junior high school. *The School Counselor*, 1971, *18*, 356–361.

Johnson, M., Busacker, W. E., & Bowman, F. Q. *Junior high school guidance*. New York: Harper & Row, 1961.

Jones, A. J. *Principles of guidance* (6th ed.). New York: McGraw-Hill, 1970.

Kandor, J., Pulvino, C., & Stevic, R. R. Counselor-role perception: A method for determining agreement and disagreement. *The School Counselor*, 1971, *18*, 373–382.

Keat, D. B. *Fundamentals of child counseling*. Boston: Houghton Mifflin, 1974.

Keith, C. R. Self-referral of elementary school children. *The School Counselor*, 1978, *26*, 50–54.

Kempler, W. Gestalt therapy. In R. Corsini (Ed.), *Current psychotherapies*. Itasca, Ill.: F. E. Peacock, 1973.

Kimmel, D. C. Adult development: Challenges for counseling. *Personnel and Guidance Journal*, 1976, *55*, 103–105.

Kincaid, M. Identity and therapy in the Black community. *Personnel and Guidance Journal*, 1969, *47*, 884–890.

Kirk, B. A., Johnson, A. P., Redfield, J. E., Free, J. E., Michel, J., Roston, R. A., & Warman, R. E. Guidelines for university and college counseling services. *American Psychologist*, 1971, *26*, 585–589.

Kirschenbaum, H. Sensitivity modules. *Media and Methods*, 1970, *6*, 34, 36–38.

Kramer, H. C., Berger, F., & Miller, G. Student concerns and sources of assistance. *Journal of College Student Personnel*, 1974, *15*, 389–393.

Krumboltz, J. D. (Ed.). *Revolution in counseling*. Boston: Houghton Mifflin, 1966.

Kunze, K. R. Business and industry look out for their own. *Personnel and Guidance Journal*, 1973, *52*, 145–149.

Lakin, M. *Interpersonal encounter: Theory and practice in sensitivity training*. New York: McGraw-Hill, 1972.

Lamb, D. H., & Clack, R. J. Professional versus paraprofessional approaches to orientation and subsequent counseling contacts. *Journal of Counseling Psychology,* 1974, *21,* 61–65.

Lazarus, A. A. *Behavior therapy and beyond.* New York: McGraw-Hill, 1971.

Levitt, M., & Rubenstein, B. (Eds.). *The mental health field: A critical appraisal.* Detroit: Wayne State University Press, 1971.

Levy, D. M. Beginning of the child guidance movement. In M. Levitt & B. Rubenstein (Eds.), *The mental health field: A critical appraisal.* Detroit: Wayne State University Press, 1971.

Lewis, F. C. Some of my best friends are counselors. *Phi Delta Kappa,* 1972, *53,* 372.

Lewis, J. A. & Lewis, M. D. *Community counseling: A human services approach.* New York: Wiley, 1977.

Litwack, L. Testimonial privileged communication: A problem re-examined. *The School Counselor,* 1975, *22,* 194–196.

London, P. *The modes and morals of psychotherapy.* New York: Holt, Rinehart & Winston, 1964.

Loughary, J. W., & Ripley, T. M. *Helping others help themselves: A guide to counseling skills.* New York: McGraw-Hill, 1979.

Loughary, J. W., Stripling, R. O., & Fitzgerald, P. W. (Eds.). *Counseling: A growing profession.* Washington, D.C.: American Personnel and Guidance Association, 1965.

Lundquist, G. W., & Chamley, J. C. Counselor-consultant: A move toward effectiveness. *The School Counselor,* 1971, *18,* 362–366.

Mahon, B. R., & Altmann, H. A. Skill training: Cautions and recommendations. *Counselor Education and Supervision,* 1977, *17,* 42–50.

Mann, P. A. *Community psychology: Concepts and approaches.* New York: Free Press, 1978.

Marsella, J., & Pedersen, P. (Eds.). *Cross-cultural counseling and psychotherapy: Foundations, evaluations, cultural considerations.* New York: Pergamon Press, 1980.

Martin, J. C. Locus of control and self-esteem in Indian and White students. *Journal of American Indian Education,* 1978, *18,* 23–29.

Maser, A. L. Counselor function in secondary schools. *The School Counselor,* 1971, *18,* 367–372.

Mathesen, D. W. *Introductory psychology: The modern view.* Hinsdale, Ill.: Dryden Press, 1975.

Mathewson, R. H. *Guidance policy and practice* (3rd ed.). New York: Harper & Row, 1962.

McArthur, C. C. Comment on "Effectiveness of counselors and counselor aides." *Journal of Counseling Psychology,* 1970, *17,* 335–336.

McCully, C. H. Professionalization: Symbol or substance? *Counselor Education and Supervision,* 1963, *2,* 106–112.

McDavis, R. J., & Parker, M. A course on counseling ethnic minorities: A model. *Counselor Education and Supervision,* 1977, *17,* 146–149.

Mears, F., & Gatchel, R. J. *Fundamentals of abnormal psychology.* Chicago: Rand McNally, 1979.

Meeks, A. R. *Guidance in elementary education.* New York: Ronald Press, 1968.

Messina, J. J. Why establish a certification system for professional counselors? A rationale. *American Mental Health Counselors Association Journal,* 1979, *1,* 9–22.

Mezzano, J. Concerns of students and preference for male and female counselors. *The Vocational Guidance Quarterly,* 1971, *20,* 42–47.

Miller, D. J. Guidance associates: Description and implications. *The School Counselor,* 1979, *24,* 182–186.

Miller, F. W., Fruehling, J. A., & Lewis, G. J. *Guidance principles and services* (3rd ed.). Columbus, Ohio: Charles E. Merrill, 1978.

Miller, L. L. *Counseling leads and related concepts.* Laramie, Wyo.: Developmental Reading Distributors, 1970.

Miller, T. K., & Prince, J. S. *The future of student affairs: A guide to student development for tomorrow's higher education.* San Francisco: Jossey-Bass, 1976.

Mills, D. H. Referral and case management consultation. In B. M. Schoenberg (Ed.), *A handbook and guide for the college and university counseling center.* Westport, Conn.: Greenwood Press, 1978.

Morrill, W. H., Ivey, A. E., & Oetting, E. R. The college counseling center: A center for student development. In J. C. Heston & W. B. Frick (Eds.), *Counseling for the liberal arts campus.* Yellow Springs, Ohio: Antioch Press, 1968.

Mosher, R. L., & Sprinthall, N. A. Psychological education in secondary schools: A program to promote individual and human development. *American Psychologist,* 1970, *25,* 911–924.

Muro, J. J. *The counselor's work in the elementary school.* Scranton, Pa.: International Textbook, 1970.

Nelson, R. C. *Guidance and counseling in the elementary school.* New York: Holt, Rinehart & Winston, 1972.

Nelson, R. C. Counseling: A frontier in elementary school guidance. In W. H. Van Hoose, J. J. Pietrofesa & J. Carlson (Eds.), *Elementary-school guidance and counseling: A composite view.* Boston: Houghton Mifflin, 1973.

Nugent, F. A. Implementing an appropriate counselor image in schools: An educative process. *Counselor Education and Supervision,* 1962, *2,* 49–51.

Nugent, F. A. A rationale against teaching experience for school counselors. *The School Counselor,* 1966, *13,* 213–215.

Nugent, F. A. A framework for appropriate referrals of disciplinary problems to counselors. *The School Counselor,* 1969, *16,* 199–202.

Nugent, F. A. School counselors, psychologists and social workers: A distinction. *Psychology in the Schools,* 1973, *10,* 327–333.

Nugent, F. A., & Pareis, E. N. Survey of present policies and practices in college counseling centers in the United States of America. *Journal of Counseling Psychology,* 1968, *15,* 94–97.

Ohlsen, M. M. *Guidance services in the modern school* (2nd ed.). New York: Harcourt Brace Jovanovich, 1974.

Pallone, N. J. Counseling psychology: Toward an empirical definition. *The Counseling Psychologist,* 1977, *7,* 29–32.

Parsons, F. *Choosing a vocation.* Boston: Houghton Mifflin, 1909.

Patterson, C. H. The place of values in counseling and psychotherapy. *Journal of Counseling Psychology,* 1958, *5,* 216–223.

Patterson, C. H. (Ed.). *The counselor in the school: Selected readings.* New York: McGraw-Hill, 1967.

Patterson, C. H. *Humanistic education.* Englewood Cliffs, N.J.: Prentice-Hall, 1973. (a)

Patterson, C. H. *Theories of counseling and psychotherapy* (2nd ed.). New York: Harper & Row, 1973. (b)

Patterson, C. H. *Theories of counseling and psychotherapy* (3rd ed.). New York: Harper & Row, 1980.

Pedersen, P., Draguns, J., Lonner, W., & Trimble, J. *Counseling across cultures.* Honolulu: University of Hawaii Press, 1980.

Pepinsky, H. B. The selection and use of diagnostic categories in clinical counseling. *Applied Psychological Monographs,* 1948, No. 15.

Pepinsky, H. B., & Pepinsky, P. N. *Counseling: Theory and practice.* New York: Ronald, 1954.

Perls, F. S. *Gestalt therapy verbation.* Lafayette, Calif.: Real People Press, 1969.

Peters, H. J., & Shertzer, B. *Guidance: Program development and management* (3rd ed.). Columbus, Ohio: Charles E. Merrill, 1974.

Peth, P. E. A critical examination of the role and function of the nonprofessional in rehabilitation. *Rehabilitation Counseling Bulletin*, 1971, *14*, 224–233.

Pietrofesa, J. J., Hoffman, A., Splete, H. H., & Pinto, D. V. *Counseling: Theory, research and practice*. Chicago: Rand McNally, 1978.

Pine, G. J. Let's give away school counseling. *The School Counselor*, 1974, *22*, 94–99.

Randolph, D. L. The counseling-community psychologist in the CMHC: Employer perceptions. *Counselor Education and Supervision*, 1978, *17*, 244–253.

Rappoport, L. Adult development: "Faster horses . . . and more money." *Personnel and Guidance Journal*, 1976, *55*, 106–108.

Redfering, D. L., & Anderson, J. Students' problems as perceived by students, counselors, and counselor educators. *The School Counselor*, 1975, *22*, 198–201.

Robinson, F. *Principles and procedures in student counseling*. New York: Harper & Row, 1950.

Rogers, C. R. *Counseling and psychotherapy*. Boston: Houghton Mifflin, 1942.

Rogers, C. R. *Client-centered therapy: Its current practice, implications, and theory*. Boston: Houghton Mifflin, 1951.

Salisbury, H. Counseling the elderly: A neglected area in counselor education and supervision. *Counselor Education and Supervision*, 1975, *14*, 237–238.

Satir, V. *Conjoint family therapy*. Palo Alto, Calif.: Science and Behavior Books, 1967.

Schlossberg, N. K. Programs for adults. *Personnel and Guidance Journal*, 1975, *53*, 681–685.

Schlossberg, N. K., & Entine, A. D. *Counseling adults*. Monterey, Calif.: Brooks/ Cole, 1977.

Schoenberg, B. M. (Ed.). *A handbook and guide for the college and university counseling center*. Westport, Conn.: Greenwood Press, 1978.

Seiler, G., & Messina, J. J. Toward professional identity: The dimensions of mental health counseling in perspective. *American Mental Health Counselors Association Journal*, 1979, *1*, 3–8.

Shah, S. A. Privileged communications, confidentiality and privacy: Privileged communications. *Professional Psychology*, 1969, *1*, 56–69.

Shapiro, D., Maholick, L. T., Brewer, E., & Robertson, R. N. *The mental health counselor in the community*. Springfield, Ill.: Charles C Thomas, 1968.

Shaver, J. P., & Strong, W. *Facing value decisions: Rationale building for teachers*. Belmont, Calif.: Wadsworth, 1976.

Shaw, M. C. *School guidance systems: Objectives, functions, evaluation, and change*. Boston: Houghton Mifflin, 1973.

Sheehy, G. *Passages: Predictable crises of adult life*. New York: Dutton, 1976.

Shelton, J. L., & Madrazo-Peterson, R. Treatment outcome and maintenance in systematic desensitization: Professional versus paraprofessional effectiveness. *Journal of Counseling Psychology*, 1978, *25*, 331–335.

Shertzer, B., & Stone, S. C. *Fundamentals of counseling* (2nd ed.). Boston: Houghton Mifflin, 1974.

Shertzer, B., & Stone, S. C. *Fundamentals of guidance* (3rd ed.). Boston: Houghton Mifflin, 1976.

Shertzer, B., & Stone, S. C. *Fundamentals of counseling* (3rd ed.). Boston: Houghton Mifflin, 1980.

Simon, S. Sensitizing modules: A cure for "senioritis." *Scholastic Teacher*, 1970, *29*, 42.

Simpson, E. L., & Gray, M. A. *Humanistic education: An interpretation*. Cambridge, Mass.: Ballinger, 1976.

Sinick, D. Rehabilitation counselors on the move. *Personnel and Guidance Journal*, 1973, *52*, 167–170.

Sinick, D. (Guest Ed.). Counseling over the life span. *Personnel and Guidance Journal*, 1976, *55*, 100–147.

Skovholt, T., Schauble, P., Gormally, J., & Davis, R. (Guest Eds.). Counseling men. *The Counseling Psychologist*, 1978, 7, 2–67.

Smith, E. J. Counseling Black individuals: Some stereotypes. *Personnel and Guidance Journal*, 1977, 55, 390–396.

Solomon, C. Elderly non-Whites: Unique situations and concerns. In M. Ganikos (Ed.), *Counseling the aged: A training syllabus for educators*. Washington, D.C.: American Personnel and Guidance Association, 1979.

Sprinthall, N. A. A curriculum for secondary schools: Counselors as teachers for psychological growth. *The School Counselor*, 1973, 20, 361–369.

Stanford, G., & Roark, A. E. *Human interaction in education*. Boston: Allyn and Bacon, 1974.

Stripling, R. O. ACES guidelines for doctoral preparation in counselor education. *Counselor Education and Supervision*, 1978, 17, 163–166.

Super, D. E. A theory of vocational development. *American Psychologist*, 1953, 8, 185–190.

Super, D. E. Transition: From vocational guidance to counseling psychology. *Journal of Counseling Psychology*, 1955, 2, 3–9.

Super, D. E. *Career development: Self-concept theory*. New York: College Entrance Examination Board, 1963.

Tanney, M. F., & Birk, J. M. Women counselors for women clients? A review of the research. *The Counseling Psychologist*, 1976, 6, 28–32.

Thoresen, C. E., & Mahoney, M. J. *Behavioral self-control*. New York: Holt, Rinehart & Winston, 1974.

Tiedeman, D. V. Shame on me! And maybe a little on us? *Association for Counselor Education and Supervision Newsletter*, December, 1979.

Tolbert, E. L. *An introduction to guidance*. Boston: Little, Brown, 1978.

Trotzer, J. P., & Kassera, W. J. Do counselors do what they are taught? *The School Counselor*, 1971, 18, 335–341.

Truax, C. B., & Carkhuff, R. R. *Toward effective counseling and psychotherapy: Training and practice*. Chicago: Aldine, 1967.

Truax, C. B., & Lister, J. C. Effectiveness of counselors and counselor aides. *Journal of Counseling Psychology*, 1970, 17, 331–334.

Tyler, L. E. *The work of the counselor* (2nd ed.). New York: Appleton-Century-Crofts, 1961.

Tyler, L. E. *The work of the counselor* (3rd ed.). New York: Appleton-Century-Crofts, 1969.

Van Hoose, W. H. *Counseling in the elementary schools*. Itasca, Ill.: F. E. Peacock, 1968.

Van Hoose, W. H., & Pietrofesa, J. J. (Eds.). *Counseling and guidance in the twentieth century: Reflections and reformulations*. Boston: Houghton Mifflin, 1970.

Van Hoose, W. H., Pietrofesa, J. J., & Carlson, J. (Eds.). *Elementary-school guidance and counseling: A composite view*. Boston: Houghton Mifflin, 1973.

Van Kaam, A. Counseling from the viewpoint of existential psychology. *Harvard Educational Review*, 1962, 32, 403–415.

Van Riper, B. W. Student perception: The counselor is what he does. *The School Counselor*, 1971, 19, 53–56.

Vontress, C. E. Counseling middle-aged and aging cultural minorities. *Personnel and Guidance Journal*, 1976, 55, 132–135.

Wagner, C. A. Elementary school counselors' perceptions of confidentiality with children. *The School Counselor*, 1978, 25, 240–248.

Wann, T. W. (Ed.). *Behaviorism and phenomenology: Contrasting bases for modern psychology*. Chicago: University of Chicago Press, 1964.

Warnath, C. F. *New myths and old realities*. San Francisco: Jossey-Bass, 1971.

Warnath, C. F. College counseling: Between the rock and the hard place. *Personnel and Guidance Journal*, 1972, 51, 229–235.

Warnath, C. F. (Ed.). *New directions for college counselors.* San Francisco: Jossey-Bass, 1973. (a)

Warnath, C. F. The school counselor as institutional agent. *The School Counselor,* 1973, *20,* 202–208. (b)

Warnath, C. F. Whom does the college counselor serve? In C. F. Warnath (Ed.), *New directions for college counselors.* San Francisco: Jossey-Bass, 1973. (c)

Waterland, J. C. Actions instead of words: Play therapy for the young child. *Elementary School Guidance and Counseling,* 1970, *4,* 180–187.

Waters, E. B. Career guidance and women. In G. R. Walz, R. L. Smith, & L. Benjamin (Eds.), *A comprehensive view of career development.* Washington, D.C.: American Personnel and Guidance Association, 1974.

Williamson, E. G. *How to counsel students: A manual of techniques for clinical counselors.* New York: McGraw-Hill, 1939.

Williamson, E. G. *Counseling adolescents.* New York: McGraw-Hill, 1950.

Williamson, E. G. Vocational counseling: Trait-factor theory. In B. Stefflre (Ed.), *Theories of counseling.* New York: McGraw-Hill, 1965.

Woellner, E. H. *Requirements for certification for elementary schools, secondary schools, junior colleges* (44th ed.). Chicago: University of Chicago Press, 1979.

Wolpe, J. *The practice of behavior therapy* (2nd ed.). New York: Pergamon Press, 1973.

Woodring, P. *Let's talk sense about our schools.* New York: McGraw-Hill, 1953.

Worthington, J. A parent's view of school counselors. *The School Counselor,* 1972, *19,* 339–340.

Wrenn, C. G. *The counselor in a changing world.* Washington, D.C.: American Personnel and Guidance Association, 1962.

Wrenn, C. G. Preface to W. H. Van Hoose & J. J. Pietrofesa (Eds.), *Counseling and guidance in the twentieth century: Reflections and reformulations.* Boston: Houghton Mifflin, 1970.

Yamamoto, K. Counseling psychologists—who are they? *The Counseling Psychologist,* 1963, *10,* 211–221.

Zunker, V., & Brown, W. Comparative effectiveness of student and professional counselors. *Personnel and Guidance Journal,* 1966, *44,* 738–743.

Name Index

Subject Index

Accountability, 69

Accreditation of Counselor Training, 10, 11

ACES, *see* Association for Counselor Education and Supervision

ACES Commission on Accreditation, 10, 11

Administrative psychological consultation, 46–47, 155–156, 248–249

Administrators, school:
  perceptions of counselors' role, 15, 106

Advisory committees, 235, 245

Affective curriculum specialist, primary role of psychological educators, 47

Affective education, *see* psychological education

Agents of social change, 16, 229–232

Alcohol, 1, 109, 167, 204, 223, 225

American Association of Marriage and Family Therapy (AAMFT), 2

American College Personnel Association (ACPA), 26

American Mental Health Counselors Association (AMHCA), 2, 3, 6, 10, 11, 34, 36, 188–189

American Mental Health Counselors Certification Committee, 6

American Personnel and Guidance Association (APGA):
  compared to Division 17, APA, 2, 3, 26, 37
  counselor role definitions, 2, 7–8, 34
  definitions of counseling, 5–7
  ethical code, 12, 54, 63
  licensing activities, 2, 4, 34, 37, 189, 191
  Licensure Commission Action Packet, 6, 34, 204
  merger with AMHCA, 2, 34
  model licensure law, 2–3, 6, 10–11, 34–35
  origin, 3, 26
  Registry Committee, 36
  registry for counselors, 36
  role in counseling, 2
  standards, difficulty implementing, 29–30
  training standards for counselors, 2, 10, 62–63

American Psychological Association (APA), 27, 189
  Committee on Training Standards, 11

American Psychological Association (APA), Division 17, Counseling Psychology, *see* Division 17, APA

American Psychologist, 165

American Rehabilitation Counseling Association (ARCA), 26, 37

American School Counselor Association (ASCA), 6
  counselor role definitions, 5, 7, 28, 34
  definition of counseling, 5, 28
  ethical code, 12
  origin, 26

AMHCA, *see* American Mental Health Counselors Association

APA, *see* American Psychological Association

APGA, *see* American Personnel and Guidance Association

Appraisal and information services, 226–229

Appraisal and testing, 227–228

ASCA, *see* American School Counselor Association

Assertiveness training, 99, 153, 223

Association for Counselor Education and Supervision (ACES), 5, 10, 26, 28, 34, 62, 63

Association for Specialists in Group Work (ASGW):
  ethical and training guidelines for group leaders, 12

Behavioral counseling, 75–76, 82–84

Behaviorism:
  compared to humanistic psychology, 78–82

The Bennett Mechanical Comprehension Test, 170–171

Blacks and counseling techniques, 67

Buckley Amendment, 62, 231

Business and industrial counselors, 190

California Psychological Inventory (CPI), 118

California Short Form Test of Mental Ability (K-8), 142

California Test of Personality (K-8), 142

Career education, 143, 219, 223, 228–229

Career Education Incentive Act, 38

Case studies, 111–129, 143–151, 171–180, 196–203

Certification, school counselors, 15, 27, 107

Certified professional counselors, 36